W9-CES-476

sinclair a. macrae,
mount royal college

an introduction to ethics

Theories, Perspectives, and Issues

Bruce Plcombs

Prentice
Hall

Toronto

To Lisa, Clara, Jack, and Will.

National Library of Canada Cataloguing in Publication Data

MacRae, Sinclair, 1962
    An introduction to ethics: theories, perspectives and issues

Includes bibliographical references and index.
ISBN 0-13-061911-6

1. Ethics. I. Title.

BJ1025.M32 2002   170   C2002-901463-8

Statistics Canada information is used with permission of the Minister of Industry, as Minister responsible for Statistics Canada. Information on the availability of the wide range of data from Statistics Canada can be obtained from Statistics Canada's Regional Offices, its World Wide Web site at www.statcan.ca, and its toll-free access number 1-800-263-1136.

ISBN 0-13-061911-6

Vice-President, Editorial Director: Michael J. Young
Acquisitions Editor: Lori Will
Executive Marketing Manager: Christine Cozens
Senior Developmental Editor: Martina van de Velde
Production Editors: Tara Tovell/Tammy Scherer
Copy Editor: Karen Rolfe
Proofreader: Claudia Forgas
Production Manager: Wendy Moran
Page Layout: Michael Kelley
Interior and Cover Design: Amy Harnden
Art Direction: Julia Hall
Cover Image: Centrifugal Pink by Steve Gouthro, 1982

1 2 3 4 5   06 05 04 03

Printed and bound in Canada.

Prentice Hall

Contents

Preface

An Introduction to Ethics: Theories, Perspectives, and Issues is a philosophical enquiry into a broad range of ethical questions, theories, perspectives, and issues. It examines fundamental ethical questions about the nature, purpose, justification, scope, origins, and application of morality, and the place of ethics in society and nature. Balancing theoretical and practical concerns, and historical and contemporary outlooks, it critically considers a number of ethical perspectives and practical moral problems from a distinctively Canadian standpoint. It is also a study of well-being and Value Theory, especially insofar as ethics impacts on these. Clearly written, accessible, and engaging, this book is suitable as an introductory text for courses in ethics and moral philosophy, contemporary moral issues and problems, and for courses in values and society/contemporary issues.

An Introduction to Ethics has been written specifically for students who are new to philosophy, and is mindful that many students who take introductory courses in the discipline are non-majors. As a result, my assumption is that you have no prior experience in the philosophical study of ethics, and no familiarity with the terminology and many theories discussed by professional philosophers.

My goal has been to make this book accessible and interesting. The philosophical study of ethics is compelling mainly because of its relevance to our lives. Anyone interested in living well is either directly or indirectly concerned with the sort of basic ethical questions and issues that are raised in philosophy. Every student in a post-secondary educational institution should take a course that asks the fundamental question: How should one live? No other question could be more suitable for driving a higher-education course.

Some of you might note that even without a background in Philosophical Ethics, we all have our own extensive experiences of morality to draw on and guide us. Thus, you might argue that a book posing the question "How should one live?" is redundant, and that it is arrogant to think that philosophers can teach us anything useful about the practical questions of day-to-day life. For example, one might wonder what a long-dead and life-long bachelor like Immanuel Kant or a medieval saint like Thomas Aquinas could teach us about how to live in the twenty-first century. Indeed, some readers might believe the issue of how to live well is so basic that there isn't much more to know about it, that the trick is to put into practice what we all know already.

One goal of this book is to challenge this view. We can learn a great deal by addressing fundamental questions about how we should live our lives. The discussion and exercises in this book are designed to encourage you to identify and think about your values and beliefs, and to shape them into ones you would accept and defend. This book seeks to provoke you into questioning and either altering or reaffirming your most basic beliefs and values. So, to speak dramatically, a central aim of this text is to change your life for the better.

Organization

In *An Introduction to Ethics: Theories, Perspectives, and Issues,* I approach a variety of practical questions about our values and moral beliefs from a philosophical standpoint. I explain that standpoint in the introductory chapter by identifying our subject matter and considering the nature of our learning. This is necessary to orient us to the methods of this book, methods that are usually unfamiliar to those new to the study of philosophy and Normative Ethics.

This book is divided into three main parts, as the subtitle suggests. Although all the three parts of the text are designed to work independently, material is frequently cross-referenced. My hope is that this will help those who are working through only some chapters to fill out their understanding of terms and ideas introduced elsewhere.

Part One, on theory, outlines the various areas of study within ethics that we will consider. To further clarify and develop our understanding of the nature of our subject, in Chapter 2, Ethics, Religion, and Law, I locate the study of ethics relative to these other areas. We then examine some historically important questions in the field of Meta-Ethics, including questions about subjectivity, objectivity, and relativity in ethics. These preliminary discussions lead us to the main task of Part One: explaining and contrasting a number of useful and influential theories in morality, including Natural Law Theory, Utilitarianism and Consequentialism, Kant's Deontology, Virtue Theory, and Feminist Ethics. In explaining and contrasting these views, I focus on their accounts of the basic categories in ethics. The progress we make in Part One will help inform our discussion in later sections of the book and provide us with some resources and conceptual tools for critically considering the various puzzles and issues we subsequently encounter.

Introductory books in ethics commonly examine the sorts of philosophical theories and questions we consider in Part One. In Part Two, however, I depart from the norm somewhat by examining ethics and ethical questions from various perspectives that move progressively from the individual to the entire planet. This approach enables us to consider several issues from different vantage points, and it helps round out our enquiry. Examining ethics from different perspectives also enables us to integrate a number of advances in ethics made in recent times. Specifically, Part Two is organized around the following five perspectives:

1. ethics and the individual;

2. ethics in interpersonal relationships;

3. ethics, law, and social policy;

4. ethics and non-human animals; and

5. ethics and the environment.

Although these divisions are somewhat rough and overlapping, each draws our attention to various aspects of ethics worthy of our consideration. Although many of the questions we consider in Part Two are theoretical and meta-ethical

(e.g., Why be moral? Who or what can be given moral consideration? How much consideration should be given?), we will also address issues in Applied Ethics. For example, Chapters 11 and 12 examine several issues in the area of Environmental Ethics.

Whereas few references are made to distinctively Canadian issues in Part One, many more are made in Part Two. This progression extends to the third part of the book. Part Three deals specifically with some topics in Applied and Professional Ethics that are of current interest to Canadians. In the area of Bioethics (Chapter 13), we'll examine the question of the just allocation of scarce medical resources. In Chapter 14, we look at a number of topical issues in the field of genetics and ethics, including the debates in Research Ethics about cloning, genetic alteration, ectogenesis, and stem cell research. In Chapter 15, we'll consider an issue in Business Ethics, namely the question of the morality of affirmative action. Finally, in Chapter 16, we examine several issues in ethics and the law concerning the value of freedom and the rightful use of the law to enforce morality.

Features

Clarity and Accessibility

A familiarity with moral philosophy, even at the introductory level, requires a basic understanding of the terminology philosophers have used to express their ideas. To assist you, text boxes highlighting important definitions have been placed throughout the text, and a glossary of terms can be found at the back of the book.

The need to introduce new terminology has been balanced with the more pressing goal of making this book accessible. In addition to contending with new subject matter, students new to philosophy often must deal with required readings that are written at rather advanced levels. In this text, however, I have used clear and straightforward language, specifically for students who are encountering this material for the first time.

Throughout the book, I have endeavoured to present ethical issues and positions fairly and clearly, without sacrificing philosophical rigour. I want to present the various views in some richness and detail, so as to convey some sense of the subtlety and power of the arguments advanced by those who have contributed to our understanding of ethics. To further assist your understanding, many of the discussions develop from the examination of a central example, scenario, or thought experiment. Some of these are of my own design; some are borrowed from others.

Finally, to facilitate reading comprehension, each chapter contains an overview of topics and a brief introduction to the content of the chapter. In each chapter, learning outcomes are stated at the beginning, and a review section summarizes the key points at the end.

Questions and Group Work Exercises

To further develop your understanding of the discussions, and to stimulate your thinking about the issues, most chapters include three types of exercises:

1. *Progress Check Questions* test your reading comprehension of the claims and arguments set out in the text.

2. *Questions for Further Reflection* address some of the deeper points and problems raised in each chapter. These questions are more demanding than the progress check questions. Instructors may find many of them suitable as essay topics.

3. *Group Work Activities*, also included in most of the chapters, are designed to complement solitary reading and reflection.

Suggested Further Reading and Weblinks

As this is an introduction to ethics, I have assumed that most students who use this book will not be expected to write advanced research papers in moral philosophy. Thus, I have limited the inclusion of extra resources for doing further research. However, most chapters include useful suggestions both for further reading and for exploring topics on the Internet.

Appendices

1. **Writing an Ethics Paper** The first appendix is written for those with little or no experience in writing papers on ethics.

2. **The *Canadian Charter of Rights and Freedoms*** A copy of our *Charter* has been appended for quick reference.

Contact the Author

I thank you for your interest in this text and welcome any comments, criticisms, and suggestions for improving future editions. You may contact me by e-mail at smacrae@mtroyal.ab.ca. Alternatively, you can send regular mail to me: Sinc MacRae, EA3141 Humanities Department, Mount Royal College, 4825 Richard Road, SW, Calgary, Alberta, T3E 6K6.

Acknowledgements

I have benefited immensely from the expert instruction and guidance of many teachers and philosophers in my own post-secondary education. I would especially like to thank Norman Brown and Ted Bond (both now Emeritus), Henry Laycock, and Alistair Macleod at Queen's University; Nathan Brett, Duncan MacIntosh, and Rich Campbell at Dalhousie University; and Calvin Normore, Arthur Ripstein, and Wayne Sumner at the University of Toronto.

Some of my colleagues at Mount Royal College generously commented on parts of the manuscript or helped me in discussion. Michael Hawley and Steven Engler offered me excellent advice and suggestions on Chapter 2, Todd Nickel commented on Chapter 14, and Peter Morton offered useful advice on the Group Work Activity in Chapter 16. Furthermore, this book is substantially better than it otherwise would be as a result of the constructive comments and suggestions of a number of reviewers: Calvin Hayes, University of Windsor; Ronald de Sousa, University of Toronto; Susan Dimock, York University; Andrew Sneddon, University of Calgary; Robin Tapley, University College of the

Cariboo; and Peter Trnka, Memorial University. I am solely responsible for any shortcomings or errors that may remain.

I also wish to acknowledge the efforts of the many friendly professionals at Pearson who helped with the production of this text at every stage of its creation. They are Andrew Wellner and Lori Will, acquisitions editors; Martina van de Velde, senior developmental editor; Tara Tovell and Tammy Scherer, production editors; Wendy Moran, production manager; Karen Rolfe, copy-editor; and Claudia Forgas, proofreader. Thank you. Without your help, this book would not be.

The Scholarly Pursuits Committee at Mount Royal College has generously provided me with two one-term course release awards to help with my writing. Thanks to the committee for the time I needed.

Education is truly a co-operative enterprise. Just as I have benefited from my teachers, I have also learned much from the thousands of students who have taken courses in ethics and Applied Ethics from me over the years. I hereby gratefully acknowledge their help. Finally, I would like to thank my children, Clara, Jack, and Will, for their understanding over the past many months and especially my wife, Lisa, for her love, patience, and invaluable encouragement and support.

Introduction: Toward Enlightenment in Ethics

Learning Outcomes

This chapter introduces you to the methods and subject matter of this book. We briefly examine both the nature of philosophical investigation in ethics and our subject matter.

Upon the successful completion of this chapter, you will be able to

1. explain the process/product distinction and how it applies to this book;

2. distinguish between descriptive and normative ethics;

3. identify Immanuel Kant's concept of enlightenment and apply it here; and

4. present arguments for the view that the philosophical study of ethics is controversial, complex, and incomplete.

I.1 Introduction

The question "What is philosophy?" is itself a philosophical question. This self-reflexive quality about the subject distinguishes it from other disciplines where the question of the nature of the discipline is not what we might call an internal question to it. Thus, one can be an expert in mathematics, physics, or history and not have a good answer to the question "What is mathematics?" "What is physics?" or "What is history?" Of course, many mathematicians, physicists,

and historians have excellent answers to the question about the nature of their discipline, but insofar as they do, they demonstrate their philosophical acumen as opposed to their discipline-specific expertise. For example, the question "What is physics?" is a question in the philosophy, of science, and as such, it is a question that is external to the actual study of physics.

Since this is a textbook in philosophy, it thus seems fitting to begin by asking what this book is about. More specifically, since this is a textbook in the philosophical study of ethics and some related areas, we should begin by asking what ethics is. Although we will begin to complete an answer to this question in this introductory chapter, we will only begin. The reason is because despite some broad agreement among philosophers about the answer to this question, there is considerable disagreement too, and filling out this disagreement, or more precisely these disagreements, will take time. Most agree that, generally speaking, the philosophical study of ethics is concerned with the right and wrong conduct of beings like us. Beyond this, however, there is controversy.

For example, there is controversy about the scope of ethics, that is, about who is owed our concern, and about the purpose of morality. Some argue that all and only human beings deserve moral consideration. Others contend that logically only beings that can suffer can be given moral consideration, and since many non-human animals can suffer, we should consider their interests too. Going even further, still others argue that we morally ought to consider the interests of all living beings including those beings, like plants, that apparently cannot suffer. As for the question about the point of ethics, some argue that we should promote the good of individual creatures, whereas others maintain that we should promote the diversity, integrity, and stability of entire biotic communities, including the planet as a whole. Although these perspectives overlap to some extent, we will see that they are different too.

These sorts of disagreements over the answers to some very basic questions in ethics are typical of philosophy. Noting this helps orient us to what we can expect in the pages ahead, namely, plenty of critical discussion, debate, and analysis.

> **Critical reasoning or analysis** refers to the process of identifying, clarifying, understanding, and evaluating the strength, truth, or rightness of a claim, view, or argument.

I.2 The Process/ Product Distinction

New students in philosophy usually start with a preconception about how to learn, and they are often surprised by how different the study of philosophy is from what they are used to. The difference is not solely due to the subject matter of the discipline but also due to the way we learn or the method we follow in making progress in our understanding. To help explain this point, consider the distinction between the act of making something (the process) and what we make (the product). Similarly, we can roughly distinguish between our approach to learning (the process) and the subject matter of our learning (the product).

I.3 The Process: Critical Analysis

"A very popular error: having the courage of one's convictions; rather it is a matter of having the courage for an attack on one's convictions!"

Friedrich Nietzsche

Unlike academic disciplines where the emphasis is mostly on remembering facts, in philosophy a central part of our focus is on **critical reasoning or analysis.** This is especially true in areas of philosophy that involve assessments of value, as is the case in the philosophical study of ethics. So in addition to learning the subject matter of part of philosophy, in our case mostly ethics, working through this book will help develop your analytical reasoning skills. Throughout the text you will gain experience in identifying and evaluating arguments supporting various controversial positions in ethics. This process of evaluating an argument is a skill, and like other skills it is one that you can work at improving. Moreover, since ethics is concerned with practical matters, improving your reasoning skills can help improve your life. One of the tasks of this text is to explain exactly how.

In the spirit of critical analysis, one might wonder about the aptness of this process/product distinction. If part of our aim is to improve our reasoning skills, and if reasoning well involves acquiring knowledge and cultivating various skills, as it does, then isn't improvement in critical analysis also part of the product of this book? In other words, if our focus is on analytical reasoning, then isn't this too our subject matter? It is true that indirectly at least using this book will improve your analytical reasoning skills. However, the formal study of the art and science of reasoning is not part of our subject matter. Although we all can benefit from the careful study of informal and formal logic, we have no space to pursue this directly here. There are a number of fine books in these subjects and you should consult with them if you wish to make improved reasoning the product of your learning.

I.4 The Product: Ethics

". . . it is the greatest good to discuss virtue every day and those other things about which you hear me conversing and testing myself and others, for the unexamined life is not worth living . . ."

Plato
Apology 38a

This emphasis on identifying and defending arguments that examine our beliefs and values about life is nicely complemented by our subject matter. The study of ethics takes two different forms. A cultural anthropologist might be interested in what is called **Descriptive Ethics**—the task of describing or reporting on the moral code that a society accepts. This is a scientific undertaking. If cultural anthropologists misdescribe a group's morality, they have failed in their task. In contrast, we are engaged in **Normative or Prescriptive Ethics.** Philosophers are not scientists. Our goal is not to describe our moral code, to say what our morals are; rather our aim is to say what moral positions or norms we should or ought to take. In order to do this we must defend our views, and here we appeal to both our commonly held values, and to carefully reasoned arguments.

Throughout this book our concern will be with Normative Ethics, or just "ethics" for short. Unless explicitly noted otherwise, "ethics" will henceforth mean "Normative Ethics."

The claim that philosophers are not scientists is not an insult. We need insight into the way that things are, but we also need direction to hold views and shape public policy and laws in ways that are reasonable and ethical. This is a job for philosophers. Consider an example. We could take a poll to see whether Canadians think that abortion during the second trimester of pregnancy is morally justified. This would be a task of Descriptive Ethics. But the question whether abortion during this period *should* be permitted is a normative question. This question invites argument and value judgments. It cannot be reasonably and fairly settled merely by pointing to facts about what a fetus is, what abortion is, how abortions are performed, and so on. Of course, these facts are important for informing the debate about the justifiability of abortion, but an appeal to them alone does not settle the issue. To do this we must also say something about our values. For instance, in this debate, judgments about the value of life and autonomy, and the badness of pain, suffering, and loss also enter into the discussion.[1]

Part of our work in ethics is to recognize and carefully articulate and defend our values. Indeed, one way to achieve some enlightenment in ethics is to interpret this personally. Thus, I encourage you to identify your values and beliefs about ethics and the prudentially good life and shape them into ones you would accept and defend upon careful philosophical reflection.

> **Descriptive Ethics** is the study of the morals of a group. This is a scientific enterprise as is done, for example, by cultural anthropologists.
> **Normative or Prescriptive Ethics** is the study of what the morals of some group should or ought to be. This is a philosophical enterprise as is done, for example, by philosophers specializing in Philosophical Ethics.

I.5 Why Critical Analysis? Toward Enlightenment in Ethics

"Enlightenment is man's release from his self-incurred tutelage. Tutelage is man's inability to make use of his understanding without direction from another. Self-incurred is this tutelage when its cause lies not in lack of reason but in lack of resolution and courage to use it without direction from another. *Sapere aude!* 'Have courage to use your own reason!'—that is the motto of enlightenment."

Immanuel Kant
Foundations of the Metaphysics of Morals, and
What is enlightenment?

"Have courage to use your own reason" is also the motto of this book, and one of my goals is to encourage you to achieve some enlightenment in ethics. This means that although many concepts, distinctions, historical facts, and background information will be presented, you will not be told what to think about the issues. Since my approach is informal and straightforward, I will sometimes explain and briefly defend my views. However, the main aim is to present a balanced treatment of the issues and allow you to decide for yourself what positions to provisionally accept and what values to provisionally endorse. Thus, competing and somewhat conflicting positions are presented, and arguments for and against these views are considered throughout. If you are used to a method of learning where you are instructed on what you must remember and know, you may well find this approach disorienting at first. But as you work your way through this book, you should find it easier to follow.

Our motto refers to having courage to use one's reason. At first glance this might seem strange. What is courageous about thinking carefully about ethics? While it might be admirable to think carefully when studying other subjects like math, it hardly seems appropriate to label this thinking "courageous." Upon reflection, however, we can see that one thing that distinguishes our subject is the personal stake most of us have in it. The study of ethics has relevance for the values most of us prize in life. Thinking carefully about ethics requires holding our present beliefs and values up to the light of critical scrutiny. If we prize resting our values, including our moral values, upon reasonable beliefs, then we must open ourselves up to criticism by engaging in the process of critical enquiry into ethics. If, furthermore, we care about being moral, then thinking carefully about ethics can lead us to conclusions that demand of us that we make changes in our lives. This certainly can require courage. Indeed, upon further reflection you can appreciate why Kant thought that it generally takes courage to think for oneself. Those who think for themselves take responsibility for their choices and their actions in ways that those who merely defer to the direction of others to explain their actions do not. Taking responsibility means holding oneself accountable. It is easier to act like an innocent child than to act like a mature and responsible adult. The passage to this kind of adulthood is not merely a matter of aging. Arguably, it takes courage too.

In addition to requiring some courage, as Kant further notes, one also needs to have some determination to achieve enlightenment. Frankly, some people are put off by the idea of having to decide for themselves which positions to accept in ethics, and which values to embrace. It is easier to leave the difficult thinking for others to do and uncritically believe whatever you are told by the experts. Certainly many find comforting the idea that some group of experts has all the answers to the hard questions in life and that we should defer to them because they are the experts. Since such deference is common and sensible in many other areas of life, why not this one too? When my doctor diagnoses the pain in my knee as a torn ligament, I don't presume to dispute his expertise. I don't hobble down to my nearest medical library to begin research that might challenge his professional judgment. So it is too with a whole host of other experts—auto mechanics, science professors, airline pilots, tax lawyers, dentists, engineers, research scientists, computer programmers, and so on. In all these cases, the wise course is to trust the professional and follow her advice.

It may appear that philosophers are professionals and experts too; they share many of the characteristics that distinguish other such groups in society. They seem to have mastered a recognized body of knowledge, belong to professional associations, do consultative work in hospitals and for Royal Commissions, possess advanced graduate university degrees, and research and teach in departments of colleges and universities. Perhaps we should defer to their judgments, especially considering that we are here to learn. Considering all these reasons then, and in the absence of reasons for thinking that professional philosophers who specialize in the philosophical study of ethics are not experts in ethics, when it comes to their wisdom, prudence suggests that we should drink in their knowledge.

Professional philosophers do have expertise, and it is wise to consider and weigh their opinions before reaching one's own conclusions whenever possible. However, the model of expertise noted above does not simply and smoothly apply to our subject matter for a number of reasons. To help appreciate why not and to appreciate the value of developing your critical reasoning skills, let's consider three of these reasons concerning the controversial nature of ethics, its complexity, and its incompleteness.

1. Ethics is controversial.

It is important to develop your critical reasoning skills when studying ethics because the philosophical study of the subject often involves controversies, and to sort through these controversies you need to think well. Although there is widespread agreement about the general kinds of skills, virtues, and learning philosophers need, there is considerable disagreement over the value judgments philosophers use their training to make. Understanding why there is such controversy involves appreciating the nature of value questions, including questions about moral and prudential values. Questions about values are questions about what is good and bad, but what is good and bad for different individuals, groups, societies, countries, non-human animals, and ecosystems is contentious. Why is this? Why isn't there an indisputable answer, however complex, about what we should do, how we should be, how we should help others, and so on?

We will have to defer a detailed study of this to Chapter 7 when we take up these matters in a concerted way. In the meantime, consider a few points. Part of the domain of ethics is human well-being. When we study Normative Ethics, we are interested in learning about how to promote the welfare of individual humans. The question

"What makes human life go well?" is controversial. There is no generally agreed-upon and universally applicable answer to it. If everyone were the same, then once we knew what made one person's life go well, what constituted his or her happiness, then we would know for everyone else too. There would be no controversy; we could just go to our local human well-being expert, like we go to our local garden centre, and get the specific instructions for living a good life, just as we get the instructions for caring for our plants from a qualified horticulturist. Life would then be a straightforward matter of following the relevant advice.

Alas (or fortunately, depending on your outlook), the formula for living well is not so easily obtained. We all know that despite our similarities there are varied and considerable differences between us. As a result, there is no one specific formula or set of instructions to follow to live a good life. There are many ways that lives can go well, and since we need to discover which way is best for us, we need to develop our critical powers of analysis to help us along. When you consider how different individuals can differently answer the question of what they should do to live well, you can see how matters become even more complex and disputable as we widen our focus. You can see how we are led to disagreement and controversy about how to relate to others, about how to organize and fairly govern our society, and about how to conduct ourselves in relation to the biotic communities and ecosystems that comprise the natural world.

To further illustrate the controversial nature of ethics that is due to differences over value judgments, consider the following example from Canadian constitutional legal history. In the early and influential *Canadian Charter of Rights and Freedoms'* case *R. v. Oakes,* heard before the Supreme Court in 1986, then-Supreme Court Chief Justice Brian Dickson considered the issue of the rightful legal limits of our *Charter* rights. Section 1 of the *Charter* states that "The *Canadian Charter of Rights and Freedoms* guarantees the rights and freedoms set out in it subject only to such reasonable limits prescribed by law as can be demonstrably justified in a free and democratic society."[2] In other words, according to the *Charter*, we have guaranteed legal rights, but these rights are not inviolable. They can be limited or overridden in the interests of the collective good of Canadian society, specifically in the interests of promoting a free and democratic society. But what makes a society free and democratic? In developing what is known as the Oakes Test, the test that helps the courts determine when a law may override our *Charter* rights, then-Chief Justice Dickson took on the challenging task of trying to outline the basic values and principles that underlie our society. He wrote that these values and principles are "to name but a few, respect for the inherent dignity of the human person, commitment to social justice and equality, accommodation of a wide variety of beliefs, respect for cultural and group identity, and faith in social and political institutions which enhance the participation of individuals and groups in society."[3]

Former Chief Justice Dickson, who died in 1998, was a good example of an expert, someone supremely knowledgeable about the law. But his statement of our basic values engenders numerous controversies, debates, and further questions, rather than simple acceptance of his opinion. We disagree about the identity, interpretation, application, and relative importance of these values and principles. Consider again the list of basic Canadian values and principles that he identified:

- respect for the inherent dignity of the human person;

- commitment to social justice and equality;

- accommodation of a wide variety of beliefs;

- respect for cultural and group identity; and

- faith in social and political institutions that enhance the participation of individuals and groups in society.

Identity

How does one go about drawing up a list of the basic values and principles that underlie our society and our *Charter*? Should we take a poll or a set of polls? This is unlikely to lead us to unanimity. Do we rather defer to the judgment of the chief justice of the Supreme Court or of the prime minister? Should we defer instead to the judgment of the leader of the Official Opposition? Securing agreement on the identity of our basic values looks challenging.

Former Chief Justice Dickson claimed that his is only a partial list. How does one complete it? Is it even possible to complete it? Another difficult question is how one identifies changes in the list. Arguably our society's values and underlying principles have changed over time and will change again in the future, though here too perhaps some would disagree.

Interpretation and Application

As we delve deeper into this example, we get a better sense of just how controversial questions about values, especially ethical and political values, can be. Even if you thought that securing agreement on the question of what our basic social and political values are is not so challenging, there is the further issue of how to interpret these values. Assuming that former Chief Justice Dickson's list is correct, in the case of each item, we can ask for clarification and interpretation. So, for instance, what exactly is social justice and equality? What does a commitment to these require of us? Does this mean, for example, that all Canadians are entitled to a minimum yearly income, or not? Does it mean that we think that all Canadians should have equal access to a reasonably high standard of health care? Who is the expert who can answer these questions for us?

Relative Ranking

How should we weigh the relative importance of these values and principles? Does one always trump the others? Is one relatively more important most of the time? Are some more important sometimes and others other times? If so, how do we proceed when these values and principles conflict? For example, how do we balance accommodating a wide variety of beliefs with showing respect for cultural and group identity when these clash? Which is more important? Why? Should extremists who deny the Holocaust have a right to voice their opinions when such views are an affront to others?

These are just a sampling of the questions raised when we consider this judgment. Notice the difference between the question of our basic societal values and the relatively uncontroversial questions in other areas of expertise. How do the various systems in a car work? Qualified auto mechanics don't fundamentally disagree about the answer to this question. Likewise, dentists generally agree about how to maintain good oral health, and experts in human anatomy agree about the names and location of all the bones in the human body. And so it is with many other fields of expertise. But the field of Normative Ethics is different due in part to the central role that controversies about values play in it. Thus, to make as much progress on the issues as we can, and to realize the prudential value of studying ethics and applied ethics, we need to develop our critical thinking skills. Hence our focus on critical analysis.

2. Ethics is complex.

Another reason why we focus on developing our critical reasoning skills is because the subject matter of Normative Ethics is often complex, as the *Charter* example above demonstrates. To usefully sort through the many issues raised in ethics, we need to think clearly and carefully. If ethical problems were controversial but simple, we would not need to focus so much on developing our thinking skills to solve them. But as many of the issues discussed in this book show, moral questions and dilemmas are often quite complex, involving many factors and competing and conflicting interests. It is often difficult to solve ethical problems because doing so frequently involves identifying, interpreting, and weighing the values and interests of those involved and patiently and sensitively sorting through the various facets of the problems.

3. Ethics is incomplete.

We place so much emphasis on critical analysis because the study of ethics is incomplete. We need to become better thinkers to make further progress on the difficult moral questions that remain to be answered and the unforeseen challenges that we will have to face in the future. This is true both for us as individuals and for society in general. We noted before that some people are put off by the thought of having to work out the answers to ethical questions for themselves partly because they assume that others have already done the work and have the answers.

However, as much as the writings of those who have contributed to Normative Ethics can help guide us, they did not, nor could not, write specifically for our lives and particular circumstances. As we just observed, we are different. Furthermore, our differences extend beyond differences in personal values to encompass differences in personalities, qualities, and character. All of these differences contribute to the uniqueness of many of the situations we encounter in the course of our lives. A book on ethics can do no more than give us general guidance, and it must necessarily be incomplete, at least sometimes. For these times, we will need to work out our beliefs and conduct for ourselves, and to do this well, it will be useful to have the sort of resolution and courage to think for ourselves to which Kant referred.

This incompleteness in ethics as it applies to our future lives extends more generally to the subject as a whole. Although considerable progress has been made in dealing with various moral problems and questions in life, there are good reasons for thinking that much more work remains to be done. Thus, even though there are experts in Normative Ethics who can provide us with much insight, they don't have all the answers. Partly this is due to the presence of new moral issues that have arisen as a result of advances in technology and science. Although moral outlooks and frameworks from the past can offer us much useful direction and guidance, they were not designed to speak to some of the previously unanticipated issues with which our society must now deal. Plato, Aristotle, and Kant did not consciously develop their ethical views to respond to troubling questions about the ethics of cloning, xenotransplantation (cross-species transplantation), or intellectual property rights in computer software, to name just a few.

These points offer some support for the view that the philosophical study of ethics is controversial, complex, and incomplete. In turn, this helps explain both why we focus so much in philosophy on developing our critical reasoning skills and why such skills are useful for us. As we proceed you will be exposed to many opposing viewpoints. The process of identifying, understanding, and weighing arguments in ethics, and relating this to one's own values is challenging. This means that to benefit most from the study of this text, you must be prepared to work. The material is interesting and fun, and the subject matter is relevant for our lives, but there is no escaping the fact that to improve your analytical reasoning skills, and to make substantive progress on the issues in ethics, you must apply yourself.

I.6 The Limited Depth of Our Investigation

The process of weighing arguments and reaching conclusions on the many different issues and topics we will be examining is a long one, longer than we have space to work with in this book. This means that although we will make considerable progress, we will not reach final and settled positions on most of the topics that we will be examining. On most issues there will be more viewpoints, criticisms, and arguments to consider. In general, there will be more thinking left to do, thinking I hope you are stimulated to pursue after you leave these pages behind.

It might seem odd to think that despite the lengthy discussions we will engage in here that we will not be reaching final answers to many of the questions we pose. However, there are some good reasons for this. *An Introduction to Ethics: Theories, Perspectives, and Issues* is a general introduction to ethics. The breadth of our analysis limits our space to consider the issues we will be encountering in the sort of depth we would need to reach ultimate conclusions on most of our topics. Considering that there is an extensive philosophical literature that is continuously

growing on the complete range of questions that we will raise, it is unsurprising that we won't be arriving at the last word on most of the issues. This is not to say that there are no right or correct answers in ethics. This is a common misconception, fostered perhaps by the brevity of introductory courses and introductory textbooks in our area, and by the nature of our investigation. We will be considering the idea that there are right answers in some detail in Chapter 3, though this is the subject of a lively debate too. Rather, the point is that the process of investigation is ongoing and there is insufficient space to consider and evaluate all the arguments in the debates that we will raise. Therefore, it is up to you to make up your mind about the various subjects and questions. I also encourage you to continue your philosophical investigations by reflecting further on the issues, discussing them with your colleagues and friends, and by reading the work of others.

I.7 The Spirit of Philosophical Investigation

"Disputes with men, pertinaciously obstinate in their principles, are, of all others, the most irksome; except, perhaps, those with persons, entirely disingenuous, who really do not believe the opinions they defend, but engage in the controversy, from affectation, from a spirit of opposition, or from a desire of showing wit and ingenuity, superior to the rest of mankind."

David Hume
An Enquiry Concerning the Principles of Morals

Given the constant flow of argument and counter-argument, of criticism and rebuttal, heated philosophical debate sometimes veers off topic. Add on to this the controversial and personal nature of many ethical disagreements, and debates in ethics sometimes transform into nasty personal attacks and counterattacks. This process is perhaps further aided by an unfortunate ambiguity in the meaning of the word "argument." In one common sense of the word, an "**argument**" is a fight or a dispute, as in the sentence: "The couple next door broke up after they had a terrible argument." It is a common misperception that philosophers' arguments are of this sort. In contrast, the word "argument" sometimes refers to a set of claims, called the *premises* of the argument, that are advanced to support a further claim, the *conclusion* of the argument. Philosophers advance arguments to rationally persuade those to whom they address their remarks.

In this book, as you have no doubt noted, the word "argument" is used in the second sense. Likewise, we use this sense of the word in philosophy generally. Thus, an argument is not a bad thing; rather, it is a tool we can use to help us achieve deeper understanding. In the passage quoted above, Hume cites examples of those who engage in discussions with closed minds or in bad faith. Discussions in what he calls a "spirit of opposition" are unlikely to realize the full value of philosophical enquiry. In contrast, this text is best read and used in what might be called the "spirit of philosophy." Philosophical investigation is a co-operative enterprise that aims at improving understanding. Arguments advanced in the spirit of philosophy are presented with a view to gaining insight and knowledge. So it is too with counter-arguments and reasoned enquiry generally.

In the spirit of philosophy, you are invited to consider the arguments presented in this book as friendly challenges to your present opinions and beliefs. Consider these challenges as part of a co-operative endeavour to aid us in reaching the most ethical and reasonable beliefs we can and in positively shaping our values. Approach this book with an open mind. Insofar as is reasonable, regard your present beliefs and values as provisional and subject to revision or even rejection subject to further study, reflection, discovery, and counter-argument.

You are also encouraged to regard the work of those writing in the past in a similar spirit. Philosophical work, as with work in other academic disciplines, takes place on a foundation of enquiry and discussion laid down by those who have come before us. The past study of ethics provides us with ways of conceiving of the issues

and problems we face now, with conceptual tools for dealing with these problems, and with numerous insights into them. Given the critically reflective nature of our enquiry, we would be amiss to passively accept the claims, arguments, and values endorsed by the influential figures of the past. But we are wise to begin by thinking about their views. To this end, a fair bit of discussion generated from the history of philosophy has been placed throughout the book.

In the spirit of philosophy, consider the various historical positions and points with a critical eye and an open mind. In addition to working with the texts of the past toward achieving enlightenment in ethics, I encourage you to weigh the arguments of those you disagree with here and in your classes in the spirit of philosophy. Given that our goal is improved understanding, constructive argument and criticism are useful aids.

> In one sense an **argument** is a fight or dispute. In a second sense an argument is a set of claims in which one or more of these claims, called the premise or premises, is or are offered as support for another claim, called the conclusion. Except where explicitly noted otherwise, we will use the word in this second sense.

I.8 Review

This introductory chapter was mostly devoted to briefly identifying our subject matter and to explaining the nature and limits of our learning. We noted specifically that due to the controversial, complex, and incomplete nature of normative ethical debates, we pay special attention to developing our critical reasoning skills. The example involving the *Charter* and the question of the basic values that underlie our society and legal system helped underscore the need for reasoned and sensitive debate in aspects of our lives that involve judgments about our values. To advance that debate, we use our powers of critical analysis, and thus, both to work through the material of this book and make more progress on the issues, we engage in debate and critical reasoning. We do so in "the spirit of philosophy" or what Kant called "achieving enlightenment."

Notes

1. The idea that ethics is properly a subject of philosophical study, as opposed to an area of scientific enquiry, is a matter of greater debate than is suggested here. We revisit this issue and examine the various arguments with greater care and in more detail in Chapter 1 and Chapter 3.

2. The *Canadian Charter of Rights and Freedoms*, *Constitution Act*, 1982, Part 1, Section 1.

3. Bickenbach, ed. (1993), p. 45.

Exercises

Progress Check

1. Explain the process/product distinction and how it applies to this book.

2. What is critical reasoning? Briefly explain.

3. Explain the distinction between Descriptive Ethics and Normative Ethics. How is the philosophical study of ethics unlike the scientific study of it?

4. According to Immanuel Kant, what is enlightenment? Explain in your own words.

5. Why is ethics controversial? What is the value of developing one's critical reasoning skills to help achieve enlightenment in ethics?

6. According to former Supreme Court Justice Brian Dickson, what are the basic values and principles that underlie Canadian society?

7. Why is ethics complex?

8. Why is the study of ethics incomplete?

9. What is the spirit of philosophical investigation?

10. Why should we bother reading the work of philosophers from the past?

Questions for Further Reflection

1. In their sweeping paper, "Toward *Fin de siècle* Ethics: Some Trends" [*The Philosophical Review*, Vol. 101, No. 1 (January 1992), pp. 115–189], Stephen Darwall, Allan Gibbard, and Peter Railton argue that "Too many moral philosophers and commentators on moral philosophy—and we do not exempt ourselves—have been content to invent their psychology or anthropology from scratch and do their history on the strength of selective reading of texts rather than more comprehensive research into contexts. "Assuming that their complaint is a valid one, how can you foresee improving one's work in Normative Ethics by being better informed about research in psychology, anthropology, and history? More generally, what connections do you see between Normative Ethics and these other disciplines?

2. Are you a reasonably enlightened person? If you think so, give an example of when you have recently demonstrated this and show how your example demonstrates enlightenment. If you think not, explain why. Whether you think that you are reasonably enlightened or not, explain any specific ways that you can become more enlightened.

3. What expertise do you think professional philosophers who specialize in Normative Ethics and Value Theory have? What do you think is the closest match to this expertise among other professional academics? Defend your view.

4. What problems can you foresee with trying to identify, interpret, apply, and rank the fundamental values and principles that underlie Canadian society? Discuss each of these points in ways that extend beyond the discussion in the text.

5. Can the study of ethics ever be complete? Will there always be unanticipated situations that will require further work to be done in the subject? Discuss.

6. What factors will limit our progress on the issues we will consider in this book? Defend your view.

7. Explain and critically assess the idea that the study of ethics, Applied Ethics, and Value Theory can lead to social progress.

Group Work Activity:

The Problem of Identifying the Fundamental Values and Principles of Canadian Society

As noted in this chapter, former Supreme Court Chief Justice Brian Dickson identified what he considered to be some of the fundamental values that underlie Canadian society in his landmark decision in the case *R. v. Oakes*. Once again, here is the list of values and principles that he identified:

- respect for the inherent dignity of the human person;
- commitment to social justice and equality;
- accommodation of a wide variety of beliefs;
- respect for cultural and group identity; and
- faith in social and political institutions that enhance the participation of individuals and groups in society.

Former Chief Justice Dickson noted that this was only a partial list. Your group work task is to try to reach some consensus among the group members and draw up your account of the fundamental set of values and principles that guide our society. These values and principles should not only be consistent with the rights and freedoms described in the *Canadian Charter of Rights and Freedoms* but also serve as a guide for lawmakers and judges to help determine when our rights should be limited or over-ridden. Be prepared to defend your list.

Feel free to amend, delete, or add to the items on former Chief Justice Dickson's list, but remember that you will have to defend any changes or additions. You may also feel free to draw on any sources for compiling your list, but again remember that you must defend your use of these sources. In addition to identifying our values and principles, your task is also to critically evaluate them. Therefore, you should develop an argument for adding, amending, and deleting any values and principles that you think we should or should not have or be committed to that we do not currently accept. For example, as we shall see in Chapter 9, many people believe that we should be committed to a principle of extending more concern to sentient non-human animals.

Advice on How to Proceed

First, don't be intimidated by the apparent enormity of this task. Remember that you are being asked to identify the basic values of your own society and to critically evaluate them. Proceed either by drawing up your own list and then discussing it with the other members of your group after they have also done so, or try collaborating on a common list together. Dickson's list can serve as a useful starting point for your deliberations and discussions. To help fill out your list, you might try to identify some characteristically Canadian traits and then consider how they might be reflected in your list. For example, we pride ourselves on being a peaceful nation. How about including a commitment to the non-violent resolution of conflict where this can be achieved without compromising our other basic values? Together you can then proceed with your evaluation.

Insofar as you can reach a consensus, next present your group's list to the other groups in your class. Once all the groups have presented their lists, try to reach a large-group consensus by working first from the items that appear on all the lists to discussing other candidate items that appear on only some lists.

Some Final Questions

Based on your small- and large-group discussions, do you think it is possible to compile a list for our entire society? Do you think there is a fair bit of consensus about this? Some consensus but some significant disagreement too? Do you see other barriers to drawing up a list for all of Canadian society that didn't present themselves in your particular discussions? If so, what are they, in your opinion?

Suggested Further Reading

I owe the point about the question "what is philosophy?" being a philosophical question to Arthur C. Danto, *What Philosophy Is: A Guide to the Elements*. New York: Harper & Row Publishers, 1968, Chapter 1. I also recommend this book as a useful and lively general introduction to philosophy along with Professor Danto's other introductory book, *Connections to the World: The Basic Concepts of Philosophy*. New York: Harper & Row, 1989.

There are many good introductory books in informal and formal logic. One that focuses mostly on informal reasoning is Trudy Govier's *A Practical Study of Argument*, 5th ed., Belmont, California: Wadsworth, 2001. Two books that introduce both subjects are I. Copi and C. Cohen, *Introduction to Logic*, 11th ed., Upper Saddle River, New Jersey: Prentice Hall, 2002, and Patrick Hurley, *A Concise Introduction to Logic*, 7th ed., Belmont, California: Wadsworth, 2000.

Weblinks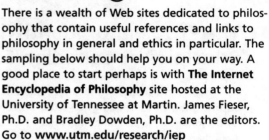

There is a wealth of Web sites dedicated to philosophy that contain useful references and links to philosophy in general and ethics in particular. The sampling below should help you on your way. A good place to start perhaps is with **The Internet Encyclopedia of Philosophy** site hosted at the University of Tennessee at Martin. James Fieser, Ph.D. and Bradley Dowden, Ph.D. are the editors. Go to **www.utm.edu/research/iep**

For a wealth of references and links to philosophy sites, go to EpistemeLinks.com at **www.epistemelinks.com/index.asp**

Also see the Web site of the Philosophy Department of Valdosta State University at **www.valdosta.peachnet.edu/~rbarnett/phi/resource.html**

A useful place to start searching for ethics-related sites and information is Lawrence Hinman's Ethics Updates at **www.ethics.acusd.edu**

Also see the Web site of the Centre for Applied Ethics at the University of British Columbia at **www.ethics.ubc.ca/resources**

Part 1

Theories

Our focus in Part One is on ethical theory. More specifically, we examine an assortment of basic issues in philosophical ethics, with an emphasis on ethical theory. After outlining in Chapter 1 the territory within the subject, including its major subtopics of Meta-Ethics and Normative or Prescriptive Ethics, we distinguish ethics from religious studies and law in Chapter 2. In the course of tracing the emergence (or re-emergence) of the secular study of ethics in the West in the past several hundred years, we encounter our first ethical theory, Natural Law Theory. Turning from how ethics is distinct from religious studies and law, we discuss a number of elemental questions in Meta-Ethics in Chapter 3. These questions raise issues about the role of both reason and sentiment in morality,

and they ask whether, and if so to what extent, ethical relativism is true. We also address the question whether there are moral facts.

From these basic issues in Meta-Ethics, we turn in the final three chapters of Part One to consider a number of ethical theories or frameworks. Among these are Consequentialism, Utilitarianism, Kantian Theory and Deontology, Virtue Theory, and Feminist Theory. These varying perspectives are the principal outlooks used in the philosophical analysis of ethical issues. Our treatment of them in Part One will provide us with some guidance and ideas when we consider the various practical issues and problems we examine throughout Parts Two and Three.

Ethics

Learning Outcomes

This chapter introduces ethics by presenting the fields of study within Philosophical Ethics, namely Normative or Prescriptive Ethics and Meta-Ethics. These fields are themselves sorted into a number of areas and topics. Within Normative Ethics we distinguish ethical theory, Relationship Ethics, Applied Ethics, and Professional Ethics. Within Meta-Ethics we address questions about the nature, justification, purpose, scope, and origins of morality.

Upon the successful completion of this chapter you will be able to

1. distinguish between two senses of the word "ethics";
2. identify the various fields of study within ethics and their interrelations; and
3. explain the distinction between top-down and bottom-up approaches to Prescriptive Ethics.

1.1 Our Subject Matter

Before we can begin the process of methodically working through the many ethical questions and issues we will consider, we first need a solid appreciation of ethics. At first glance this may seem odd. After all, what is the point of introducing us to what we already know? We all have extensive experience doing the right thing, caring about others, and knowing right from wrong. Morality is something we are taught from early childhood. Why introduce the subject matter of ethics?

It is true that we all have experience with morality in the course of our everyday lives. This mitigates the need to introduce our subject matter compared to, say, geophysics or neurophysiology, subjects about which most people know little. But keep in mind that our concern is with Normative Ethics—the systematic and philosophical study of ethics. "Ethics" as it refers to our practices and beliefs about how to get along in life is distinct from the philosophical study of ethics, which is our concern in this book.

1.2 Ethics

In the Introduction we distinguished between Descriptive Ethics and Normative Ethics and noted that our concern is with the normative study of ethics, that is, with the study of questions about how we ought to be and live our lives. As a rough description this was a decent start, but we need to develop and further refine our account. The word "ethics" can refer to the particular principles, teachings, or codes that guide our practices in life. Thus, of a criminal someone might say, "his ethics leave a lot to be desired," or "he has no ethics." The word can also refer to the general study of these principles, teachings, and codes. This is the sense used when someone says, "Kant's contribution to ethics should not be underestimated." Despite our ultimately practical orientation, our discussion of ethics will be focused mostly on ethics as a field of study. So unless it is clear from the context that the word "ethics" refers to someone's practices, throughout this book we will use the word in the second sense, to refer to the field of study we have identified as Philosophical Ethics.

"Ethics" and "Morality"

Since confusion over the meaning of "ethics" extends to the meaning of "morality," we should clarify our use of this term too. Some reserve the word "morality" to pick out an individual's or group's ethical beliefs and practices, and they reserve the word "ethics" to refer to the academic general study of this. We sometimes speak of a professional code of ethics as opposed to a professional code of morality, and we talk of business ethics as opposed to business morality. Moreover, some use the word "morality" more narrowly to refer to an individual's ethical beliefs and practices and use the word "ethics" to refer to the collective moral beliefs and practices of identifiable groups.

No doubt there are these subtly different shades of meaning, and others besides, in the use of the two words. There is also some point in preserving these differences and using the terms carefully in these ways, so the decision to not follow these conventions comes at some price of subtlety. However, "ethics" and "morality" will be used interchangeably here for the sake of simplicity and ease of exposition.

1.3 The Range of the Study of Ethics

So far we have noted that the subject matter of ethics is the right and wrong conduct of individuals. Although this is indeed part of its domain of study, it is only part. In the study of ethics we are concerned not only with conduct, behaviour, and actions but also with motivation, character, beliefs, and feelings. In general we are interested in the full assortment of ways that ethics bears on individual life. One way ethical theories sometimes differ is in terms of their focus. For example, under the general heading of "Utilitarianism," a theory considered in Chapter 4, we can distinguish an array of more specific theories including versions of Act, Rule, Motive, Character, and Conscience Utilitarianism, to name only a few.

It is also somewhat vague to say that we will be concerned with ethics as it bears on the life of individuals. This could be taken to mean that our interest in ethics is limited to reflecting on what individuals should think and feel, how they should act, and how they should shape their character for living their everyday lives. Although this will comprise a significant part of our concern, it will not exhaust it. Rather, our concern is with the wide range of areas and perspectives in life upon which ethics bears. So although much of our attention will be devoted to personal issues of morality, we will also examine ethics as it pertains to questions about many other spheres in life. Ethical issues arise in the formation and development of social policy and law, in the consideration of our treatment of non-human animals, and in the consideration of our treatment of the environment in general. We will consider each of these perspectives and issues arising from them.

In response, you might argue that all these areas of life are areas of individual concern. As individuals we wear many hats, and have many kinds of interests. Responsible citizens in society take an active interest in and some responsibility for the formation of the social policies and laws of their governments and legal institutions. Likewise, they take an active interest in policies and laws that affect non-human animals and the environment. Furthermore, when we talk about moral agency we must talk about the agency of individuals. Indeed, you might add, the consideration of ethics makes sense only for those beings, individuals every one, who can make a difference in the world, who can act. So, it might be argued, it is not limiting to insist that our concern with ethics is as it relates to individuals.

Although this is true, our concern in this book is with ethics beyond those that arise in our everyday lives. This is not to say that the issues we examine are not issues for individuals; they are. It is rather to remind us that ethical concerns impact the wider world around us and that we can view these concerns from different perspectives. So, for example, in Part Two we will consider the issue of weighing and ranking the value of human life and how this should impact social policy. We will also examine, from different perspectives, the issue of giving non-human animals moral concern. Although these issues have some connections to our everyday lives, most people are not in the position of determining what social policy and law should be in these areas. Thinking consciously about these problems can widen our outlook on life.

Related to this point about widening our outlook is a more general point about the value of education in ethics. I have emphasized the practical import of studying this text, but this is not its only value. Our concern is also with answering general questions, including questions about the nature, purpose, justification, scope, and origins of morality. Making progress on these questions and issues is valuable in itself or just for satisfying our curiosity and desire to know about these matters. Indeed, a good part of the value of the work you will do here will likely not directly impact your day-to-day life, nor should it.

1.4 The Elements of Ethics

As with many other issues in philosophy, the divisions of study within Normative Ethics are somewhat controversial. We will consider some rationale for identifying and organizing the subfields as we do, but this defence will be brief, and you should consider it with a critical eye. For a schematic overview of ethics, see Figure 1.1. Remember that these categories are rough and intended only to help us better appreciate the divisions of study within the subject and the approximate relations between these various subfields. They are not offered as mutually exclusive subdivisions because the areas overlap in several ways.

Philosophical Ethics

We noted in the Introduction that ethics as a subject of study can be roughly divided into two main subfields: Descriptive Ethics, as is pursued by cultural anthropologists, and Normative Ethics, the area of study within philosophy. As a rough account this is fine, but the philosophical study of ethics involves not only the study of norms or prescriptions but also the study of the set of background and framing issues in Normative Ethics. This area of study is known as Meta-Ethics, and we will consider it in the "Meta-Ethics" section later in the chapter. Normative Ethics is also referred to as "Prescriptive Ethics." Both terms convey the idea that the philosophical study of ethics includes the study of moral norms and ethical prescriptions and proscriptions, as opposed to describing the particular moral code of some group.

Facts and Values and the Is/Ought Divide

The distinction between the descriptive approach to the study of ethics and the normative or prescriptive approach has been the subject of much debate and controversy.

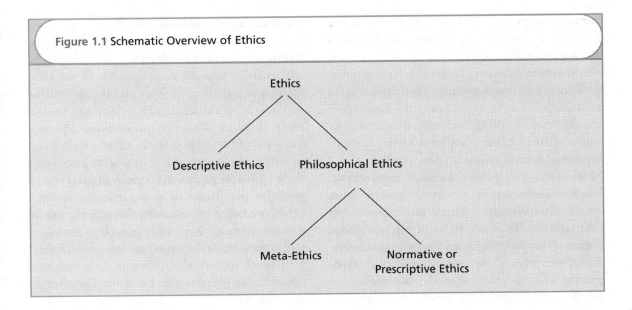

Figure 1.1 Schematic Overview of Ethics

Philosophers in the past distinguished between Descriptive and Normative Ethics in terms of the fact/value and is/ought distinctions. For our purposes Descriptive Ethics is concerned with what is—the study of facts about the world, like, for example, whether euthanasia is accepted or not from society to society. In contrast, Normative Ethics is concerned with values, especially moral values, and with moral norms—with what humans ought to do, like, for example, whether euthanasia should be accepted. It is important to stress that these concepts are presented only as rough guides intended to offer some initial clarification of the distinction between Normative and Descriptive Ethics, no more.[1]

1.5 Normative or Prescriptive Ethics

Ethical Theories and Approaches

Normative or Prescriptive Ethics refers to the specific approaches, theories, frameworks, and views about how we should be, how we ought to live, and what we should and should not do. Thus, here Normative Ethics and Prescriptive Ethics refer to the particular approaches, theories, views, and frameworks that consist of

specific prescriptions and proscriptions, the dos and don'ts of morality. So, for example, Ethical Egoism is a particular prescriptive ethical theory or outlook that states that people should act to promote their own self-interests.[2] "Always look out for number one" could be an example of an egoist prescription. "Don't sacrifice your happiness for the sake of another" could be an example of an egoist proscription.

As a normative theory, Ethical Egoism is a theory about how we should be and how we should act. Like many other ethical theories it offers some unified account of how we should live our lives. Defenders of various prescriptive theories and frameworks argue that we need to systematically align our behaviour with their theory to be moral. In chapters 2, 4, 5, and 6, and to some extent in chapters 7, 11, and 12, we will examine a number of different theories or approaches in Normative Ethics. By learning about the various prescriptive views, you can consider a range of arguments to help better inform your practices. Prescriptive ethical theories and outlooks are valuable mainly

Normative or Prescriptive Ethics is the study of the particular moral theories, views, approaches, and frameworks that consist of the specific prescriptions and proscriptions of morality. More generally, the study of Normative Ethics is the systematic study of ethical conduct, character, and practice. It is also the study of practical ethical questions and issues that encompasses the fields of *Applied Ethics*, *Professional Ethics*, and *Relationship Ethics*.

because they provide us with practical guidance in resolving the moral problems and dilemmas we face in our daily lives.

We follow common usage in referring to the various normative approaches and frameworks as "theories," but we should note the loose sense in which we are using this term. In the stricter sense "theory" carries common conceptions of science of a more or less unified, predictive, and general account of some range of phenomena. On this understanding we devise theories based on the observational evidence and experiments we perform with an eye to acquiring knowledge about all similar situations and circumstances. Thus, for instance, we speak about a theory of gravity and appeal to the idea of gravity to explain why objects like apples fall to the ground under specific circumstances. We also appeal to our theory to make predictions about what will happen to objects similarly situated in the future.

This stricter use of the word "theory" fits only some conceptions of ethics and ethical knowledge. The mere use of the term to describe ethics presupposes a particular account of the nature of morality. Some begin from the assumption that the goal of a theory in Prescriptive Ethics is to provide us with the general rules or principles that we can then apply to concrete situations to distinguish right from wrong and to determine what we should do. The ancient Greek philosopher Plato (427–347 BC) defended this sort of approach in his account of moral epistemology, according to which the truths about ethics are abstract, immutable, and eternal. In contrast, Plato's student Aristotle (384–322 BC) argued that the goal of ethics is not to provide us with theoretical knowledge but to help us get along in life. He argued that the study of ethics helps us develop our judgment and virtues so that we can better judge how we should act in different circumstances and situations. For Aristotle, ethics is not top-down; rather it is bottom-up, so general rules, principles, and ethical theories in the strict sense are of limited value.

> **Applied Ethics** is the field of study within Normative Ethics that is devoted to examining ethical questions and issues that arise in distinct spheres of life. Bioethics, Business Ethics, Environmental Ethics, and Computer Ethics are all examples of areas within Applied Ethics.

It should be stressed that this characterization of different approaches to ethics (top-down, bottom-up), and the linking of these with Plato and Aristotle offer only a general way of thinking about and assessing the various ethical theories we will be considering. The strict or narrow sense of the term "theory" presupposes a particular set of assumptions about the nature of morality. Since part of our goal is to investigate these assumptions, we don't want to preclude or prejudge the fitness of any particular account before we begin by assuming through the use of a word that one kind of approach is the right one. Thus we use the word "theory" only loosely. If you prefer, think of the theories as approaches, outlooks, or frameworks. I will use these terms interchangeably.

Among the theories or outlooks we will consider are Ethical Egoism; Utilitarianism; Consequentialism; duty-bound approaches to ethics including Natural Law Theory and rights theories; common-sense morality; Virtue Theory; and feminist theories.

Applied Ethics, Professional Ethics, and Relationship Ethics

In addition to the study of particular prescriptive theories, Normative Ethics encompasses the general examination of practical moral issues, questions, and problems from various perspectives. In the past 30 years in Anglo-American philosophy, a number of fields within Prescriptive Ethics have been greatly expanded and developed. Among these have been the subjects of Applied Ethics, Professional Ethics, and Relationship Ethics. Although there is some overlap between these areas, the distinctions between them remain useful. In Chapter 8 we will consider some issues in Relationship Ethics. Part Three is devoted to considering the areas of Applied and Professional Ethics.

Applied Ethics

Applied Ethics refers to the practical study of ethics from within particular spheres of life in which moral problems and issues arise that are distinctive and sometimes unique to those particular spheres. In the expanding field of Applied Ethics some of the most commonly studied subjects are Bioethics, including the ethics of the practice of medicine, health care, and scientific research; Business Ethics; Environmental Ethics; and Computer Ethics and Ethics and Information Technology. Most of Part Three is devoted to Applied Ethics, although a host of Applied Ethics issues and problems are discussed throughout the book.

Professional Ethics

Professional Ethics comprises the study of ethical issues and concerns as they impact various areas of the lives, and especially the work, of professionals. Professionals are commonly distinguished by their independence, their mastery of a recognized body of knowledge, and by the special rights and duties they have in virtue of their work and education. As a result of these work-related rights and duties, many professions are formally or informally bound by specific ethical codes of conduct. The subject of Professional Ethics is thus an area within Prescriptive Ethics that examines and evaluates the specific moral concerns of these groups of working people, like, for example, the concerns physicians have in allocating scarce health care resources, examined in Chapter 13. Among these groups are doctors, lawyers, engineers, accountants, nurses, dentists, counsellors, journalists, and architects.

Relationship Ethics

The field of **Relationship Ethics** is the study of the ethical issues and problems that we confront generally as social beings in the run of our daily lives. Alternatively referred to as "Personal Ethics" or "Interpersonal Ethics," the area of Relationship Ethics broaches the moral issues involving family and friends, love and sex, and such topics as trust and truth-telling, lies, and deceptions as these impact our workaday lives. We address some of these topics in Part Two.

Ethical theory, Relationship Ethics, Applied Ethics, and Professional Ethics overlap in a number of ways. For example, various ethical theories can and are used to help answer questions in each of the other three areas of Prescriptive

Ethics. Also, the issue of the ethics of lying and deceiving is prominent in Professional Ethics and many of the fields within Applied Ethics. Likewise, several matters dealing with sex enter discussions of Professional and Applied Ethics. Nevertheless, maintaining the distinctions between these four areas is a useful and accepted practice. With this brief survey of the domain of Normative or Prescriptive Ethics, we can now supplement our schematic overview of ethics (see Figure 1.2).

1.6 Meta-Ethics

As with the other distinctions in our schematic overview of ethics, the distinction between Normative Ethics and Meta-Ethics is loose and presented as a guide only. Within philosophy there is no universally accepted understanding of what Meta-Ethics is, although for many years an influential group of analytic philosophers regarded Meta-Ethics as the study of the meaning of moral terms like "good" and "right." These thinkers argued that their expertise extended only to meta-ethical questions and they viewed normative questions that arise in Prescriptive Ethics as beyond the expertise of philosophers.

Epistemology is the study of the nature of knowledge and justification. Questions such as "What is knowledge?" and "What is truth?" are basic epistemological questions. Included in the study of epistemology are questions about the scope of knowledge and the basis or bases of justification. Skeptics raise doubts about the possibility and especially the limits and foundations of knowledge.

> **Professional Ethics** is the field of study within Normative Ethics that examines ethical issues and concerns as they impact various areas of the lives, and especially the work, of professionals like physicians, lawyers, and engineers. Professionals are often subject to specific codes of conduct.

> **Relationship Ethics,** also known as Personal or Interpersonal Ethics, is the field of study within Normative Ethics that examines the ethical questions and issues faced by individuals in the course of their lives as social beings. Questions about the ethics of family and friend relations and issues involving the morality of sex and love are among those that are prominent in this area.

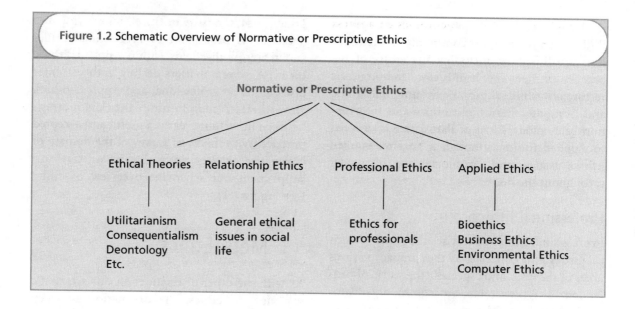

Figure 1.2 Schematic Overview of Normative or Prescriptive Ethics

Normative or Prescriptive Ethics

Ethical Theories

Utilitarianism
Consequentialism
Deontology
Etc.

Relationship Ethics

General ethical
issues in social
life

Professional Ethics

Ethics for
professionals

Applied Ethics

Bioethics
Business Ethics
Environmental Ethics
Computer Ethics

Nevertheless, we will follow more recent practice and define "Meta-Ethics" more broadly. Generally we will understand **Meta-Ethics** to be the area concerned with the broad background and framing issues arising in connection with the concerns of Normative Ethics. We noted that Normative Ethics is the study of the practical and immediately pressing questions concerning how we should be, what we should and should not do, how we should shape law and policy, and so on. Put simply, Normative Ethics is concerned with spelling out the specific dos and don'ts of morality. In contrast, Meta-Ethics is the study of questions about the underpinnings and limits of questions in Normative Ethics. These include questions about the analysis of moral language and epistemological and metaphysical questions about morality. But Meta-Ethics as we will understand it extends beyond posing these traditional questions to asking a broader range of questions about morality.

> **Non-Cognitivism** in ethics is the view that moral judgments do not express propositions. As such, they have no truth-value (they are neither true nor false) and therefore there is no such thing as ethical knowledge. **Ethical Subjectivism** is a non-cognitivist theory about ethics according to which moral judgments are really only the reports or statements of the attitudes of those making the judgments. **Emotivism** is a non-cognitivist theory about ethics according to which moral judgments are really only the expressions of the feelings of those making the judgments. Typically, these expressions are ones of approval or disapproval.

Three examples of views within Meta-Ethics are Non-Cognitivism, Ethical Subjectivism, and Emotivism. **Non-Cognitivism** in ethics is the view that moral judgments do not assert propositions or make verifiable claims. As such they have no truth-value (they are neither true nor false) and therefore there is no such thing as ethical knowledge. So, for example, the Non-Cognitivist theory known as **Ethical Subjectivism** (see Chapter 3) asserts that when someone claims "That action is morally good," she is merely reporting her own pro-attitude toward the action. She is not asserting that it is true that the action is morally good. **Emotivism** is another non-cognitivist theory about ethics according to which moral judgments and so-called moral claims are really only the expressions of the feelings of those making the judgments. Typically these expressions are ones of approval or disapproval. On this view, someone's judgment that "That action is morally good" really expresses that person's approval of the action. Thus the judgment translates into "Hurray for that" or "You should do that!" Notice that Non-Cognitivism, Ethical Subjectivism, and Emotivism are not normative theories about ethics because they do not offer particular prescriptions or proscriptions. Rather, they are theories about the nature of morality. As such they fall within the domain of Meta-Ethics.

As with most of the other topics we address in this book, the field of Meta-Ethics as we are conceiving of it here is rather large, and the literature on it is quite extensive. Although we cannot discuss the full range of issues within the area, we will consider some of the basic questions that we need to address to present a well-rounded introduction to ethics. In particular we will address questions about the nature, justification, purpose, scope, and origins of morality.

The Nature of Morality

The question of the nature of morality is central to this book and one that we have already examined at some length. In the Introduction we noted that partly as a result of its relation to questions of individual well-being, ethics is controversial, complex, and incomplete. More generally we can discern two sorts of approaches to answering this basic question. We can illuminate the nature of ethics by considering it as a whole and trying to locate it relative to other fields of study. Alternatively we can answer the question about the nature of morality by analyzing its various elements and noting the contribution each makes to ethics as a whole.

In Chapter 2 we take the former approach by contrasting the philosophical study of ethics with religious studies, theology, and law. In this chapter we have pursued this latter approach, and we will extend what we started here in Chapter 3 by considering some fundamental metaphysical and epistemological questions about morality. We take up the question of the metaphysical status of moral goodness and moral properties in general by considering a version of Subjectivism in ethics, and a related question concerning moral objectivity and moral realism. We also consider some meta-ethical theories about the nature and justification of moral claims and judgments, namely Ethical Relativism and Ethical Absolutism. Three views we just identified, Non-Cognitivism, Ethical Subjectivism, and Emotivism, are meta-ethical theories about the nature of morality that likewise address epistemological issues in Meta-Ethics; specifically, they address questions about the possibility of acquiring ethical knowledge.

The Justification of Morality

Another set of meta-ethical questions focuses on the project of justifying morality. In recent times this project has been conceived of in two distinct ways, and we will consider each of these. The theories and debates that arise in discussion of the metaphysical and epistemological questions we address in Chapter 3 are traditionally associated with one conception of justification, according to which the project of justifying ethical claims and judgments is akin to theory justification as occurs in science. On this model, justifying morality concerns issues of truth, knowledge, and correctness, and one way of regarding a justified theory of morality is to see it as the true theory.

> **Meta-Ethics,** broadly conceived, is the field of study within philosophical ethics that addresses the general background and framing issues that underlie Normative or Prescriptive Ethics. Thus Meta-Ethics examines the underpinnings and limits of questions in Normative or Prescriptive Ethics. These include questions about the analysis of moral language and epistemological and metaphysical questions about morality. More generally, Meta-Ethics addresses questions about the nature, justification, purpose, scope, and origins of morality.

In Part Two we consider another model of justification in ethics, the so-called **Practical Reasoning Approach,** according to which the goal of justification is not to prove some theory correct or true but to show that some way of life or course of action in life is rational. On this model, ethics is associated with action and practical reason, and questions like "Is it rational to be moral?", "To what extent is it rational to be moral?", and "What is the relation between being rational and being ethical?" take centre stage.

> The **Practical Reasoning Approach** to the justification of morality indicates that the problem of justifying morality involves showing the rationality or practical benefit of being moral or leading a moral life.

The Point or Purpose of Morality

Another fundamental meta-ethical question we will address is the purpose of ethics or morality. In the course of considering this question, we survey and examine arguments of some competing views.

The Scope of Morality

Related to this question of the purpose of morality is the question of its scope. To whom or what can we have moral obligations? Why? These are conceptual questions about the kinds of beings for whom it makes sense to say that we owe moral consideration. In the course of answering these questions we assess arguments for a number of competing views including Anthropocentrism, Welfarism, Biocentrism, and Holism. Examining these last three views takes us into Environmental Ethics where the question of the scope of morality is much contested. We pursue this in chapters 11 and 12.

The Origins of Morality

Meta-ethical questions about the origins of morality ask where morality came from. Traditionally, the main competing answers appeal either to supernatural or natural explanations. So, on the one hand, there is a long stream of theologians and philosophers who have argued that God is the source of morality and, as a result, ethics is in one way or another based on religious teachings. In contrast, naturalist explanations of the origins of morality are found in natural science. Thus there are sociobiological and Darwinian accounts of the origins of morality that thinkers working in the area of environmental philosophy quote to help support their particular ethical outlooks. In chapters 2, 11, and 12, we consider these competing views.

1.7 Review

In this chapter we expanded our understanding of ethics by examining its various elements or subfields. The philosophical study of ethics (our area of concern) divides into two subfields, Normative or Prescriptive Ethics and Meta-Ethics. Normative Ethics is the study of the particular moral theories, views, approaches, and frameworks that consist of the specific prescriptions and proscriptions of morality. It is the systematic study of ethical conduct, character, and practice. It is also the study of practical ethical questions and issues that encompasses the fields of Applied Ethics, Professional Ethics, and Relationship Ethics. Meta-Ethics is the subfield of study within philosophical ethics that addresses the general background and framing issues that underlie Normative Ethics. Furthermore, Meta-Ethics is concerned with the underpinnings and limits of questions in Prescriptive Ethics, including questions about the analysis of moral language and epistemological and metaphysical questions about morality. More generally, Meta-Ethics is concerned with questions about the nature, justification, purpose, scope, and origins of morality.

Notes

1. The eighteenth-century Scottish philosopher David Hume (1711–76) famously drew attention to the distinction between *is* and *ought* as it applies to ethics. See Hume (1739), Book 3, Part I, Section 1.

2. We will examine Ethical Egoism in greater detail in Chapter 7.

Exercises

Progress Check

1. Explain the distinction between the two senses of the word "ethics."

2. Identify the various subfields within ethics and explain their interrelations.

3. Explain the controversy over describing the various views within Prescriptive Ethics as "theories."

4. Explain the distinction between top-down and bottom-up approaches to Prescriptive Ethics.

5. What is Non-Cognitivism in ethics?

6. What is Ethical Subjectivism?

7. What is Emotivism?

8. What sort or type of theory is Non-Cognitivism?

9. What sort of theory is Ethical Subjectivism?

10. What sort of theory is Emotivism?

Suggested Further Reading

There are a number of fine introductions to ethics. James Rachels, *The Elements of Moral Philosophy*, 3rd ed., presents the basic concepts of ethics in clear and accessible language with a number of useful illustrations. See Rachels (1999). Lawrence Hinman's *Ethics: A Pluralistic Approach to Moral Theory*, 2nd ed., is impressive for its scope, balance, and attention to detail. Hinman's book also has excellent bibliographic essays and a wonderful supporting Web site. See Hinman (1998). Another good introduction to ethics is Michael Boylan's *Basic Ethics*. Boylan has a number of books in the accompanying series, but this first one deals broadly with ethical theories. See Boylan (2000). For two very good brief introductions to ethics see Douglas Birsch's *Ethical Insights: A Brief Introduction* (Birsch [1999]) and Robert Solomon's *A Handbook for Ethics* (Solomon [1996]). Mike W. Martin's *Everyday Morality: An Introduction to Applied Ethics*, 3rd ed. (Martin [2001]), is a very good introduction to Applied Ethics. It also discusses topics not typically considered in such introductory texts. Finally, for an excellent reference book in ethics, consult the volume edited by Peter Singer, *A Companion to Ethics* (see Singer, ed. [1993]).

Weblinks

For some Web sites on ethics, see the Weblinks in the Introduction.

Ethics, Religion, and Law

Learning Outcomes

In this chapter we examine the nature of ethics by contrasting it with, and considering its place within, the areas of religious studies and theology on the one hand, and the study of law on the other.

Upon the successful completion of this chapter, you will be able to

1. identify and present some arguments for locating various views of the relation of ethics to religion and philosophy;

2. explain and critically evaluate Divine Command Theory;

3. explicate the Euthyphro Dilemma and its relevance for the subject matter of the chapter;

4. define Natural Law Theory and outline its metaphysical assumptions;

5. trace some historical developments of classical Natural Law Theory;

6. articulate and evaluate the natural law account of the connection between ethics, religion, and law; and

7. distinguish Legal Positivism from Natural Law Theory and assess an influential criticism of Legal Positivism advanced by Ronald Dworkin.

2.1 Introduction

In this chapter we address two questions to develop our understanding of ethics:

1. How is Normative Ethics related to religion?
2. How is Normative Ethics related to law?

Consider the first question. Many people experience and learn about morality through religious teachings, but are the two areas of study distinct? If so, how and why? In many societies, including Islamic ones, no distinction is drawn between ethics and religion because religion encompasses ethics. From this sort of outlook one might think that there is no place for the philosophical study of ethics that is independent of religious beliefs and assumptions. In contrast, many atheists argue that religion has no place in Normative Ethics. These views locate ethics entirely in philosophy. A compromise view recognizes the value of studying ethics both within philosophy and within the study of religion. Which is the best approach to take? Why? In the first half of this chapter we address these and other related questions.

Our investigation into the relation between ethics and religion leads us to examine natural law theories, and this in turn leads us to our second question. According to Natural Law Theory, something doesn't qualify as a law, properly speaking, unless it is at least consistent with the dictates of morality. Therefore, the goal of a civil society should be to entrench the principles and rules of morality into the legal code so that that code embodies morality, insofar as this is possible. In contrast, we briefly compare two other views of law and ethics. Legal Positivists argue that the questions "What is ethics?" and "What is law?" are conceptually distinct and that the overlap between the two areas can be quite minimal. In this view the idea of immoral law makes perfect sense as is evidenced by the many immoral laws in fundamentally unjust legal systems. In opposition to this is a third view, expounded by the American philosopher and legal scholar Ronald Dworkin, who argues against the posi-

tivist severing of morals and law for an account of the nature of law where moral principles are law at its foundation. Unlike Natural Law Theory, however, Dworkin accepts that there can be and are immoral laws.

By contrasting these accounts of the nature of law and its connections to ethics, we clarify our understanding of ethics. In addition, our examination of the relation of Normative Ethics to religion and law will advance our progress about both the origins and the point of ethics. In Chapter 1 we identified these meta-ethical questions as ones to pursue. Our treatment of the topics of religion and law allows us to begin to do that.

2.2 The Threat to Philosophical Ethics

Gandhi, Mother Teresa, Bishop Desmond Tutu, and the Dalai Lama are examples of deeply religious people whom we regard as moral exemplars in our society. Although certainly not true of all religious leaders, generally we hold such figures in high regard when it comes to moral matters, more so than, say, political leaders. This esteem is both for their personal character and for the ethical and spiritual guidance they offer. This connection between ethics and religion extends too to the way we formally teach ethics in Canada. Theological ethics courses are an established part of the curriculum of religious studies departments and schools of theology across the country, and for good reason.[1] These course offerings reflect people's experiences of different religions and religious ways of life all over the world. Indeed, one would be hard pressed to identify a religion where ethical considerations, however defined, were not an important concern.

In light of these facts, and given the central role that ethical issues and concerns have played in so many different religions, there is a strong initial case for linking ethics and religion in higher education. The apparent compatibility of ethics and religion presents a challenge for those who would teach philosophical ethics to articu-

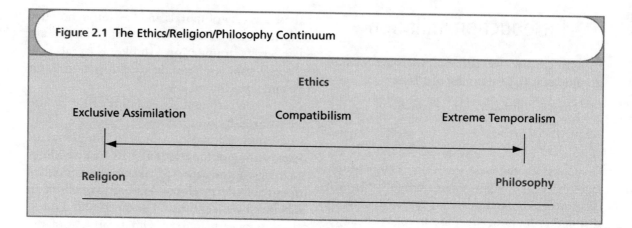

Figure 2.1 The Ethics/Religion/Philosophy Continuum

Ethics

Exclusive Assimilation   Compatibilism   Extreme Temporalism

Religion   Philosophy

late and defend an account of their subject that holds out the promise of being useful and insightful, but is nonetheless distinct from theological treatments of ethics.

To help clarify, let's survey a range of possible positions that you could take on this issue of the relationship of morality to religion and philosophy. At one end of the spectrum (see Figure 2.1), we have this strongly assimilatory stance according to which the study of ethics is somehow dependent upon some particular religious doctrine, as we noted in the case of Islam. Let's call this **Exclusive Assimilation**. At the other end we have a position advanced by some atheists who argue for the complete rejection of religion, or at least religions based on a belief in a supernatural being or beings, and who regard the study of ethics as properly a field of philosophical enquiry. Since this group of atheists regards ethics as a worldly field of study properly divorced from religion, let's call this **Extreme Temporalism.** Between these two extremes we have a range of outlooks that value and recognize a meaningful place for ethics in both religious studies and philosophy. To signify that such views accept the study of ethics within both disciplines, let's call these **compatibilist outlooks.**

Our continuum leaves room for different accounts of the relationship of ethics to religion and philosophy. Given the many varieties of religious worldviews and competing accounts of the nature of religion, it would be overly simplistic to suggest that there is just one way that ethics is related to religion. Human religious experience and understanding spans a diverse range of practices, experiences, and beliefs, and the task of locating some commonality among all religions is surprisingly difficult. The word "religion" derives from a Latin word denoting the bond between humans and the gods, and this root provides us with the most common definition of the word nowadays. This is the view that religions are distinguished by a belief in the existence of a supernatural god or gods.[2] Although this belief helps distinguish many religious outlooks, it is far from comprehensive because there are many notable exceptions. Some variants of Buddhism, Confucianism, and Taoism either do not posit or do not depend upon the existence of any supernatural being or beings.

Happily, we can accept that there is a range of religious outlooks that are not easily categorized under some simple description. Since the challenge to the wisdom of studying ethics philosophically is made from the exclusive assimilation view, we need respond only to those religious outlooks that embrace this position. Consistent with recognizing that some religious positions adopt this strongly assimilatory view, we can see that that there are others that reject it and argue for different connections.

Exclusive Assimilation is the view that the study of ethics is somehow dependent upon a particular religious doctrine.
Extreme Temporalism is the view that ethics is a worldly field of study, properly divorced from religion.
Compatibilist outlooks assign a meaningful place to the study of ethics in both religious studies and philosophy.

2.3 Exclusive Assimilation

The best known example of an exclusive assimilation view is **Divine Command Theory**, according to which morality is completely subsumed by religion, specifically religion based upon obeying the will of God. More precisely, Divine Command Theory is a theory of moral rightness according to which what God commands is morally right simply and only because God commands it.[3] If a secular ethical view happens to recommend that we follow the correct principles of morality, it must have a flawed and incomplete explanation of why those principles are right since by definition it does not make reference to the fundamental role God plays in the story of morality. The best known examples of Divine Command Theories are fundamentalist interpretations of Christianity and Islam.

2.4 Objections

Epistemological Concerns

The obvious practical appeal of Divine Command Theory is that it seems to offer us a clear and straightforward formula for living rightly. Since what is right is what God commands, to live rightly one must simply follow those commands. However difficult this is to put in to practice, at least with Divine Command Theory we seem to know what we have to do. In contrast, those lacking this conviction about the nature of moral rightness and obligation must determine for themselves what they must do in life to be moral. Given the apparent complexities and uncertainties of ethical issues and questions, not only is this a difficult task but also there are no guarantees that the answers will be found.

One well-known set of objections to Divine Command Theory raises concerns that undermine the theory's practical appeal. According to these objections, even if we concede that what is right is determined by what God commands, we are still faced with the daunting problem of determining and knowing what God's commands are. We need to know what we should do and how we should be in life, but how can we be certain that our beliefs about God's will are correct? For example, Divine Command Theory is manifested in many different religions. Is the will of God what the Muslim, the Jew, or the Christian claims, to cite three possibilities? Or is it what some other religious outlook asserts?

> According to **Divine Command Theory**, ethics is completely subsumed by religion because what is morally right, good, or obligatory is so simply and only because God commands or wills it to be so.

Assume that Divine Command Theory is correct and that God's will has been revealed. How do we know that it has been revealed as *God's will*? In other words, how do we correctly recognize God's commands? There are many purported sources of God's will and since some contradict others, they cannot all be genuine. How does one choose from among these many competing alternatives?

Even if we imagine that God's will has been revealed and that it is expressed in some agreed-upon and authentic source, there is the further question of correctly determining the right interpretation of that source. For example, there are many views within Christianity and many different interpretations of God's revelations. Even if one was to concede that the Bible was the source of God's commands, which interpretation of the Bible is the right one? Insofar as it is open to different interpretations, the Bible is a representative example of a sacred text, so this worry is not limited to Christianity.

The Euthyphro Dilemma

Apart from these epistemological concerns, the best known challenge to Divine Command Theory is also among the oldest. In his dialogue *Euthyphro*, Plato presents a discussion between two characters, Socrates and Euthyphro. Euthyphro explains to Socrates that he is prosecuting his father on a charge of murder. Upon discovering that one of Euthyphro's workers had murdered a servant, Euthyphro's father had the killer bound and tossed into a ditch while he sent another servant to the authorities to receive guidance about how to proceed. In the meantime, according to Euthyphro, his father neglected to care for the killer and by the time the servant had returned, the killer was himself dead. Euthyphro concludes that his prosecution of his father is a pious act in accordance with divine law. This leads Socrates to question Euthyphro about the nature of piety, and in response Euthyphro asserts that what is agreeable to the gods is pious or holy. In the course of seeking clarification of Euthyphro's position, Socrates asks: Is what is pious, pious because the gods love it, or do the gods love it because it is pious?[4]

In response to the related question, "Is what is morally right right only because God commands it or does God command it because it is right?", the Divine Command Theorist must say the former. Whatever is right is so simply and *only* because God wills it so. There is nothing further to be said. In taking this position, we can see how believers in Divine Command Theory try to limit the use of reason in examining basic ethical issues, including questions about the nature of moral rightness and the grounds of ethical obligation. However, this stance proves disappointingly unsatisfying to those who believe that the application of critical reasoning skills to basic moral questions is not pointless. For example, when we wonder why murdering people for money is immoral, the notion that it is futile to even pursue this question, beyond accepting that it just is because God wills it so, is hardly convincing.

These objections to Divine Command Theory provide us with merely a flavour of the debate. Rather than delve deeper into it, let's instead move on to consider some other positions on the continuum.

2.5 Extreme Temporalism

As a first step in making a positive case for locating ethics within philosophy as opposed to religious studies or theology exclusively, we can consider the view at the opposite end of our continuum, Extreme Temporalism.

There are two parts to the extreme temporalist response to the challenge of arguing for the placing of ethics in philosophy. Extreme Temporalists present a positive argument for locating ethics in philosophy and a negative argument for divorcing ethics from religious studies.

The Positive Argument: The Enlightenment Tradition and the Belief in the Independence and Value of Reason

In our brief discussion of the Euthyphro Dilemma we noted that the Divine Command Theorist endorses the claim that what is right is so because God commands it. In contrast, Socrates' question entertains an alternative account of the possible foundations of ethics, one that promotes the independence and value of reason and reasoning about moral matters. It also speaks to the heart of the issue of linking ethics to philosophy because it extends a place to rational enquiry in the study of ethics. We noted in the Introduction that one aim of this book is to promote some enlightenment in ethics and that for Kant such enlightenment requires independence of thought. Such enlightenment also presupposes the value of such thought. Enlightenment thinkers like Kant believed that although there were certainly limits to the value of thinking about ethics, there was much to be said for it too.[5]

In keeping with the Enlightenment tradition, we begin from the belief that through the careful use of reason and reasoning we can discover answers to the basic questions of ethics. However, balanced against this conviction in the value of reason we also recognize the contributions of those who have challenged this Enlightenment influence. Among this group are some notable nineteenth-century European continental philosophers including Arthur Schopenhauer (1788–1860) and Georg Wilhelm Friedrich Hegel (1770–1831). While generally sympathetic to Kant's moral philosophy, which we will consider in Chapter 5, Schopenhauer argued that the Enlightenment view of reason overvalues its proper place in ethics. Instead, he emphasized the importance of suffering and compassion in our moral lives. Likewise, Hegel took exception to the Enlightenment emphasis on the value of reason in ethics, arguing that the defence of reason and rationality in Kant's moral philosophy discounts the important connection between the ethical and the social. For Hegel, ethics is meaningful in particular social contexts, and this point becomes obscured if too much emphasis is placed on an abstract idea of rationality.

More recently many philosophers, including many virtue theorists, antitheorists, and feminists, have drawn our attention to the proper place of virtue, sentiment, context, compassion, and caring in ethics, and they have identified connections between sexism and traditional Enlightenment approaches to ethics.[6] In light of these balancing critiques, we can identify a distinctively philosophical approach to ethics that seeks to strike a balance regarding the role of reason and the efficacy of reasoning in answering questions in the subject. This unified approach to the **philosophical study of ethics** presupposes that the answers to the fundamental questions of ethics are not dependent on matters of faith and belief in the existence of a supernatural god. In this respect the philosophical study of ethics is distinct from much work in theological ethics.

These reasons provide us with some grounds for identifying a distinctively philosophical approach to the study of ethics, but this approach is best judged after you consider some philosophical treatments of ethical issues and questions. Hence, we leave open the question of the value of Normative Ethics as a field of study for now.

Thus far we have considered some reasons for distinguishing the philosophical study of ethics from the theological study of it. We have briefly examined the threat to Philosophical Ethics posed by Exclusive Assimilation, and we have identified some of the features of Normative Ethics that distinguish it as a field of philosophical enquiry. However, the question of the best conception of the relationship between religious studies, ethics, and philosophy remains. Since settling this question is not necessary for

the argument of this chapter, I leave it to you to reflect upon the matter and decide for yourself. To help you along you might want to consider some of the following alternatives and some arguments for and against them.

2.6 The Extreme Temporalist Rejection of Religion

We have appealed to a positive argument consistent with Extreme Temporalism for identifying a distinctively philosophical approach to the study of ethics. However, for a number of reasons Extreme Temporalists also reject the idea of a theological study of ethics in favour of the philosophical study of it.

1. Disbelief in God

An obvious challenge to Divine Command Theory is that it depends on God's existence, and Extreme Temporalists commonly reject the so-called proofs of the existence of God.

2. Social Scientific Accounts of Religion

Another influential stream of reasoning advanced in support of Extreme Temporalism can be traced to nineteeth-century work analyzing the role and place of religion in life from a social scientific perspective. The German philosopher Ludwig Feuerbach (1804–72) criticized belief in God as representing the projecting of all that is good about humanity onto some supernatural being and away from actual humans. Instead, Feuerbach argued, we should reclaim our humanity by adopting an ethic of community based on love and focused on life grounded in the world of experience. Feuerbach's work influenced Karl Marx (1818–83), who developed

> The **philosophical study of ethics** seeks to strike a balance regarding the role of reason in answering ethical questions and sorting through ethical issues. This approach presupposes that the answers to the fundamental questions of morality are not dependent on matters of faith and belief in the existence of a supernatural god. In these respects the philosophical study of ethics is distinct from much work in theological ethics.

the idea of alienation present in Feuerbach's work and extended it to the economic analysis of society. Famously referring to religion as the "opium of the people," Marx added, "The immediate *task of philosophy*, which is in the service of history, is to unmask human self-alienation in its *secular form* now that it has been unmasked in its *sacred form*."[7] In other words, Marx believed there was a need to extend the analysis of the alienating effect of religion to the appearance of alienation in wider social life, specifically as this appears in the form of the pursuit of money and material gain.

Feuerbach's emphasis on human life anticipated a similar concern of followers of the twentieth-century movement known as **Existentialism.** Although it has its roots in the nineteeth-century in the Danish thinker Soren Kierkegaard's (1813–55) writings on Christianity, Existentialism nowadays is primarily seen as a post-World War II philosophical and literary outlook that emphasizes consideration of the concrete lives of individuals over reflections on so-called essential human qualities. The famous Existentialist Jean-Paul Sartre (1905–80) championed the cause of freedom in his work and argued that belief in God threatens our freedom.

> **Existentialism** is primarily recognized as a post-World War II philosophical and literary outlook that emphasizes consideration of the concrete lives of individuals over reflections on so-called essential human qualities.

3. Hubble, Darwin, and the Rise of Science

Place a dime, with the queen's profile toward you, between your thumb and index finger and hold it at arm's length up to the sky. The space occupied by the queen's eye approximates the region in space that was recently photographed by the Hubble Space Telescope. The astronomers picked an area of space that was undistinguished by astronomical standards. They just wanted a look at an apparently average region in space. They set their camera on a long-term exposure of several days and then they counted the number of galaxies appearing in their picture. They counted in this one tiny space of the night sky

approximately 1300 galaxies. There are roughly 100 billion stars in a galaxy.

Especially since the publication of Charles Darwin's (1809–82) *On the Origin of Species* in 1859, atheists have pointed to the rapid expansion of science and the rise of our understanding of the world and the universe to help support their case. They argue that, as the Hubble story helps show, as our appreciation of the incredible vastness of the universe develops, the idea that there is an omniscient, benevolent God concerned about the lives of humans on earth seems less and less likely, even preposterous. The only sensible course is to divorce the study of ethics from religious studies and theology and to locate it instead in an exclusively secular study of the world as occurs in philosophy.

Response: (1) Extreme Temporalist Arguments Have an Overly Narrow Understanding of Religion

One line of response for those who defend a compatibilist approach to ethics holds that all the extreme temporalist reasons just noted, along with others like them, are parochial in their application. They are all reactions to a limited selection of religions that adhere to a belief in a single god. However, as we noted earlier, religious studies is diverse and encompasses religions that either do not assert or depend upon the existence of a supernatural being. Therefore, the extreme temporalist objections do not apply to these religions. Moreover, since many of these religions are concerned with ethics as it applies to secular life, the study of theological ethics within these religious views is a worthwhile pursuit.

Counterresponse

The Extreme Temporalist can try to respond to this argument by insisting that for a set of practices and beliefs to qualify as a religion it must include a belief in the existence of some god or gods. By this criterion non-theistic religions do not qualify. Alternatively, if this seems too narrow-minded, the Temporalist can concede that these non-theistic views are religions but that the critical study of ethics within these outlooks is "theological" in name only since they are philosophical in content. Thus, the Extreme Temporalist insists that the sorts of courses in theological ethics that are offered based on non-theistic religions are in fact courses in philosophical ethics and to label them "theological" ethics courses is uninformative.

Response: (2) Extreme Temporalist Arguments Are Irrelevant

Compatibilists also respond to the extreme temporalist arguments by maintaining that they are all irrelevant. The idea that we can expect to prove the existence of God is a misguided project that fails to appreciate that God's existence is properly accepted as a matter of faith. Therefore, showing that the proofs for the existence of God are flawed in no way proves that God does not exist. Likewise, arguments about the effect of science on religion are similarly beside the point. As scientific investigation is limited to examining the physical world, results in the areas of astronomy, biology, physics, and all the other sciences cannot prove or even demonstrate that there is no God or that there are only physical substances.

Finally, the argument noting the alienating effect of religion and more generally arguments that point to the bad social consequences that are claimed to have followed from the effect of major religions like Christianity are also either irrelevant or weak. They do not pose arguments against the value of courses in theological ethics, but are more properly regarded as criticisms of some past particular religious practices. There is nothing necessarily bad about religion that would justify the call for its complete rejection. Moreover, these criticisms of religion conveniently overlook all the benefits that followers of various religions enjoy. A case could be made that many religious movements have been powerful forces of positive social change. Also one might note that believers tend to live longer, enjoy more peace in life, and enjoy the benefits of community life that Feuerbach called for but have mostly gone missing in capitalist democratic societies.

2.7 Compatibilist Alternatives

We are amazingly diverse in our religious outlooks. Canadians accept a wide range of beliefs about religion, from none at all to those that predominate in different cultures and countries all over the planet. Many of us believe in some sort of god or gods. In view of this diversity, Compatibilists argue that we should accept Extreme Temporalism only if there is convincing evidence for it, which there is not.

Compatibilists thus accept two ideas. They believe that the study of ethics can be profitably and consistently undertaken both through philosophy departments and through religious studies departments or schools of theology. On the one hand, they agree that the non-theistic study of ethics in philosophy is worthwhile since ethics can be understood to have an independent basis in reason, feeling, and everyday social life. But they also accept the possibility of ethics pursued from a characteristically religious perspective that may be grounded in faith and presented through revelation.

Toward the philosophy end of the continuum are agnostics who believe that the existence of a supernatural god or gods cannot be either proved or disproved. Confident of the value of studying ethics philosophically, agnostics nonetheless entertain the idea that the theological study of ethics may also be valuable. Further toward the centre of the continuum are those who believe that both ways of studying ethics are potentially equally valuable. Hegel is an example of a thinker who adopted this sort of position because he believed that the truth about morality as discovered through philosophical methods is entirely consistent with the truth about a universe created by God. In his view there is harmony between the natural and divine orders.

The influential Indian social reformer and leader M.K. Gandhi (1869–1948) also held a view that is near the middle of the continuum. Gandhi held that we should seek after truth (*satya*), which we can express and attain through non-violence (*ahimsa*). *Ahimsa*, in turn, is both religion and the basis of all particular religions. In other words, Gandhi taught that the best at the core of all religions is ethics, embodied in his philosophy of non-violence. "Religions," he wrote, "are different roads converging to the same point."[8] Gandhi's idea that ethics is the best at the core of all religions points to a practical reason for embracing a compatibilist outlook in Normative Ethics. The philosophical study of ethics requires only that you remain neutral, to the extent that you can in good conscience, to the various possible views that followers of various religions take with respect to supernatural beings and phenomena. On this compatibilist view the philosophical study of ethics is secular because it is grounded in the affairs of the world and the experience of life as we know it. Since our experience of life can provide us with some common starting points for the philosophical study of ethics, the wise and inclusive view is the one that admits students from a multitude of religious backgrounds into the discussion.

Toward the religion end of the continuum are those who accept and follow a religious worldview but who acknowledge the value of the philosophical study of ethics too, though they believe this value is limited. Kierkegaard respected the value of reason in determining the morally right course of action in our normal social lives. However, he insisted that acceptance of God means acceptance of God's will even if that sometimes contradicts the demands of reason in the life of society. Similarly, the influential medieval theologian and philosopher St. Thomas Aquinas (1225–74) accepted the value of the philosophical investigation into human affairs, including ethical matters. However, Aquinas believed that understanding achieved through divine revelation exceeds what is possible through the mere use of reason and philosophical methods of investigation.

2.8 Natural Law Theory

Aquinas's version of Natural Law Theory is the classical statement of the view, and it is also the first of a number of moral theories that we will examine. The theory presents a set of answers to the basic questions of ethics, including the questions of the nature, justification, origins, and purpose of morality. Although specific natural law views offer guidance on the prescriptions and proscriptions of ethics, our concern with Natural Law will be limited to examining its answers to some of these other basic questions. We will also consider it for its account of the relation between ethics, religion, philosophy, and law, and for its historical influence on our understanding of both morality and law.

Classical Natural Law Theory is unusual in that it has played a pivotal role in philosophical debates in both ethics and law in the history of Western thought, and more generally it exerted tremendous influence for several hundred years after Aquinas's death. Leading figures of the Protestant Reformation like Martin Luther (1483–1546) and John Calvin (1509–64) held versions of it, as did many influential Catholic theologians.[9] However, perhaps because it is mostly out of favour these days, philosophers sometimes overlook its role in the shaping of Normative Ethics and law. In our examination of Natural Law Theory, we will consider its strengths, especially its key insights into the relation between ethics and law. An appreciation of these insights and an appreciation of the debates spawned by Natural Law Theory will help develop our understanding of the nature of morality.

Natural Law Theories maintain that there are universally applicable and objectively right moral principles that are discoverable by human reason, like, for example, the principle that stealing is

Natural Law Theories maintain that there are universally applicable and objectively right moral principles that are discoverable by human reason. These objective moral principles, which are the natural laws, apply uniformly to all people at all times and in all places. Aquinas's view rests on an Aristotelian metaphysical view of the world that is contrary to our modern understanding. Most of us believe that there are regularities in nature that scientists endeavour to discover and describe. The laws of Newtonian mechanics are examples of such laws of nature insofar as they serve to try to explain the motion of objects. Although as objects our bodies are subject to these laws, we are also subjects with free will. Unlike objects like billiard balls and apples, we can choose to obey the laws of our society or not. Thus we commonly say that the natural laws of science are descriptive whereas human law has a prescriptive element to it. We can distinguish between asking what the law in our society is and whether we should obey it or not. About mere objects, such talk is nonsensical.

wrong. These principles are the natural laws. Natural laws thus apply uniformly to all people at all times and in all places. They should govern our behaviour, and their binding nature imposes obligations on all of us. On Aquinas's classical account God promulgates the natural laws, and God imposes the ultimate sanctions on those who choose to either obey or disobey them.[10]

Aquinas's worldview is somewhat foreign to us partly because he does not make this distinction between the character of Natural Law and human law. More generally, on Aquinas's outlook there is no distinction between the natural order and the moral order. The true moral principles that are discoverable by the proper use of human reason are grounded on natural facts, particularly facts about human nature. Aquinas believed that everything in the universe, including humans, is subject to the laws appropriate to it. Whereas most people accept the idea that there are natural laws or regularities in nature that help explain why events unfold as they do ("It fell because of gravity"), Natural Law Theory is unusual in that it extends this account to us too. So although humans can use their reason and exercise their will not to follow the laws appropriate for them, Aquinas maintained nevertheless that there are still laws that apply to us. Following Aristotle, Aquinas believed that every kind of thing in the universe has its own distinctive *telos,* or end. Each thing's *telos* is determined by its nature, and a good thing of its kind performs its function or realizes its nature well. So, for example, on the Aristotelian view the *telos* or end of a watch is to keep time. A good watch fulfills this function well. Since according to Aristotle we are by nature rational animals, Aristotle believed that our *telos* is to lead a life that is in accord with reason.

And what is a life lived in accord with reason? Generally, Aquinas defined law as an ordinance of reason that is directed toward promoting the common good promulgated by one who has responsibility for the community. Therefore, the human life lived in accordance with reason is the one that obeys the natural laws that promote the common good of humans. More broadly, Aquinas conceived of three kinds of law that are created and promulgated by God in addition to the law humans create:

- Divine Laws: These are laws created by God that direct us to our eternal ends. These laws are not discoverable through the use of reason, but are rather presented through God's revelations.

- Eternal Laws: Eternal laws govern the universe and direct each kind of thing to its particular end. The laws of science are eternal laws on Aquinas' account.

- Natural Laws: Natural laws are those laws created by God that direct us to our end in this life. These laws are discoverable through the use of reason, and they are the manifestation of the true principles of morality.

- Human Laws: Human laws are the laws that we create to govern our societies.

Aquinas's account of natural law fits into his larger teleological outlook, an outlook that is held together by God. He argued that our goal should be to develop human laws so that they mirror the natural laws that God created for us to direct us to our ends on earth. Even stronger than this, on Aquinas's natural law view there is an essential connection between law and morality. According to Aquinas "*lex iniusta non est lex*"—an unjust law is not a law. Aquinas thus used the concept of law normatively. He believed that for a human "law" to be, properly speaking, a law, it must be in accord with the Natural Law ordained by God.

2.9 Natural Law Accounts of the Purpose, Origins, and Proper Functioning of Morality

According to classical Natural Law Theory, then, ethics, religion, philosophy, and law are related in the following ways. There is a class of truths revealed through the divine laws that direct us to our eternal end that cannot be discovered through the use of reason. Apart from these truths, however, God has created the universe such that the natural laws that direct humans to their ends in this world are discoverable through the right use of reason, and thus Natural Law Theory values the philosophical study of ethics. Furthermore, the human laws should be modelled on the immutable moral truths that constitute the set of natural laws. On classical Natural Law Theory there is therefore a strong and necessary connection between law and morality. Indeed, Natural Law Theory does not distinguish between law and morality. On this account, the answer to our opening question "How is Normative Ethics related to law?" is that they are identical. Thus, on the natural law view morality consists of discharging one's duty to obey the law, and virtue is understood as the habit of doing this.

From this sketch we get a better sense of Aquinas's Compatibilism, which values both the philosophical investigation into ethics and revealed truth about ethics as it affects our eternal existence. The respect for the value of reason demonstrated by this view helped Christian philosophers contend with a problem posed by those who worried that Divine Command Theory undermined belief in God's benevolence. If Divine Command Theory is true, then it seems that only those who have been exposed to God's teachings can consciously live a moral and good life. However, Christian theologians knew that many humans had not been exposed to the teachings of Christ through no fault of their own. How are we to regard God's attitude toward them? On Natural Law Theory, there is no problem. As long as some people use their reason to organize society such that most are led into obeying the law, we can live morally good lives. Furthermore, since God created the universe and the natural laws, in obeying the rightful laws of our society, we are indirectly obeying God. According to Natural Law Theory, ethics originates from God.

To fully appreciate the value of Natural Law Theory and its role as a forerunner to modern accounts of ethics and law, one needs to see how laws are supposed to function to facilitate our good. A community that operated under a system of law that approximated Natural Law would be organized in such a way as to promote the good of all its citizens. It would ensure that all members of the society could express their love for God by both fulfilling their *telos* and by co-operating with others. In Aquinas's view, the purpose of morality is to express our love for and promote the greater glory of God, and to love each other. These aims of loving and glorifying God and loving each other are the Christian foundation of Aquinas's Natural Law Theory.

Given our philosophical focus, for our purposes the main value of Natural Law Theory is in appreciating how law functions to advance the greater good of the citizens of a state. As we have noted, according to natural law doctrine, the good of each individual is promoted by following the natural laws that effectively function to promote the good of society. How does law connect the good of the individual to the good of the community? Many traditional natural lawyers attributed the Christian idea that we are motivated to love our neighbours as ourselves. However, two influential thinkers in the tradition, the Dutch lawyer Hugo Grotius (1583–1645) and the English philosopher Thomas Hobbes (1588–1679), emphasized the benefits to individuals of obeying the law.[11] The problem is to explain how a self-interested agent is better off submitting to the will of God and obeying the law rather than not obeying it. Are you not best off by living in a world where others obey the law but you do not? Isn't it rational to break the law when possible, since the law imposes limits on us in the pursuit of our ends in life? Consider two examples where we face choice situations where we might be inclined to break the law.

1. The Water Shortage Example

Imagine you are a homeowner in a large city. There has been a prolonged heat wave and the city's water supply reserves are dangerously low. To ensure that everyone has enough water to drink, the city authorities enact a law forbidding citizens from watering their lawns. You reason, however, that the best state of affairs is one where everyone has enough water to drink and your lawn is green and healthy. Since the amount of water that you use on your lawn is so little compared to the overall city supply, what harm is there in turning on your sprinkler?

2. The Public Taxation Example

Think more generally about the idea of taxation. In theory, governments use personal income tax monies to help pay for public goods like schools, transportation infrastructure, and public security. Imagine you like these benefits, but you dislike paying for them. So you reason that if everyone else pays their income taxes but you don't, the overall negative effects on these public projects from you not contributing will be minimal given the relatively little amount you pay in taxes. So you can enjoy these public goods and keep all your income!

The main problem with each scenario is that your choice is not just between you co-operating along with everyone else or everyone else co-operating while you take advantage of their restraint. The other likelier possibility is that you and many others like you will not co-operate and the benefits of co-operation will not be enjoyed if there is no way to reasonably guarantee compliance. This would be a worse state for you than the one in which you co-operate with everyone else. If there is no general co-operation, then there will likely be widespread hoarding, waste, panic, and violence in the first example. A similar analysis applies in the taxation example. Hobbes appreciated that to ensure the superior state where citizens in society enjoy the widespread benefits of co-operation, each of us must agree to forsake the apparent advantages of exploiting others, provided they do likewise. The resulting general system of co-operation will greatly benefit all, especially in the long term. However, Hobbes also recognized that to achieve this co-operation, society needs a sovereign powerful enough to enforce compliance with the laws. If co-operation can be enforced, then it is reasonable to co-operate.

Even stronger than this, Hobbes recognized that law and its enforcement is valuable because there are benefits available to individuals acting together not available to individuals acting on their own. As he famously argued, life in the state of nature, that is life without co-operation, would be "solitary, poor, nasty, brutish, and short."[12] Indeed, given the reliance we have on our caregivers from birth, in the absence of co-operation no one would survive. Even if we somehow managed to survive, without co-operation life would lose much of its value. There would be no love, friendship, education, art, commerce, or society. Try to imagine life like that for a moment. Just look at this book, or around at your surroundings. Unless you are reading this in the wilderness, you would be hard pressed to avoid the products of the co-operative efforts of many humans. They are everywhere. Who could build the structures we live and work in alone? Or the many machines and tools we use in the course of a normal day? The co-operative benefits that we enjoy and that we usually take for granted make our high quality of life possible.

These considerations help illustrate how law functions to promote both the greater good of the individual and the greater good of the community. On the classical natural law account, God is at the centre of the story because God created the universe such that the natural laws work in this way to advance our natural ends, and God also serves as the source of the sanctions that makes compliance with the laws reasonable. Specifically, God ensures compliance with the demands of morality through the imposition of eternal rewards and punishments. On this view, we should obey the law because we will enjoy eternal rewards for doing so. Conversely, if we disobey the law, we will suffer eternal punishments.

2.10 The Emergence of Secular Accounts of Morality and Law Out of Natural Law Theory

Aquinas's Natural Law Theory nicely demonstrates a basic link between promoting one's own good and promoting the good of others through the reasonable following of laws that realize co-operative benefits for all. Natural Law Theory shows that provided there is a reasonable guarantee that co-operation can be enforced, a guarantee on the theory that is supplied by God, it is rational or in each person's self-interest to co-operate. However, trying to reconcile robust roles for both reason and God in the story of morality introduced tensions into Natural Law Theory. These tensions eventually led to the general separation of ethics from religion and the development of wholly secular theories of morality and law in the West. The basic problem is revealed in the Euthyphro dilemma. If God commands what is right because it is right, then God's central role in ethics appears threatened. Why not just develop a theory of rightness independent of what God commands? In essence this is what happened.

By the seventeenth and eighteenth centuries, tensions of the sort just noted began to surface in the writings of three thinkers who all advanced versions of Natural Law Theory that effectively undermined the central role that God plays in the story of morality. Grotius famously declared that the laws of nature would impose obligations on us even if God did not exist. He believed that God did exist, but he appreciated the force of Plato's argument. He was the first to hold that all persons possess rights that demand respect in all communities and even from God himself. Hobbes, the author of *Leviathan* (1651 in English, 1668 revised Latin edition), regarded his moral philosophy as a version of Natural Law Theory, and he further extended Grotius's position by holding that the purpose of ethics is to promote the good of individual persons. The English philosopher and bishop Richard Cumberland (1632–1718) disagreed with much of Hobbes's view, but he also undermined the place of God in Natural Law Theory by arguing that the sanctions for not complying with the laws of nature are natural.

Consider briefly how these ideas helped lead to a version of Natural Law Theory that places God in the background and that leads ultimately to secular theories of ethics and law. If we take Grotius and Hobbes's idea that the point of morality is to promote the good of the individual, then law and morality are justified ultimately by whether they in fact do this. And we determine this not by considering whether systems of law and morality express love for God or promote God's glory, but by whether they actually make people better off. Similarly, Hobbes's and Cumberland's remarks on sanctions undercut any need for God in this part of the account too. Although he believed in God, Hobbes argued that for compliance with a society's laws to be reasonable, one needs only an earthly sovereign powerful enough to enforce the laws. On this outlook the sanctions of the afterlife are mostly superfluous. In a similar vein, Cumberland argued that since we are inclined to care for each other and since we experience guilt and shame when we harm others unjustly, our own conscience supplies us with the necessary sanctions for complying with law and being moral.

We can further develop our understanding of the relation of law and ethics by connecting Hobbes's and Cumberland's remarks on sanctions to the two kinds of ways that we actually achieve co-operation in life. Thus we can better appreciate how secular accounts of law and morality emerge from classical Natural Law Theory. Turning again to our water shortage example, we can see each of these sanctions at work. Initially at least, people typically say that they would not water their lawn in the water shortage example because they don't want to be fined. This sort of incentive corresponds to Hobbes's sovereign's threat of punishment backed by the coercive power of law. But this is only part of our motivation because most people would obey the prohibition because they want to do the right thing too, as Cumberland noted. And in this case the right thing means not sacrificing life and health for green grass. How would you feel, to take an extreme scenario, if the water you and your selfish cohorts wasted on your lawns meant that young children in hospitals had nothing to drink? Guilty? Ashamed? Here we have identified a different kind of motivator. This kind of motivation, widely felt, can contribute to making co-operation reasonable in life. Though we have expressed this negatively so far, we can put the point more positively. Thus we would say that we want to conserve water because we take pride in doing the right thing. We also respect other moral people and admire those who, like us, do what's right in the face of temptation. This talk of doing the right thing roughly marks out the territory of ethics, in contradistinction to the territory of law. Indeed, ethics is commonly defined as the field of study concerned with principles of right and wrong conduct.

Most seventeenth-century natural lawyers agreed with the classical natural law view that people must be made to comply with the law, and thus for them the concepts of duty and obligation were central. They referred to such duties as perfect duties, but they also believed that there were imperfect unenforceable duties in life associated with virtues like kindness and charity. Acting on these duties was a matter of conscience and internal motivation, and philosophers began to distinguish morality from law in a way that had not been recognized by the classical natural law perspective. Christian Thomasius (1655–1728) first clearly distinguished between law and morality by arguing that perfect duties are a matter of law and imperfect duties are a matter of morality. Whereas we can explain our desires to obey the law in terms of our self-interest, Thomasius argued that the internal motivation to fulfill imperfect duties springs from direct concern for others for their sake. He regarded this concern for others as the hallmark of ethical motivation.

We can clarify Thomasius's idea with the help of a rough but useful distinction between **prudential value** and moral value.[13] An assessment of the prudential value of your life is a measurement of its value to you. An assessment of the moral value of your life is a measurement of its value to others. Generally, prudential value refers to what is *good for you;* moral value refers to what is *good for others.* For example, if an apple is prudentially good for you, it contributes to your happiness, welfare, or well-being. If a terrible shock is prudentially bad for you, it contributes to your unhappiness. This distinction between prudential value and moral value is useful and is one we can build upon. However, we should remember that it is useful primarily for

distinguishing between assessments of our motivations and the consequences of our actions, and we should not take this distinction too far. The spheres or dimensions of moral value and prudential value overlap because although a moral concern is a concern for someone else for his or her sake, we count morally, too. Agents can and should be given moral consideration. Our distinction merely helps us keep these dimensions of value distinct in our minds.

> **Prudential value** refers to the good or well-being of the person or being in question. Thus, an assessment of the prudential value of your life is a measurement of its value to you.

2.11 Alternative Accounts of Law and the Connection between Law and Morality

Our brief examination of Natural Law Theory presents us with some interesting answers to our question about the relation of Normative Ethics to law. Whereas the classical account argues that law, properly understood, is identical to ethics, later versions of the theory began to open up a gap between the two and regard them as different but still connected. This question of the relation between law and morality has been central in the debates among competing accounts of the nature of law in the discipline known as the philosophy of law. Although a detailed study of the various views and answers to the question is beyond our scope, we can at least survey some of the other main accounts and raise some of the central issues.

2.12 Hart and Legal Positivism

Although there are a variety of versions of Legal Positivism, Positivists generally reject the classical natural law view that law and morality are identical. They typically argue for a much weaker connection between the two and claim that law and ethics are conceptually distinct areas of study. This is sometimes referred to as the

Separability Thesis. By separating these questions about the nature of law and morality, Positivists distinguish the idea of a legal system's viability from the question of its justness. Thus they argue that it makes perfect sense to speak of an oppressive legal system because valid and functional legal systems need not be morally good. Whereas the natural law view tends to regard a legal system as functioning to serve the common good of the citizens who are subject to it, Legal Positivists have argued that law can also be a tool of oppression used to exploit the powerless. The coercive power of law, they note, can be used for both good and bad ends.

This separability thesis is connected to the second defining feature of **Legal Positivism**, the idea that laws acquire their status as laws not because of their content but because of their pedigree. This is sometimes referred to as the **Pedigree Thesis.** In other words, according to the Positivist, a law becomes a law as a result of some official process, not because of its moral content. On the classical version of the theory, developed by the Englishman John Austin (1790–1859), laws are commands issued by a sovereign to political inferiors. On the most influential modern version of the view developed by the English philosopher H.L.A. Hart (1907–92), laws are rules. On Hart's account there are two kinds of rules, primary rules and secondary rules. The primary rules are the laws directed to ordinary citizens that impose duties like, for example, the duties to stop at red lights, not steal, and not kill.

Secondary rules help provide order and continuity to the legal system by empowering officials to enforce and adjudicate the law (the rules of adjudication), by facilitating changes in the system of primary rules (the rules of change) and by identifying the primary rules of the system (the rule of recognition). Thus on Hart's account, a law is valid if its creation or enactment can be traced to the procedures specified by the rule of recognition. So, for example, a country's constitution might be its rule of recognition. Furthermore, it might state that only laws duly enacted by a democratically elected parliament are valid. Hart notes that in a complex legal system a rule of recognition can likewise be quite complex, but it is true for every valid rule of the system that it derives its validity through its pedigree to the rule of recognition.

2.13 Hart on the Minimum Moral Content of Law

Although there is a wealth of detail and much more sophistication to Hart's Legal Positivism than our brief overview suggests, our main interest is in answering our question about the relation of Normative Ethics to law. Hart's remarks on law's minimum moral content are most relevant for us. In his analysis of Natural Law Theory, he argued that natural lawyers were right to recognize a minimum necessary content to law but that they greatly exaggerated this. Hart argued that due to five truisms about humans, all functioning legal systems need to have some laws with moral content in order to be viable. Given that the purpose of a legal system is to facilitate the association of humans for mutual survival, there must be laws that promote this aim. However, beyond this bare minimum, he insisted, there is no necessary connection between law and morality.

Hart's five truisms follow:

1. We are vulnerable to harm.

2. We are approximately equal in physical strength and intellectual capacity.

3. We demonstrate limited concern for others, especially strangers.

4. We live in societies with limited resources.

5. There are limits to our understanding and strength of will.

Hart believed that all legal systems need rules that protect "persons, property, and promises" and to this extent at least, laws must have

> This **Separability Thesis** is linked to the **Pedigree Thesis.** According to this latter thesis a law's validity is a matter of its pedigree, not its content. In other words, the Positivist argues that what makes a law a valid law of a system is determined by a social fact or social facts about the law coming into being in the right sort of way. **Legal Positivism** is a theory about the nature of law according to which law and ethics are conceptually distinct areas of study that refer to distinct social phenomena.

some moral content.[14] He thought that as a result of truism 1, all legal systems must have some prohibitions against unjustified killing. If someone among us was immune to attack from everyone else and if that person was greatly superior in terms of strength or intellect, then there could be a viable legal system where everyone else was oppressed by this single person. In that immoral system there might be no need for even a minimal moral content in the laws. However, Hart notes that even the most ruthless dictator must sleep. Thus the legal system in which the dictator rules must make provisions for protecting the interests of some critical mass of persons who benefit from and are protected by the system, and who in turn ensure the continued smooth functioning of the system. An interesting question for legal and political philosophy is what this critical mass must comprise.

Truisms 3, 4, and 5 also help explain laws' necessary minimum moral content. A legal system designed to promote the good of some critical mass of persons requires mutual forbearance and compromise. If we were all saints disinclined to harm each other, then laws requiring mutual forbearance would be unnecessary. If we were devils, Hart observes, they would be impossible. He adds that since we live in conditions of moderate scarcity, we also need laws that respect property. Since we have limited understanding and strength of will, we also cannot rely on voluntary compliance with the moral rules, hence we need laws backed by the coercive power of enforcement.

2.14 Ronald Dworkin's Critique of Positivism

With Natural Law Theory and Legal Positivism we have before us two very different accounts of the relation between ethics and law. Each contributes to our ongoing project of clarifying our understanding of the nature of morality. Rather than defend Natural Law against Positivism, it might be more interesting to briefly consider another contemporary view of law that is distinct from these two theories, namely Ronald Dworkin's theory of law. Dworkin was a professor in jurisprudence at the University of Oxford from 1969–98 and then a professor of law at New York University. Through an influential series of books and articles, he articulated and defended his own theory of law distinct from the positivist view. Although we do not have sufficient space to examine Dworkin's full theory, let's consider one of his influential objections.

Dworkin argued that the Positivist's Separability Thesis and insistence that laws are rules overlook the actual complexity of modern legal systems such as ours. He maintained that in addition to rules, legal systems consist of laws that are indistinguishable from moral principles. Moreover, since these moral principles are at the very foundation of law and part of its spirit, and since they are not rules, they cannot be traced to any rule of recognition. Since the positivist outlook fails to account for the place of legal/moral principles in law, as a theory about the nature of law it is therefore incomplete and flawed.

Dworkin's criticism suggests that the tidy account of the relation between law and morality defended by Hart is too simple and that, as we saw with our attempt to completely distinguish ethics from religion, a similar effort to completely distinguish ethics from law is also likely to fail. In support of Dworkin's argument, we can reconsider a point we noted in the Introduction in our discussion of morality's complexity. We noted there former Supreme Court Chief Justice Brian Dickson's attempt to articulate some of the principles that underlie our rights in the *Canadian Charter of Rights and Freedoms* and specifically the idea in section 1 of the *Charter* that Canadian society is to be free and democratic. Consider again the list of basic Canadian values and principles that he identified:

- respect for the inherent dignity of the human person;

- commitment to social justice and equality;

- accommodation of a wide variety of beliefs;

- respect for cultural and group identity; and

- faith in social and political institutions that enhance the participation of individuals and groups in society.

As we observed, Dickson thought that these values and principles should guide the Supreme Court when it decides cases determining the limits of our basic rights. In other words, he envisioned these values and principles as forming part of the foundation of the *Charter*. As such, he thought that one of their functions was to help determine whether particular laws were constitutional; whether, in other words, particular laws enacted by Parliament are in fact valid laws of Canada. So it seems both that these values and principles are an integral part of our legal system, but that they do not fit into Hart's positivist conception of laws as rules. The Positivist must show either that these values and principles are somehow separate from our legal system or that they are part of it because they are in fact rules.

This regrettably brief treatment of the debate between three influential theories of the nature of law is far from comprehensive, but it does serve to highlight some thoughtful accounts of the nature of the relation between Normative Ethics and law. With this understanding we can move on to consider other questions in Meta-Ethics in Chapter 3.

2.15 Review

In this chapter we further developed our account of the nature of ethics by considering its relation to, and overlap with, the areas of religious studies or theology and law. In the first part of the chapter we focused on outlining and evaluating various positions along the ethics/religion/philosophy continuum. We noted that the case for completely subsuming Normative Ethics within religious studies or theology, at least as presented by Divine Command Theory, appears lacking. In addition to this admittedly weak conclusion, we also considered a positive case for locating the study of ethics in philosophy. Beyond making this case, we canvassed a range of views that one might take along the continuum and some reasons for and against supporting these views.

In the second part of the chapter we turned our attention to the question of the relation of

Normative Ethics to law. We began by considering our first moral theory, Natural Law Theory. We examined the classical view of this theory as presented by St. Thomas Aquinas, and we explained the natural law accounts of the justification, origins, and purpose of morality. By tracing some developments in the classical view, we were able to uncover a basic connection between ethics and the law; namely the idea that both ethics and law serve to some extent to facilitate co-operation in society. Beyond this minimal agreement of the connection between the two, we noted that in the philosophy of law there is considerable debate about the precise nature of the relation between ethics and law. In this debate we considered the legal positivist view as developed by H.L.A. Hart and one criticism of Hart's account advanced by Ronald Dworkin.

Notes

1. Although I will refer to both religious studies departments and schools of theology throughout this chapter, it should be noted that these are distinct disciplines. Theology is the systematic study of a particular religion as occurs, for example, at seminary colleges that educate and train priests and rabbis. The theological study of religion thus begins from a position of acceptance of the basic tenets of the religion being taught. In contrast, instructors and professors of religious studies departments of colleges and universities teach courses in religion from within the perspective of the religion without presupposing, or necessarily presupposing, those basic tenets. So, for example, one need not be a Buddhist to teach a course on Buddhism in a religious studies department.

2. I owe this way of explaining this point about the difficulty of defining "religion" to David Stewart (1998), p. 1. For more on this problem, see the remainder of Stewart's introductory essay. See also Arnal (2000).

3. There are actually many interpretations and accounts of Divine Command Theory. The one presented here is just one prominent version on the theory.

4. Plato, *Euthyphro*, 10a.

5. The Enlightenment as an historical period is categorized differently by geographical location

and to some extent by subject, but roughly it refers to the period from 1690 (specifically John Locke's publication of *An Essay Concerning Human Understanding*) to about 1800.

6. We examine these views later in Part 1.

7. Both quotations are from Marx (1844), p. 54.

8. Gandhi (1997), p. 53.

9. The historical period known as the Reformation refers to the uprising of Protestant challenges to the domination of the Roman Catholic Church from about 1517–55.

10. Although on the classical view natural laws are conceived of as having been issued by a supreme, benevolent deity, there are other versions of the theory where this is not the case. Some contemporary accounts of Natural Law dispense with claims about the role of a deity and it is likewise with some ancient Greek and Roman accounts.

11. Some might wonder about including Hobbes within the natural law tradition. On the one hand, he is connected with egoist accounts of ethics for his moral views and his account of human nature, and subsequent Egoists embraced him. On the other hand, Hobbes is also embraced by Contractarians like David Gauthier, who view moral codes as socially accepted contracts and who see Hobbes's account as "the true ancestor" of his own contractarian view. See Gauthier (1986), p. 10. Although this is not the place for a full defence, I see no inconsistency with placing Hobbes in the natural law tradition and regarding his view as offering support to both Egoists and Contractarians. Hobbes was working in the natural law tradition and regarded his view as a natural law account.

12. Hobbes (1668), Part 1, Chapter XIII, Section 9.

13. The expression "prudential value" is from Griffin (1986).

14. Hart (1961), p. 193. Hart explains and defends his view of law's minimum moral content in this part (Chapter 9, section 2) of his book.

Exercises

Progress Check

1. Explain the ethics/religion/philosophy continuum and briefly outline the views along it.

2. What is Divine Command Theory and why is it an Exclusive Assimilation View?

3. Explain the Euthyphro Dilemma.

4. What is Existentialism?

5. What is Natural Law Theory?

6. Explain how classical Natural Law Theory rests on an Aristotelian metaphysical worldview.

7. What role does God play in classical Natural Law Theory?

8. Explain the classical natural law accounts of the (1) justification, (2) purpose, and (3) origins of morality.

9. Outline how developments of classical Natural Law Theory in the seventeenth and eighteenth centuries led to the emergence of secular theories of ethics and law.

10. Why should we co-operate generally in life? Under what condition or conditions is co-operation in society reasonable, according to Hobbes?

11. Explain the distinction between the two kinds of motivations for co-operating.

12. What is Legal Positivism? Briefly explain H.L.A. Hart's version of the view.

13. Explain Hart's account of the minimum moral content of all viable human legal systems.

14. Explain the criticism of Hart's account by Ronald Dworkin that is presented in this chapter.

Questions for Further Reflection

1. What is religion?

2. Explain and critically evaluate the idea that Divine Command Theory is false.

3. Distinguish the philosophical study of ethics from the theological study of it. Defend your view.

4. Explain and critically evaluate the extreme temporalist rejection of the theological study of ethics.

5. Explain and assess the strongest case you can think of for taking a compatibilist approach to Normative Ethics.

6. Explain and critically evaluate the idea that the proper function of morality is to promote the good of individual people.

7. Explain and critically evaluate the idea that we achieve co-operation in society in two distinct ways that correspond to ethics and law.

Group Work Activity:

The Story of the Ring of Gyges

In Book Two of Plato's *Republic,* the character Glaucon relates the story of Gyges, a shepherd from Lydia. According to the legend, one day Gyges was tending his flock when there was a great storm and an earthquake, causing a chasm to open in the ground. Descending into the chasm, Gyges saw many amazing things including a bronze, hollowed horse in which was a corpse with a gold ring on one of its fingers. Gyges took the ring and later discovered that by turning the ring's bezel he became invisible. He then arranged to be in a party to report to the king, and once there he seduced the queen and plotted the overthrow of the king. Using his newfound power, he was able to murder the king and assume the throne.

Glaucon wonders whether it would make sense for anyone who has such a power to use it justly. Why, in other words, would anyone choose to be just and moral when they could avoid the societal constraints we have in place to force people to obey the law? Furthermore, doesn't this in turn show that people are moral simply because they cannot get away with being immoral? Would it not be better for us to exploit our fellow citizens if possible? Glaucon and his brother Adeimantus ask the character Socrates in the dialogue to defend the idea that justice is its own reward. Your task is to answer the following questions in your groups. Be prepared to defend your answers to the other groups in your class.

1. What reasons do people have for being moral when they confidently and rightly believe that they can act immorally without being detected and punished?

2. Are any of these reasons good enough to convince you that you should act immorally in such circumstances? Why or why not?

3. What does it mean to say that justice is its own reward? Is this reward reason enough to be just when you can get away with being unjust? Why or why not?

4. If you could exploit your friends, that is, harm them and use them for your own selfish gain, without being caught would you do so? Why or why not?

8. Explain and critically evaluate the idea that a moral concern is a concern for another person for her or his sake.

9. Explain and critically evaluate Hart's argument for law's minimum moral content.

10. Critically assess Dworkin's critique of Hart's account of Legal Positivism.

11. Explain and critically evaluate the view that former Supreme Court Chief Justice Brian Dickson's decision in *R. v. Oakes* supports Dworkin's view of the nature of law.

Suggested Further Reading

Apart from the works cited in the notes, I have benefited from and highly recommend two works by Jerome Schneewind that discuss the history of Natural Law Theory. The first is his paper "Seventeenth and Eighteenth Century Ethics" (see Schneewind [1992]), and the second is his excellent book *The Invention of Autonomy: A History of Modern Moral Philosophy* (Schneewind [1998]).

I also recommend the chapters on ethics and religion in Lawrence Hinman's *Ethics: A Pluralistic Approach to Moral Theory,* 2nd ed. (Hinman [1998]) and James Rachels' *The Elements of Moral Philosophy,* 3rd ed. (Rachels [1999]).

Weblinks

Kenneth Himma's entry on Natural Law in **The Internet Encyclopedia of Philosophy** is at **www.utm.edu/research/iep/n/natlaw.htm#source**

Joseph Magee's Web site on St. Thomas Aquinas includes useful links to other sites on Aquinas and a discussion of Aquinas's classical Natural Law Theory. It is at **www.aquinasonline.com**

Richard Nolan maintains a Web site on philosophy and religion with some useful resources at **www.philosophy-religion.org**

The **Journal of Religious Ethics,** published by the Department of Theology at Georgetown University, has its Web site at **www.fsu.edu/~religion/jre**

Ethical Subjectivism, Relativism, and Absolutism

Overview

Learning Outcomes

The main aim of this chapter is to examine some basic issues in Meta-Ethics. Specifically, we will rebut two commonly accepted meta-ethical views, Crude Ethical Subjectivism and Crude Ethical Relativism, by considering the place of reason and sentiment in morality. This will also help us clarify why Normative Ethics is distinct as an area of study from science. Furthermore, by pursuing an answer to the question of the purpose of ethics, we will gain insight into two more sophisticated meta-ethical views, Sophisticated Ethical Relativism and Ethical Absolutism.

Upon the successful completion of this chapter, you will be able to

1. explain and critically evaluate Crude Ethical Subjectivism, Crude Ethical Relativism, Sophisticated Ethical Relativism, Ethical Absolutism, and Etiquette Relativism;

2. explicate both Cultural Relativism and Sociobiology;

3. appreciate the central place of feeling or sentiment in morality;

4. provide an explanation of the meta-ethical nature of some versions of Ethical Relativism and Ethical Absolutism; and

5. outline a basic argument for and criticisms of the view that there are moral truths and moral facts.

3.1 Introduction

The question of the nature of morality has long been contested in the history of philosophy, and disagreements about the roles played by reason, sentiment, truth, and value judgment add to the confusion. We need a basic understanding of these issues to make further progress and decide for ourselves what we think about the many debates among moral philosophers.

In this chapter we examine the issues of whether there are moral truth and moral facts, and the place of reason and sentiment in ethics. We consider and then reject two rather popular views, Crude Ethical Subjectivism and Crude Ethical Relativism, and we also assess more sophisticated versions of Relativism and the view known as Ethical Absolutism. In our analysis we are guided by a simple question, one that Ethical Relativists have generally mishandled or avoided at their peril, namely, What is the purpose of morality? By pursuing an answer to this question, we are led to a place for reasons and reasoning in ethics, and at least a sketch of an argument for Cognitivism.

3.2 The Sociopaths and the Cat

Consider the following example presented by Gilbert Harman in the first chapter of his book, *The Nature of Morality: An Introduction to Ethics*.[1] Imagine that while on the way to a friend's house we take a shortcut through some alleys. As we turn a corner, we witness two 12-year-old boys with their backs to us pouring gasoline on a cat. Before we can react, they set the cat on fire. Horrified, we watch this gruesome scene unfold, unable to aid the hapless cat as it dies an excruciating death. Turning our attention from the cat to the boys, we ask them why they did that. "For fun," one boy says. "For fun?" you reply. "How can that be fun?" "I don't know," he says, "It just is." He explains that he was feeling a little bored and, setting out to relieve his boredom, he happened to come across this cat and decided to set it on fire for fun. It worked; he found the experience mildly amusing. "What's wrong with that?" he asks. "What's wrong with it?" you reply, "It's evil. Don't you understand?" The boys say that they understand that people like us think it is evil to set cats on fire for fun, but that they don't see the immorality. It is just your opinion that what they did was immoral, one tells you. "No," you insist, "it is a fact." "Show me," he replies. Thinking there still might be some hope for the boys, we decide to show them the wrongness of their behaviour. What should we say?

It certainly seems to be a fact that what the boys did is immoral, but until we can explain the nature of facts of this sort, our analysis will be subject to doubt. The challenge then is to show the boys it is indeed a fact that what they did was wrong. Part of the difficulty with this is that most people would accept it as obviously true. However, since the boys are not like most people, a good strategy for trying to show them the error of their ways is to first determine how they are unlike the rest of us. If we can understand our difference or differences, we might gain some insight into showing them their mistake.

We can see the badness of the boys' action, but they claim not to see any such thing. If we see something they don't, then perhaps their problem is perceptual? Are their senses deficient in some way? It seems not. Like us, they see the cat, smell the gasoline, feel the heat of the fire, and so on. But they don't see any badness, and there are no eyeglasses that would enable them to detect this thing that is so obviously right in front of the rest of us. Perhaps instead, then, their problem is some sort of cognitive deficiency. Is there some information or reasoning they lack that explains their failure to appreciate the wrongness of their behaviour?

With the goal of uncovering this we set out to convince the boys to change their ways. What should we say to them? You ask them if they understand that setting the cat on fire hurts and kills the cat. "Oh yes," one replies, "that's the point, otherwise, why bother?" Still a little unsure whether they understand, we ask the boys whether they would like to be set on fire. "That would be awful," the other replies, "but I'm very careful not to set myself on fire." When we enquire whether he is not worried that he might meet the fate of the cat, he shakes his head and says that he tortures only defenceless creatures. "And besides," he adds, "I live in a place where people can't be tortured." He also tells us that they are usually careful to avoid getting caught but were just unlucky today.

It looks as though the boys' problem is neither perceptual nor cognitive. Their senses work fine, and they seem to understand what they are doing. Shocking as it may be, they also reason clearly. So what is the difference between them and us? What else is there to distinguish us? To uncover this, try to imagine what the scene just described would really be like. Most of us would find it truly horrifying. We might feel nauseous at the sight and sound of the cat's suffering. We would feel pity for the cat, anger and confusion toward the boys, and a deep sense of sadness at the whole sorry mess. In stark contrast, the boys feel only a mild sense of amusement. They are unlike us in that they don't care about the cat, whereas we do. Each of the two boys thinks only his suffering is bad, whereas we think all such suffering is. Most of us care about others, at least to some extent, but each of these boys cares only about himself. As sociopaths, they are incapable of caring for others, and since feeling for or caring about others is a prerequisite for being moral, the boys cannot be morally motivated. The Scottish philosopher David Hume (1711–76) recognized the central place of caring in ethics when he argued that ethics rests on natural feeling or sentiment.

3.3 Crude Ethical Subjectivism

The example involving the boys shows that you cannot always use reason to convince someone to be moral. Since the boys lack the requisite concern for others, they cannot appreciate the wrongness of their behaviour. Overly impressed by examples like this, or perhaps lacking the wherewithal to show why some action is immoral, some take this point to an extreme and claim that ethics is solely a matter of sentiment. According to this view, which we shall refer to as **Crude Ethical Subjectivism,** when people make moral judgments they are merely stating their feelings. So the Crude Ethical Subjectivist would say that your judgment that what the boys did to the cat was evil is just another way of expressing your personal feelings of disgust and disapproval over their behaviour. Crude Ethical Subjectivism is not an account of the prescriptions and proscriptions of morality. Rather, it is a meta-ethical theory about the nature of moral judgments. As such, it stands in direct opposition to the explicit aim of this book—to achieve enlightenment in ethics through the critical investigation of ethical problems and issues. Since Crude Ethical Subjectivists deny reason any meaningful place in ethics, the idea of critically enquiring into a moral problem makes no sense. For one thing, there is no possibility of meaningful disagreement about morality on the crude ethical subjectivist outlook. Since all moral judgments are mere statements of feelings, although two people might have different feelings about some event, there is no factual disagreement. Likewise, talk of rightness and wrongness is meaningless on this view. All such claims about actions being right or wrong are only statements of approval or disapproval. According to the Crude Ethical Subjectivist, it isn't true that what the boys did was evil; some of us just feel bad about their actions.

This account of the incident involving the cat fails to capture the force of our conviction that what the boys did was wrong. When we make this sort of moral judgment we think that it is true that the boys behaved evilly, and we can advance reasons to support our judgement. For example, we might think that we have a duty to not gratuitously inflict suffering on innocent creatures because in doing so, we fail to show them the respect they deserve as sentient beings.

> **Crude Ethical Subjectivism** is a non-cognitivist meta-ethical view about the nature of moral judgments. According to it, all moral judgments are merely expressions of feelings because there are no moral facts or moral truths.

Alternatively, we might argue that it is wrong because the minimal value to the boys of torturing and killing the cat is greatly outweighed by the disvalue to the cat of its suffering and loss of life. Even if we disagree about the right or best reason for showing the wrongness of their actions, we think both that the project of advancing reasons to justify our judgments is meaningful and relevant and that it is possible to disagree about how one should act toward cats.

Although these points, based on our shared view about the role of reason and the possibility of disagreement in ethics, provide a presumptive case against the Crude Ethical Subjectivist, to fill out our argument we need to explain the ideas of moral truth and moral facts. A comprehensive account and defence of these ideas is beyond the scope of our introductory treatment of Meta-Ethics; however, we can add to our case by saying more about how a defence of Cognitivism in ethics might unfold. Before we turn to this, however, we should discuss another flawed view in Meta-Ethics, namely crude versions of Ethical Relativism.

The Crude Ethical Subjectivist says that morality is merely a matter of feeling, and in the example involving the boys, we can explain our differences by saying that whereas we feel one way, the boys feel differently. It is a short step from saying this to accepting the related crude relativist position that such behaviour is right for the boys (they approve of it) but wrong for us (we don't).

3.4 Crude Versions of Ethical Relativism

Confusion about Ethical or Moral Relativism is probably the main source of trouble among students new to the study of ethics. It's easy to get lost in the subtleties of Meta-Ethics and Normative Ethics, and even in its cruder forms Ethical Relativism can be a tempting view, more so than even Crude Ethical Subjectivism. Part of the problem with dispelling this confusion is saying carefully what Ethical Relativism is because there are different views of varying levels of

sophistication. It will be useful to briefly survey some of these views and expose their strengths and especially their shortcomings. We will begin by examining some cruder versions of Ethical Relativism, and after some analysis of these views, we will turn our attention to more sophisticated forms of the theory.

It is fair to say that all Ethical Relativists share the belief that any truths about morality are relative to someone's or some group's beliefs and values. Furthermore, relativistic accounts share a basic conviction in the belief that there is a lack of universality in ethics. This conviction is expressed in two general ways. Sometimes it is expressed through the assertion that the Relativism in Ethical Relativism is Relativism to the beliefs and values of particular individuals; and sometimes it is expressed through the assertion that the Relativism in Ethical Relativism is Relativism to the beliefs and values shared by a group. In the first case, this is expressed in the assertion that ethics is "subjective," that there are no "objective" moral truths or moral facts, or if there are moral facts, then these facts are facts only relative to the beliefs of different individuals. Put crudely, this version of Ethical Relativism is the view that "I'm OK, you're OK. You believe X, I believe not-X, and since morality is personal and subjective, and since we are different, each view is right or true for us." Since some Crude Ethical Relativists accept that there are truths about morality, and since some claim that there are not, there are, therefore, both non-cognitivist and cognitivist versions of the view.

Alternatively, the relativistic belief that there is no universality in ethics is sometimes expressed in the claim that morality is relative to particular societies, cultures, or groups of individuals. The crude version of this relativistic view is captured in the saying "When in Rome, do as the Romans do." The idea here is that, since there are no universal truths about ethics, we should follow the local practices of those who live wherever we find ourselves. Within this outlook, morality is like etiquette because it is a simple matter of learning and then following the local conventions or customs. This view is crude in part because these customs are regarded as being arbitrarily decided. In principle, any set of moral customs would do, but since we are where we are, we should follow the local rules.

In both its cruder and more sophisticated forms, **Ethical Relativism** is a normative theory about morality. Specifically, the versions we are examining are meta-ethical theories about the nature and justification of moral claims and judgments. Like Crude Ethical Subjectivism, they are not sets of particular ethical "dos" and "don'ts." Rather, Ethical Relativists try to explain how the normative claims that people make should be understood and justified. According to the Ethical Relativist, such judgments are in some sense relative and are justifiable only by reference to the views of someone or some group of people. So, for instance, an Ethical Relativist would say that a moral judgment such as "you should not torture defenceless creatures" is not simply wrong; it is wrong relative to someone's view or the shared views of some group. Thus it just is wrong for me and not for you, or alternatively, it is wrong because I feel it is, because it violates my moral code, because it contravenes our shared way of life or set of values, or because we say so and agree that it is wrong.

3.5 The Appeal of Crude Versions of Ethical Relativism

We can take a first step toward diagnosing the problems with Ethical Relativism by considering why people adopt crude versions of the view. Here are two connected contributing explanations:

1. The Appeal of Tolerance

Many of us want to be tolerant of others and respect our differences. We regard tolerance as a virtue, and indeed there are some good reasons for this. We should be tolerant because apart, perhaps, from some basic needs that most of us share, we are different. Humans derive value from a wide variety of things and activities. For example, some of us like to take risks and some of us are risk averse. The view that everyone must participate in risky activities like skydiving,

mountain climbing, or racecar driving in order to be happy contradicts common sense. Typically, those who are narrow-minded insist that whatever way of life is prudentially good for them is prudentially good for everyone. In contrast, Crude Ethical Relativists acknowledge that we are different and that we should live our lives differently as a result and accommodate the broad scope of interests that humans have. Thus, Crude Ethical Relativists say we shouldn't be so judgmental and that everyone is entitled to his or her own point of view.

While there is some merit to this outlook, Crude Ethical Relativists take this much too far. They suggest that we should be free to do whatever we want regardless of the consequences to others, provided it is morally acceptable according to our personal standards. With Crude Ethical Relativism, what starts out perhaps as a morally proper tolerance of our differences slides into a lax, wide-open permissiveness. On this view, since I can't judge your immorality by any non-relative standard, anything goes. If it is morally OK for you, then although I might not agree, I can't say that you really act immorally.

Generally speaking, however, morally proper tolerance for our differences should extend only as far as the point where the exercising of our choices does not unjustly harm others. So, for instance, it is one thing to say that people should be free to engage in activities of varying degrees of risk because we have varying levels of risk-taking comfort. It is quite another to say that I should be free to take risks with other people's lives and well-being because I enjoy doing so. Being tolerant of others means that, as a result of our differences, I can appreciate that some people might derive value from engaging in activities that I, prudentially speaking, disapprove of. It does not mean that I should morally approve of any such activity, regardless of its harmful effects on others.

Crude Ethical Relativists fail to make this crucial distinction, and as a result they take their

> **Ethical Relativism** is a normative and meta-ethical theory about the nature and justification of moral judgments. According to the Ethical Relativist, moral judgments and any truths about morality are relative to someone's or some group's beliefs and values.

good-intentioned willingness to be tolerant too far. There is a difference between being flexible and being spineless.

The laudable desire to be tolerant of others that expresses itself in a commitment to some version of Crude Ethical Relativism reveals another laxness in the view. Crude Ethical Relativism is now starting to look like a specific prescriptive ethical theory according to which one should be tolerant of others. But we just noted that Ethical Relativism is a theory about how we should understand moral judgments. As such, it is a theory in Meta-Ethics, and it should be silent on the specific "dos" and "don'ts" of morality. "Be tolerant of others" is a moral prescription or imperative. Thus it would be an instance of conceptual confusion for an Ethical Relativist to claim that his theory commits him to endorsing tolerance for others.

Meta-ethical theories and prescriptive ethical theories are different in kind and thus should not be confused. As we noted in Chapter 1, Meta-Ethics is the study of particular prescriptive ethical views, it is not an area within Prescriptive Ethics. More specifically, Meta-Ethics includes the study of the nature and justification of the moral beliefs that comprise particular prescriptive ethical theories or outlooks. Thus particular meta-ethical views, like Ethical Relativism, are views about the status of the truth of the beliefs that comprise prescriptive ethical outlooks as opposed to views with specific prescriptive and proscriptive ethical imperatives. The answers to questions in Meta-Ethics provide a foundation upon which prescriptive ethical theories are constructed.

This failure to consistently classify their theory leads to another problem for Crude Ethical Relativists. How can the Ethical Relativist consistently endorse both the claim that we should be tolerant of others, where this is taken to be true of all Ethical Relativists, and the claim that the truths of morality are relative? There are two possibilities, both of which are problematic. Either the claim is to be understood as a necessary truth about Ethical Relativism or a contingent truth. In other words, either the belief about tolerance is taken to be definitional—to be a

Relativist, one must be tolerant—or it is claimed that, coincidentally, all Relativists believe we should be tolerant of others. If the idea that tolerance is morally good is a necessary truth about morality, then it is an absolute truth because it must be true of all moral outlooks. It would hence directly contradict Ethical Relativism and therefore it could not be endorsed by the Ethical Relativist. If, on the other hand, it is a relative truth, then whether all individuals and groups believe it is a dubious empirical assertion, one for which we would need empirical proof.

2. Ignorance about How Moral Claims Are Justified

Another reason why people are inclined, at least initially, to accept some crude version of Ethical Relativism is that they are ignorant about how moral claims and judgments are justified. Lacking confidence in their own beliefs, they acquiesce to some version of Crude Ethical Relativism and accept the idea that anything goes, or at least that they cannot prove that someone else's view is wrong. Others think that because the subject of ethics is so subjective, because it is such a perplexing mix of reasoning and feelings, there is therefore no single truth about morality. Certainly, there is no one correct view. The complex and longstanding debate over the morality of abortion is a good case in point. In the face of the sort of apparently hopeless disagreements engaged in by those in debates about the ethics of abortion, the Crude Ethical Relativist concludes that we are left with determining only what is morally best or true for us. Given our differences in values, opinions, and feelings, this is all there is.

The problem with explaining how ethical claims are justified is best met by thinking carefully about our question about the point or purpose of morality because ethical claims are justified with respect to this purpose, as we shall see. However, since this problem also plagues more sophisticated versions of Ethical Relativism and versions of an opposing meta-ethical view, Ethical Absolutism, we would do well now to broaden our discussion and also consider these views. More sophisticated versions of Ethical Relativism and correspondingly sophisticated versions of Ethical Absolutism give better answers to our question about the purpose of morality, but their answers are still weak. By revealing this weakness, we will be well placed to fill out our argument against Crude Ethical Subjectivism.

3.6 More Sophisticated Versions of Ethical Relativism

Typically, more sophisticated versions of Ethical Relativism assert that whatever truth there is about ethics is relative to a shared belief system and set of principles and values that are themselves the product of a shared way of life. This view is more sophisticated than Crude Ethical Relativism because it rejects the simple notion that the moral customs of a culture are arbitrarily decided. However, it remains a relativistic view because it endorses the idea that what is morally right and wrong for a group of people is relative to its particular way of life. Harman has defended this view. In a series of papers, he advanced and supported a sophisticated version of Ethical Relativism that "denies that there are universal moral demands and says that different agents are subject to different basic moral demands depending on the social customs, practices, conventions, values and principles that they accept."[2]

Sophisticated versions of Ethical Relativism consist of ideas drawn from different sources. One source for these views comes from the work of scientists. Thus, for example, anthropologists and sociologists have observed that different societies and cultures follow different codes of morality. Although there may be some moral principles common to many, or even all, human cultures, no two cultures are identical. This view is known as **Cultural Relativism**. Another example of scientific support for sophisticated versions of Ethical Relativism is drawn from the work of scientists who have advanced **sociobiological explanations of ethics,** that is, explanations of ethics from the perspective of

the study of the biological foundations of human social behaviour. So, for instance, some have argued that we can provide an ecological explanation of our species' flourishing by pointing to the role played by our ability to co-operate in small groups, groups that have expanded beyond our immediate and relatively small families. This sort of explanation draws on facts about our biology, namely, that we care about each other and that our caring can extend beyond our kin. Furthermore, it regards ethics as growing out of local human associations, which speaks against the idea of a universal moral code.

Sophisticated versions of Ethical Relativism appeal to both Cultural Relativism and sociobiological explanations of ethics for support, but these views are, strictly speaking, not identical with Ethical Relativism. Non-Relativists can accept Cultural Relativism and sociobiological explanations of ethics because each view is descriptive. Regardless of one's normative ethical position, one can accept both the fact that human cultures are diverse and this sociobiological explanation that appeals to ethics to help explain why we have flourished as a species. Sophisticated versions of Ethical Relativism add a normative claim to these sources to reach their position. Specifically, defenders of more sophisticated accounts of Ethical Relativism take these anthropological and sociobiological facts about us as their starting point. They then make the claim that not only is morality the product of a shared way of life but also that the claims and judgments of morality *should* be judged as right or good *because* they are accepted. Sophisticated Ethical Relativists maintain that since there is no culturally independent and "objective" set of truths about ethics, there is no culturally independent correct morality. All we have are the differing views of different cultures. Sophisticated Ethical Relativists reject supernatural accounts of ethics, like those that hold that ethics is universal because God created and revealed the truth about morality to us. Instead,

> **Cultural Relativism** is the view that different societies and cultures follow different moral codes. A **sociobiological explanation of ethics** explains ethics from the perspective of the study of the biological foundations of human social behaviour.

they embrace Ethical Relativism as a superior view, one that appeals directly to science and scientific methodology for support, specifically to the work of anthropologists. Thus we can see how what begins as work in Descriptive Ethics, merely describing the moral codes of various groups of humans, lends itself to a theory in Normative Ethics, specifically a meta-ethical theory about the nature and justification of the claims of morality.

3.7 Ethical Absolutism

In contrast to Ethical Relativism, **Ethical Absolutism,** a meta-ethical theory, asserts that at least some truths about morality are absolute. The Moral Absolutist asserts that under suitably similar circumstances, a moral judgment is true for all people at all times and in all places. The qualification "under suitably similar circumstances" is important because Absolutists think that the contexts in which we make moral judgments are relevant and that differences in circumstance lead to differences in judgments by Ethical Absolutists. Thus, for example, Absolutists who believe that murder is morally wrong think that the circumstances of killing are relevant. Absolutists can distinguish between murder or unjustified killing, and killing in self-defence. Moral Absolutism is not a simple-minded view.

Although they might disagree about the number of absolute moral truths, all Ethical Absolutists accept that at least some moral truths are absolutely true; that is, they are not relative to people's beliefs and values. They argue that there is the sort of universality in ethics denied by Ethical Relativists for various reasons. Universality in ethics is sometimes explained by pointing to the purported role that a deity played in our creation and plays in our lives. On this view, since we were all made according to an image created by God, there are universal truths about morality that apply to each of us. Alternatively, universality is sometimes explained without appealing to a deity, but by appealing again to some alleged universal quality or qualities common to all humans, like the possession of free will or reason. Thus, on these views, there are absolute truths about morality because of our common status as beings with free will or because of our common status as rational beings. Moreover, these universal truths are deducible, in principle, by anyone who uses his reasoning abilities well.

Sometimes universality in ethics is explained by reference to both ideas, as we saw in the case of classical Natural Law Theory in Chapter 2. Aquinas's Natural Law Theory is absolutist because the truth about morality is not relative to the beliefs and values of different people or different groups of humans. Whereas, for example, an Ethical Relativist might point to differences in circumstances between different societies to explain differences in relative and correct moral codes, the Thomistic view is that there is one set of correct natural laws ordained by God that distinct societies discover to varying degrees of success. The difference between Ethical Relativism and Ethical Absolutism is a difference over universality. The Relativist denies that there are universal moral demands, and the Absolutist asserts that there are.

> Ethical Absolutism is a normative and meta-ethical theory about the nature and justification of ethical claims and judgments. According to the Ethical Absolutist, there are universal moral demands for various reasons. Furthermore, under suitably similar circumstances a moral judgment is true for all people at all times and in all places.

Exercises 3.1

Progress Check

1. What is the main point of the story involving the boys and the cat?

2. What is Crude Ethical Subjectivism? Why does it pose a threat to the aim of this text to promote some enlightenment in ethics?

3. What is Ethical Relativism? Describe two crude versions of the view.

4. Why is Ethical Relativism a meta-ethical view?

5. Why is tolerance a virtue?

6. Why does the Crude Ethical Relativist's endorsement of tolerance go too far?

7. Explain the conceptual confusion that results from the Crude Ethical Relativist's endorsement of tolerance.

8. Explain the distinction between crude and sophisticated versions of Ethical Relativism.

9. What is Cultural Relativism?

10. What is a sociobiological explanation of ethics?

11. Explain the distinction between Cultural Relativism and Sophisticated Ethical Relativism.

12. What is Ethical Absolutism?

13. How do Ethical Absolutists defend their view that ethics is universal and not relative?

Questions for Further Reflection

1. Is the fact that the boys set a cat—as opposed to a human or some other creature—on fire relevant to our moral analysis of this example? Critically discuss.

2. What is the best explanation of why the boys' actions are immoral? Why?

3. Crude Ethical Relativists demonstrate a willingness to be tolerant that goes too far. Why?

4. Briefly sketch out and defend your own account of the morally proper limits of tolerance. What principle or idea guides your account of where we should draw the line? Why?

5. To what extent, if any, are sophisticated versions of Ethical Relativism correct? Why?

6. To what extent, if any, are ethical absolutist views right? Why?

3.8 Appreciating the Meta-ethical Nature of Ethical Relativism and Ethical Absolutism

It is easy to lose sight of the difference between Ethical Relativism and Ethical Absolutism and the fact that the versions of the views that we are considering are meta-ethical. We noted how Ethical Relativism moves from accepting a view in anthropology, namely Cultural Relativism, to being a view in Normative Ethics, but it is worth pausing to emphasize this important shift. Actually, the fusion of the descriptive with the normative can occur in arguments for both Ethical Relativism and Ethical Absolutism, so we would do well to examine each sort of case. For instance, one might be tempted to argue for Ethical Absolutism by noting that all human societies and cultures share certain basic prescriptions and proscriptions. One might cite the universal prohibition of murder in all human societies to show that there are universal moral demands and that, therefore, the Ethical Absolutists are right. Alternatively, one might point to the cultural relativist insight that there are sensible differences in practices between cultures to show that Ethical Relativism is the right view. Let's consider each of these arguments in turn, beginning with the one for Ethical Relativism.

The differing attitudes to abortion we see in different cultures provides us with a good example of the type of practice that the Ethical Relativist sometimes uses to support her view. Ethical Relativists note that we can explain how different societies can have different attitudes toward a practice like abortion and how they can both be right for their situation or relative to their circumstances. In a society like China, abortion is not only tolerated but also encouraged as part of an ethical solution to the problem of overpopulation. The Chinese policy of "one couple, one child" makes sense for their situation and, as a result, according to the Sophisticated Ethical Relativist, by their agreement and by their practices, abortion is morally acceptable. In contrast, the Relativist notes, a society living in different conditions, say one where a distinct way of life was vanishing because of a problem with depopulation, might agree to regard abortion as immoral. To insist in the face of these different circumstances that abortion is either universally right or wrong for all humans is a mistake, according to the Ethical Relativist. On this outlook, the truth about morality is relative. Abortion is morally right for the Chinese because they generally agree that it is, and it is morally wrong for the members of the other society because they generally agree on that.

In this argument we see how the Ethical Relativist appeals to facts about cultural or societal differences to help support Ethical Relativism. A similar sort of argument is made by Moral Absolutists who point to the fact that all human societies in fact have some moral prohibition against murder to justify their belief that there are universal moral demands. The Absolutist might argue that by using our reason we can see that such a prohibition is necessary for humans to co-exist peacefully in any society and thereby achieve the benefits of co-operation. Again, an appeal to a fact about how the world is, is cited to support a normative view in ethics.

The problem in each of these kinds of arguments is that they fail to appreciate the nature of the meta-ethical project. The meta-ethical project of classifying and justifying ethical claims and judgments does not proceed simply and directly from an appreciation of the way things are. For example, the fact that practices like stealing and bribery are common in a society does not permit us to infer that those practices are morally justified. The prevalence of these actions could be attributable to the fact that the society is unjust and suffers from widespread vice and corruption. One can't infer that just because it happens, it is good or justified. When we ask meta-ethical questions about the nature and justification of moral claims, we are not simply asking about how things are. That is the job of the scientist. Rather, we are engaging in the philosophical process of judging or assessing how things should be. This is a straightforward difference between Descriptive Ethics and Normative Ethics, as we noted in the Introduction.

In light of this point, reconsider the two examples we have just examined. An Absolutist who concluded that murder is absolutely immoral because there is in fact a prohibition against it across all human societies would make a poor argument for Ethical Absolutism. It is poor because it blends description with proscription. Another way to appreciate this is to see how the Ethical Relativist interprets the facts differently. The Relativist would say that the fact that all human societies prohibit murder does not justify Ethical Absolutism, it shows only that each society turns out to have a prohibition against murder. But this does not prove anything about universality. The Relativist would say that for each society murder is wrong by that society's agreement and circumstances. Furthermore, we can explain why there is this common prohibition from the fact that each group would prosper

by agreeing to its inclusion in its code. We do not need to posit God's existence or some mysterious universal reasoning ability to explain this fact.

The same sort of mistake undermines the argument for Ethical Relativism that we just considered. The Relativist asserts that to determine whether abortion is morally justified or not, one must refer back to the shared beliefs and values of the group in question. So on this analysis, abortion is justifiable in China but not in another differently circumstanced society. The problem here again is inferring from a fact about a society to a claim about what is ethically justified. The Ethical Relativist asserts that abortion is ethically justified in Chinese society because it is generally accepted there. But we've already noted the danger in making this sort of inference.

In response, an Ethical Absolutist can embrace Cultural Relativism to help us see that the truth of Cultural Relativism does not necessitate or guarantee the truth of Ethical Relativism. The Absolutist can accept the fact that there are differences in moral practices regarding abortion between different cultures and societies. But, he could insist, this does not prove Ethical Absolutism wrong. Rather, we can explain the different practices of the two societies regarding abortion by arguing that in each society there is actually a common commitment to a deeper and more important ethical value, namely a commitment to promote the common good of the group. The Absolutist can argue that in order to promote the good of the group, in one society abortion is accepted and in the other it is rejected. The differences in the circumstances of the two societies explains why there are these differences in practice and attitudes toward abortion, but the underlying universal moral demand remains the same. Specifically, in order to promote fairness and the collective survival of the group, Chinese society approves of abortion. To stem the depopulation problem and to ensure its collective survival, the other society disapproves of abortion. In each case, the goal is to promote the collective good.

This brief argument does not prove that Ethical Absolutism is the right view about Meta-Ethics, nor is it designed to do this. Rather, the point is that whether Ethical Absolutism is the right view or not is not determined by whether Cultural Relativism is correct. Since they are different kinds of theories, in principle both the Ethical Relativist and the Ethical Absolutist can embrace this descriptive account. More generally, we need to remind ourselves that these meta-ethical theories are theories about the nature and justification of moral claims and judgments. As such, their success will turn on how well they explain moral claims and how well they explain what justifies specific moral prescriptions and proscriptions.

We have noted that there are various weaknesses in crude versions of Ethical Relativism, including the problem Crude Ethical Relativists have with explaining why particular moral judgments are justified or not. Their problem or mistake is in falsely believing that moral choices cannot be judged so they go further than simply accepting moral choices. This problem also handicaps sophisticated versions of Ethical Relativism and Ethical Absolutism. To see this, we need to answer our question about the purpose of morality.

3.9 Etiquette Relativism

As a descriptive account of human moral practices, Cultural Relativism seems right. There is compelling evidence for the view that different human societies and cultures follow (however slightly) different moral codes. However, as a normative moral view, Ethical Relativism maintains that we should regard whatever truths there are about ethics as relative to the beliefs and values of different groups of humans. What support is there for this? Why should we understand moral truth in this way?

The idea that moral codes are relative to different groups of humans can lead to the possibility that similar actions can be right on one code but wrong on another. The extent to which this happens is a matter of debate, with critics of Ethical Relativism rightly noting that it is easy to exaggerate such differences. Thus it is argued that one must first gather all of one's facts and

understand the contexts in which different judgments are made about apparently similar actions. Sidestepping this debate about the actual number of real conflicts for a moment, it will be useful to examine the idea of apparently conflicting moral judgments more carefully. It seems odd to think that similar practices ought to be accepted as wrong for one group of humans yet right for another group. How can this be? Philosopher Bernard Williams has argued that the aim of Relativism in its various forms is to explain away conflict.[3] Relativism's defenders must say why there appears to be the sort of inconsistency we just noted and then why this inconsistency is only apparent and not real. Can defenders of Ethical Relativism do this for their versions of Relativism? For comparison purposes, let's consider a version of Relativism that passes Williams's test, namely, Etiquette Relativism.

The old phrase "When in Rome, do as the Romans do" makes sense when applied to straightforward cases of etiquette, because here at least we can see that it is really entirely consistent to act in ways that appear to be inconsistent. In the case of etiquette it can make sense to perform act X in one place and act not-X elsewhere in relevantly similar circumstances. So, for example, in North America the custom when eating is that one engages in conversation. In contrast, we can imagine a country, call it Elsewhere, with a different code of etiquette that requires that during meals people remain silent. When I do business with strangers in North America I talk at the dinner table. When I do business with strangers in Elsewhere I don't talk at the dinner table. Do I act inconsistently? No. It looks like I am acting inconsistently by performing X in one place (talking at the dinner table in North America) and not-X in another place (not talking at the dinner table in Elsewhere). But this apparent conflict is not real because in each place in order to be polite I must engage in behaviour determined by the local code of etiquette. As it turns out, each local code requires that I do something (talk in one place, not talk in the other) that superficially seems to be inconsistent. However, since in each place I adhere to my goal of being polite, my behaviour is really consistent. So when it comes to etiquette, when in Rome, do as the Romans do.

Etiquette Relativism makes perfect sense as a normative meta-etiquette theory about how we should regard the truths about etiquette. According to **Etiquette Relativism** we should understand the claims about etiquette relatively, specifically, relative to the relevant local code. In contrast, an absolutist normative meta-etiquette theory is silly. It says that some favoured set of practices is really right or true wherever one goes in the world. On this view it is right to talk at any dinner table on the planet. An absolutist meta-etiquette theory rests on an inherently flawed understanding of the nature of etiquette. We know that as a matter of fact, codes of etiquette vary from place to place, and Etiquette Relativism is based on an appreciation of this. The absolutist view that only some single set of practices is polite is dogma with no basis in fact.

> **Etiquette Relativism** is a normative meta-etiquette theory about how we should regard the truths of etiquette. According to this view, the truths of etiquette are relative to particular and different local codes of etiquette.

3.10 The Case of Jane and the Alien Invaders

Can we extend the sort of analysis we see in the etiquette case to Ethical Relativism? Can we make sense of the idea that some action can be morally right in one place yet immoral somewhere else? Consider the following bit of science fiction to test our intuitions. Imagine that aliens arrive on earth intent on taking several thousand humans back to their home planet to breed us for food. The human-like creatures on their planet are dying off because of some infectious disease the aliens have been unable to contain. Since the aliens depend on eating beings like us for their survival, they desperately need to find a new source of nourishment. Imagine further that they are impervious to our efforts at resisting them and that they are oblivious to our suffering and wishes. They don't care about us.

The aliens discover that one person on Earth, Jane, has a unique skill or talent they would like to learn. They offer Jane the opportunity to teach them her skill in return for some suitable payment. They invite her to alien world to negotiate a mutually acceptable agreement and subsequently begin the lessons. Jane appreciates the potential benefits of bargaining with them: they could provide her with amazing and highly profitable technology. So she agrees to go. Imagine furthermore that Jane's interest in going is fuelled by her desire to become fabulously wealthy and live an opulent, easy life of leisure back here. She has no desire to acquire the technology to improve our lives; she is selfish.

It is customary on the aliens' planet to have a banquet prior to the commencement of business negotiations at which the guest of honour is the chief foreign negotiator. At the banquet at which she finds herself guest of honour, Jane learns of another alien custom. Guests of honour at alien banquets are expected to kill and consume the evening's first human-like creature. Jane learns, and let's imagine further she reasonably believes, that if for whatever reason the negotiation either doesn't take place or fails, she will be sent safely back to Earth so that she doesn't have to kill. She also discovers that despite their apparent lack of sensitivity to our suffering, the aliens are quite a formal and touchy bunch. They would regard any effort by Jane to not observe their banquet customs as a terrible slight, and all business with them would abruptly come to an end. Although she doesn't want to offend her hosts, she finds the idea of murdering and cannibalizing for profit morally repugnant. (She is selfish, not evil.) Thus, when she is presented with her duty at her banquet, she hesitates. The question is: What, morally speaking, should she do?

The aliens, of course, don't appreciate her dilemma. On the alien moral code, only aliens have standing. Since humans don't deserve moral consideration, it isn't immoral to kill and consume us. This is understandable in light of the fact that we fulfill a dietary need of theirs that they could otherwise not meet. Given their interest in breeding and killing us, the aliens' actions are entirely reasonable. They have no vegetarian option. Thus it is quite clear to Jane that in the aliens' society she is not being asked to do anything immoral. By their code, this sort of thing happens, quite rightly, every day. What, they wonder, is she waiting for?

Before we answer the question about what, morally speaking, Jane should do, let's answer this question from the perspective of Ethical Relativism. Does the "when in Rome, do as the Romans do" response make sense here? Certainly on a cruder understanding of Ethical Relativism, it seems that she should feel no moral compunction about murdering and cannibalizing in this situation. She is in Rome. On Harman's more sophisticated account of Ethical Relativism, it seems that she would have to say that proceeding would be immoral by her local agreement back on Earth, but not immoral on the alien code. Remember that on Harman's view of Ethical Relativism, different agents are subject to different moral demands depending on the social customs, conventions, values, and principles that they accept.

The idea that it could be morally wrong for her to do something that would be morally right for an alien in exactly her position might seem odd, but this is a very unusual example. The aliens are not like us. What we would see as murder, they would regard as self-defence. Jane doesn't have to kill and cannibalize in self-defence to survive; she can go home. Imagine that, as a strict vegetarian, she planned ahead and brought her own supply of organically grown legumes and nuts for her nourishment. Thus, she has a vegetarian option.

3.11 The Difference between Etiquette Relativism and Ethical Relativism

The sophisticated ethical relativist directive that Jane not murder and cannibalize for profit accords well with our intuitions, but Ethical Relativism does a poor job of explaining why this is the morally right response to our question. To help appreciate this, it will be useful to complete our comparison with Etiquette Relativism. According to the Etiquette Relativist, there is no inconsistency in performing action X in one place and another action, not-X, under similar circumstances somewhere else. Is this also true in the case of ethics? The apparent inconsistency in Jane's case is that she would not murder and cannibalize in her local community back on earth for profit, but she is thinking about doing this on the aliens' planet. Would it be a real inconsistency or only an apparent one if she performed these actions on the aliens' world but not back home? Can we explain away this apparent inconsistency as we did in the etiquette case?

To answer these questions, we need to look deeper into the nature of etiquette and ethics. The reason why it can be polite to perform actions X and not-X in different places under similar circumstances is that, in the case of etiquette, what is regarded as polite behaviour in a community is determined by what people agree about. If we either implicitly or explicitly agree that talking at the dinner table is polite or placing one's fork on one's plate when one is finished eating is polite, then it is. If we agree that to demonstrate one's respect for one's host and to show satisfaction with one's meal after eating one should smash one's dinnerware against the nearest wall, then that, too, would become polite behaviour. In the case of etiquette, the rules or customs to which we agree constitute polite behaviour. This makes sense given the purpose of codes of etiquette. Such codes are designed to facilitate co-operation, especially between strangers. We can demonstrate our goodwill toward a stranger by following a mutually accepted code of behaviour that governs our actions.

In contrast, what makes an ethical judgment right or wrong is not simply determined or constituted by what people agree about. The reason why murder and cannibalism for profit are wrong is not because we say they are. We do say they are wrong, but that's not *why* they are wrong. At best, Ethical Relativism provides us with an incomplete account of how moral claims are justified, and at worst, it provides us with a misleading account. We should be careful here to avoid any confusion. Anthropologists who make claims about a group's "moral code" are, when they are engaging in Descriptive Ethics, describing the implicit and/or explicit rules or agreements that the group lives by. Whether the rules or agreements are morally correct is a separate question, one not simply answered by reporting on a group's way of life. Now we are judging others.

Some people are uncomfortable with the idea of evaluating or judging others. As we noted earlier, some might be tempted to accept the Ethical Relativist's analysis that since they do it, it is therefore morally right for them out of a combination of a misguided desire to be tolerant and ignorance about how moral claims are justified. The idea that we can and should judge other people's behaviour, especially those from other cultures, societies, and times, carries with it, some think, the ring of a kind of intolerant moral imperialism. But again we need to make more careful distinctions. There is a difference between morally judging others well and doing it poorly, on the one hand, and the question of whether evaluating others' ethics is possible, on the other. We should not infer that because some judge poorly that therefore we cannot judge at all. We can, though admittedly this can be difficult. Once we know how moral judgments are justified, we can move on to the task of evaluating them. The notion that evaluating another person or group's morality is impossible rests on a failure to appreciate how moral judgments are justified. We can make progress on this critical question by returning to our opening question: What is the point of morality?

3.12 The Question of the Point of Morality

The question of the point or purpose of morality asks what morality is for. Ethical Relativists typically do not directly address this question. As for Moral Absolutists, in Chapter 2 we briefly surveyed two different answers to this question given by Absolutists who accept Natural Law Theory. According to Aquinas's classical account

of the view, the purpose of morality is to express our love for, and promote the greater glory of, God. Later interpreters argued more directly for a view that held that the purpose of morality is to promote the good of individual people. In Part Two we will consider various competing answers to this question, but for now let's assume that some version of a view that holds that the purpose of ethics is to promote the good of individuals is at least partly correct. Of course, if we discover or come to accept an opposing answer to our question later that conflicts with the one we are provisionally accepting now, we will have to revisit whatever conclusions we drew.

The idea that ethics is for promoting the good of individuals cuts across many different positions on this issue, and it also accords well with common sense. When we consider this idea of promoting the good of individuals in connection with Jane's dilemma, we are able to appreciate that her killing and cannibalizing for profit would be morally wrong. Certainly, murdering someone and then consuming him to make money is not acting out of a concern for his welfare. This is true here and on the aliens' planet. Whether someone like us is murdered and eaten on Earth or on the aliens' planet makes no difference. The result is bad for that person, regardless.

Notice how appealing to the idea that the point of morality is to promote the good of individuals helps support the judgment that murdering and cannibalizing for profit is immoral, at least in a case like Jane's. The idea that all beings with a good of their own, or a prudential good or welfare (see Section 2.10), deserve consideration invites the further question of how we are to balance the competing goods of two individuals when these goods come into conflict. As we shall see, this can be very complicated. For the moment we can at least roughly see that the good to Jane of living a lazy life of leisure does not offset the disvalue to her unfortunate victim of being killed and eaten. To justify this, we would have to weigh Jane's pleasure as having much greater value than the potential victim's life. Of course, we could cook up the example to make this happen, but that would just obscure our main point. We could imagine that the human-like creature offered up to Jane was really a heinous criminal on alien world and that, regardless of what Jane does, he will be killed and consumed anyway. We could also imagine that Jane's mission was the noble one of serving humanity upon her return to Earth. But let's leave these potentially complicating considerations aside. Instead, let's suppose, in addition to our assumption about Jane's selfish designs, that her potential victim will, under an odd alien law (amazingly known to Jane!), be set free and go on to live a happy and peaceful long life if Jane declines the aliens' invitation to murder and cannibalize. Let's further assume that the potential victim is not a heinous criminal, that he doesn't wish to die, and that he enjoys the human capacities and potential that we would classify as being more or less average. Given these assumptions, it also makes no difference whether the potential victim is from alien world or whether he was just taken off the ship that travelled from Earth. The relevant point is the effect of Jane's actions on his welfare, not where he is from.

It should be clear now that what people in her local community agree about, or what the aliens in their world agree about, does not determine the potential rightness or wrongness of Jane's actions. As a normative moral view, Ethical Relativism maintains that we should regard whatever truths there are about ethics as relative to the beliefs and values of different groups of humans. But humans are fallible. We can misidentify our interests and fail to appreciate what will best advance our prudential well-being. Saying and then agreeing that an action is good or bad does not make it so. To understand whether an action is moral or not, we must determine how it will affect those involved. This explains, too, how we can see Jane's killing and cannibalizing as immoral, but the aliens' killing and eating of the same victim as morally acceptable. The consequences to the aliens of not eating humans or human-like creatures is that they will die. Jane, on the other hand, will just have to work for a living.

3.13 Fictional Facts

With our provisional acceptance of the idea that the point of morality is to promote the good of individuals, we can now return to the question of the factual nature of ethics that we deferred in our discussion of Crude Ethical Subjectivism. Recall that to complete the case against Crude Ethical Subjectivism we would need to explain the basis of factual claims and judgments about ethics. Although we do not have the space to offer a comprehensive defence of this notion, we can at least point the way to such a defence.

In our discussion of the question whether Normative Ethics might someday be subsumed by science, we noted that feeling or sentiment plays a role in ethics that it does not seem to in science. In order for you to appreciate that what the boys did in our cat example is evil, you first must care about others. In contrast, it seems that feeling plays no such similar role in science. You need not feel for or care about an object to detect its presence in a straightforward scientific experiment. The force of gravity is not detectable to just those who care about it; indeed, in science such talk makes no sense. So it seems that our points about the role of feeling in ethics help us locate a difference between the philosophical study of ethics and areas of scientific investigation.

Although this insight is cheering for those who would continue to regard Normative Ethics as a characteristically philosophical endeavour, it complicates our present task of trying to defend a cognitivist outlook in ethics. If our model of a fact is drawn from science, and if ethics is distinct from science, then how are we to explain the factual nature of moral claims?

On the scientific model, roughly speaking, an assertion is a fact if it truly describes something that anyone with functioning senses can witness. On this model, what the boys do is not truly evil because the supposed immoral character of their actions is not evident to them. However, rather than insisting that what the boys do is not really wrong, or that it is not a fact that what they do is evil, we can instead look to an alternative conception of the nature of a fact to help us along. In this vein, then, consider an alternative to the straightforward perceptually based facts of science, namely fictional facts. Consider the following variation of an example of Arthur Danto's. Imagine you and I attend a performance of Shakespeare's *Hamlet*. Partway through the play I tell Polonius to shut up. I think he is too full of himself, and I can't stand listening to his self-important speeches. "Look," I shout, "shut up, or else." He continues. To try to quiet him I throw a tomato at him. I hit him in the head, and that does the trick. Concerned about my behaviour, you usher me outside. "Well, I hit him," I say. "Hit whom?" you ask. "Polonius, of course." "No," you explain, "you did no such thing." You proceed to inform me that I hit an actor playing Polonius and that my claim that I hit Polonius is false. I don't understand.

I ask you where Polonius is. You tell me there is no such person. "So, he's dead then, right?" I ask. "No," you explain, "Polonius is just a character in a play, and no matter how hard you throw your tomato or where you throw it, you will never hit him." I still don't understand. "Listen," I ask you, "is it true or false that Polonius is the father of Laertes?" "That's true," you reply, "that is a fact." When you go on to explain that the person on the stage wasn't really Laertes, and that he too never lived, I am doubly confused. "How can it be a fact that Polonius is Laertes' father if neither of them ever existed?" I wonder. "They exist in fictional Denmark with the other characters," you reply. "Where is that?" I ask. "You can't get there from here," you explain, "at least not in any conventional way." Now I'm really confused. What evidence do you have to prove the existence of this fictional place, if you can't get there from here? What could possibly cause you to make the observation that Polonius is Laertes' father if there were never people named Polonius and Laertes related in this way?

My problem is an odd one for people of our culture, or at least for adults. However, it is not unheard of. An anthropologist colleague of mine claims that there is at least one tribe of humans, and possibly more, that believe that events that occur in dreams really occur in physical space in the way in which everyday events do. Apparently they take everything literally. They don't have or comprehend a distinction between dreams, imagination, and pretense on one side and reality on the other. With respect to the idea of a fictional world or worlds, they don't get it. Nevertheless, in most societies the distinction between a dream or pretend world and the real one is one we must learn, and to grasp this we must make an imaginative leap. Children, for example, come to appreciate and engage in pretend play. They aren't born understanding this distinction, and the example of the rare tribe shows that not everyone acquires it. Not everyone can take the imaginative leap that we make unreflectively when we go to a play or see a movie.

The presence of some people who don't appreciate fictional facts in no way compromises their standing. Fictional facts are facts, though to appreciate them one must be able to make the requisite imaginative leap of understanding. Fictional worlds have their own order and logic, and not anything goes. It is false that Laertes is Hamlet's brother, that Ophelia is his mother, and that another character named Bob slays Hamlet in the final act. Also, to say that fictional facts aren't "really" facts is ambiguous. In one sense, this is true but misleading. In another, more relevant sense, it is false. If the claim is that fictional facts aren't real in the way facts about gravity are, then this is true, though somewhat misleading. More precisely, gravity is a force, and claims about it can be factual. In contrast, though real events may have served as a kind of model for the events in Shakespeare's play, they aren't entirely or directly based on them. Though there may have been a Corambis, there literally was no Polonius. Nonetheless, if the claim is that there aren't really fictional facts in the sense that no fictional claims are facts, then this is false.

Of course, if you believe that only claims about physical objects and events can be the basis of facts, then you will not accept the claim to facthood made on behalf of some fictional assertions. But why should we accept such a narrow understanding of what a fact is? Talk about fictional facts is useful and meaningful and, so long as we don't confuse the various kinds of facts, can expand our understanding.

3.14 Subjectivity and Moral Facts

Just as one must make an imaginative leap of understanding to appreciate the facts of fiction, you must likewise have some concern for others to appreciate moral facts. If you are like me in the Hamlet example, then you will not understand the facts of the play. Likewise, if you are like the boys in our earlier example, you will not appreciate the moral fact that what they do is wrong. You will not see that what the boys do is evil, though you may be able to discern that others think such behaviour is bad. How are we to deal with doubts in the face of claims about these facts? We would not say that a force such as gravity didn't exist if someone who was incapable of perceiving its effects claimed that he could not experience it. Likewise, in the Polonius example, just because I didn't understand the fact that Polonius is Laertes' father, therefore it is not a fact that he is. By the same reasoning, we should not say that it isn't really a fact that what the boys do in the case involving the cat is wrong because they don't care about the cat. This is not to deny that there are different kinds of facts. There are. But we need an independent argument for thinking that some kinds of facts are somehow or other superior to other kinds. Why should we think this? Why should we think that moral facts are inferior to the facts of science?

Those who doubt the facts of ethics commonly claim that ethics is subjective in a way that science is not. The inference is that the claims of ethics lack objectivity and thus are somehow or other inferior to the objective claims of science. Leaving aside criticisms of the idea that the claims of science are objective, we can explain why people are prone to devalue moral facts.

You might be inclined to devalue the status of moral facts for the reason we have noted in this chapter, namely, not everyone appreciates them. This is simply the point that ethics is different from science. You might devalue the facts of ethics because you are confused over the role that feeling plays in appreciating these facts. Thus it might be claimed that ethics is subjective because it is a matter of feeling, or because it rests on feeling. In contrast, it is assumed, objectivity rests on fact or reason held to recognized standards.

This is indeed one sense in which subjectivity and objectivity are contrasted. Unfortunately, this distinction is multiply ambiguous, and it is easy to confuse the various different senses in which claims are said to be subjective or objective. Subjectivity is regarded in one sense as equivalent to arbitrariness, as when someone says that the vicious and unpredictable dictator's sentence was subjective. If so-called moral facts were really arbitrary, we might indeed be skeptical about them, let alone devalue their relative standing to the facts of science. However, we need to distinguish between saying that ethics is arbitrary and saying that appreciating the facts of ethics requires that one feels for others. These are not the same. It is not just my arbitrary opinion that setting the cat on fire is contrary to the cat's interests. It is, and most of us, including the boys, understand this. However, this fact does not deter the boys, given their lack of concern for the cat. What they do is wrong, and since the fact that their actions harm the cat provides us with a basis for making this judgment, our judgment is not arbitrary. Thus it is not subjective in this sense.

Alternatively, subjectivity is sometimes understood as meaning "not subject to rational scrutiny or rational standards," as when someone says that the daredevil's predilection for danger is a subjective thing. It may indeed just be a fact that some people like to court risk and that the rest of us cannot argue them into enjoying safer pursuits. In this sense, perhaps a subjective preference is not subject to rational arbitration. However, here again this is not the sense in which ethics is subjective. We must distinguish between saying that ethics is irrational and saying that ethics rests on feeling or concern for others. Moral claims are subject to rational standards. In our analysis of the wrongness of setting the cat on fire, we just applied one. We appealed to the notion that the prudential good to the boys of setting the cats on fire is outweighed by the harm to the cat. Therefore, what the boys did was immoral. Of course, this moral judgment is open to debate. It is not free from rational scrutiny and thus subjective in that sense, and no doubt some would take issue with it. However, to appreciate moral claims at all, one must first care about someone other than oneself. Rational debate begins only once we enter the domain of morality. Once there, that is, once we feel concern for others, we can apply rational standards in our judging of our own behaviour and the behaviour of others in a wide range of cases.

3.15 A Source of Controversy in Ethics

The idea that we can apply rational standards in our moral judgments in a wide range of cases brings us finally to a place where there is legitimate and perplexing disagreement about not just the specific moral judgments we make, but about the basis of those judgments. This is another reason why one might think that the truths of ethics are inferior to the truths of science. Here the apparent difference between ethics and science perhaps suggests that there is a limit to how confident we should be when we make assertions about the facts of morality, at least in some cases. The problem is that different moral theories disagree about how much we should care about others, and the question is how to choose rationally among these competing accounts. Notice that our progress so far does not resolve this issue. Knowing that ethics rests on sentiment does not help us decide how much we should, morally speaking, care about others as we make our way through life.

We will survey some of this debate, but consider an example for the moment to illustrate the difficulty. Is there a single correct answer to the question of how much we morally should consider a stranger's interests when we decide how to behave toward him? Imagine that you find yourself forced to choose between a stranger's life and the life of your sister. Are you ethically justified in choosing your sister or should you,

morally speaking, flip a coin to choose between them? Of course, you might from the perspective of your prudential welfare prefer that your sister live, but the question here is whether morally this decision is defensible. Admittedly this example is very sketchy, but different ethical theories answer this question differently. The problem is deciding which view, if any, is the right one. And the problem reduces to a debate about how much, morally speaking again, we should care for others. On one view, Utilitarianism, we should consider the stranger's interests as equally valuable as our sister's or our own for that matter, assuming no unusual qualifying considerations. According to another theory, Common Sense Morality, we are morally justified in choosing our sister because we care more for her than we do for the stranger. Which of these views is morally right, or is there perhaps another better theory? And most interestingly, why is one right or better than the other or others?

At this point in the debate, we may have reason for doubting ourselves. Notice, however, that we have to go fairly far into the story of morality before we reach this place where people can reasonably say not only that they disagree but also that they aren't sure that there is a correct way of resolving their disagreement. Here ethics is genuinely perplexing. We will begin to pursue this when we consider Utilitarianism in the next chapter.

3.16 Review

We began this chapter with the example of the sociopaths and the cat to help locate the central place that concern or feeling for others plays in morality. From this, we considered the idea of the Crude Ethical Subjectivist that ethics is solely a matter of such feeling, and we spent a good part of the rest of the chapter rejecting this notion. Through the examination and criticism of Crude Ethical Relativism, Sophisticated Ethical Relativism, and Ethical Absolutism we located space for both reason and feeling in ethics, and we considered how an argument for the cognitivist ideas of moral truth and moral facts might be developed.

With the help of the story of Jane and the alien invaders we revealed limitations in relativist and absolutist views, and by comparing the ideas of Ethical Relativism and Etiquette Relativism, we made good progress on our question about the point or purpose of ethics. Finally, we considered a source of controversy in ethics relating to the question of the right extent of the scope and depth of our concern for others. This, in turn, leads us into the rest of Part One and an examination of various competing theories in ethics.

Notes

1. Harman (1984), p. 35.
2. Harman (1977), Chapter 1.
3. Williams (1985), pp. 156–157.

Exercises 3.2

Progress Check

1. How do Ethical Relativists appeal to Cultural Relativism for support? Explain how the abortion example works in this regard.

2. How do Moral Absolutists appeal to certain facts about human societies for support? Explain how the murder example works in this regard.

3. Explain why these arguments for Ethical Relativism and Ethical Absolutism rest on a misunderstanding of the meta-ethical project.

4. Why would the truth of Cultural Relativism not guarantee the truth of Ethical Relativism?

5. Explain Bernard Williams's test for Relativism.

6. What is Etiquette Relativism?

7. Explain how Etiquette Relativism passes Williams's test.

8. What does the story of Jane and the alien invaders show?

9. What is the point of the example involving Polonius?

10. Explain the distinction drawn between scientific facts, fictional facts, and moral facts.

11. In what sense is ethics subjective? In which senses is it not subjective?

12. Briefly explain the controversy over the proper scope and depth of our concern or feeling for others.

Group Work Activity:

The Dilemma over Darkie Toothpaste

David Olive, in his article "When in Rome" (in *The Globe and Mail Report on Business Magazine*, May 1994, p. 12), reports that the North America-based company Colgate-Palmolive in 1985 acquired a half-interest in a Hong Kong firm, Hawley and Hazel Chemical Co., that marketed in Asia a popular toothpaste called Darkie, whose logo was a minstrel in blackface. Colgate resisted for several years pressure from shareholders, religious groups, and African Americans to stop promoting a racial stereotype.

Finally, in 1990, the product was renamed to "Darlie," and the logo was redesigned.

In your groups, answer the following questions:

1. Given the widespread acceptance of the product in Asia and its offensiveness to North American consumers, is this an example of a situation where different morals are accepted by different cultures and societies?

2. Explain the offensiveness of the original name and design.

3. How do you account for the popularity of the product in Asia?

4. In the case involving Jane and the alien invaders, we saw how a Sophisticated Ethical Relativist could justify both Jane's regarding the ceremonial killing as immoral and the aliens regarding it as moral. Is the Darkie Toothpaste case like this? Why or why not?

5. Could a Sophisticated Ethical Relativist morally justify not changing the name and logo of the toothpaste? Why or why not?

Questions for Further Reflection

1. Explain and critically evaluate the idea that Cultural Relativism supports Ethical Relativism over Ethical Absolutism.

2. To what extent, if any, are sophisticated versions of Ethical Relativism right about the nature and justification of moral judgment? Defend your view.

3. To what extent, if any, is Ethical Absolutism a correct view in Meta-Ethics? Defend your view.

4. Critically compare Ethical Relativism and Etiquette Relativism.

5. Briefly outline and defend your answer to the question of the purpose of morality.

6. Explain and critically evaluate the argument presented in this chapter for the view that there are ethical truths and facts.

Suggested Further Reading

James Rachels has accessible and useful discussions of the topics of Cultural Relativism and Ethical Subjectivism in his *Elements of Moral Philosophy* (see Rachels [1999]). Two of the more influential sources of debate in the past 25 years on the topic of the objectivity of morals and values are J.L. Mackie's *Ethics: Inventing Right and Wrong* (see Mackie [1977]) and Gilbert Harman's *The Nature of Morality* (see Harman [1977]). For a rich historical overview of the issues, see Darwall, Gibbard, and Railton (1992). For a good collection of papers on Mackie's views, see the anthology *Morality and Objectivity: A Tribute to J.L. Mackie* edited by Ted Honderich (Honderich [1985]). John McDowell's paper "Values and Secondary Qualities" (McDowell [1985]) contains an interesting and much discussed response to Mackie. Harman has explained and defended his views on moral objectivity and relativity in a number of his writings (see Harman [1975, 77, 78a, 78b, 82, and 85]). The anthology edited by David Copp and David Zimmerman contains one of Harman's papers and a number of others on this and some related topics in Meta-Ethics (see Copp and Zimmerman [1984]).

Weblinks

There are several Web sites that discuss Moral Relativism. A good place to start is with **The Internet Encyclopedia of Philosophy** entry on Moral Relativism at **www.utm.edu/research/iep/m/m-relati.htm**

Lawrence Hinman's Internet Resources on Moral Relativism is a rich source of information and links. It is at **ethics.acusd.edu/theories/relativism/**

For those interested in learning more about the group work activity topic on Darkie Toothpaste, The History Net's **African-American History** Web site has an informative section with links on the history of minstrels in America at **afroamhistory.about.com/cs/minstrelsy/**

4 Consequentialism and Utilitarianism

Learning Outcomes

In this chapter we begin to examine two influential moral theories, Consequentialism and Utilitarianism. We discuss the basic elements of the two views and how they are connected. We also consider their major strengths and weaknesses, and some of the critical debates over them.

Upon the successful completion of this chapter, you will be able to

1. identify Welfarism and consequentialist moral theories, including Utilitarianism;

2. explain the debates over monistic versus pluralistic theories of value, between mental state accounts and state of the world accounts of value, and between aggregative and distributive approaches to promoting utility;

3. outline and intelligently discuss influential criticisms of Utilitarianism advanced by John Rawls, Robert Nozick, Bernard Williams, and Samuel Scheffler; and

4. explicate some of the important developments in the history of utilitarian thought.

4.1 Introduction

In the first three chapters of Part One, we have identified the subject matter of Normative Ethics by both locating it within the study of philosophy and by distinguishing it from religion and law. In Chapter 1 we also observed that there are various areas of study within ethics, including Meta-Ethics and Prescriptive Ethics. Whereas we focused on addressing some questions in Meta-Ethics in Chapter 3, in this chapter and the following two we turn our attention to some specific moral theories or frameworks. We pay special attention to the meta-ethical assumptions of these frameworks, including their view of the basic categories of ethics.

In this chapter we examine Consequentialism and Utilitarianism. Since its appearance as a moral theory, Utilitarianism has sparked passionate debate, with its critics more than once advancing an objection and then proclaiming that the view is fundamentally flawed and should be put to rest. Yet it has persisted in various forms for over 200 years. As thinkers have developed and presented their doubts about Utilitarianism, the spotlight has shifted to Consequentialism and its basic assumptions. Although Consequentialism stands to Utilitarianism as genus to species (it is the more encompassing view) specific defences of Consequentialism appeared long after Utilitarianism was a dominant and widely discussed moral theory. So although Consequentialism is the more general view, it is also the more recent one.

The basic utilitarian idea seems appealing enough. As John Stuart Mill put it, Utilitarians accept the Principle of Utility or the "Greatest Happiness Principle" according to which "actions are right in proportion as they tend to promote happiness, wrong as they tend to produce the reverse of happiness."[1] Many have found sensible the idea that a moral theory should direct us to promote people's happiness, or perhaps less controversially, people's well-being. However, critics have taken issue with utilitarian attempts to move from this simple notion to a complete, detailed theory at every stage of Utilitarianism's development. Some of the debates over Utilitarianism have focused on the question of how best to understand it. Is it best seen as guiding our daily decision-making? Is it rather a moral theory that will help us determine right from wrong? Perhaps it is better regarded as a theory about how we should organize our society and major social institutions?

Since our concern is with Prescriptive Ethics, we will mainly examine Utilitarianism and Consequentialism as theories or frameworks for guiding us to distinguish right from wrong and morally good from bad. Our interest in looking to moral philosophy is to gain some further insight into learning about how we should live our lives, if we want to be ethical beings. A prescriptive theory should provide us with a framework for understanding the moral life and perhaps some organizing principles to provide some coherence and order to our many, and sometimes conflicting, intuitions about ethics. Does Utilitarianism or Consequentialism fit the bill?

Unsurprisingly, this question is too ambitious for us to fully answer here. However, we can at least begin to answer it and consider some of the central ethical issues and questions raised by a serious look at these views. By examining some of the influential criticisms that have led to the development of utilitarian thought, and by considering some of the objections that have challenged the consequentialist basis of Utilitarianism, we can at least make some useful progress in addressing our larger question. We will begin by identifying the three defining features of all consequentialist views. This will help us clearly distinguish consequentialist from non-consequentialist frameworks. We will then map out the terrain within Consequentialism and locate classical Utilitarianism in relation to these conceptual markers. This will allow us to both appreciate the possible consequentialist alternatives to classical Utilitarianism, and it will help us put the scope of the various criticisms in context.

After we move from examining the main objections to classical Utilitarianism, we will begin the process of considering some deeper objections to the consequentialist bases of utilitarian thought. As we will see, many of the criticisms that Utilitarianism's critics have advanced are not as damaging as they have sometimes been made out to be. Of greater interest to us are these deeper objections to Consequentialism.

Since Consequentialism is the more general view, the criticisms against the basic elements of Consequentialism have greater impact and warrant more careful scrutiny. In this chapter we take up this project, which will be further pursued both in the remainder of Part One and through a good deal of Part Two.

4.2 Consequentialism

As often happens in philosophy, our first challenge in considering the moral theory known as **Consequentialism** is to identify it. The definition of Consequentialism is a matter of some controversy. It is sometimes understood very broadly to include all those moral views that maintain simply that some consequences matter morally in some way.[2] Understood in this very broad way, Consequentialism is sometimes contrasted with Immanuel Kant's ethic, which is understood as emphasizing the moral importance of our intentions as opposed to the moral impact of our actions. So on Kant's outlook what we will or intend is morally more basic and significant than what happens. Furthermore, on this broad interpretation, Consequentialism encompasses a diverse range of more specific moral theories including various versions of Virtue Theory, Ethical Egoism, various feminist theories, Common Sense Morality, and Utilitarianism.

Although there is some point and some precedent for characterizing Consequentialism in this broad way, it will be more instructive and useful for us to follow the practice of many philosophers who understand the theory more narrowly. For them, Consequentialism remains a moral outlook that encompasses more specific theories, but it is distinguished by some defining traits that exclude some of the other moral theories that accept consequences as morally important. Specifically, Consequentialism is marked by three defining traits:

1. Consequentialism is good-based. It rejects the view that some kinds of acts are intrinsically or inherently immoral. Instead, on Consequentialism the right is defined in terms of the good. Consequentialism endorses or renounces acts solely on the basis of the contribution that the acts make to furthering the overall good.

2. Consequentialism is a welfarist theory. The good Consequentialism aims to promote is the well-being of particular individuals.

3. Consequentialism is committed to a principle of equal respect and consideration. Consequentialists aim to promote individual welfare in a way consistent with their commitment to this principle.

Let's consider each of these traits more carefully.

1. Consequentialism is good-based.

We can identify and distinguish between ethical theories by the positions they take with respect to our basic ethical categories. Two of these categories are the right and the good. We talk about principles of right and wrong conduct and about actions or states of affairs that are morally good or bad. One respect in which ethical theories differ is in terms of their ordering of these categories. If a moral theory affirms the priority of the good over the right, then it holds that its theory of the good is ethically basic. What is morally right is a function of, or is determined by, what promotes the good. In other words, the theory's theory of the good presupposes no prior account of what is right or wrong. Since consequentialist theories hold that what is good is ethically basic, Consequentialism is good-based, as opposed to right-based.[3] According to the Consequentialist, there are no inherently or intrinsically right acts because what is right or wrong is determined by Consequentialism's view about moral goodness. Moreover, what is right can change depending on the circumstances. So, for

> **Consequentialism** is marked by three defining traits.
> **(1)** Consequentialism is good-based. It endorses or renounces acts solely on the basis of the contribution that the acts make to furthering the overall good.
> **(2)** Consequentialism is a welfarist outlook. The good Consequentialism aims to promote is the well-being of particular individuals.
> **(3)** Consequentialism aims to promote individual welfare in a way consistent with its commitment to a principle of equal respect and consideration.

instance, for the Consequentialist, lying is not inherently right or wrong. Whether a particular act of lying or habit of lying is right or wrong is determined by whether it sufficiently promotes the good or not. According to the Consequentialist, then, the right is that which promotes the good somehow. In contrast, right-based theories, like the Kantian view we examine in Chapter 5, maintain that some acts are simply or intrinsically right. They are not right because of their consequences, or because they promote the good.

2. Consequentialism is a welfarist theory.

We have noted that Consequentialism is a theory that encompasses a range of distinct views. In turn it is encompassed by a more general theory itself, namely Welfarism. **Welfarism** is the foundational view in ethics according to which the purpose of morality is to promote the good of those beings that have a good of their own. On the welfarist view, only the welfare or well-being of sentient and potentially sentient beings matters for ethics.[4] To use a concept from Chapter 2, we can say that welfarist theories are thus concerned with the promotion of prudential value (see Section 2.10).

> **Welfarism** is the foundational view in ethics according to which the purpose of morality is to promote the good of those beings that have a good of their own. According to the Welfarist, only welfare matters for ethics.

3. Consequentialism is committed to a principle of equal respect and consideration.

The final distinguishing feature of consequentialist theories is their basic commitment to some principle of equal respect and consideration. One way in which this commitment is expressed is through the consequentialist theory of the good, or the theory of value. For example, Consequentialists often explain their view through a distinction made popular by Thomas Nagel. Nagel distinguishes between agent-neutral and agent-relative reasons and values, and he argues that neutral and relative values provide agents with neutral and relative reasons respectively for acting. He characterizes a reason as agent-relative if the general form of the reason includes an essential reference to the person who has it. To illustrate this point, Nagel mentions the case of two rivals, Jones and Smith, who each have a relative reason for wanting something to happen that is contrary to the other's interest.[5] In contrast, an agent-neutral reason makes no essential reference to the person who has it.[6] As an illustration he considers the notion of wretchedness in the world: if anyone has a reason to want it reduced, then that is a neutral reason. Nagel believes that in addition to having a reason for relieving our own pain, we all also have a reason for relieving anyone's pain, namely the fact that suffering is awful.

While we might agree that suffering is awful from the perspective of the person or persons who experience it, why should we think that this gives all of us a reason to relieve the suffering? Why should the fact that someone half a world away is in distress give you a reason to interrupt your life to alleviate his pain? Underlying the acceptance of agent-neutral values and reasons is a commitment to a principle of equal respect and consideration. As Nagel puts it, "the fundamental thing leading to the recognition of agent-neutral reasons is a sense that no one is more important than anyone else."[7] If you accept this principle of equality, you will have some sympathy toward recognizing agent-neutral values and reasons.

4.3 Sumner and the Consequentialist's Global Goal

We know that consequentialist theories are all good-based, welfarist, and committed to promoting a principle of equal respect and consideration. On this understanding, then, any view that denies any of these three conditions is non-consequentialist. Although this helps us to distinguish between consequentialist and non-consequentialist ethical theories, how can we distinguish between the many different possible views within Consequentialism? To help us appreciate some of the different possibilities, consider the following analysis.

L.W. Sumner connects the three defining traits of Consequentialism by explaining that in addition to being a good-based moral outlook, Consequentialism is also goal-based.[8] According to Sumner, for consequentialist theories, the decisive factor determining whether some action should be performed is whether it would sufficiently advance the Consequentialist's global goal. Sumner understands this global goal as being constructed in three stages. The first stage involves specifying the Consequentialist's basic agent-neutral theory of value. Insofar as this first stage specifies that whatever is valuable for Consequentialists is agent-neutrally valuable, and insofar as this captures the consequentialist commitment to equality, all Consequentialists must accept it.[9] However, there is room for much disagreement here over the specifics of the theory. Although all Consequentialists agree that we should promote the welfare of individuals, Consequentialists disagree about the number of different kinds of ultimate goods that constitute an individual's well-being. They also disagree about the nature of value.

Monistic theories of value assert that there is just one ultimately valuable kind of good that constitutes our welfare, whereas pluralistic theories hold that there are many ultimately valuable different kinds of goods that combine in different combinations to make up our welfare. On the pluralistic accounts, the different goods cannot be compared in terms of some common element because they are fundamentally different. Competing theories also understand the nature of value in different ways. According to one influential view, **Mental State Accounts,** the only ultimately good things are states of mind. A monistic Mental State Account maintains that all valuable states of mind share some common experience or quality so that this can be the basis of a ranking of all of them. A pluralistic Mental State Account maintains that only states of mind are ultimately valuable, but that there are many different states of mind that share no common experience or quality. Critics of Mental State

Accounts of value typically argue that such views are too narrow, that there are other bearers of value that contribute to our well-being besides our own mental states. We will take up some of these issues further when we examine Utilitarianism.

> **Mental State Accounts** are accounts of well-being or prudential value according to which well-being can be understood entirely in terms of the mental states of sentient beings.

Once they have their theory of value, Sumner argues that Consequentialists then need to explain how we should move from promoting the good of an individual to promoting the good of individuals. In other words, at Stage 1 we identify what sort of good or sorts of goods we should promote—the elements of individual welfare—and at Stage 2 we explain how we should promote this sort of good or these sorts of goods for all the beings who count. How are we to combine the separate basic goods identified at Stage 1 into a global value for us to advance? Here again, Consequentialists have many options from which to choose. The two most popular contenders have been aggregative accounts and distributive accounts. Those who favour aggregation say that the Consequentialist's global goal consists of the summing of the individual goods of individuals.

Distributive accounts say we should aim not simply to add total individual good, but we should aim to distribute value across individuals in some fair manner. For example, on one distributive approach, we should aim to ensure that all individuals reach some basic minimum level of welfare instead of just trying to promote as much welfare as possible regardless of who benefits. Alternatively, we might favour a stronger version of distribution, which requires that we promote the well-being of all beyond the point at which minimum needs are met. Whereas Aggregative Consequentialists think that the more goods we advance or promote the better, Distributive Consequentialists believe that more is not necessarily better. Instead, we should attend to the pattern of distribution of goods in addition to the total of the goods (shared with everyone). Sumner argues that Consequentialists can disagree about which combinatory operation is best, and that the range of possible consequentialist global goals is bound only by our mathematical ingenuity.[10]

Once we know what our global aim or goal as Consequentialists is, we also need direction about what we should do about this goal. Calling this Stage 3 of constructing the goal, Sumner notes that although Consequentialists may agree that the goal is to be promoted, they may disagree about how much it should be promoted. The best-known directive is to maximize the promotion of the goal. However, some have defended alternative views, including that we should aim to satisfice or go for a satisfactory promotion of the goal. On a satisficing consequentialist outlook, morality requires that we create a satisfactory amount of value as opposed to a maximal amount.[11]

One virtue of Sumner's account of Consequentialism is that it leaves room for a diverse range of consequentialist views, all of which share some defining traits. While Consequentialists are united in their commitment to a good-based theory, to Welfarism, and to furthering equal respect and consideration, they may differ in their understanding of what their theory requires of them to live up to these commitments.

4.4 Classical Utilitarianism

Just as there is a debate over the nature of Consequentialism, there is also controversy over the nature of Utilitarianism. Although there are many versions and variations of the theory, the classical statement of the view (including perhaps the name "Utilitarianism") can be traced to the English philosopher and social reformer Jeremy Bentham (1748–1832). Bentham's was not the first account of Utilitarianism, but it was widely discussed and criticized in both the nineteenth and twentieth centuries. Before Bentham, elements of Utilitarianism appear in the work of Francis Hutcheson (1694–1746) and David Hume (1711–76). Furthermore, for many years Bentham's account of Utilitarianism competed for recognition and acceptance with a theological version of the view expounded by William Paley (1743–1805). Some argue that after Bentham the classical version of Utilitarianism evolved as a result of the influence of John Stuart Mill (1806–73) and Henry Sidgwick (1838–1900).

Bentham's classical expression of Utilitarianism, printed in 1780, was published in his *Introduction to the Principles of Morals and Legislation* in 1789. In this work he defended the basic idea of Utilitarianism that we should maximize utility. "By utility," Bentham writes, "is meant that property in any object, whereby it tends to produce benefit, advantage, pleasure, good, or happiness (all this in the present case comes to the same thing) or (what comes again to the same thing) to prevent the happening of mischief, pain, evil, or unhappiness . . ."[12] The principle of utility that Bentham defends is known as the Greatest Happiness Principle, according to which we should promote "the greatest happiness of the greatest number."[13] Furthermore, Bentham understands this aggregatively. In order to maximize utility, we should try to create as much utility as possible irrespective of who benefits.

Bentham's classical expression of Utilitarianism provides us with a useful initial characterization of the view, from which we can understand some of the debate over the theory. Although it is questionable from the passage we just noted, Bentham has been taken to hold a monistic theory of value according to which there is only one ultimate value, namely pleasure and the absence of pain. Furthermore, this is a Mental State Account of value. On it, utility or happiness is reduced to the mental states of conscious creatures. Bentham's Utilitarianism is also marked by a commitment to aggregation and maximization. So Bentham constructs the consequentialist global goal by starting with a Mental State Account of value at Stage 1, specifying that we should add these individual goods at Stage 2, and that we should maximize the promotion of this goal at Stage 3. Bentham's Utilitarianism also clearly falls within Consequentialism. He endorsed an agent-neutral theory of value that expresses his basic commitment to a principle of equal respect and consideration (in his famous phrase: "Each to count for one and none for more than one"). His view is also good-based since what is right for Bentham is what would best promote utility. Finally, his view is welfarist since he recognized the moral standing of all sentient beings, that is, all beings that have a good of their own.[14]

4.5 Stage 1 Criticisms: Utilitarian Theories of Value

Although Bentham defended a Mental State Account of value that was arguably monistic, many, both within the consequentialist and utilitarian camps and outside these camps, have rejected his view. There has been considerable debate over the best theory of value for Utilitarians.[15] Utility has sometimes been interpreted as being best understood in terms of mental states; sometimes it has been understood in terms of states of the world. Alternatively, some critics of Utilitarianism have challenged the notion that our welfare is best understood in terms of utility at all. Besides these, there are many other competing views.

Smart's Electrode Operator

To begin to appreciate this debate, consider again Bentham's monistic mental state theory of value. Since he favoured the promotion of happiness, and he understood happiness in terms of the experience of pleasure and the absence of pain, Bentham is sometimes referred to as a proponent of **Hedonistic Utilitarianism.** Bentham's monistic account of value ranks all kinds of pleasures as comparable in terms of their quality. In other words, on Bentham's account, the pleasure one derives from appreciating an elegant and brilliant mathematical proof is not intrinsically different than the pleasure one receives from watching the latest horror movie, provided the quantity of pleasure is the same in each case.[16] For this view classical Utilitarianism was much criticized as being a doctrine worthy only of swine.

In his reformulation of Utilitarianism, John Stuart Mill rejected this idea and asserted that "It

is quite compatible with the principle of utility to recognise the fact, that some *kinds* of pleasure are more desirable and more valuable than others."[17] Mill argued that some kinds of pleasure are intrinsically superior to other kinds and that those with experience of both would rightly favour pursuing the "higher" sorts of pleasures. More than a hundred years later (Mill's *Utilitarianism* was first published in 1861), J.J.C. Smart defended Mill's point with his example of the electrode operator.[18] Smart notes, as did Mill, that Bentham and his supporters defended Utilitarianism against the swine charge by pointing out the utilitarian reasons for cultivating the very "higher" sorts of pleasures to which Mill referred. Since the utility principle calls on us to maximize happiness, we should cultivate the so-called "higher" pleasures because doing so will provide us with a greater overall sum of pleasures over pain.

To appreciate this, consider the social value of encouraging people to develop their mathematical abilities over spending their time viewing the latest horror movies. Such efforts will more likely result in practical benefits to society through the development of mathematics. As Smart puts it, the progress of our species depends on the progress of mathematics, and more generally the most complex and intellectual pleasures are the most fecund.[19] In contrast, the determined pursuit of the "lower" pleasures, like eating and drinking, will tend to decrease overall utility in part because of the bad effects of the overindulgence of these pleasures. So although the experience of the kinds of pleasures may be equal, Bentham's supporters argued that Utilitarianism is not a low or base theory because it will recommend that we devote our time to more productive and more intellectual pursuits than the critics appreciate.

Mill asserted that although this argument was reasonable, Bentham and his supporters were arguing for the "higher" pleasures for extrinsic reasons, that is, for reasons disconnected from the actual experience of these

> **Hedonistic Utilitarianism** is the view that utility consists of the experience of pleasure, and that moral rightness should be understood in terms of the maximization of utility.

pleasures. In fact, Mill claimed, these pleasures are intrinsically different and superior to the "lower" or "cruder" pleasures. To help, Smart asks us to imagine a scenario where the determined pursuit of the "lower" pleasures was not socially counterproductive. Imagine a machine consisting of some apparatus connected to electrodes that can be inserted into your brain. By pressing levers on the machine, you can use electrical currents to stimulate various areas of your brain resulting in the experience of the pleasures of sex, eating, or drinking. Smart recognizes that people might use these machines in self-destructive ways. They might become electrode operators at the expense of all else, behaving like addicts with predictably bad long-term consequences. But, he adds, imagine that someone could use the machine responsibly such that he could work productively most of the time and then attend to his pleasure tapping for a few hours in the evening. Would he be happy? More generally, would a society that worked toward producing this machine be the kind of future society we should strive for?

Mill would say that such a state would not be the happiest one for humans because Mill distinguishes between the "higher" and "lower" pleasures, and the machine offers only the "lower" ones. In contrast, Smart argues that those who, like Bentham, accept a monistic theory of value that regards all kinds of pleasures as intrinsically equal would have to say that this goal would be one that Utilitarianism would endorse. He thinks that the fact that Hedonistic Utilitarians like Bentham would support this goal shows a deficiency in their view because the goal is one that we should not recommend because such a state would not offer us, as operators, happiness. Smart holds that the concept of happiness is partly evaluative. Although the electrode operators would feel contentment, and might enjoy their time at the machines, such contentment, he says, is not true happiness. He adds that there is something more long-term about happiness that would be lacking in the electrode operator society. We can see this, he believes, by noting that although the experience of the machine would be enjoyable, it makes perfect sense for us to turn down an opportunity to live our lives like that.

Nozick's Experience Machine

Mill and Smart believe that Bentham's monistic account of value is too simple. They hold that there are many different kinds of pleasures and that we should be pluralists about value. However, some have questioned Smart's analysis of his example. What exactly is so bad about spending some time each day experiencing pleasure? Even Smart acknowledges that some contentment and enjoyment is a necessary part of living a happy life, but he suggests that to be truly happy, humans should aspire to more than the electrode operator society offers. What more could this be? To locate this true happiness, some have argued that we must abandon the theory of value that Mill and Smart accepted. Although they were pluralists about value, both Smart and Mill accepted Mental State Accounts.[20] However, on the Mental State Account only mental states are valuable, and to be happy we should thus strive for a life that offers us the best set of mental states.

In response, Robert Nozick asks us to consider his idea for an experience machine.[21] Imagine that some brilliant scientists have created a machine that can give us any set of mental states we could desire. Perhaps you may have wondered what it would be like to discover a cure for cancer, write a great novel, be a talented jazz musician, or win a gold medal at the Olympics. Although in real life these dreams may never be realized, in the experience machine you can have all of this and more. The machine might be a vat in which hoses and wires attach to your body and brain in various ways to give you the feeling of having any set of experiences. While you are in the machine, your memory has been altered such that you do not understand that you are there. Instead, you experience whatever experiences you have pre-programmed, and you think these are real. You can choose to blot out all or part of your pre-machine life when you pre-program your future experiences. To help you select these, you can consult with assorted experts in history, psychology, or whatever.

If you are put off by the idea of planning all of your future now, imagine that you can hop out of the machine periodically to set up the next few months or years of your life. Of course, every time you go back in you have no recollection of the programming, the scientists, the actual machine, and so on. Again, you think it is all real. Should you plug in? Does the experience machine offer you a better chance at living a prudentially good life than the one you are currently living? Since we are different, we may perhaps answer this question differently, but if the mental state account of value is right, and if we use the machine wisely, then it seems obvious that we should plug in. Yet many people resist. Why is this? Is such resistance sensible?

Notice that there are a number of advantages to choosing the machine. Life is safer in it. In real life a bus might hit you tomorrow, but since the experience machine is located deep inside the Canadian Shield you will not suffer this fate (unless you choose it). Another advantage of life in the machine is that it would help you overcome your limitations. Life out here is not fair. No matter how hard you try, for reasons beyond your control perhaps you will never be an Olympic champion, a brilliant research scientist, or a great musician. In the machine, however, you need not live with these inequities. While I actually run at a plodding pace, in the vat I experience running as the fastest man in the world in the 100-metre final.

Some say that they would not plug in because the achievements in the machine would come too easy, and that they would therefore be hollow. In real life we learn from our hard knocks, and our accomplishments and successes are more valuable to us because we have suffered hardships and setbacks along the way. However, the likelihood of this undermining our experience machine experiences would depend on how easy we made our achievements. There is no reason why one would not program in obstacles and failures for oneself on one's way to one's glorious future. In the experience machine we can learn from our mistakes too. Others worry that life in the machine would be sedentary and physically unhealthy, but again this need not be the case. You would receive nourishment and any necessary medical attention from those attending to your maintenance and the maintenance of the machine. You would sleep and live as rich,

healthy, and varied a life as you wish. You can program in plenty of exercise, which you would perform in the vat. Some worry that life in the machine would be lonely. But of course you could experience having as much contact with as many other people as you wish.

So why would someone hesitate and choose not to enter for the rest of her life? Nozick notes that we would lose by going in too. He argues that entering the machine would be like committing suicide. From the perspective of everyone on the outside you would be dead. You would have no further contact with all the people in your life. Although you could program experiences with your loved ones and friends, these experiences would not be real, since they would not actually be in there with you. Living the remainder of your life in the machine would be very selfish. Similarly, although in the machine you might experience achievements like discovering a cure for cancer, you would have only the experience of the achievement, not the cure. While you might grow and develop in the machine, and while you might even make discoveries, advance human knowledge, push the limits of human endurance, and so on, if you remained inside, no one else would ever benefit from your efforts. Finally, there is another way in which your efforts are cut off from the real world in the machine. In life you might value making a difference in the world, for example, you might value saving some marshland. Although the machine could offer you the feeling of having saved the marsh, you could not actually do it from there.

Nozick argues that it would be sensible to refuse to enter because we value more in life than just our own mental states; we also value making a difference in the world. Although once inside we would not be able to distinguish between the appearance of making a difference and actually making one, we would know before we entered. Hence our resistance. Since, moreover, the experience machine offers us any set of mental states in the course of our life, and since we are interested in our well-being, our reluctance to enter shows up the inadequacy of Mental State Accounts of value or utility. Similarly, one could argue that the chief shortcoming of being an electrode operator every evening is not that engaging in this is mere indulgence in lower over higher pleasures, but that this pursuit offers only mental states, albeit pleasurable ones. As Smart himself notes, we want to be more than electrode operators. We also want to do things like write books and join cricket teams.

Whereas Smart and Mill value these sorts of pursuits for the mental states they produce, Nozick argues that his experience machine example shows that we really value more than just the experience of doing things. We also value states of the world beyond our own mental states. Specifically, we have noted two sorts of values in life that do not reduce to our own mental states. First, we value our relationships of love, friendship, fellowship, and solidarity with others. We don't just value the feeling of loving or caring about another, the thought that we have improved a friend or loved one's life, we value their lives actually going better. In other words, their good is part of our good. Secondly, we value accomplishment and making a positive difference in the world rather than just the experience of making a difference. What you value is not just thinking that you helped preserve the marsh; you value the state of the world where the marsh is actually saved. Likewise, we value actually discovering a cure for cancer (a state of the world) over the mere experience of believing (a state of mind) that we discovered a cure.

4.6 Stage 2 Criticisms: Aggregation and Justice

In the first part of our critical examination of Utilitarianism and Consequentialism, we noted some shortcomings in the theories of value employed by Bentham, Mill, and their followers. These criticisms do not prove that Utilitarianism and Consequentialism are wrong-headed views. They show only that Utilitarians and Consequentialists need to build their moral position on a better theory of value. Once we develop such an account—and we have managed only a few steps toward this in our discussion—at Stage 2 of constructing our consequentialist global goal we will have to say how we are to promote the individual goods of all those who deserve equal consideration. According to the classical Utilitarian view, we should aggregate individual well-being; that is, we should just add it up.

In his celebrated criticism of this aggregative approach, John Rawls explains why someone might be attracted to it.[22] In our own lives, we aim to add up the various components of our well-being over the long term, sometimes accepting sacrifices now for the sake of realizing benefits in the future. Classical Utilitarianism, Rawls holds, merely applies this model of rational individual choice to society in general. Just as we balance present and future benefits and losses, so too society is seen as balancing the benefits and losses of its individual members. However, Rawls observes that on this outlook, it does not directly matter how these benefits and losses are distributed across the members of society because what is right is determined by what is good. And for the classical Utilitarian, the more benefits the better. In other words, on the classical Utilitarian view, there is nothing wrong with imposing costs on some people for the sake of greater gains for others. Since this maximizes utility, it is right.

According to Rawls, this shows that "Utilitarianism does not take seriously the distinction between persons."[23] Moreover, he believes that this reveals a deep moral flaw in the theory: Utilitarianism fails to respect our individual rights not to be harmed or sacrificed for the sake of others for the sake of the greater good. Rawls expresses this conviction underlying our status as bearers of rights with his assertion that "Each person possesses an inviolability founded on justice that even the welfare of society as a whole cannot override."[24] Although he later qualifies this assertion by saying that it is somewhat overstated, according to Rawls, the main problem with classical Utilitarianism is that it is fundamentally unjust. Needless to say, if Rawls is correct about this, this would be a fatal defect in the theory.

McCloskey's Example of the Sheriff and the Scapegoat

Critics of Utilitarianism have sometimes tried to demonstrate the force of objections like Rawls's by describing examples in which the utilitarian course of action is both counterintuitive and unjust. H.J. McCloskey's case of the sheriff and the scapegoat illustrates Rawls's point.[25] Imagine that you are the sheriff of a racially divided and charged town that has just been witness to a terrible crime. An angry vigilante mob is threatening to start a race riot that will cause considerable loss of life and suffering to many innocent people if the perpetrator of the crime is not quickly brought to justice. You determine that you can defuse the tension and eliminate the threat of the riot by framing and executing an innocent man from among the group targeted by the mob. Should you do it?

Critics of Utilitarianism point out that the Utilitarian will recommend the unjust course of action in this example and in other similar cases where we are faced with choosing between utility and justice. Utilitarianism's defenders have pursued three kinds of responses.

(1) Sometimes they have argued that these cases are so unusual that in real life they will not occur. Even in McCloskey's example, it isn't clear that the Utilitarian would recommend that the sheriff scapegoat the innocent man. After all, we must consider the bad consequences of this too. Although in the short term it may appease the angry mob and at least temporarily spare the lives of those who would be threatened by the riot, there are also long-term consequences to consider. First of all, although it might be expedient to appease the angry, racist mob, how wise is this? Utilitarians might wonder about the utility of dealing with the systemic injustice of racism by subverting the rule of law to satisfy the misdirected bloodlust of a wild bunch of bigots. Such an act will not only not remedy the underlying causes of racism, but also perhaps make things worse. The scapegoating will help cement the racist suspicions of the mob, and it might embolden them to take justice into their hands again. Will the sheriff too be swayed by the voices of prejudice and ignorance in the future? Why not? If the sheriff is tempted to subvert justice in this case, would he not be so inclined in other ones where it looks like doing so would be for the better?

What if the sheriff's action is discovered? Wouldn't this undermine faith in the system? Perhaps those who were among those victimized this time will see the case as further evidence that the law does not afford equal protection to all regardless of race. Perhaps this will strengthen the hand of those among the minority to take up arms, in the form of general rebellion or acts of terror, against the oppressors. How will this promote general utility? One might also note that the real criminal would still be at large and free to strike again.

(2) In counterresponse, critics of Utilitarianism might note that further unusual conditions could steer the Utilitarian to recommend the scapegoating. Perhaps the scapegoat has a history of violent crime and no family or friends who might suspect the scapegoating, and maybe there is circumstantial evidence convincing enough to sway those who would have doubts about his guilt. Perhaps the sheriff's guilty conscience will encourage him to redouble his efforts to defuse racist tension in his country and he might be inspired to help lead a peaceful civil rights movement that would help send violent bigotry packing. Again, the point is that there certainly could be circumstances that would force the Utilitarian to recommend that the rights of some be trampled in the cause of overall utility since Aggregate Utilitarians place no restrictions on how utility should be distributed across separate individuals.

In counterresponse to the insistence on the possibility of Utilitarianism recommending injustice, Utilitarianism's defenders have sometimes admitted that it is logically possible that this could happen. However, pointing to the oddness of the supposed damaging examples, they have asserted that the times when this would actually occur will be very rare, if ever, indeed. H.M. Hare, for example, argues that while these anti-utilitarian examples seem to have an initial veneer of plausibility, as they become more realistic and more specific they lose their force.[26]

(3) James Griffin advances a more interesting response to the charge that Utilitarianism recommends favouring utility over justice.[27] The issue, he claims, is more complex than this because we commonly accept that justice sometimes

requires that we promote utility. Rather, he maintains that we should see the conflict Rawls and McCloskey are pointing to as one between competing commitments to utility and equality, not utility and justice. Underlying Rawls's commitment to justice is some commitment to a principle of equality. Rawls's view, justice as fairness, begins from strongly egalitarian assumptions that accord all citizens an extensive set of equal rights. Remember, however, that like Rawls, Utilitarians including of course Bentham ("Each to count for one and none for more than one") are also committed to a principle of equality. Thus both must specify what showing people equal respect and consideration exactly means, and thus both must resolve the problems of finding the right place in their theories for utility and equality.

That justice will not always involve favouring equality over utility is clear from examples like the following. Imagine that doctors are faced with having to choose between saving the life of a 107-year-old blind, deaf, and immobile man in the advanced stages of senile dementia and a healthy young mother of three. There is only one necessary supply of whatever is needed to save each, be it an organ or whatever. If justice always favoured equality over utility, then we would have to say that the only fair solution to this problem is to flip a coin. But most of us, including the Utilitarians and Rawls, would say that we should give it to the woman over the man. One reason is because this would be a better use of the resource. In other words, in cases like this, utility trumps equality. This is to be sure an extreme case, but the point is that we do commonly endorse utility over equality over a fairly broad range of cases and situations. More generally, in the area of medicine we think that emergency medical care should be apportioned according to some principle of triage. Health care providers in emergency medical situations should weigh both the urgency of need of patients competing for their limited time and resources and the best use of those resources. Griffin argues that Rawls's objection appeals to our unreliable and inconsistent intuitions over a selected range of examples, like the one McCloskey describes. However, the deeper problem facing Utilitarianism and Rawls too is to spell out the tension between our commitments to utility and equality when they conflict, and to revise our theory in light of the progress we make on this. This deeper problem is a real one for lawmakers and framers of social policy, and one that we examine in some depth in chapters 9 and 10.

Some see a commitment to aggregation as definitional of Utilitarianism. If this is true, one might argue that Rawls's criticism shows that Utilitarianism is fundamentally flawed. In response, critics can deny that Utilitarianism should be defined in this way. They can add that Rawls's criticism usefully shows that the best version of Utilitarianism will move away from the classical account that accepts simple aggregation to accept some distributive principle or combination of aggregative and distributive principles at Stage 2 of constructing the global goal. In other words, Utilitarians can adapt their view to be more responsive to the sort of consideration for justice and individual rights that Rawls advocates. Utilitarianism can evolve to be fairer for individuals. Alternatively, critics can agree that aggregation defines Utilitarianism, but that Consequentialists who are not Utilitarians can continue to develop their theory by rejecting aggregation.

4.7 Stage 3 Criticisms: Maximization and Integrity

Apart from various Stage 1 and Stage 2 objections, classical Utilitarianism has been criticized at Stage 3 for adopting the goal of utility maxi-

The **Demandingness Objection** is an integrity objection to Utilitarianism. According to this objection, the problem with Utilitarianism's demandingness can be traced to its conception of *the right*. Act Utilitarianism, for example, has a criterion of moral rightness that always requires agents to perform acts that will produce impersonally best states of affairs. Thus, Utilitarianism requires that individuals devote energy to their personal commitments, projects, and relationships only when and to the extent that doing so is most productive of *the good*, impersonally construed. The theory, it is argued, threatens that integrity or the continuity of the lives of all persons who, to meet this requirement, must lessen their personal commitments, or perhaps even abandon some of them.

mization. Perhaps the best known of these objections is Bernard Williams's integrity objection. We sometimes use the word "integrity" to describe an aspect of a person's character, for example, when we say that she is a person of integrity because she is morally upright and truthful in her dealings with others. This, however, is not the sense of "integrity" that Williams accused Utilitarianism of attacking. His concern was with how "integrity," in the literal etymological sense of "wholeness," applies to individual lives, not an individual's character. Generally speaking, a life exhibits the relevant kind of integrity if it has some discernible unified structure, if there is some continuity in the values, projects, and relationships to which the person living the life is committed.

Williams originally argued that Utilitarianism attacks integrity because it apparently places boundless obligations on individuals to promote the good, impersonally construed, with no allowances for the unique ways in which individuals rank their projects. He claimed that the sheer weight of the preferences that determine the utilitarian sum will sometimes sweep aside the preferences of any particular person, regardless of the value that person places on them. Williams acknowledged that in cases of less important preferences this is acceptable, but in cases where the utility network directs individuals to forsake commitments with which they are most closely identified, Utilitarianism compromises integrity for what it takes to be the greater good. In doing so, he argued, it alienates individuals from their actions and the source of their actions in their own convictions.[28]

Commentators on Williams's work have argued that the integrity objection actually has two distinct parts, a Demandingness Objection and an Impersonal Motivation Objection. Together, these objections present Utilitarians and Consequentialists with an integrity dilemma. According to the **Demandingness Objection**, the problem with Utilitarianism's demandingness can be traced to its conception of the right. Thus it is said that Act Utilitarianism, for example, has a criterion of moral rightness that always requires agents to perform acts that will produce

impersonally best states of affairs. So, for example, critics insist that according to Utilitarianism, it is immoral to treat a friend to a movie when there are people in the world who lack adequate food and clothing. Utilitarianism thus requires that individuals devote energy to their personal commitments, projects, and relationships only when and to the extent that doing so is most productive of the good, impersonally construed. The theory, it is argued, threatens the integrity or the continuity of the lives of all those persons who, to meet this requirement, must lessen or abandon their personal commitments or perhaps even abandon some of them.[29]

In addition to the Demandingness Objection, Utilitarians have had to defend their theory against another, the **Impersonal Motivation Objection.** This objection claims that Utilitarianism threatens integrity by requiring that individuals adopt an impersonal motivation toward their personal commitments. According to this argument, even if Utilitarianism permits individuals to develop and maintain their personal commitments, it does this to promote the overall good: agents with such ties, it is claimed, are better able to promote impersonally good states of affairs than agents without such concerns. The problem, however, is that Consequentialism requires individuals themselves to adopt this attitude, and this mediating, impersonal motivation has a destructive, or at least inhibiting,

The **Impersonal Motivation Objection** is an integrity objection to Utilitarianism. According to this objection, Utilitarianism threatens integrity because it requires that individuals adopt an impersonal motivation toward their personal commitments. Although Utilitarianism permits individuals to develop and maintain their personal commitments, it does so to promote the overall good: agents with such ties, it is claimed, are better able to promote impersonally good states of affairs than are agents without such concerns. The problem, however, is that Utilitarianism *requires* individuals themselves to adopt this attitude. This mediating, impersonal motivation has a destructive (or at least inhibiting) effect on the character of an individual's personal commitments. Thus, for example, rather than being committed to a friend as a friend, one is instead committed to a friend as a means or instrument for promoting impersonal value. But this mediating motivation undermines the essentially personal character of one's commitments, thereby destroying much of their (personal) value. This objection is an integrity objection because this change in motivation must reflect a change in values, which in turn threatens the integrity of a person's life.

effect on the character of an individual's personal commitments. Thus, for example, rather than being committed to a friend as a friend, you are committed to a friend as a means or instrument for promoting impersonal value. But, it is objected, this mediating motivation undermines the essentially personal character of your commitments, thereby destroying much of their (personal) value. This objection is an integrity objection because this change in motivation must reflect a change in values, which in turn threatens the integrity of a person's life.[30]

4.8 Criticisms of Consequentialism: Equality and Impersonal Value

One might respond to Williams's objection on behalf of Consequentialism by dropping the classical utilitarian commitment to maximization and replacing it with a less demanding requirement. However, as our discussion of the integrity dilemma reveals, some of Consequentialism's critics have argued that the problem here is not simply with a dispensable feature of classical Utilitarianism, but that it runs deeper to reveal a flaw in Consequentialism. Samuel Scheffler argues that the feature of Utilitarianism, in particular, and Consequentialism, in general, that is responsible for the attack on integrity is the consequentialist conception of the right, which "requires each agent in all cases to produce the best available outcome overall."[31] According to Scheffler, this means that individuals may pursue their own personal projects and commitments only when, and to the extent that, doing so best promotes impersonal value. The problem, though, is that agents typically develop their commitments independently of and out of proportion to the value of those commitments from the impersonal point of view. So, Scheffler explains, by requiring people to pursue their commitments in strict proportion to their value from the impersonal standpoint, Consequentialism threatens integrity.

4.9 Subjective Consequentialism, Objective Consequentialism, and Sophisticated Consequentialism

So far in our discussion in this chapter, we have avoided distinguishing between the many kinds of Utilitarianism and Consequentialism that differ over the objective of utilitarian or consequentialist theory. There are many possibilities, including Act, Rule, Character, Motive, and Conscience Utilitarianism or Consequentialism, to name but a few. Utilitarianism's and Consequentialism's defenders have made use of some of these possibilities in developing responses to the integrity dilemma. Consequentialism's defenders have challenged both horns of this dilemma.

Let's consider the first challenge. At the heart of the Demandingness Objection is the idea that Consequentialism's demands far exceed our shared, common sense expectations of what morality requires of us. Although we might think it reasonable that morality sometimes requires that we sacrifice pursuing our personal commitments in the interests of promoting some greater good when these two conflict, it seems unreasonable to require agents to always make such sacrifices. Yet Act Utilitarianism demands just this. Consequentialists, backing away from Act Utilitarianism, have argued that their theory's demandingness is more apparent than real. They note that Consequentialism's global goal can be best achieved indirectly by agents maintaining their intimate commitments to themselves and to those in their intimate circle of family and friends ("think global, act local"). This can be better than the direct method of having agents sacrifice these commitments to devote themselves exclusively to aiding those in the greatest need. Thus, according to this response, the problem with the Demandingness Objection is that it falsely holds that Consequentialism requires individuals to compromise their personal commitments.

A number of arguments have been offered in support of this view. For example, the argument has been made that friendships are a central component of a good human life and that, as such, the Consequentialist's global goal must include this value.[32] However, since differential valuing is a constitutive part of friendship, Act Utilitarianism, with its "strict proportionality requirement," must give way to an interpretation of Consequentialism that leaves room for striking up and maintaining friendships. In addition to its intrinsic consequentialist value, the instrumental value of friendships to Consequentialism has also been emphasized. Thus, the argument has also been made that rather than devote ourselves to equally helping needy intimates and needy, perhaps distant, strangers, Consequentialism requires us to differentially attend to intimates because we are better able to see to their needs than to the needs of strangers. Henry Sidgwick argues that the "theoretical impartiality of Utilitarianism" is limited by the consideration that "generally speaking, each man is better able to provide for his own happiness than for that of other persons, from his more intimate knowledge of his own desires and needs, and his greater opportunities of gratifying them."[33]

These arguments present Consequentialists with an interpretation of their theory that differs from the type of interpretation presented by Scheffler, which draws upon the notion of a "strict proportionality requirement" that we just examined. Peter Railton refers to Scheffler's kind of interpretation of Consequentialism as **"Subjective Consequentialism,"** the view that "whenever one faces a choice of actions, one should attempt to determine which act of those available would most promote the good, and should then try to act accordingly."[34] Subjective consequentialist views present agents with one way of calculating the effects of their behaviour on the promotion of the Consequentialist's global goal. They require agents to measure their contribution to the global goal by summing up the effects of their discrete actions. These views then instruct agents to perform the action that will lead to the greatest promotion of the global goal, calculated in this way.

In contrast, Railton argues that in addition to being a Subjective Consequentialist, one may also be an Objective Consequentialist. **"Objective Consequentialism,"** he explains, "is the view that the criterion of rightness of an act or a course of action is whether it in fact would most promote the good of those acts available to the agent."[35] He adds that a **Sophisticated Consequentialist** is someone who has a standing commitment to leading an objectively consequentialist life. Unlike Subjective Consequentialists, Objective Consequentialists are not committed to any particular form of decision-making in the course of promoting their consequentialist aims. Their goal is to live a life that best promotes Consequentialism's goals, and they are free to adopt whichever motivations and commitments would do this. Thus, if the Consequentialist's global goal will be better promoted if agents sometimes relax from always promoting impersonal value, then Sophisticated Consequentialism will endorse this.[36]

The Sophisticated Consequentialist's liberation from direct act utilitarian decision-making forms the basis of a response to not only the Demandingness Objection but also the Impersonal Motivation Objection. The Impersonal Motivation Objection is based on agents adopting a mediating consequentialist motivation toward their personal commitments. For instance, according to this objection, the Utilitarian should help his friend only to the extent that insofar as doing so promotes the overall good of society rather than doing things for his friends' sakes. However, Sophisticated Consequentialists claim that they need not adopt consequentialist motivation. Thus, the argument goes, by separating their consequentialist justification for having the personal commitments they do from their integrity-preserving, non-impersonal motivation for acting on

> **Subjective Consequentialism** is the view that "whenever one faces a choice of actions, one should attempt to determine which act of those available would most promote the good, and should then try to act accordingly."
>
> **Objective Consequentialism** "is the view that the criterion of rightness of an act or a course of action is whether it in fact would most promote the good of those acts available to the agent."
>
> A **Sophisticated Consequentialist** is someone who has a standing commitment to leading an objectively consequentialist life.

the commitments, Sophisticated Consequentialists can avoid this objection too. This move is a variation on the standard response to the Impersonal Motivation Objection, advanced by Sidgwick and a number of others since him, which claims that Consequentialism provides us with an ultimate criterion of moral rightness; it need not, however, be taken to imply that agents adopt a direct motivation to act in accordance with this criterion. Indeed, the defence continues, if it is true that a direct motivation to act in accordance with the consequentialist criterion of rightness would lead to overall worse states of affairs than if there was no such motivation, then Consequentialism would require the rejection of such a strict consequentialist moral motivation. Thus, it is argued, Consequentialism does not make the mistake of confusing the truth-conditions of an ethical theory with its acceptance-conditions in particular contexts.[37]

Whereas Subjective Consequentialists cannot be motivated to perform the right act without being aware of the consequentially justified status of the act, Sophisticated Consequentialists, it is claimed, can. Act Utilitarians interested in discovering the right (or a right) course of action look for the act justified by their theory. In other words, Utilitarians consciously decide how to act in light of what their moral theory regards as right. However, Rule Utilitarians interested in discovering the right (or a right) course of action need only follow a justified rule. Unlike Act Utilitarians, Rule Utilitarians can do the right thing without knowing why it is right. The key point, according to this line of argument, is that to follow their theory Rule Utilitarians need not be directly motivated by the aim of performing consequentially justified acts. They can separate their consequentialist justification for adopting some set of consequentially justified rules from their non-consequentialist motivation for acting in accordance with the rules they adopt. So, for instance, rather than help a friend because Utilitarianism requires that they do so, they can help a friend in accordance with their rule that they should do so and because they care for the friend. On this analysis, Rule Utilitarianism does not require its adherents to

be directly motivated by utilitarian considerations. So, for example, Rule Utilitarians argue that the rule that agents ought to maintain their personal commitments is consequentially justified but, they hold, they can separate their consequentialist justification for adopting this rule from their integrity-preserving, non-consequentialist motivation for maintaining and developing these commitments.

4.10 Other Objections

In this chapter we have surveyed some of the debate over Utilitarianism and Consequentialism. Although we have mostly focused on considering the objections that have been specifically levelled against classical Utilitarianism, non-Consequentialists challenge the three bases of Consequentialism too. In this last part of the chapter, we have considered some criticism of the Consequentialist's commitment to a principle of equality as it appears in the form of a commitment to the promotion of impersonal or agent-neutral value. However, there is much more to the debate. We consider some of this in the remainder of Part One, where we examine some competing moral theories. We also consider some of these issues in further detail in Part Two. Consequentialists interested in promoting a commitment to equal respect and consideration need to spell out who deserves this. On the surface it seems that there is a tension between the consequentialist commitment to Welfarism and the commitment to equality. Welfarists argue that we should give consideration to all beings that have a good of their own, but this group includes both more and less than the group of all humans; more because many non-humans have a good of their own, and less because not all humans have a good of their own. (For more on this, see Chapter 11). How can Consequentialists reconcile their commitment to this basic feature of their theory with what has been a tendency to view Consequentialism as encompassing only humans? We take up this puzzle in Chapter 11. We also take up broader challenges to Welfarism in Chapter 12 from those who dispute the welfarist emphasis on promoting welfare and the welfarist emphasis on individuals.

4.11 Review

In this chapter we introduced and critically examined Consequentialism and Utilitarianism. We noted that consequentialist theories are marked by three defining traits: they are good-based, welfarist, and endorse some principle of equality. After seeing how consequentialist theories can be understood as constructing a global or comprehensive goal in three stages, we defined Bentham's classical utilitarian view in this way. We noted that he endorsed a Mental State Account of value, and principles of aggregation and maximization. Our discussions of Consequentialism and Utilitarianism explained both why all utilitarian views are Consequentialist and why many consequentialist views are not Utilitarian.

To gain some insight into the development of utilitarian thought and the increasing acceptance of Consequentialism, we considered some influential criticisms of Bentham's theory made by John Stuart Mill, J.J.C. Smart, Robert Nozick, John Rawls, and Bernard Williams. According to these criticisms, classical Utilitarianism is wrong-headed because

- it accepts a flawed and incomplete theory of value;

- it sanctions the promotion of utility at the expense of justice; and

- it threatens the integrity of the lives of utilitarian agents.

Although we mostly focused on examining objections to Utilitarianism, toward the end of the chapter we began to take up some objections to Utilitarianism's underlying Consequentialism. We will pursue this project further in Chapter 5 and in Part Two.

Notes

1. Mill (1861), p. 7.

2. For example, see Griffin (1986), p. 195.

3. See Sumner (1987a), p. 167. The notion that Consequentialism can be described as affirming the priority of the good over the right can be traced back to John Rawls's *A Theory of Justice*. See Rawls (1971), pp. 24–31. It should be noted also that Rawls himself does not defend a theory that asserts the priority of the good over the right.

4. See Sumner (1996), chapters 6 and 7. The term "Welfarism" is Amartya Sen's. See Sen (1979). We will examine Welfarism more carefully in Part Two.

5. Nagel (1986), p. 153. Derek Parfit coined the terms "agent-neutral" and "agent-relative." See Parfit (1984), p. 143. However, Nagel (1970) originally made the distinction to which they apply.

6. Nagel (1986), p. 152.

7. Nagel (1986), p. 171.

8. See Sumner (1987a), p. 168.

9. This is the case, unless they can both reject this theory of value and express their commitment to equality in some other way.

10. Sumner (1987a), p. 171.

11. For example, see Slote (1985) and (1989) for more on this option.

12. Bentham (1789), p. 12.

13. Although Bentham is famously associated with this phrase, he owes it to the eighteenth-century Italian judicial reformer Cesare Beccaria (1738–94). See Shackleton (1972).

14. For clear support for the view that Bentham recognized that sentient non-human animals also deserve moral consideration, see Bentham (1789), pp. 44, 58, and 282b.

15. For excellent accounts of these debates, see Griffin (1982) and (1985), and Sumner (1996).

16. See Bentham (1843), pp. 253–254.

17. Mill (1984), p. 8.

18. Smart (1973), pp. 12–25.

19. Smart (1973), p. 18.

20. Mill, for example, explains the Utilitarian's Greatest Happiness Principle as holding that actions are right insofar as they promote happiness and, he explains, "By happiness is intended pleasure, and the absence of pain; by unhappiness, pain, and the privation of pleasure." Mill (1984), p. 7.

21. Nozick (1974), pp. 42–45.

22. See Rawls (1971), pp. 22–27 and 183–192.

23. Rawls (1971), p. 27.

24. Rawls (1971), p. 3.

25. McCloskey (1963), p. 599.

26. He writes,
    I have done quite a lot of work on serious practical problems in medicine, war, politics, urban planning and the like, and have never come across any actual example in which this kind of anti-utilitarian argument was in the least convincing. (Hare [1981], pp. 139–140.)

27. Griffin (1982), pp. 354–357.

28. Williams (1973), pp. 114–117.

29. Several people have discussed this objection in various forms. See Brandt (1979), p. 276; Scheffler (1982), p. 9; Shelley Kagan (1984), p. 239; Railton (1984), pp. 160–163; and William Langenfus (1990), pp. 132–134.

30. Langenfus briefly discusses this objection. See Langenfus (1990), pp. 132–135. The way in which consequentialist impersonal motivation adversely affects friendship is explained at greater length by Michael Stocker (1976), and by Railton (1984), pp. 135–140. Susan Wolf examines the wider adverse affects of this motivation. See Wolf (1982), pp. 430–431.

31. Scheffler (1982), p. 9.

32. By, for example, Neera Kapur Badhwar (1991), pp. 484, 485, and 489.

33. Sidgwick (1907), p. 431.

34. Railton (1984), p. 152.

35. Railton (1984), p. 152.

36. Smart uses this example. See Smart (1973), p. 55.

37. Sidgwick's contribution to this objection consists of his discussion of the distinction between Utilitarianism's standard or criterion of rightness and utilitarian motivation. See Sidgwick (1907), p. 413. Railton makes the point about the distinction between the truth-conditions and the acceptance-conditions of an ethical theory in his account of the response (see Railton [1984], pp. 152–160. Scheffler (1981), pp. 43–52; Parfit (1984), pp. 24–29; and Langenfus (1990), p. 131, also discuss the response. Railton (1984), pp. 140–146; David Brink (1986), pp. 421–427; and Will Kymlicka (1990), p. 29 endorse it.

Exercises

Progress Check

1. What is the controversy over identifying Consequentialism?

2. What are Consequentialism's three defining traits?

3. What is Welfarism?

4. What are the distinctions between agent-neutral and agent-relative reasons and values?

5. Outline the three stages in constructing the Consequentialist's global goal.

6. Explain the distinction between monistic and pluralistic theories of value.

7. What are Mental State Accounts of welfare?

8. Explain the distinction between aggregative and distributive accounts of Consequentialism.

9. Describe Bentham's classical utilitarian view in terms of the three stages of constructing the Consequentialist's global goal.

10. What is Hedonistic Utilitarianism?

11. What are the advantages and disadvantages of using Nozick's experience machine?

12. What is Rawls's criticism of classical Utilitarianism?

13. What is Williams's integrity objection against Utilitarianism?

14. What is the integrity dilemma?

15. Explain the distinctions between Subjective, Objective, and Sophisticated Consequentialism.

Questions for Further Reflection

1. Utilitarians who accept monistic Mental State Accounts of value believe that all valuable mental states share some common experience or quality. What could this be? If you disagree with this idea, how would you argue against it? Explain.

2. What point is Smart's electrode operator example designed to illustrate? Is it successful? Defend your view.

3. What point is Nozick's experience machine designed to illustrate? Is it successful? Defend your view.

4. How, if at all, would you use the experience machine?

5. If you were the sheriff in McCloskey's example, what should you do? Why? What would a Utilitarian say the sheriff should do? Defend your answer.

6. Explain James Griffin's response to the charge that Utilitarianism sometimes recommends favouring utility over justice.

7. Why does Scheffler think the integrity dilemma reveals a problem with all consequentialist theories, rather than just classical Utilitarianism? Is he right? Defend your view.

8. Explain the distinction between Consequentialism viewed as providing agents with a decision procedure with direct consequentialist motivation for acting, and Consequentialism viewed as providing us with a criterion of moral rightness. Explain, using the distinction between a moral theory's truth-conditions and its acceptance-conditions.

9. Explain and critically evaluate the view that Sophisticated Consequentialism, since it does not require direct and conscious consequentialist reasoning, is no longer a theory in Prescriptive Ethics.

10. Can Consequentialism adequately respond to the integrity dilemma and remain a prescriptive ethical theory? Explain.

Suggested Further Reading

The three sources of classical Utilitarianism are Jeremy Bentham's *An Introduction to the Principles of Morals and Legislation*, John Stuart Mill's *Utilitarianism*, and Henry Sidgwick's *The Methods of Ethics*, 7th ed., Book IV. These are available in a number of editions, including the three mentioned in the Bibliography. For a list of works cited in this chapter, check the notes in this chapter and the Bibliography at the end of the book. These cited works also provide various useful avenues into the critical discussion of Utilitarianism and Consequentialism. Besides these, there are three other collections of essays that contain useful, interesting, and sometimes influential discussions of the main topics of this chapter. They are (1) Wesley Cooper, Kai Neilson, and Stephen C. Patten, eds., *New Essays on John Stuart Mill and Utilitarianism*, *Canadian Journal of Philosophy*, Supplementary Volume V, 1979; (2) Amartya Sen and Bernard Williams, eds., *Utilitarianism and Beyond* (Cambridge: Cambridge University Press, 1982); and (3) Samuel Scheffler, ed., *Consequentialism and Its Critics* (Oxford: Oxford University Press, 1988).

Weblinks

David Pearce operates a Web site with an impressive wealth of resources on Utilitarianism and Consequentialism, including a substantial number of links at **utilitarianism.org**

Dan Bonevac and Paul Lyon, both of the University of Texas at Austin, have a growing site on classical Utilitarianism at **www.la.utexas.edu/cuws/**

Kantian Ethics

Learning Outcomes

In this chapter we outline the basics of Immanuel Kant's account of the foundations of ethics. Kant's deontological (or duty-bound) approach to ethics contrasts sharply with the teleological (or good-based) views we have been considering, which are explained by their emphasis on promoting the well-being of individuals. Kant grounds ethics in reason and free will and defends a view that emphasizes autonomy, dignity, and respect for rational agents.

Upon the successful completion of this chapter, you will be able to

1. describe the Dilemma of Determinism and the challenge it poses to believing in determinism and free will;

2. explain the main elements of Kant's metaphysics of morals, including its basis in the idea of free will;

3. contrast Kant's deontological approach to ethics with the teleological approaches we have been considering;

4. identify several formulations of the categorical imperative and the role it plays in Kant's Meta-Ethics; and

5. explicate the place and importance of the ideas of autonomy, dignity, and equal respect for persons in his account.

5.1 Introduction

In Chapter 3 we considered the view that morality rests on feeling or sentiment. As we noted there, the boys who set the cat on fire for fun lack compassion for others and therefore seem incapable of being morally motivated. In making this claim, we are assuming that a condition of being morally motivated entails that one will have some concern for others, that one cares about them.

As we noted, David Hume endorsed the view that ethics rests on sentiment, and he believed further that all humankind is endowed with similar "passions" or feelings. This view has other advocates, too. It accords well with most people's experience of the moral life and so seems like simple common sense. Elsewhere in philosophy, it has been defended in one form or another by critics of traditional male-dominated approaches to ethics like Nel Noddings (see Section 8.10) and by Holists in Environmental Ethics (see Section 12.7). Despite this, the notion that ethics rests on feeling or sentiment remains controversial. Most famously, Immanuel Kant challenged this view by arguing that morality rests, instead, on reason and free will.

In this chapter we examine Kant's influential and philosophically deep alternative account of the foundations of ethics.

5.2 The Dilemma of Determinism

Most of us assume that we have free will. This, we think, distinguishes us from mere objects. But this belief is subject to a great deal of philosophical doubt and debate. Insofar as we are composed of matter and, as it is in terms of being material objects that we explain the motions of objects in space, it seems that we are like billiard balls and other such things subject to the laws or regularities of nature. If you push me off a cliff I fall, not because I choose to but because, like billiard balls and rocks, I, too, "obey" the Law of Gravity. Obviously the sense in which objects

"obey" the laws of nature is different from the sense in which we think we obey human laws. We believe that we freely choose to obey our laws, that when we do obey them we could have chosen otherwise. How is it, then, that we can consistently accept our apparently dual status as beings free to obey some laws and as material bodies inescapably subject to others?

The apparent tension between these two standpoints has been captured in an argument that concludes from this tension that we are never responsible for anything that happens. It is a commonplace of our times that, in addition to making assumptions about human free will, people are also inclined to accept **determinism,** the view that there is a causal explanation for all worldly events.[1] Determinists claim that all events can be fully explained by reference to their causes; in other words, that given these antecedent causes, all events are necessitated to happen.

However, determinists must also believe that this is true for events apparently caused by us. This belief, in turn, entails that our choices are causally necessitated to happen, which seems to suggest that given these causes, we could *not* have chosen otherwise. Yet our everyday commitment to free will also seems to imply that we could have chosen otherwise. Isn't this what we mean when we say that we have *free* will? It appears that believing in free will is not compatible with believing in determinism. Moreover, if determinism is true, then it must follow that contrary to our beliefs, we do not have free will and we are not responsible for what happens.

One way to respond to this problem would be to reject determinism and accept indeterminism instead. **Indeterminism** is the view that proposes that not all events are caused. For example, we might hold that there is no causal explanation for human choices and actions. We can maintain that although there is a deterministic explanation for events involving mere objects, this sort of explanation does not extend to events involving human agency. Does this strategy enable us to consistently accept a modified

> **Determinism** is the view that there is a causal explanation for everything that happens. **Indeterminism** is the view that some events are not caused.

version of determinism and believe in free will? Again, it seems not.

Although insisting that human actions are not determined opens up the possibility that we have free will, it seems that if our actions are not caused, then there is no explanation for their occurrence and thus we cannot claim responsibility for them. In other words, to maintain the connection between having free will and being responsible for our choices and actions, we need to assume that there is a causal link between the two.

These considerations seem to lead to the conclusion that whether determinism or indeterminism is true, we are never responsible for anything that happens. This problem has been expressed in the form of a dilemma, the Dilemma of Determinism, by Joel Feinberg and Russ Shafer-Landau:

1. If determinism is true, we can never do other than we do; hence we are never responsible for what we do.

2. If indeterminism is true, then some events—namely, human actions—are random, hence not free; hence, we are never responsible for what we do.

3. Either determinism is true or else indeterminism is true.

4. Therefore, we are never responsible for what we do.[2]

We have briefly explained the problem with challenging the dilemma by contesting either the first premise or the second one. Notice that the third premise also seems true. Furthermore, since the argument is deductively valid, it seems that unless we can mount a different challenge to either of the first two premises, we are led to accept the disheartening conclusion that we are never responsible for what we do!

5.3 Our Common Assumptions about Moral Agency and Free Will

The Dilemma of Determinism strikes at the very heart of our everyday assumptions about our status as free agents and as moral agents. To see this, consider the presuppositions implicit in the judgments we make about our actions and behaviour. When we work hard and achieve success, we take some pride in our accomplishment. On the other hand, when we fail to reach a goal or otherwise fall short of our expectations for ourselves, we say that we are to blame, that we are at fault. Such judgments of praise and blame for our actions are common.

They extend, too, to our judgments about our moral and immoral behaviour. We take credit for our good deeds, and we think that we are morally culpable for our bad ones. Our attributions of praise and blame presuppose that, sometimes at least, we are responsible for what happens, and more specifically that we are responsible for what we do. We believe, furthermore, that since we can formulate and act on our own life plans, our lives are purposeful. Our lives have meaning for us as a result of our choices and actions.

As agents responsible for our actions, we believe that we are unlike mere objects. Whereas you would rightly give me credit for, say, carrying you down the street, we think that it makes no sense to say that our cars are responsible for conveying us to and from our destinations. Cars, we believe, are objects acted upon by various forces. Automobiles and other such machines do not *choose* to operate. They are objects subject to the laws of nature rather than agents responsible for their actions. In contrast, we believe that we do so choose, and it is by virtue of our choosing that we think we are responsible. So, to take Jane English's example, if a mad scientist was to render innocent people into automatons programmed to attack others, we would hold the scientist accountable, not the zombies.[3] Since they lack agency, since they have no power over what happens and do not choose to attack others, we regard the innocent automatons as victims, too. Agents who are rendered into automatons are deprived of the will to choose and act.

However, the Dilemma of Determinism challenges our assumption that we have free will, or at least it challenges our belief in the compatibility of determinism and free will. If we are so quick to supply a deterministic explanation of the car's motion, why do we not also do so in our own cases? Upon what grounds do we think that *we* are not automatons? We believe that we are unlike the mad scientist's victims who, formerly free agents, are turned into mere things. But the Dilemma of Determinism forces us to respond to the charge that it is an illusion inconsistent with our faith in the regularity of nature that any of us has free will in the first place.

5.4 Kant's *Foundations of the Metaphysics of Morals*

The view that ethics rests upon free will is most famously defended by Immanuel Kant, who also provides an ingenious response to the Dilemma of Determinism. Kant presents his account of the foundations of ethics in his brief book, *Foundations of the Metaphysics of Morals,* first published in 1785. By setting Normative Ethics upon a sound metaphysics of morals, Kant believed that one could thereby best respond to skeptical critics of morality. Following his view about this, then, we will outline the basics of Kant's theory in stages, beginning with his metaphysical argument.

Many are put off by Kant's metaphysical approach to morality. They regard his writings on ethics as being dry, formal, and disconnected from our experience of human relationships and the ethical life. However, it is a mistake to dismiss his view and ignore the problem that he addressed. For, loathe as some are to seriously examine Kant's moral philosophy, or ready as we may be to dismiss it as the obscure system of a long-dead and life-long bachelor, the problem he responds to remains after his view is rejected.

As we have noted, ethics presupposes free will, for without free will it seems there would be no agents and hence no choices or actions to be judged as morally good or bad. But how can we explain this presupposition, and how can we reconcile it with our deterministic explanations of other natural phenomena? It is to Kant's credit that he faced this issue directly. Furthermore, by approaching his account from the perspective of

the problem raised by the Dilemma of Determinism, we can see that his account is perhaps not as obscure and difficult as it is often made out to be.

5.5 The Doctrine of the Two Standpoints

To assert that Kant believed that ethics rests upon free will is not quite accurate. Rather, he claimed that we live, and must live, on the unprovable assumption that our will is free. As we have noted, ethics presupposes belief in free will, and one can understand Kant's argument about the foundations of ethics as taking this point seriously. Rather than deny either free will or deterministic explanations of natural phenomena and events, Kant proposes a reconciliation between the two beliefs. He seeks to achieve this by arguing that we can see ourselves from two different but compatible perspectives. As physical bodies, like other objects in the world, we move in the **phenomenal realm** of worldly, sensible experience. Here deterministic explanations apply. We can discover the laws of science that enable us to predict events that occur in nature, and it is as an object that we can explain our falling bodies by appeal to such as the Law of Gravity.

However, since we also believe that we have free will and since, as Kant proposed, there is no place for the idea of such a will in the phenomenal realm, we can also regard ourselves from the perspective of a noumenal realm of will and pure reason. The **noumenal realm** is the antithesis of the phenomenal realm and within it, the possibility of freedom, agency, and morality arise not just for human beings but, if there are other beings who have free will and are agents, for all rational beings.

In confronting this peculiar idea of a noumenal realm, note first that such a perspective is

> The **phenomenal realm** is used by Kant to refer to the world of sensible experience. The **noumenal realm** is Kant's term for the antithesis of the phenomenal realm of worldly experiences. In this realm (and from this perspective), the possibility of freedom, agency, and morality arise.

possible. Since the noumenal realm is the antithesis of the phenomenal one, we cannot in principle dismiss the possibility of the noumenal by reference to investigations carried out within the phenomenal realm. Nothing science tells us can lead us to reject this alternative standpoint because scientific enquiry employing the law of cause and effect pertains to the phenomenal realm. As such, science is incapable of investigating and advancing physical evidence against the possibility of the noumenal. To look for physical evidence to disconfirm the noumenal is to misunderstand the distinction between the two perspectives.[4] In addition to noting the possibility of the noumenal realm, we might also wonder why we would think that the phenomenal realm of sensible objects and experiences must be all there is. Certainly we cannot draw this inference merely from our experience.

Just as there is, in principle, no physical evidence to prove that there is no noumenal perspective, we also cannot offer physical proof of its existence. But without proof, how do we know that there is such a perspective? Kant argues we do not know this, but we must assume that there is a noumenal realm because we must assume that we have free will, and we cannot acquire our idea of our free will from our experiences in the phenomenal world of experience. Kant claims that to make use of our reason as a guide to conduct, the concept of freedom cannot be based on our experiences. Instead, it must be derived independently of experience. To use the philosophical terminology, instead of being an *a posteriori* (empirical) concept, it must be an *a priori* (independent of experience) one. We have already noted a reason for this. The idea of the free use of reason based on experience contradicts our deterministic explanations of events in nature. It seems instead that we must derive this idea independently of experience.

As rational beings occupying the noumenal realm, we must believe that we can direct ourselves in the world of experience. Insofar as we have the power to act according to our own plans and wishes, we stand in contrast to most occupants of the phenomenal realm, all mere objects.

Another implication of the doctrine is that, in order to be consistent, we must take care to apply the concepts that pertain to each realm and not confuse the two. So, for example, it makes no sense to seek causal explanations for our free choices or to look for causal links between our choices and our actions, since causality applies only in the domain of the phenomenal.

5.6 Kantian Deontology

According to Kant, then, not only should causal explanations of events be restricted or applied to their proper domain—the phenomenal, sensible world of experience—but also the concepts of the noumenal realm should be applied to their proper domain. This means the ideas of free will, agency, pure reason, and morality should be examined and understood by reference to the perspective of the noumenal realm. If this is correct, the implications for ethics are considerable. For example, within Kant's account, it makes no sense to try to explain the foundations and underlying presuppositions of morality by examining or referring to the world of experience. Morality is properly a subject of study from the noumenal perspective, and Kant argues that all moral theories that base their conclusions solely on our life experiences must be mistaken, since they fail to appreciate that ethics presupposes free will.

Kant broadly classifies areas of study according to the two realms. Physics is the science of the laws of nature, and ethics is the science or study of the laws of freedom. The study of these laws of freedom considered a priori, or independent of empirical enquiry, is what he calls the metaphysics of morals. Since this involves an enquiry into the a priori principles or rules of reason as they relate to freedom, the Foundations of the Metaphysics of Morals is an enquiry into pure reason as it applies to ethics. Notice how this is unlike most other approaches to ethics, which direct us to what they say should be our moral goals by reference to some empirical account of welfare or human perfection, or by reference to some external authority. Since these views all regard ethics in terms of its function of guiding us to some independent end or goal, they are all teleological theories.

Teleological ethical theories are good-based. They regard the promotion of some good or end as being the purpose of ethics. According to teleological outlooks, the right is defined in terms of the good. Teleological theories tell us what is morally right by reference to the good or end, which, they maintain, it is the purpose of ethics to promote. In other words, what is morally right, what we morally should or ought to do or be, is determined by the logically prior account of the good. Thus philosophers sometimes say that in teleological theories, the concept of the good is prior to the concept of the right.

There are many teleological theories. Consider classical Natural Law Theory from Chapter 2. On the surface it seems that this approach shares with Kant's view a respect for the place of reason in ethics and the idea that we can use our reason to discover or determine our duties. Furthermore, it seems that both views share a belief that ethics is grounded on universal laws. Despite these apparent similarities, however, classical Natural Law theory is teleological because, although Aquinas and his followers believed that we can use our reason to discover our duties, the natural laws we should discover are grounded on empirical facts, particularly facts about human nature. As we noted in Chapter 2, classical Natural Law Theory is based on Aristotle's teleological notion that humans have their own proper end or function. According to Aquinas, this proper end or function is to live our lives in accordance with reason, to follow the natural laws that were created by God and that embody the true principles of morality.

Thus we can detect three significant differences between classical Natural Law Theory and Kant's deontological view. On Aquinas's view

- what is ethically right is determined by reference to an empirical account of human perfection;

- this in turn is ultimately determined by an external authority, namely God; and

- the function of ethics is to guide us to this independent end.

Kant repudiates each of these ideas.

Just as classical Natural Law Theory is teleological, so too is Aristotle's account of morality. As we will see in Chapter 6, Aristotle developed and defended a Virtue Theory of ethics based on the notion of our good. According to this outlook, the development of the moral virtues will guide us to realize the characteristic excellences of humans, which is determined empirically and based on Aristotle's theory of human nature.

Likewise, all welfarist theories in ethics are teleological. According to the Welfarist, what is morally right is a function of what promotes the good of sentient or potentially sentient beings. As we noted in Chapter 4, consequentialist theories are in this respect good-based. Utilitarians accept the Greatest Happiness Principle or some variation thereof. Ethical Egoists, as we shall see in Chapter 7, similarly embrace the teleological view that the right is determined by reference to what promotes welfare. However, although Ethical Egoists endorse Welfarism, they reject the utilitarian commitment to a principle of equality. Rather than endorsing the Greatest Happiness Principle, or some other similar notion, Ethical Egoists say that each agent ought to act to promote his or her own good. Therefore, as with other teleological accounts, Ethical Egoists derive our duties and their theory of the right from a prior account of the morally good.

In contrast, **deontological ethical theories** such as Kant's moral theory are right-based. In light of his account of the metaphysics of morals, Kant thought it was a confusion to base ethics on an empirical examination of some aspect of the phenomenal realm, like the theories that appeal to ideas of human goodness and perfection do. According to his theory, our duties are determined through the exercising of

> **Teleological ethical theories** are good-based theories about the foundations of ethics. According to them, the morally right is determined by reference to the logically prior notion of what is morally good.
> **Deontological ethical theories** are right-based theories about the foundations of ethics. According to them, the morally right is logically prior to the good, and it is determined other than by appeal to the notion of what is morally good.

pure reason, not reason based on empirical study. Thus, within his deontological account the concept of the morally right is not derivative, it is primary. The right is not explained in terms of the good. Instead, what is morally good must be consistent with what reason tells us about the logically prior category of the morally right. So, for example, on Kant's analysis, we should not lie because it is wrong to do so, not because lying causes harm. Kant's deontological account is thus right-based instead of good-based.[5]

Kant's moral theory is deontological because, according to it, we determine what is morally right not by appeal to a prior and empirical account of human goodness or perfection, but by determining what pure reason considering the laws of freedom judges the moral law to be.

5.7 Will, Maxims, and the Laws of Freedom

What are the main implications of Kant's deontological approach to ethics? Since he emphasizes the place of ethics in the noumenal realm of pure reason, free will, and agency, Kant insists that claims about the underlying nature of ethics must be traced to these notions and this realm. He rejects the view we considered in Chapter 3 that a necessary condition of being morally motivated is that we feel for or care about each other. The idea that feeling is a necessary element in moral motivation must be mistaken if having concern for others is an aspect of our phenomenal selves. In Kant's understanding, our compassion for others is not grounded somehow in our free will, reason, or agency. If this is correct, then it follows from Kant's metaphysics of morals that caring about another is not an essential requirement for being morally motivated.

To support this view, a Kantian might observe that although feeling for others is not a necessary aspect of moral motivation, we can accept that the two often go together. That is, we can admit that often when we are morally motivated we also care about those whom we help. For example, usually parents want to help their children, and doing so is frequently morally right, too. However, the point is that feeling for others and moral motivation need not go together. An act need not be motivated out of a concern for someone in order for it to be morally motivated. Kant argues that we can and do speak of actions performed out of duty, and in being motivated out of duty, we need not care about those whom we help. Take, for example, the case of the ship captain who feels indifference toward—or even dislikes—the passengers on his vessel, but for whom he sacrifices his life when disaster strikes. We might judge his decision to sacrifice his own life to be the morally right choice given his situation, and we might say that he was morally motivated despite his lack of feeling or negative feelings for those he helped save. Indeed, we might especially admire and respect people who do what is right contrary to their personal wishes and feelings.

Not only can we imagine cases where someone was morally motivated in spite of negative feelings or indifference toward others but also we can imagine circumstances where duty requires that we act contrary to our strongest feelings of love and concern for another. Imagine now that our captain has to contend not only with the disaster involving the sinking of his ship but also with the knowledge that his much beloved teenage son is also on board. Although he loves his son, his duty as ship's captain is to all his passengers, and the rule for filling the lifeboats dictates that spaces should be awarded on the basis of age, with the youngest to be selected first. By this rule, and contrary to his strong feelings for his son (and his duty as a father), he might have to award the limited spaces in the remaining undamaged lifeboats in such a way that denies his son a place.

Of course, someone might hold that in acting in this way the captain acts immorally, or alternatively, that there is no morally right choice for him to make given the circumstances. If you want to defend either of these options, then to support your view you will need to explain the basis upon which you reject the Kantian analysis. Kant's argument regarding the morally right choice rests upon his account of his metaphysics of morals. These examples illustrate another problem with trying to base ethics on our compassion or feelings for others. Our feelings are flawed guides to morally right action. If we simply follow our heart in these and many other cases besides, we will act wrongly, at least according to the Kantian analysis.

If caring about another is not an essential requirement for being morally motivated, then what does it mean to say that someone was motivated out of duty? To answer this question, we need to look more carefully at Kant's account of the metaphysics of morals. Earlier we noted that this concerns the study of the laws of freedom considered *a priori*, or independently of experience. The idea is that for a rule or principle to be moral in nature, it must be a law or command of reason. But what is a law of reason? And how exactly does Kant conceive of the relationship between reason, morality, and freedom?

We can begin to understand this relationship by considering the concept of will. In the phenomenal realm, we believe that all events involving phenomenal objects can be explained in terms of the laws or regularities of nature. Similarly, we can understand events involving rational beings in terms of law, but in the case of rational beings such as ourselves, Kant argued that we act according to the *conception* of laws. We can act according to laws or principles that we give to ourselves. Thus Kant held that our **will** refers to our capacity for acting according to the conception of laws. Furthermore, since we must use our reason to conceive of these practical laws or principles, our will can be understood as practical reason.

Kant explains our acting according to our conception of laws as acting according to "maxims." A **maxim** is simply a rule of conduct. Consider the following example. Think of someone intentionally performing an action, say picking up the mail. Imagine that this person picks up her mail each weekday after work. Since she does this of her own free will, she acts according to a rule of conduct—a maxim—that she gives to herself. Kant argues that generally we can characterize our intentional behaviour in terms of the many and various maxims we follow. Even if we do not consciously conceive of our behaviour in this way, the point is that describing our intentional behaviour in this way fairly and accurately picks out the intentional nature of much of what we do.

5.8 The Categorical Imperative

For Kant, a maxim is simply a precept under which we act. To understand when a maxim has moral import, we need to introduce the idea of an imperative. An imperative is a command. The sentence "Take out the garbage!" is an example of an imperative. Most imperatives command us to act relative to a worldly goal or aim. In our example, the assumption is *if* you don't want it to rot in your home, then you ought to take out the garbage. Since these sorts of imperatives refer to empirical, worldly goals based on our worldly desires (like our desire to not live among rotting garbage) they lack moral import. Kant refers to them as **hypothetical imperatives.** Notice that since these hypothetical imperatives are commands, we can act under maxims that respond to them. So, to extend our present example, one can act according to the maxim that one regularly takes out the trash. However, this sort of maxim lacks moral import, according to Kant.

Hypothetical imperatives lack moral import because they are empirical and derived from the phenomenal world. In contrast to hypothetical imperatives the **categorical imperative** presupposes no phenomenal end. Therefore, it is unconditional or categorical. Rather than being derived from our worldly experiences, the categorical imperative is derived from pure reason alone. Since our exercise of pure reason is based on the assumption that we reason freely, the categorical imperative therefore expresses the autonomy of the will of rational beings such as ourselves. This is how it acquires its moral import. According to Kant,

> **Will,** according to Immanuel Kant, refers to our capacity for acting according to the conception of laws. Since we must use our reason to conceive of these practical laws, will is practical reason. A law that is conceived is a **maxim,** or a rule of conduct.

> **Hypothetical imperatives** are commands based on fulfilling worldly desires.
> The **categorical imperative** commands unconditionally and is derived from pure reason alone. As such, it expresses the autonomy of the will of rational beings. According to Immanuel Kant, it is the supreme principle of morality.

the categorical imperative is the supreme principle of morality.

A maxim acquires moral worth when it is done out of duty, that is, out of respect for the categorical imperative, the moral law. Another way of putting this is to say that a maxim acquires moral worth only when it is carried out based on the belief that it is right, that it is in accordance with the categorical imperative. For example, a maxim willed and performed out of duty is moral. Putting it this way enables us to see that the categorical imperative functions as a filter, identifying maxims and principles of conduct that lack moral worth. The categorical imperative provides us with a criterion for determining whether the maxims we act on are morally right. To see how it does this, we must examine the imperative more carefully.

Kant argues that the categorical imperative can be expressed in several different ways. The first form runs as follows: "Act only according to that maxim by which you can at the same time will that it should be a universal law."[6] In this formulation, we can see that the categorical imperative rejects all maxims that are not universalizable. The idea is that the principles of morality, since they express our common nature as autonomous beings, and since they are derivable from the exercising of pure reason, should be the same for all rational beings. Therefore, whatever principles we live by should be such that they can be willed as universal laws by all rational beings for all rational beings. To put it simply, to act rightly we must act consistently. We must abide by principles that can be willed and acted upon by all agents. Consider an example. The maxim, "Steal others' property whenever you can get away with it," cannot be willed by everyone as a maxim because if everyone endeavoured to steal personal property, then no one could enjoy the use of their own property. Someone who lives by this maxim thus acts inconsistently because he fails to respect everyone else's property rights but assumes that everyone else will respect his.

Kant's account of the categorical imperative and the view he outlines in his *Foundations of the Metaphysics of Morals* does not detail a normative theory of ethics. It does not provide us with a specific recipe for being moral. It does not tell us how we should live our lives. Rather, it is an account of the foundations of ethics that provides us with a guide for judging the moral worth of the maxims by which we live. The categorical imperative functions as a constraint on our maxims. It provides us with a useful test to help us along. To be moral we must still use our judgment, and we must be sensitive to the circumstances of life. Since it was not designed to be a normative theory, the common criticism that Kant's account is too general, or worse, that it is completely lacking in content, misses its mark. These are objections to a normative theory, but Kant was not pursuing this project in the *Foundations of the Metaphysics of Morals*. This is not to say that his view cannot be criticized. The point, rather, is that to properly take issue with it, one must challenge it as an account of the foundations of morality. It is a meta-ethical theory.

The sense in which Kant's ethical theory is deontological should now be evident. Kant's outlook asserts the priority of the right over the good. A moral maxim is one that is willed for the sake of duty as opposed to being willed out of a desire to promote the good, whether this is conceived as improving the lot of the needy, increasing total happiness, or any other worldly desire. In our theft example, the reason why the maxim "Steal others' property whenever you can get away with it" is wrong is not because of the bad effects of acting on the maxim. It is wrong because not all rational agents can consistently will it.

5.9 Equal Respect for Persons, Human Dignity, and Autonomy

Kant understood that, despite what we might discover through the free use of pure reason, we are sensual beings, too. We are subject to temptation and vice, and we all respond differently to these temptations. However, since all rational beings have free will, Kant maintained that all rational beings are capable of following maxims that they can will to be universal laws. There is, therefore, a strongly egalitarian and democratic element to his meta-ethical perspective. We can appreciate this through two other concepts made famous by Kant: the idea of the price/dignity distinction, and the notion of rational beings as ends in themselves.

Kant sharply distinguishes between mere objects in the phenomenal realm and agents in the noumenal realm. Whereas objects have a price and can be used as tools, Kant argues that we must remember that we are lawgivers. We can live by our own conception of law and as agents with free will capable of living by our own dictates; we have *dignity* as opposed to *price*. Since we are subjects as opposed to objects, consistency requires that we not treat each other as if we were things. So although of course we can avail ourselves of the services of others, we must never treat a subject as if he or she is a mere object or tool. We must never treat a being with dignity as we would treat an object with a price. Whereas we can treat objects as mere means to our ends, we must always live conscious of the fact that all other agents are ends in themselves. Since we, too, are ends in ourselves, we must also uphold our own self-respect. Kant expresses this in the second formulation of the categorical imperative: "Act so that you treat humanity, whether in your own person or in that of another, always as an end and never as a means only."[7] Notice the imperative states that we must *always* act in this way. Since this is a categorical imperative, there are no exceptions. Kant's approach does not permit the sort of calculations about persons that Rawls criticized Utilitarianism for endorsing (see Section 4.6).

Kant's meta-ethical approach is grounded on an ideal of equal respect for the dignity of all agents. Its egalitarian and democratic emphasis is further developed through the notion that we are simultaneously subjects and lawgivers in the noumenal realm. This idea is expressed in the next two formulations of the categorical imperative: We should always remember that all rational agents are capable of making universal laws, and we should always act as lawgivers in the kingdom of ends. This kingdom of ends equally includes all rational agents.

The view that we are equal members in a realm of ends where each person can live by the same universal moral laws follows, as we have noted, from Kant's deontological viewpoint and, especially, from his assertion that ethics rests on free will. It is his thoroughgoing emphasis on human autonomy that ultimately distinguishes Kant as a moral philosopher in the history of philosophy. Other thinkers in the eighteenth century believed that we are capable of identifying our moral duties by exercising our reason. Welshman Richard Price (1723–91), Scot Thomas Reid (1710–96), and German Christian August Crusius (1715–75) all held this view. However, as theologians, they also believed that the demands of morality derive from God. In contrast, Kant's Meta-Ethics locates the source of morality in us. On Kant's account, we determine the demands of morality through the free and careful use of our reason. Unlike his contemporaries, Kant gave pride of place to human autonomy in the story of ethics, and it is for this reason that he is mostly celebrated by those who have been influenced by him in our own times.

5.10 Criticism and a Look Ahead

In our discussion of Kant we have focused on outlining the main elements of his metaphysics of morals. Not surprisingly, in light of its radically different outlook and strong assertions, Kant's view has been much disputed. Although there is no denying his amazing influence on later thinkers, it is also true that Kant has often been the subject of withering attacks and challenges from those who have taken issue with his meta-ethical and normative ethical beliefs. Among these critics are those who endorse the other ethical frameworks we examined in chapters 2 and 4. Rather than develop further criticism here, in Part Two we turn, instead, to a more careful critique of some of Kant's main claims. In Chapter 9 we critically examine the egalitarian emphasis of Kant's outlook. Alternatively, we examine the views of Kant and those influenced by him in the context of specific issues in Part Three. For example, in Chapter 14 we examine some of the implications of maintaining a strongly Kantian respect for life in the various debates in bioethics involving ethics and genetics.

5.11 Review

In this chapter we focused on explaining Immanuel Kant's influential and challenging Meta-Ethics. To provide a context for appreciating Kant's argument, we began by outlining the problem raised by the Dilemma of Determinism. The dilemma seems to force us to conclude that we are never responsible for anything that happens. Yet our judgments about morality rest on the presupposition that we have free will, that we are at least sometimes responsible for what happens. The problem raised by the dilemma is that it seems impossible to believe at the same time in free will while endorsing a deterministic explanation of natural events.

We then considered how Kant responds to this problem by distinguishing between two realms: the noumenal realm of free will, reason, agency, and morality, and the phenomenal realm of events occurring according to the predictable regularities of nature. Kant argues that although we cannot prove that we have free will, we must live our lives under the assumption that we do, and we must therefore see ourselves as occupying both of these perspectives in our lives. As subjects with free will, we take the noumenal standpoint and as material bodies we are subject to the laws of nature. Furthermore, since morality is rooted in the noumenal realm, Kant believes that we must adopt a Meta-Ethics that recognizes this.

In turn, this led us to appreciate the sense in which his approach to ethics is deontological rather than teleological. According to Kant's analysis, the concept of the right is logically prior to the concept of the good. This means that we should determine how we should act not by appeal to the potential good that we could do (however this is interpreted), but by reference to what pure reason demands.

One upshot of this concerns Kant's account of moral motivation. Contrary to many people's

views, Kant says that moral motivation does not require feeling compassion or sympathy for others. We tried to illustrate this point with our example involving the captain and his son. Rather, Kant argues that to be morally motivated, we must be motivated out of duty. To explain this notion we introduced the ideas of a maxim, or a principle of conduct, and a command or imperative. Kant distinguishes between hypothetical imperatives that derive from our worldly goals and desires, and the categorical imperative, which is derived from the exercising of pure reason alone. Maxims that are done out of duty are done purely out of respect for the categorical imperative. In other words, we act out of duty when we act of respect for the moral law, a law that is derived from pure reason. Furthermore, we noted that the categorical imperative rejects all maxims that are not universalizable. Since the moral law expresses our common nature as autonomous beings, and since it is derivable from the exercising of pure reason, it should be the same for all rational beings. This means that whatever principles or maxims we live by should be such that they can be willed as universal laws by all rational beings for all rational beings.

In the final part of the chapter we examined Kant's standing as a philosopher who stresses the moral importance of human autonomy and how this distinguishes him from his contemporaries, who believed that morality derives from other sources besides our own free will and reason. We also observed how the emphasis that was evident in Kant's Meta-Ethics is expressed through his distinction between the price of objects and the dignity of rational subjects, and through the importance he places on always showing respect for persons.

Notes

1. Determinism is commonplace relative to earlier times—consider, for example, the views of those living before the Scientific Revolution, say societies in the Dark Ages or people living in pre-Homeric Greece.

2. Feinberg and Shafer-Landau (1999), p. 412.

3. See English (1975), Section II.

4. We should not understand the idea of a noumenal realm or perspective literally as implying a space or a spatial standpoint. Rather, the words are used metaphysically neutrally as when metaphysicians use the word "thing" to refer to the concepts of substance or universals. So, for example, in the sentence "Orange is a warmer colour than blue," one might be led by the grammar of the sentence to suppose that orange and blue are literally physical things like books and shoes. But when metaphysicians ask whether there are universals and, if there are, what sorts of things are they, or when they wonder what are the basic substances, and what sorts of things they are, they don't presuppose that all things must be like the medium-sized dry goods with which we are most familiar.

5. Although this distinction between teleological and deontological theories in ethics can be traced to John Rawls [see Rawls (1971), pp. 24–31], the way the distinction is drawn in this text differs from the way Rawls draws it. For criticism of Rawls' account of the distinction, see Kymlicka (1988).

6. Kant (1785), p. 39.

7. Kant (1785), p. 47.

Exercises

Progress Check

1. What is determinism?

2. What is indeterminism?

3. Explain the Dilemma of Determinism. What is the problem with challenging the first premise? What is the problem with challenging the second premise?

4. Explain our common assumptions regarding the connection between free will, agency, and morality.

5. What is Kant's Doctrine of the Two Standpoints, and how does this provide a response to the dilemma?

6. Why can there be no physical evidence for or against the idea of a noumenal realm?

7. Why does Kant think we must believe in a noumenal realm even though we do not know for certain that there is such a thing?

8. What does Kant mean by the idea of a metaphysics of morals?

9. Explain the distinction between teleological and deontological theories in ethics.

10. Why is Aquinas's classical Natural Law Theory teleological but Kant's moral theory deontological?

11. Why does Kant reject the view that caring about or having some concern for another person is a necessary condition of being morally motivated?

12. Explain the point of the example involving the captain and his teenage son.

13. Explain Kant's account of will.

14. What is a maxim?

15. What is an imperative?

16. Explain Kant's distinction between hypothetical imperatives and the categorical imperative.

17. What is the first formulation of the categorical imperative? How is this related to the idea of universalizability?

18. Why does the maxim "Steal others' property whenever you can get away with it" violate the first formulation of the categorical imperative?

19. What is the second formulation of the categorical imperative?

20. Explain Kant's distinction between price and dignity.

21. Why does Kant's emphasis on human autonomy distinguish him from his contemporaries like Price, Reid, and Crusius, who also believed that we could use our reason to discover the demands of morality?

Questions for Further Reflection

1. Does the captain who denies his teenage son a place in the lifeboat act morally? Explain and defend your view.

2. On Kant's view, what is the point or purpose of morality? Do you agree? Why or why not?

3. (a) What is Kant's account of the scope of morality; that is, which beings does he believe are owed moral consideration? Why?
   (b) Do you agree? Why or why not?
   (c) How do you think Kant's view of the proper scope of morality differs from the welfarist perspective? Explain.

4. Some philosophers working in the area of Environmental Ethics and philosophy argue against Kant's account of the foundations of morality by claiming that it is ahistorical. The

problem, they argue, is that his view could not explain our survival as a species, and it therefore cannot be the right story of ethics in light of the importance of the development of ethics for our survival. Their argument rests on a number of premises. The first is the claim that we can explain our collective flourishing as a species only by assuming that we were able to develop bonds and associations that enabled us to co-operate. Furthermore, these bonds must have developed very early on in our history. Given, moreover, that our ability for the sort of advanced reasoning that Kant emphasizes evolved relatively recently, it must follow that morality is based on a more basic aspect of our natures, namely our feelings of concern for each other.

Develop the strongest counter-argument that a Kantian might construct to respond to this criticism. Is your counter-argument persuasive? Why or why not? Explain.

5. Kant's view that rational beings have dignity rather than price suggests that it would be immoral to place a price on someone or to trade off someone's life for some material benefit. Do you agree? Why or why not? Defend your view.

6. It seems to follow from the second formulation of the categorical imperative that it is always immoral to take one's own life, assuming that taking one's life is an act of self-disrespect. Do you agree? Is it possible instead to argue from a Kantian perspective that suicide need not be disrespectful? Discuss.

Group Work Activity:

Stocker on Moral Alienation and Acting from Duty

In his essay, "The Schizophrenia of Modern Ethical Theories" (see Stocker [1976]), Michael Stocker points to an apparent problem with acting according to a moral theory that requires that we be motivated out of duty. The problem is that it seems that such a view requires us to live psychologically fragmented lives. The justifications we have for acting morally seem disconnected or removed from our personal motivations for caring about others. The result is a kind of moral alienation due it seems to the emphasis on doing one's duty for duty's sake as opposed to doing it for the sake of the person one helps. It thus appears that in acting out of duty, one must act impersonally.

To help illustrate his point Stocker relates the example of Smith, someone who visits you in the hospital during your lengthy recovery from some illness. Smith's visits greatly cheer you. However, when you thank him for regularly coming, he protests that in coming he has merely been doing his moral duty. You realize that he is telling the literal truth and that it is not essentially because of you that he has been visiting. It is as if you have provided him with an opportunity to do his duty, that you are essentially a placeholder for anyone.

Stocker argues that Smith's actions are lacking in moral merit. Certainly we could understand why his actions might leave you cold, why your judgment of their moral value might change once you appreciate his motivation. The problem is that his actions are impersonal.

Questions

In your groups, answer the following questions:

1. What, if anything, does this charge regarding moral alienation show about moral motivation?

2. Is Stocker correct that Smith's behaviour is lacking in moral merit? Why or why not?

3. We have seen that Kant believes that for a maxim to be morally motivated it must be motivated out of a respect for the moral law. One must act out of duty. It seems that this precludes having the sorts of personal connections one has to one's friends and loved ones. In other words, it seems to follow from Stocker's objection that following Kant's view would lead us to become alienated from our friends and loved ones. Develop the strongest response on Kant's behalf that you can to this charge.

4. Is your response on Kant's behalf convincing? Why or why not? Defend your position.

For more on the sort of problem that Stocker raises, see Railton (1984).

Suggested Further Reading

There is a wealth of scholarship on Kant's ethics. A good place to start is with Onora O'Neill's "Kantian Ethics," in *A Companion to Ethics*, P. Singer, ed. (O'Neill [1993]). See also her two collections of essays, *Constructions of Reason* (O'Neill [1989]) and *Towards Justice and Virtue: A Constructive Account of Practical Reasoning* (O'Neill [1996]).

For an examination of Kant's moral philosophy from the perspective of the history of philosophy see Jerome Schneewind's "Seventeenth and Eighteenth Century Ethics" (Schneewind [1992]), and his excellent book *The Invention of Autonomy: A History of Modern Moral Philosophy* (Schneewind [1998]). Many contemporary thinkers have been influenced by Kant including, most notably, John Rawls. Apart from his *A Theory of Justice* (Rawls [1971]), the Kantian influence in Rawls's work is most apparent in his paper "Kantian Constructivism in Moral Theory" (Rawls [1980]).

Weblinks

Dr. Steven Palmquist maintains a Web site with numerous web-related resources and links on Kant at **www.hkbu.edu.hk/~ppp/Kant.html**

Dr. Richard Lee maintains a Web site listing Web-related resources on Kant at **comp.uark. edu/~rlee/semiau96/kantlink.html**

Rights, Virtue Ethics, and Feminism

Learning Outcomes

In this chapter we complete our main treatment of the topics within ethical theory, especially Meta-Ethics, by examining Rights Theory, Virtue Ethics, and Feminist Ethics.

Upon the successful completion of this chapter, you will be able to

1. answer the question whether Rights Theory is a meta-ethical theory;

2. outline and assess the case for the view that virtue is a basic category in ethics;

3. discuss some of the contributions made by Virtue Ethics to our understanding of morality; and

4. explain the fundamental ideas of Feminist Ethics and provide some examples of male bias in traditional moral theory.

6.1 Introduction

In this chapter we survey three more influential outlooks in ethics from the perspective of the meta-ethical questions that have guided us throughout Part One. Our first concern is with Rights Theory. Rather than focus on the conceptual analysis of rights, our interest in examining Rights Theory is to uncover its impact on Meta-Ethics. Next, we consider Virtue Theory. Again our concern is not so much with the conceptual analysis of virtue, but rather with the question of whether virtue presents us with an alternative basic category in ethics. Finally, we examine some of the influence of Feminist Ethics on Meta-Ethics.

6.2 Rights, Normative Ethics, and Meta-Ethics

Just as money is the currency of our economic lives, talk about rights is the currency of our everyday moral lives. It is doubtful whether one could find a single edition of a daily city newspaper that contains no mention of rights or that does not use the words "right" (as a noun) or "rights" at least once. This reflects our widespread and familiar practice of explaining and defending our views about all ethical matters in terms of our rights. In turn, this tendency demonstrates how comfortable we are thinking about ethics in this way. When we speak of rights we typically do so in relation to particular normative concerns. For example, we appeal to our rights to equality and equal treatment to counter efforts to privatize health care. Similarly, we appeal to our rights to privacy to oppose legislation that increases the power of governments and big business to covertly gather information about us.

Given the importance and prevalence of rights talk in our lives, it may seem odd that we have so far considered rights so little in this book. If we think and talk about ethics in terms of rights, then should not the analysis of Rights Theory be the most important or at least one of the most important topics in an introductory book on ethics? If so, then why the omission?

Think back to Chapter 1, where we distinguished between the various areas of study within ethics. We noted there that our concern in this first part of the book would be with the background and framing issues of ethics that we located within the area of Meta-Ethics. In the course of examining various moral theories and views in Part One, we considered some fundamental questions about the nature and justification of morality, and we examined the underlying assumptions of various influential moral outlooks. Likewise, moral philosophers of the past 100 years or so have primarily been interested in addressing these meta-ethical questions. Since our everyday talk about rights concerns issues in Normative Ethics—the dos and don'ts of morality—moral philosophers generally have regarded the analysis of Rights Theory as being of secondary importance. This is not to say the examination of rights and Rights Theory is uninteresting or unimportant. Rather, the point is that the appeals we make to our rights presupposes that we have them, that we are justified in our appeals. So, for example, an appeal to our right to equality effectively supports a case against privatizing health care only on the assumption that we have such a right in the first place.

More generally, then, talk about our specific rights rests on an assumed theoretical framework, and since our concern thus far has been with examining such frameworks, we have had little reason to discuss Rights Theory. Logically, we proceed from a justified meta-ethical position to a substantive view about Normative or Prescriptive Ethics. Moreover, given the differences between the various basic outlooks in ethics, it is unsurprising that there are significant differences between the views about what our specific rights are, who has them, and how strong they are. Consider, then, the topic of rights as it pertains to the three main theories we examined in Part One: Natural Law Theory, Consequentialism, and Kantian deontology.

6.3 Rights and Natural Law

The topic of rights and Natural Law is interesting, not so much for discerning the view of rights on the natural law perspective, but for understanding the history of the idea of a right. As we noted in Chapter 2, there is no single Natural Law Theory; rather, the view has developed in various ways since Roman times and has its roots in Aristotle's philosophy. Recall that according to the classical version of the view, articulated by St. Thomas Aquinas, natural laws were created by God to direct us to our end in this life. Aquinas recognized that human law falls short of the set of ideal natural laws, which constitute the true moral principles, and he did not conceive of law and morality as distinct. Furthermore, he held that the purpose of following Natural Law/morality is to express our love for and promote the greater glory of God, and to love each other.

Although the idea of a natural right in Natural Law was noted earlier, Dutch lawyer

Hugo Grotius (1583–1645) was the first to clearly and directly defend this idea. Although he was himself a believer, Grotius famously argued that we would possess rights even if God did not exist. He thus proposed an interpretation of Natural Law that helped lead to the secularization of classical Natural Law Theory. By conceiving of Natural Law Theory in terms of the rights of individuals, Grotius helped effect a shift in focus that led to our present view of ourselves as individuals with inalienable rights. These inalienable rights are unlike many of the rights we possess in that we have them simply as persons. They are not given to us by someone or some social institution, and we cannot forfeit or be stripped of them. For instance, we believe that we have a right to life regardless or what anyone says.

Rights are often understood as those powers or claims we enjoy as a result of specific laws or rules that grant the rights. For instance, consider the idea of having the right of way while driving. According to our traffic laws, drivers of vehicles who arrive first at an intersection governed by four-way stop signs have the right of way. In this case, the right enjoyed by the driver is a power to proceed first through the intersection. In contrast to this sort of legal right, Grotius identified the notion of a **natural right,** or what today we might simply call a **moral right,** an **inalienable right,** or a **human right.** Human rights, we think, are rights we have by virtue of our status as human beings, like, for example, our right to life. Although different thinkers have explained and defended the idea of human rights differently, we see the first appearance of this influential notion in the work of Grotius.

> **Human rights, natural rights, inalienable rights,** or **moral rights** are rights we have in virtue of our status as human beings.

6.4 Rights and Consequentialism

The idea that we have moral or human rights independent of any social institution granting those rights captures the conviction of many that rights are basic in ethics. Utilitarians and Consequentialists challenge this idea. Jeremy Bentham, for example, famously claimed that talk of natural or moral rights is "nonsense on stilts." As a Utilitarian, Bentham believed that claims about rights are not ethically basic. Rather, they must themselves be justified by reference to the overall good. For Utilitarians, appeals to our supposed rights cannot justifiably override the promotion of the greater good. In this we see an example of the consequentialist belief that in ethics the good is prior to the right.

In Chapter 4 we noted that, for Consequentialists, what is morally right is determined by reference to the promotion of the prior category of the overall good. Consequentialists accept Welfarism, and they understand claims about what is morally right and wrong in terms of the effects on the welfare of those beings that have a good of their own that are involved. Thus according to their view, appeals to rights are not basic or ultimate because rights themselves are justified only insofar as they promote the overall good. This was the view of John Stuart Mill (1806–73) who wrote:

> To have a right, then, is, I conceive, to have something which society ought to defend me in the possession of. If the objector goes on to ask why it ought, I can give no other reason than general utility.[1]

One might think that Utilitarians and Consequentialists must forsake talk of rights, but as we see here, they have incorporated such talk into their theory. They insist, however, that our rights are themselves justified by appeal to the welfare of individuals. Contemporary Consequentialists have also taken this approach.[2]

6.5 Rights and Kantian Deontology

The idea of a Utilitarian appealing to our moral rights will strike some as confusing. Indeed, in Section 4.6 we considered John Rawls's criticism of Utilitarianism, that it fails as a moral theory precisely because it fails to respect individual rights. According to Rawls, the idea of a right provides individuals with protections against the demands of utility. Appeals to rights are supposed to prevent the sacrificing of the good of the individual for the sake of promoting overall utility. In light of this sort of criticism, how can a Utilitarian defend his view as being about rights? Furthermore, how can a Utilitarian support his account of rights from the perspective of justice?

Rawls sees himself as following in the Kantian tradition in ethics, and the idea that appeals to rights can be derived from the category of the right can be discerned in Kant's moral theory. In Chapter 5 we considered Kant's derivation of morality from our status as agents with free will. Kant argues that the idea of the right is prior to the category of the good in morality. According to Kant's deontological theory, the category of the right is ethically basic, and it is a mistake to try to derive what is right by appeal to worldly beliefs about our good. Instead, we should understand what is morally good in terms of what is right since the idea of rightness derives from the autonomous exercising of our pure reason. In turn, rights follow from duties.

Kant's duty-based ethics is nicely captured in terms of rights talk. For instance, our observance of the categorical imperative, the supreme principle of morality, imposes various duties upon us, and we can easily understand our duties by reference to their corresponding rights. So within Kant's analysis we can see a person's right to be treated as an end in herself as following from our duty not to treat her as a mere object. This second formulation of the categorical imperative ("Act so that you treat humanity, whether in your own person or in that of another, always as an end and never as a means only") points to a further affinity between Kant's view and talk of our rights. The imperative to treat individuals as ends in themselves follows on Kant's analysis from his belief that individuals are deserving of respect as autonomous beings and as lawgivers in the kingdom of ends. Recall that, according to Kant, we must assume that we have free will and that as subjects we are equally deserving of respect and equally capable of willing universalizable maxims. By understanding and expressing our relations in terms of our mutual rights, we capture this Kantian idea of respect and his corresponding idea that we are equally possessors of dignity. Many thinkers have held that Kant's view makes sense of rights talk in part because it expresses our basic convictions about respect for persons.

6.6 Transplant and Trolley: A Puzzle about the Strength of Our Right to Life

In light of this Kantian analysis, we might think that the utilitarian account of rights is wrongheaded and at odds with our considered judgments about justice. Rights talk, we might think, makes sense only if an appeal to an individual's rights can cancel out or trump utilitarian calculations about the greater good and thereby reflect our basic moral belief that we are beings deserving of respect. Rawls objects that Utilitarianism fails because it does not treat people respectfully; rather, it treats us as tools to be used to promote general utility. Thus, on his view, the idea of utilitarian "rights" fails to express our fundamental convictions about rights. The problem with utilitarian accounts of rights, someone taking up Rawls's objection might say, is that it seems that such talk is pointless. If we cannot appeal to the concept of a right to trump utilitarian calculations about the greatest good, then what is the value of such talk? Why bother talking about rights at all?

We can understand Rawls's challenge in terms of the strength of our rights. As we observed earlier, any comprehensive theory about rights will have to say something about how strong our rights are, and this is a notoriously difficult question to answer. We have briefly noted both Rawls's view about this and the consequentialist view. Rawls initially states that the good of society as a whole cannot cancel out an individual's rights, but he then backs away from this very strong assertion. On the other hand, the Utilitarian would seem to permit the overriding of an individual's rights if it served the greater interests of society even a very tiny bit more than the value to the individual of having his rights respected.

Which of these views is better? How strong are our rights? To help focus this question, consider a particular right—our right to life. We commonly assert that we have this right, and it is contained in section 7 of the *Canadian Charter of Rights and Freedoms*. But how strong is our right to life? Can we appeal to this right to trump utilitarian calculations about the greatest good? If so, when? One problem we noted in Section 4.6 is that in addition to being concerned with treating people as equals, we are also concerned about utility. Furthermore, when our interests in promoting both of these goals come into conflict, it seems that there is no simple way of resolving the conflict. To conclude our brief discussion of rights, we can perhaps see that our intuitions about the strength of our right to life are an unreliable guide to answering our question. To see this, consider the following two examples, known respectively as Transplant and Trolley.[3]

Transplant

Imagine that you hobble into the emergency department of your local hospital after twisting your ankle. Although you are there only to receive medical attention, a brilliant transplant surgeon determines (we need not consider how) that your vital organs are a perfect match for five patients in desperate need of organ transplants. Imagine furthermore that the five patients in need of organ transplants are innocent victims of fate. They are not responsible for their need. Otherwise, they are like you: normal and at a roughly similar stage of life. Moreover, imagine that there are no other suitable potential donor organs besides yours and that without your organs, the five patients will soon die. If the transplant surgeon takes your organs, we can reasonably foresee the patients surviving and living normal lives. The transplants, however, will have the unfortunate consequence of killing you. Would the surgeon be justified in taking your organs against your will to save the other five patients? More strongly, does the surgeon have a moral duty to transplant your organs? In other words, would it be immoral for the surgeon not to kill you?

Most people will respond by answering "no" to these questions, and to support their answer they will commonly cite our right to life as cancelling out or trumping any claim the patients might make against us. In this case, at least, it seems that most of us regard our right to life as being strong enough to cancel out the lives of five others. But now compare Transplant to Trolley.

Trolley

Imagine that you have just twisted your ankle and you are hobbling along some trolley tracks on the way to your local hospital. Down the line is a runaway trolley hurtling toward a fork in the tracks. On the fork toward which the trolley is currently headed are five people at roughly the same stage in life as you. These people, like you, are innocent of any wrongdoing and find themselves in their current position through no fault of their own. As it turns out there is no chance that they will be able to avoid being struck and killed by the trolley unless the brilliant transplant surgeon standing at the switch quickly diverts the trolley from its present path to the line of track upon which you are currently hobbling. Unfortunately this will have the effect of killing you. There is no time for anyone to take any other action. Would it be a morally good thing for the surgeon to throw the switch? More strongly, would the surgeon be at fault if he did not throw the switch to save the five?

Many people respond to this example by agreeing that it would be good of the surgeon to throw the switch, and many believe even more strongly that the surgeon *ought* to throw the switch. After all, five is more than one, and all those involved are innocent. Thus, many people react differently to the two examples. The problem, however, is that there seems to be no moral difference between them. In both examples an innocent person (you) would have to be killed to save the lives of five other innocent people. If the surgeon does nothing, then you will live and five will die. But of course the surgeon can do something. He can kill you to save five lives. Shouldn't he do so? You might appeal to your right to life to save yourself, but what about the rights of the innocent five? Don't they count?

Transplant and Trolley raise perplexing but fascinating puzzles about morality. Although one might ponder why we are more inclined to appeal to our right to life in Transplant than Trolley, our present point is that we cannot appeal to our intuitions about our rights to settle the controversy. Since such appeals are unreliable, we must instead attend carefully to the underlying meta-ethical and theoretical questions to make progress. It seems that our theory about our rights rests upon these underlying beliefs, so we must look there for insight. In other words, we must construct our account of our rights on an underlying justified meta-ethical framework.

In the first part of this chapter, we have briefly discussed Rights Theory as it bears on the three main moral outlooks that we introduced in Part One. We noted that a complete theory of rights would provide us with an account of how strong our rights are, who has them, and which exactly they are. In Parts Two and Three, we will make some progress on these topics. In chapters 9 and 10 we examine more carefully the issue just raised about the strength of our right to life. In chapters 11 and 12 we consider the question of the scope of morality, a question closely related to the issue of who (or what) has rights. Finally in Part 3 we examine some specific rights, like, for example, our rights to equality and freedom.

6.7 Virtue Ethics

"Character is man's fate."

Heraclitus

In our survey of fundamental meta-ethical questions, issues, and theories we have identified two basic categories, the good and the right, in terms of which we can usefully think about ethics. In addition to distinguishing some central theories about ethics with respect to these categories, we noted how their differences over the priority of the two categories lead us to different methods for justifying moral claims and for resolving moral disputes. Although this way of distinguishing the main moral theories seems useful, some have challenged the influence of the cate-gories of the right and the good in our ethical thinking. In the first part of this chapter, we considered one such challenge, according to which we should think about moral problems not by reference to what is morally good or right but in terms of our rights. Although it seems that in our everyday lives we often appeal to our rights to try to settle moral disputes, we observed that such appeals are useful only given a developed theory about rights, including an account of their nature, scope, and strength. Furthermore, it seems that to justify our theory of rights, we must appeal to a more basic meta-ethical framework, like the ones advanced by the main outlooks that we have been considering in Part One.

Another challenge to the importance of the categories of the right and the good comes from defenders of what is known as **Virtue Ethics** or **Virtue Theory**. Sometimes Virtue Ethics refers to theories that identify virtue as basic in morality, or, less strongly, that the examination of virtue should assume a central but not foundational role in ethics. Within the first interpretation, Virtue Ethics is conceived of as a challenger to more dominant outlooks like Consequentialism and Kantian Deontology. In contrast, within the second interpretation, supporters of Virtue Ethics insist merely that virtue has been neglected by the main theories, and those theories need to redress this deficiency and recognize the important role that virtue plays in our moral lives. Usually, both interpretations of the view cite the influential moral philosophies of the ancient Greeks, especially those of Socrates, Plato, and Aristotle, as supportive of Virtue Theory. Historians also note the important role played by virtue in the theories of various medieval thinkers, and in recent times we have witnessed a revival of Virtue Ethics in philosophy.

> **Virtue Ethics** or **Virtue Theory** is the view that virtue is either a basic category in ethics or, less strongly, that virtue assumes a central role in ethics.

6.8 Is Virtue a Basic Category in Ethics?

What can be said on behalf of the stronger interpretation of Virtue Theory, according to which virtue should be regarded as a basic category in ethics? One way in which such a position could be defended is to show that the concept of virtue somehow subsumes either the idea of the good or the right or both. In other words, if one could argue that the concept of goodness or rightness makes sense only in terms of virtue, then logically virtue would be the more basic category. As it turns out, there is some evidence for attributing this view to the influential ancient Greek philosophers Socrates, Plato, and Aristotle.

Socrates

A long-admired model of virtue, Socrates (469–399 BC) casts a long shadow in the history of philosophy. We know him mostly through his influence on his most famous pupil, Plato (427–347 BC). Plato's dialogues immortalized Socrates, and, although Socrates appears in many of them simply as a character, scholars believe that the speech attributed by Plato to Socrates in the *Apology* is likely a fair recounting of Socrates' remarks to the jury at his trial. Tried and convicted on the charges of heresy and corrupting the minds of the youth of Athens, Socrates received the death penalty and thereby became a martyr for his philosophical convictions.

In his speech, the character emphasized the importance of spending one's life concerned not with acquiring wealth, glory, or power but with living a good life and with improving one's character by enquiring into the nature of the virtues. In his words and his actions, Socrates demonstrates an unshakeable integrity distinguished by a courageous and relentless pursuit of wisdom and justice.

Plato

Plato's dialogues on moral themes examine the nature of the virtues. Of special concern to Plato are the virtues so well exemplified by Socrates: courage, justice, and wisdom. In *Republic*, Plato argues that the just or morally best state, like the just or morally best man, will be characterized by a harmony of these virtues, together with the virtue of temperance. For Plato, the prudentially good life is identified with the life of virtue. Happiness or, more broadly, faring well, consists of being virtuous. In *Republic*, Socrates (the

character) famously argues that only the just man is truly happy. According to Plato's view, then, the category of the good is understood in terms of virtue. For him what is good is what is virtuous, and a necessary and sufficient condition of faring well is being virtuous.

Aristotle

Plato's student Aristotle (384–322 BC) advanced the most influential account of virtue in the history of philosophy. In his writings on ethics, especially his *Nichomachean Ethics*, Aristotle presents a detailed account of the nature of virtue and his view of its role in the prudentially good life. Contrary to Plato, Aristotle believed that merely living a virtuous life would not guarantee happiness or well-being because in addition to virtue, one needs various goods in order to fare well in life. However, he did argue that virtue was an important element in faring well and, even stronger, he agreed with Plato that it was necessary for living a prudentially good life.

Response

Although we see evidence in these views for understanding ethics in terms of virtue, the ancient Greeks' notion that living virtuously was a necessary requirement of living a prudentially good life is suspect. As we have observed, there are different ways that lives can go well, and although one might concede that there are many morally virtuous people who are also happy, the stronger claim that one must be morally virtuous to be happy seems to contradict the facts.[4] History is littered with the stories of powerful, wealthy, and long-lived immoral types who seemed not only to be quite content with their lives, but also took delight in, or regarded as a source of pride, their immoral behaviour. By what standard are we to argue that these exemplars of vice were in fact miserable, appearances to the contrary notwithstanding? It seems that the wiser strategy is to retreat to the weaker claim that often happiness and virtue go together in a life and not insist that they must go together.

A deeper worry with trying to argue that the category of virtue is prior to the category of the good is one that struck down the argument we just considered on behalf of the importance of the notion of moral or human rights. Just as it seems our appeals to rights presuppose a prior account of the good or the right, appeals to what is virtuous likewise seem to rest on a prior conception of what is good. To appreciate this problem, it will be useful to examine the concept of virtue more carefully. Philosophers traditionally have divided the virtues primarily into the self-regarding ones and the other-regarding ones. In both cases, it seems that virtues are regarded as virtues only insofar as they promote one's own good, or the good of others, or both. So, for example, it seems that we deem self-regarding virtues like self-control, self-reliance, and self-confidence as virtues and not vices precisely because the possession of them generally advances one's good. Likewise, it seems that we deem other-regarding virtues like kindness, loyalty, generosity, and tolerance as virtues rather than vices because possessing them tends to promote the welfare of others.

6.9 Virtue and Some Shortcomings in Modern Moral Philosophy

The argument that we have been examining, against regarding Virtue Ethics as outlining a meta-ethical position that can contend with the major moral theories, is obviously very brief. Still, in the absence of a strong counter-argument for conceiving of Virtue Ethics in this way, it seems prudent to turn and consider the less ambitious version of the view. Various critics of modern moral philosophy cite the relative lack of attention to virtue as a major shortcoming of contemporary philosophical ethics. In an influential 1958 paper, Elizabeth Anscombe helped usher in a reassessment of moral theory by calling for a reconsidering of the Virtue Ethics of Plato and Aristotle. In her scathing indictment of Utilitarianism and Kant's ethics, Anscombe basically accuses proponents of these outlooks of talking nonsense when they discuss morality.[5] In a series of papers and in his "Against" contribution to *Utilitarianism For & Against,* published in

1973, Bernard Williams also criticizes Utilitarianism for its neglect of the importance of character in the moral life. Finally, Alasdair MacIntyre further propelled the development of a new Virtue Ethics with the publication of his 1981 book, *After Virtue.* Since then, there has been a sustained and considerable examination of Virtue Theory by moral philosophers.[6]

Those sympathetic to Virtue Ethics argue that the dominant moral theories of our day all overlook or greatly understate the importance of character and virtue in the moral life. Natural Law emphasizes the obeying of law, Utilitarianism focuses on morally right rules and acts, and Kantian ethics emphasizes duties and obligations. But all of these views neglect the place of people in ethics. As Anscombe argued, to understand ethics, we need insight into ourselves, specifically into our moral psychology, to really understand morality. Furthermore, the best account of ethics will rest upon insight into this dimension of our lives. As Aristotle recognized, morality is learned, taught, and experienced through the development, the modelling, and the application of character and virtue to concrete situations.

6.10 Aristotle's Account of Virtue

Aristotle believed that in order to live a good life, one must be virtuous. He argued that *eudaimonia*, which roughly translates into what we mean by a life of happiness or faring well, consists in living a life of *arete*, that is, a life demonstrating excellence of character or virtue. *Arete*, he explains, is a disposition or state of character concerning a choice lying in a mean relative to us. The mean is determined by reason in the way in which the *phronomos*, or man of practical wisdom, would determine it.[7] Let's consider this view and the lessons it has for the dominant moral outlooks.

1. The focus of Aristotle's virtue ethics is practical, not theoretical.

Virtue Ethics is concerned with the development of moral character rather than with learning theory or moral truths. Unlike Plato, who identifies virtue with knowledge, Aristotle argues that we learn to act rightly through practice. Ethics is a practical study as opposed to a theoretical one. We must habituate ourselves to use our judgment consistently and well, as would the man of practical wisdom, in the unique, particular situations in which we find ourselves in life. Given its practical focus, Aristotle's Virtue Ethics eschews the learning of rules, duties, or abstract formulae for calculating morally right action. As such, it is essentially grounded in lived experience, and our goal should not be to master some theory or body of knowledge, but to model the judgment of the man of practical wisdom.

In this emphasis, we can clearly see how the focus of Aristotle's virtue ethics differs from recent dominant moral theories. Defenders of Aristotle's approach to morality insist that to improve and round out their outlooks, defenders of the main theories in ethics will need to ground their views more directly in the concrete experience of life. They will also need to develop an understanding of how ethical behaviour is taught and learned. For example, traditional theories fail to appreciate the importance of modelling and practising good judgment in the teaching and learning of good behaviour and character. People of character, like Socrates, teach by example.

2. Virtue is a state of character concerning a choice lying in a mean relative to us.

According to Aristotle, we both reveal and develop our character through our choices. Again, his focus is practical, not theoretical. We do not determine how we should act by simply or mechanically applying general rules or principles to life situations. Rather, the right choice for us in any particular situation will depend both on the particular circumstances in which we find ourselves and in our own aptitudes, limitations, and abilities. According to Aristotle's doctrine of the mean, the virtuous choice navigates between two extreme alternatives. So, for example, courage is a virtue lying between cowardice on

one side and foolhardiness on the other. But what is courageous for one person can be foolhardy for another. The trained, well-equipped, and physically fit firefighter demonstrates courage by running into the burning building to save the unconscious man, whereas given my circumstances, limitations, and abilities, I would demonstrate only foolhardiness in doing so.

3. The mean is determined by reason aided by practical judgment.

This sensitivity to the real circumstances of life, and the belief that what is right in any particular situation is best left to good judgment, stands in contrast to moral theories that prescribe the simple application of general rules or formulae for determining right action. This is not to say Aristotle thought theory was useless in promoting morally good living. After all, he wrote about ethics and believed that doing so was worthwhile. However, in his view, general treatments of ethics are of limited value in helping us actually live well. We must habituate ourselves to choosing and acting well and for this end, theory can provide us with some guidance, but we are better aided by good practical judgment, such as is demonstrated by people with practical wisdom. Again, here we see how Aristotle's Virtue Ethics emphasizes the practical nature of moral life and how this difference in emphasis marks a contrast with more abstract traditional moral theories.

Finally, defenders of Virtue Ethics have argued that their approach to ethics gives proper attention to the roles of feeling and compassion in moral life. Whereas the traditionally dominant views tend to say little about emotion, the Virtue Ethics' emphasis on practical judgment leaves proper room for this basic dimension of our experience in their account. Theories that stress the application of rules or principles to life seem to overlook or at least downplay the significance of our feelings in determining our choices and actions. In contrast, the exercising of good practical judgment requires that one be sensitive to one's own feelings and the feelings of others in deciding how to choose and act.

6.11 Feminist Ethics

The emphasis on the significance of concrete, lived experience for understanding morality is a theme also common to much work in another influential stream in ethics in the past 30 years or so, namely Feminist Ethics. Particularly since the late 1970s, many thinkers have emerged from a feminist perspective to present a groundbreaking challenge to traditional ethics that is still being sorted out. Although many different viewpoints have been labelled "feminist," and although there is much debate over what "feminism" and "Feminist Ethics" means, there are some unifying points. Alison Jaggar, for example, argues that the feminist community shares some basic assumptions including "the view that the subordination of women is morally wrong and that the moral experience of women is worthy of respect."[8]

If these points seem obvious to us now, it is due in large part to the work of feminists. For as many writers have shown, the history of philosophy, including the history of moral philosophy, is shot through with male bias. And while there have been some notable exceptions of reasonably enlightened attitudes toward women by men like Plato and Mill, most traditional work has been by men and mainly for men at the expense of women and others in the moral community. It is perhaps striking to us now that the long history of ethics in the West has been almost the exclusive preserve of men. Certainly men developed all the traditional ethical theories, and many feminists argue that this predominance has created a centuries-old build-up of male bias that will take some time yet to overcome. Annette Baier points out that

> The great moral theorists in our tradition not only are all men, they are mostly men who had minimal adult dealings with (and so were then minimally influenced by) women. With a few significant exceptions—they are a collection of gays, clerics, misogynists, and puritan bachelors.[9]

Many thinkers have analyzed the distorting effects of male domination on the study of ethics. Baier, for example, argues that this traditional domination accounts for the neglect of a concept basic to most people's moral lives, the concept of trust, at the expense of less central but decidedly male-favoured concepts like contract and obligation. It is not surprising, she adds, that men mostly uninfluenced by women would devote so much of their work to examining the moral relations between the cool dealings of more or less equally powerful strangers. Furthermore, on this conception of ethics it makes sense that the concepts of contract and obligation would assume so much importance. Nonetheless, this emphasis is not reflective of most people's lives, including most women's lives.

Baier notes we can understand our moral dealings with each other along two dimensions, in terms of relative power and in terms of intimacy. Whereas traditional theory has stressed the study of the moral dealings of roughly equally empowered male strangers, Baier contends that this narrow enquiry overlooks the broad range of power relations between members of the moral community. Consider the various ways in which adults, children, the elderly, the infirm, the mentally and physically disabled, therapists and their patients, professionals and their clients, and non-human animals stand in relation to each other. Now consider how our understanding of ethics might be distorted if we were to base our study of the moral life on the model of the relations between similarly empowered, free, adult men. We can further appreciate the broad range of relations within the moral community by also factoring in the dimension of intimacy. Individuals can be mostly disconnected, but they can also be lovers, siblings, parents, and friends. Baier argues that a complete study of morality should help us understand how to act and feel toward others across the broad range of both of these dimensions of relationships. Moreover, she holds that the concept of trust will be more serviceable in informing us in these regards than the concepts of contract or obligation.

Carol Gilligan's Work on an Ethics of Care

Baier's analysis is just one example of the distorting effects of male bias in the history of ethics. Carol Gilligan, however, revealed the best-known example of this in her early work in moral psychological development. In her 1982 book, *In a Different Voice*, Gilligan presented research that suggests that girls and women develop and experience their ethical lives differently than boys and men do. Gilligan contrasts her own research with the research of another psychologist, Lawrence Kohlberg, who founded his conclusions on the moral development of humans on the basis of research involving men. Gilligan argues that normative judgments about morally good and bad behaviour that draw exclusively or mostly on the moral experiences of males is prejudicial against females. They also fail to capture the richness and complexity of ethics, and Gilligan calls for a reassessment of our moral norms and standards in light of women's experiences.

Gilligan argues that, whereas Kohlberg makes his judgments about a person's moral development relative to a male-friendly ethic of justice based on traditional moral theory, women experience their moral lives in a way that can be best understood in terms of an ethic of care. Thus, a complete account of morality and moral development will have to take both sorts of ethics into consideration. The primarily male ethic of justice is based on abstract reasoning skills that subordinate feeling and emotion in moral judgment making. It prizes the impartial application of universalizable rules and principles to particular situations. In contrast, Gilligan argues that girls and women see morality from a different perspective, one where persons must be sensitive to their own feelings and the feelings of others in concrete circumstances. From this perspective, experiences can be understood and judged from an ethic of care that recognizes partiality based on the actual relationships of individuals. It also values caring, empathy, and sensitivity to circumstance.

Although Gilligan's research was subjected to vigorous criticism, it also exerted enormous influence on the subsequent development of Feminist Ethics in philosophy. Given its critical stance toward traditional moral theory, it is of special interest to us now. Whereas those working in Feminist Ethics have made a number of contributions to our understanding of a diverse range of particular normative issues (abortion, affirmative action, pornography, and so on), they have also forced us to rethink our understanding of moral theory. Given that this was our focus in Part One, we might also want to rethink some of the progress we have made from the critical perspective afforded us by feminism.

Our two examples illustrate some of the advances made within feminism in this area. The arguments advanced by Baier and Gilligan point to the need to revise and develop a Meta-Ethics that is respectful of women's moral experience. How do the traditional meta-ethical frameworks fare in this regard?

6.12 Feminism, Welfarism, and Kantian Moral Theory

We have noted, briefly, how traditional theory that focuses on the impartial application of general moral rules and principles is at odds with at least some Feminist Ethics. As such, Feminist Ethics poses a challenge to utilitarian, and to some extent, consequentialist moral outlooks. However, at the prior level of Welfarism, it seems that Feminist Ethics poses no such challenge. The welfarist view that the purpose of morality is to promote the good of those beings that have a good of their own seems neutral as regards feminism. Minimally, it seems that the welfarist outlook is neither inherently disrespectful of women's moral experiences, nor does it embody any belief in the subordination of women. As with Virtue Ethics, it seems that Feminist Ethics does not present us with a different basic Meta-Ethics that challenges Welfarism. The situation as regards Feminist Ethics and Kantian moral theory is not so clear. We have briefly noted how some work in Feminist Ethics challenges the male bias detected in Kant's moral theory, but as with the Kantian challenge to Welfarism and all other good-based moral views, it is not clear how a distinctively feminist outlook might respond to Kant's case. As we noted in Chapter 5, Kant argues from his premise about free will to the conclusion that the story of ethics must be told from the noumenal standpoint. What feminist counterresponse can be made to this argument?

6.13 Review

In this chapter, we briefly surveyed Rights Theory, Virtue Theory, and Feminist Ethics, paying special attention to their implications for the meta-ethical outlooks that we have considered in Part One. Although our treatment of these diverse views and the complicated questions and issues that they raise has been far from comprehensive, we have made some noteworthy progress.

After locating the idea of inalienable human rights in some work in classical Natural Law Theory, we considered the role that rights talk plays in Utilitarianism. We noted that for Utilitarians, an individual's rights claims are justified only by appeal to the more basic concept of the good. We also observed that although talk of rights fits easily into a Kantian Meta-Ethics, it still assumes secondary importance to the category of the right.

We also considered a puzzle about the strength of our right to life that led us to question our ordinary intuitions about our rights. This suggested that to resolve such questions about the nature and strength of our rights we must delve deeper into underlying meta-ethical issues not dealt with by Rights Theory.

Some defenders of Virtue Ethics present another potential challenge to the two basic ethical categories of the right and the good. However, we had little success in making sense of the idea that virtue could be a more basic category than either the concepts of the right or the good. For it seems that our judgments about both the self-regarding and other-regarding virtues presuppose prior judgments about the good. It seems, in other words, that we regard dispositions as virtuous, or not depending upon their impact on the good.

On the other hand, we also noted how the recent revival of interest in Virtue Theory has positively influenced moral philosophy by broadening our examination of ethics and the moral life. Similarly, we noted the positive expanding influence of Feminist Ethics on traditional moral theory. By overcoming the negative effects of male bias, proponents of Feminist Ethics hold out the promise of developing ethics to reflect the moral experiences of women. This project is ongoing.

Notes

1. Mill (1861), p. 56.

2. For a recent attempt to defend a consequentialist theory of rights, see Sumner (1987a).

3. Transplant is from Harman (1977), Chapter 1. Trolley is adapted by Judith Jarvis Thomson in Thomson (1990), Chapter 7 from Philippa Foot's example. See Foot (1978).

4. The idea that there is a connection between being virtuous and living a prudentially good life is controversial and stands in need of explanation and defence. We address this in chapters 7 and 8.

5. See Anscombe (1958).

6. These are just some of the main contributors to the revival of Virtue Ethics. There were, of course, others like Philippa Foot. For some references to work in this area, see the "Suggested Further Reading" section of this chapter.

7. Aristotle, EN II.6.1106b36–1107a2.

8. Jaggar (1991), p. 95.

9. Baier (1986), pp. 247–248.

Exercises

Progress Check

1. Who was the first person to clearly and directly defend the idea of natural rights?

2. What are inalienable rights? How are they unlike many of our other rights?

3. Why do Utilitarians think that rights are not ethically basic? How is this different from Kant's moral theory?

4. Why might a critic think that a utilitarian theory of rights is pointless?

5. Outline the Transplant and Trolley examples.

6. What is Virtue Ethics?

7. What are the main criticisms of traditional moral theory from defenders of Virtue Ethics?

8. Outline Aristotle's theory of virtue.

9. What beliefs unify the feminist community, according to Alison Jaggar?

10. Annette Baier argues that we can understand our moral dealings with others along two dimensions. What are these?

11. Outline Carol Gilligan's distinction between an ethic of justice and an ethic of care.

Questions for Further Reflection

1. Explain and critically evaluate the idea that Kant's ethical outlook is best understood in terms of moral rights.

2. How strong should an individual's right to life be? What difficulties arise in answering this question?

3. Explain and defend your response to the claim that there is no moral difference between the Transplant and Trolley examples.

4. Why are people more inclined to defend the single individual's right to life in Transplant rather than Trolley? Defend your answer.

5. Explain and critically evaluate the view that virtue is a basic category in ethics.

6. Critically compare Plato's and Aristotle's accounts of virtue.

7. Explain and critically evaluate the notion that in order to fare well in life, one must be virtuous.

8. Assess the main criticisms of traditional moral theory made by defenders of Virtue Ethics.

9. Explain and critically evaluate Annette Baier's critique of the traditional emphasis in moral philosophy on the concepts of contract and obligation.

10. Explain and critically assess Carol Gilligan's critique of the influence of traditional moral theory on our understanding of human moral psychological development.

11. What impact can you foresee Feminist Ethics having on Meta-Ethics?

12. Critique one of the other theories that we have examined in Part One from a feminist perspective.

Suggested Further Reading

If you are interested in the conceptual analysis of rights, you might turn to the influential work of the American law professor Wesley Hohfeld (1879–1918) (see Hohfeld [1913] and [1917]). For more recent treatments of rights from some different perspectives, see Rawls (1971), Nozick (1974), Sumner (1987a), and Thomson (1990).

As noted above, Anscombe (1958), Williams (1973), and (1981), and MacIntyre (1981) have made influential contributions to the revival of Virtue Theory, but also see Foot (1978). Railton (1988) examines some implications for Utilitarianism of work in Virtue Ethics. Finally, for an excellent bibliography of work in this area, see Kruschwitz and Roberts, eds. (1987), pp. 237–263.

In addition to Baier's "Trust and Antitrust" (1986), see also her paper "What Do Women Want in a Moral Theory" (1985), reprinted along with other essays in Baier (1995). For an interesting discussion of the debate between Gilligan (1982) and Kohlberg (1981) and (1984), see Blum (1988).

Weblinks

The Human Rights Library at the University of Minnesota has a large Web site on rights with a vast set of links to other sites at **www1.umn.edu/humanrts/**

The Internet Encyclopedia of Philosophy's (hosted at the University of Tennessee at Martin) entry on Virtue Theory is at **www.utm.edu/research/iep/v/virtue.htm**

The Stanford Encyclopedia of Philosophy's entry on Feminist Ethics, written by Rosemarie Tong, contains several links to other resources. It is at **plato.stanford.edu/entries/feminism-ethics/**

Part 2

Perspectives

We move on to more practical questions and concerns in this second part of the book. There are still some lingering theoretical issues we need to consider, but now we address a set of questions that directly impacts our lives in various ways from various perspectives. Indeed, this concept of ethics viewed from different perspectives provides this part of the book with one of its unifying themes. It is a commonplace about our lives that we view ourselves from various perspectives in varying relations to the world around us. Since morality is a pervasive part of life, it makes sense that it too can be examined from this range of perspectives. If you were asked to identify yourself you could do so in terms of your unique individual qualities ("I am funny and optimistic about life") or your relations to your immediate circle of family and friends ("I am X's daughter/son, Y's sister/brother, and Z's best friend"). You could also do so in terms of your place in your community and society ("I am a student," "I am Canadian") and in terms of

your relation to the natural world ("I am a vegetarian," "I am a conservationist/environmentalist").

To do some service to this wide range of perspectives from which we see ourselves, in this part of the book we consider a set of ethical questions and issues that encompass these expanding perspectives. Specifically, we address our questions from the following five overlapping but distinct perspectives:

1. Ethics and the Individual

One traditional way of examining ethics and ethical issues is from the perspective of the individual. In Chapter 7 we take up this perspective in addressing the basic question, Why be moral? We consider some views that have been advanced in response to our question that have traditionally taken this perspective, including Ethical Egoism, the view that each of us, morally speaking, should be motivated to promote our own self-interest.

2. Ethics in Relationships

In opposition to the answer to our question that we receive from Ethical Egoists, in Chapter 8 we move on to consider a wider view. Some argue that to explain the value of being moral, we need to fully appreciate our social natures and the contributions that love and friendship make to living a morally good and prudentially valuable life. Critics of Ethical Egoism point to a richer and wider conception of both self-interest and morality to support their views about the best answer to our question. In so doing they address a deeper skeptical worry about the prudential value of caring for others for their sakes. Although traditionally underrepresented in moral philosophy, the whole area of ethics in interpersonal relationships, or what we might call Relationship Ethics, has expanded greatly in recent times. We get some introduction to this in Chapter 8 when we discuss matters of love, family, and friendship.

3. Ethics and Society

As Canadian citizens and members of large human political communities, we face a variety of pressing ethical concerns, concerns not sufficiently understood in terms of our relations to our intimate circle of family and friends. In chapters 9 and 10 we discuss one such concern, the problem of determining the value of human life. This particular problem impacts a host of questions for public policy-makers and legislators, and our explanation of it raises some deep, practical puzzles for the two most common approaches to dealing with it. We examine these puzzles through the analysis of some imaginative examples.

4. Ethics and Non-Human Animals

Since they believe that only humans can be given moral consideration, Anthropocentrists argue that our account of the relevant perspectives in morality is now complete. Although we consider this view in Chapter 11, critics charge that any comprehensive introduction to ethics is incomplete if it excludes consideration of our obligations toward non-human animals. In addressing the question of the proper scope of morality in chapters 11 and 12, we assess some different accounts of this view. In opposition to Anthropocentrism we explain and examine the welfarist view that all sentient and potentially sentient beings can be given consideration for their own sake. As a result, we must take the interests of these non-human animals into account and look beyond our obligations to our fellow humans in telling the story of morality. We take this up in Chapter 11.

5. Ethics and the Environment

In Chapter 12 we look beyond the welfarist answer to the question of who can be given moral consideration to consider the biocentric view that all living beings count. Biocentrism thus represents a further widening of our outlook, and since it appeals to an environmental consciousness for support, our consideration of it represents a clear step into the field of Environmental Philosophy and ethics. To complete this brief foray into Environmental Philosophy, we consider an even wider outlook, the holist view that entire ecosystems can and should be given moral consideration as wholes, including the largest biotic community on our planet, the earth itself.

7 Egoism and a Skeptical Challenge to Ethics

Learning Outcomes

In this chapter we begin our survey of the various perspectives one can take in ethics by considering the perspective of the individual. From this vantage point, we examine some skeptical challenges to morality concerning ethics' practical value. We also examine two egoistic theories, Psychological Egoism and Ethical Egoism.

Upon the successful completion of this chapter, you will be able to

1. distinguish between a weak and a deep skeptical challenge to ethics;
2. explicate Psychological Egoism and differentiate between various versions of this theory;
3. apply Karl Popper's concept of falsifiability to theories in science and pseudo-science;
4. explain what Ethical Egoism is; and
5. describe the idea of the breadth of self-interest and the corresponding spectrum along this dimension of value.

7.1 Introduction

Philosophers have long tried to practically justify morality, and in this chapter and the next we consider some issues raised by this challenge and some of the theories that are typically examined in connection with it. We also examine some more recent criticism of the whole project of trying to rationally justify morality.

So let's begin with the assumption that we want to be happy. If the idea of being happy is a goal that sounds too selfish or simple-minded to you, then substitute the perhaps more neutral-sounding idea of faring well, of living a life high in welfare or well-being. From this starting point we can begin to address the question "Why be moral?", and we can explore some accounts of the connections between being moral and faring well in life. Whereas the question "Why do you want to fare well in life?" seems silly, the query "Why do you want to be moral?" has attracted a great deal of interest, and it has generated considerable debate and discussion. Skeptics have long asked this question. Their concern has been with the practical value of morality to the individual, and they wonder what contribution being moral makes to living a happy life. Maybe, they have mused, in the pursuit of happiness one can dispense with the tiresome duties of morality.

7.2 The Example of the Old Man and His Wallet

Skeptics have actually raised a number of doubts in the history of moral philosophy. Famously, for example, they have raised metaphysical doubts about the nature of moral value and epistemological doubts about claims regarding moral truth. In this chapter and Chapter 8, however, our focus will be on some skeptical doubts that have been advanced regarding the practical justification of ethics. More precisely, we can distinguish two such doubts; we will focus our attention mainly on the second one.

Efforts to provide a practical justification of morality typically try to show why it is in one's self-interest to cultivate a virtuous character and to habitually act in moral ways. Thus such attempts try to show why generally speaking it is a prudentially good thing to be ethical. Although as a rough approximation, this is fair enough, we can refine our discussion of the responses that are made to the skeptical challenge by clarifying the nature of exactly what is being contested. Indeed, when we consider the matter more carefully, we can discern at least two interestingly different skeptical challenges to ethics that fall within this area. To help illustrate the distinction between the two sorts of challenges, consider the following example.

Imagine you are walking along the street one day when the dishevelled old man in front of you accidentally drops his wallet and does not stop to pick it up. You retrieve it, call out to him, and return it. Can we describe your behaviour as ethical? Assuming no unusual circumstances (he is

not a robber baron, you are not Robin Hood), and without plunging into the depths of social and political theory, your action certainly has a morally good result. The wallet was returned to its rightful owner. But it is a separate question whether your motivation was moral. We can distinguish between judging the effects of our actions and our motivations for performing them. Although these often go together, they need not. Sometimes the bumbling evildoer saves the world from disaster.

It is worth pausing here to emphasize this distinction. It is very easy to think of oneself as displaying moral behaviour based on the effects of one's actions even when one's motivations are purely selfish. Our example can illustrate this. Based on the results, it would be easy to infer that you are ethical because you returned his lost wallet. But to determine whether your motivation is moral we need to consider what reason or reasons you might have for acting as you did. You could say that you returned the wallet for the following reasons:

1. You wanted to deceive your potential future employer, who was walking with you on the way to your big job interview, into thinking that you are an honest person.

2. You wanted to deceive your biggest customer, who was watching from across the street, into thinking that you are an honest person.

3. You wanted to keep the wallet, but you were afraid that you would get caught and punished for stealing if you did so. Surveillance cameras are everywhere these days.

4. You wanted to keep the wallet, but you didn't want to risk getting caught. A nice fat reward for "honesty" is just the balm you need to soothe your tortured lust for money.

5. You gave it back because you didn't want to feel guilty or ashamed of yourself, and you know that given the way you have been raised, you would have felt this way if you kept it.

6. Alternatively and more positively, you wanted to feel good about yourself.

7. It is the right thing to do, and you always unquestioningly do what you have been told is the right thing.

8. You valued the old man's praise and the approbation of the others passing by more than the paltry sum he was likely to be carrying around. You might even make the news.

9. You believe in the Golden Rule. You would want him to return your wallet if you dropped it.

10. Even though he is a stranger, you felt bad for him and didn't want him to come to harm.

Although they each lead to the same morally good result, notice that of all these reasons only the final one, number 10, is clearly and obviously primarily other-regarding. If you return the wallet for reason number 10, you do it out of a concern for the old man's well-being. In contrast, reasons 1–9 cite the effect on you as your exclusive or primary motivation for acting. This is not necessarily a bad thing, of course. We can make sense of the idea that acting for one's own good can be morally good. However, to help distinguish between the two sorts of motivating reasons in our example, let's say that distinctively moral motivation is marked by agents acting out of a concern for someone else for his sake, or for others for their sakes. In contrast, acting exclusively or primarily out of a concern for one's good, where one's own good is independent of the good of others, is the mark of non-moral motivation.

Some might be put off by this way of distinguishing between the two sorts of reasons, but the distinction we are drawing here is not being offered as proof of some deep insight into the nature of morality. Rather, our aim is to use this distinction to differentiate between two kinds of skeptical challenges to ethics. If you find this way of expressing the difference disagreeable, you are invited to mark it using other terms.

7.3 A Weak and a Deep Skeptical Challenge to Ethics

With our distinction in hand, we can now raise two skeptical challenges that might flow from our original question ("Why be moral?"). The first challenge is this. A skeptic might wonder about the practical value of acting in ways that have moral results regardless of the nature of one's motivation for acting in these ways. According to this challenge, which we will call the **Weak Skeptical Challenge to Ethics,** the worry is that acting in ways that benefit others is not generally rational. A skeptic adopting this view might argue that to live the best life, you should consistently and directly promote your own good. Furthermore, he might opine that there seems to be little room in such a life for pursuing projects that promote the good of others. So, for example, in the case involving the old man, the rational thing to do is to keep his wallet. This, it might be argued, is what will best advance one's good.

To meet this Weak Skeptical Challenge to Ethics, we need only show that it is rational to act in ways that benefit others, and indeed we have already done this. Recall that in Chapter 2 we recognized the prudential value of co-operating with others. We showed that in many situations in life it is rational for us to co-operate with others because there is a reasonable guarantee that they will co-operate and because there are benefits available to individuals acting together not available to individuals acting on their own. The idea here is that although it might not always be rational to act in ways that benefit others—and the case involving the old man might be such a case—conditions that make co-operation rational often exist in society. In other words, the proponent of the Weak Skeptical Challenge to Ethics cannot infer too much from the example involving the old man. Often, we do have a reasonable guarantee that others will co-operate with us, and we benefit when we co-operate too. So, for example, by following traffic laws, we enjoy the considerable benefits of travelling on our roads and highways and we avoid the costs imposed on lawbreakers.

As interesting as this Weak Skeptical Challenge to Ethics is, an even more revealing challenge is raised when one asks how it could be in one's self-interest to act out of a concern for someone else for her sake. Notice that the Weak Skeptical Challenge to Ethics encompasses cases where people act out of this sort of motivation, but these cases pose a deeper challenge to defenders of ethics than that presented to respondents to the Weak Skeptical Challenge to Ethics. Since the Weak Skeptical Challenge to Ethics wonders about the wisdom of generally acting in ways that benefits others, it includes situations where people act of a concern for another or for others. However, in order to meet what we might call the **Deep Skeptical Challenge to Ethics,** we cannot simply point to reasons like reasons 1-9 in our example involving the old man. The Deep Skeptical Challenge to Ethics asks how it can ever be rational to act primarily out of moral motivation, that is, out of a concern for someone else for her or his sake. To respond to this challenge, we cannot simply cite the sorts of co-operative benefits we noted in Chapter 2, or the sorts of selfish reasons we noted in the case involving the old man. The trick now is to show not how you can benefit from co-operating with others, or to show how you can advance your own good by performing actions that help others. The trick is rather to show how you can benefit from helping others where your motivation is primarily to act out of a concern for them.

The Deep Skeptical Challenge to Ethics asks how it could be rational to be motivated out of a concern for someone else for her sake. On the face of it, this does seem paradoxical. How can your good possibly be promoted by acting out of a concern for someone else? It seems at first glance at least that to promote your own good, you should act primarily for it and not for the good of another. In contrast, notice that you can act morally, and thereby advance the good of another or the good of others, but you can do so without any concern for him, her, or them. Thus you might act morally by co-operating with others and thereby advance some project that benefits them, but do so out of a narrow concern for yourself because advancing the project also best promotes your own well-being. So, to take another example, I might keep my end of a business deal with you, thereby helping you prosper, but do so because this makes me rich. In this case, I act in a way that benefits you, but my motivation is to advance my own good. I don't really care about you at all.

7.4 Psychological Egoism

To show that it is rational to act out of a concern for someone else for his sake, you must explain how such behaviour can be good for yourself. Any attempt to demonstrate this presupposes that we can and do sometimes act out of a concern for others; however, there is one well-known theory of human behaviour that in many of its forms disputes this. Before we directly take up the task of meeting the Deep Skeptical Challenge to Ethics, we will have to consider this theory.

> The **Weak Skeptical Challenge to Ethics** challenges the view that it is rational to act in ways that benefit others.
> The **Deep Skeptical Challenge to Ethics** challenges the view that it is rational to care for anyone else for her or his sake.

Psychological Egoism is the view that humans are motivated by their self-interest. Although all Psychological Egoists accept this claim, the view splinters into many different accounts, some of which we need to distinguish. On its more familiar, extreme interpretation, Psychological Egoism is the view that we always act to pursue our own good. This is not to say that the Psychological Egoist believes that we are always successful in promoting our good, for we can fail, for instance, to accurately identify or achieve it. Rather, the theory is a theory about our behaviour. According to it, we always aim to advance our self-interest whether we appreciate this or not.

Deterministic and Non-Deterministic Interpretations of Psychological Egoism

One respect in which different versions of Psychological Egoism can be understood is in terms of whose behaviour is being explained. We can formulate a theory about our own behaviour or we can formulate a theory about human behaviour

> **Psychological Egoism** is a theory about human motivation according to which humans are motivated by a concern for their self-interest. In its extreme form, it is the view that humans always and only aim to advance their self-interest, where an individual's self-interest is understood narrowly to be independent of the self-interest of others.

Determinism is the view that all events are caused. A deterministic explanation is an explanation that assumes that determinism is true.

generally. In our own case, when we endeavour to explain why we performed some action, we will typically sometimes mention our own reasons for acting ("I wore red today because it is Canada Day and I wanted to display my patriotism"). From the inside, we commonly assume that our actions are to some extent within our control. We can choose to do this or that. This sort of commonplace account of our self-reports of our behaviour presupposes that we have free will, that forces beyond our control do not determine our actions. In some sense, then, we provide non-deterministic accounts of our behaviour. This is not to say that there is no explanation for why we do what we do, but only that our behaviour is not determined by forces beyond our control, at least some of the time. Some think that a non-deterministic or non-causal account of behaviour is equivalent to behaviour that is inexplicable. On this outlook, all explanations must be causal explanations. There are no other possibilities.

Extreme Deterministic Psychological Egoism is the view that humans lack free will and always behave in ways that promote their own good. According to this view, humans are never motivated out of a concern for another person.
Extreme Non-Deterministic Psychological Egoism is the view that humans always act in ways that aim to promote their own good, and never act primarily or exclusively for the sake of another person.

In contrast, when we explain our own behaviour, we think we act for our own reasons and that these reasons are not causally necessitated by causes external to us. We assume that our choices (at least some of the time) are free.

In contrast, researchers sometimes provide accounts of the behaviour of their subjects that deny free will. On such accounts, the explanation of the behaviour is not based on the subjects' reasons for acting. Rather, some other explanation is provided, one inconsistent with the notion that we have free will. On such accounts reasons are offered to explain behaviour, but the reasons are not the motivating reasons of subjects. They are the asserted causes of behaviour,

causes that lie outside subjects. So, someone might say that the reason I wore red today is not because I wanted to display my patriotism, but because I have an overwhelming need to be socially accepted. Since such accounts rest upon a deterministic account of human behaviour, we can refer to these sorts of explanations as being based on **determinism.** In one extreme form, Psychological Egoism is a deterministic view. According to it, we always act to advance our self-interest, regardless of what contrary reason we might think we have for acting. Deterministic versions of Psychological Egoism are thus distinct from non-deterministic versions because, according to the non-deterministic versions, we can choose to act for our own reasons.

Extreme Deterministic Psychological Egoism

What we can refer to as **Extreme Deterministic Psychological Egoism** is the view that humans always act to promote their own good or well-being despite what they claim to the contrary. Since it is a deterministic version of Psychological Egoism, proponents of this view believe that to understand human behaviour, you must not simply rely on the motivating reasons humans mention to explain their behaviour. Rather, we need to explain the causal forces acting on us to see that we always act to promote our own good. For example, you might claim that you returned the wallet to the old man because you didn't want him to come to harm. However, the Extreme Deterministic Psychological Egoist would insist that you really did it to somehow benefit yourself and that you could not have acted exclusively or primarily for him despite what you might think to the contrary. Thus, Extreme Deterministic Psychological Egoism is not extreme simply because it denies human free will, but also for another reason. According to this theory, humans *always* act to promote their own good, that is, we never act for the sake of anyone else. Both because it is deterministic and because it precludes other-regarding behaviour, Extreme Deterministic Psychological

Egoism poses a serious threat to any attempt to meet the Deep Skeptical Challenge to Ethics.

Extreme Non-Deterministic Psychological Egoism

In contrast to Extreme Deterministic Psychological Egoism, **Extreme Non-Deterministic Psychological Egoism** accepts that humans have free will. On this view, it is not the case that we must act for our own benefit; rather, the claim is that we do act only in this way. So according to the Extreme Non-Deterministic Psychological Egoist, it is possible to act exclusively or primarily for the sake of someone else, but we just never do so, again, despite whatever we might think or say to the contrary. For instance, you might claim you returned the wallet to the old man because you were concerned about him, but you really did it to promote your own interest in some way. Like the deterministic version of the view, defenders of this account similarly hold that we should not rely on the self-reports of individuals to learn about their behaviour. In this case, however, the reason we should not rely on these reports of people's purported reasons for acting is not because these reasons are not effective, but because claims about them are not reliable. So whereas the Extreme Deterministic Psychological Egoist claims that the reasons we cite to explain our actions are not the real causes of our behaviour, the Extreme Non-Deterministic Psychological Egoist believes that our free choices and reasons can be efficacious. That is, our reasons can explain our actions. However, insofar as we tend to believe and assert that our motivations are exclusively or primarily other-regarding, our self-reports are unreliable because we are victims of our own self-deceptions. As with the deterministic view, Extreme Non-Deterministic Psychological Egoism is an extreme view because according to it, we always act to advance our own good and never do so for the sake of anyone else.

In addition to providing an extreme account of human motivation, Extreme Non-Deterministic Psychological Egoism also tells a rather simple story. We think we can often identify a complex range of reasons in our deliberations and a correspondingly complex assortment of goals that we seek to achieve through our actions. For example, a woman might say that she chose to attend university in her hometown rather than out of province for many different reasons and to accomplish a number of aims; her hometown university, though maybe not the best, is still very good. She also wanted to relieve the financial burden on herself and her family. By staying at home she could continue to help with her parents' business and retain her job. She also wanted to maintain her relationship with her closest friend who has been going through a difficult time lately and would value her company in the coming year. Similarly, she wanted to be a part of her young nephew and niece's lives. All of these familiar kinds of reasons seem to attest to the complexity of our motivations. However, on the extreme non-deterministic account, we can reduce or eliminate this list to one simple sort of reason: She chose her hometown school because she always and only acts for her own benefit, and she judged that this was best for her.

7.5 The Case for Extreme Psychological Egoism

We have briefly outlined the two accounts of Extreme Psychological Egoism, but why might someone think that they were true? Common sense tells us that we often willingly and reasonably act for selfless reasons, as when we hold a door open for someone else or when we do someone a favour at some cost to ourselves. The most common argument adduced on behalf of the two extreme views emphasizes the unreliability of these sorts of claims. Thus, the Extreme Psychological Egoist notes that our stated reason for acting belies our truly selfish aims. We can all produce examples where we might have initially thought or said that we acted for the sake of someone else and later admitted (at least to ourselves) that we really did it for some more selfish reason. What sets the extreme psychological egoist position apart, however, is that the defender of this view takes this sort of example to be representative of *every* single case of apparently selfless behaviour. In other words, Extreme Psychological Egoists maintain that in the entire history of our species, no human has ever performed a single act with the sole or primary intention of benefiting someone else. In response to the assertion that we act from such motivation on a regular basis, the Extreme Psychological Egoist insists that we are victims of self-deception if we truly believe this. In support, they note that as victims of our own self-deception we cannot appeal to what we declare is our real, selfless motivation for acting since this is precisely what we are deceiving ourselves about. Consider how the Extreme Psychological Egoist would respond to a case advanced against the position by David Hume. Hume finds the idea of Extreme Psychological Egoism absurd, and he thinks the Egoist presents a counterintuitive and overly simplistic picture of motivation. For example, he believes that our love for our children can outweigh our feelings of self-love. Thus he writes:

> What interest can a fond mother have in view, who loses her health by assiduous attendance on her sick child, and afterwards languishes and dies of grief, when freed, by its death, from the slavery of that attendance?[1]

Hume suggests here that a reasonable person would agree that the mother clearly acted out of love for her child despite the harmful effects that her devotion had on her own well-being. She obviously acted out of this motivation because if her original devotion had been insincere, then once the child had died, she would not have languished and died from grief herself. Rather, she would have resumed her life content in the knowledge that she did what she could, and that no one could have expected more of her.

Far from regarding the mother's behaviour as evidence of the sincerity of her devotion to her child, the Extreme Psychological Egoist interprets her behaviour as evidence of her selfishness. Although she might have sincerely claimed to be concerned about her child, her real motivation was to enhance her own self-esteem. She believed that her behaviour was what was required to be a good mother, and her goal was to meet her own expectations for herself. Furthermore, she sought the esteem and honour of others in her society since people generally admire the apparently self-sacrificing devotion she displayed. Finally, her headlong pursuit of glory manifested itself in the ultimate apparent sacrifice of her loss of life. In fact, the Extreme Egoist argues, she really just wanted to experience the satisfaction while she was alive that when she died she would be remembered as a great mother. Far from being motivated out of a concern for her child, she used her child's illness to advance her self-esteem, to acquire praise and honour, and to fuel her own dreams of glory.

7.6 Extreme Psychological Egoism as Pseudo-science

This sort of response by the Extreme Psychological Egoist to examples like Hume's is often met with frustration and exasperation by those who strongly believe that the view must be wrong and who struggle to provide empirical evidence against it. The idea that there must be some evidence that would count against the extreme versions of the theory is based on the presupposition that Extreme Psychological Egoism is a descriptive theory, such as is found in the field of scientific enquiry into human motivation and behaviour. At first glance it certainly looks like such a theory. It purports to describe human behaviour, and its defenders seem to offer evidence on its behalf. Furthermore, we might find it impressive that no evidence seems to count against the view. This, at any rate, is true of scientific theories generally. If we can find no evidence against a scientific theory, then this suggests that the theory is strong.

The inference that Extreme Psychological Egoism must be a strong theory because other theories in science for which there is no counter-evidence are strong is sound provided that Extreme Psychological Egoism *is* a scientific theory. However, this assumption is dubious. Upon closer examination, one can see that

Extreme Psychological Egoism falls on the pseudo-science side of the divide between science and pseudo-science, at least according to a highly regarded and widely influential theory about science advanced by the British philosopher Karl Popper (1902–94). Popper argued that for a theory to count as scientific, it must be subject to falsifiability. In other words, in principle it must at least be possible that empirical evidence could count against or falsify the theory. The strongest scientific theories are thus those that can be disconfirmed, but that have not suffered this fate. In contrast, Popper argued that any theory that cannot in principle be disconfirmed is at best pseudo-scientific. It looks like a theory in science but it is not. On this analysis what at first appeared to be Extreme Psychological Egoism's strongest point—the impossibility of there being any disconfirming evidence against it—now seems evidence of its failure to qualify as the kind of theory its supporters insist it is. Since they interpret all human behaviour from the perspective of their theory, Extreme Psychological Egoists refuse to accept any examples of human actions as evidence against their view. Any purported disconfirming counterinstances are simply interpreted away by the Extreme Psychological Egoist. Once we appreciate this distinction between science and pseudo-science, we can cease trying to find disconfirming evidence against the view; that is, we can cease regarding it as a scientific theory and regard it instead as an interpretive account of human behaviour. As such an account, we can now ask: Does the Extreme Psychological Egoist provide us with a reasonable interpretation of human behaviour?

7.7 The Breadth of Self-interest

A good place to begin our investigation into the reasonableness of the extreme psychological egoist interpretation of human behaviour is with the egoist's account of our self-interest. Our self-interest or well-being can be assessed and compared from a number of different perspectives. So, for example, we can assess our well-being in terms

of its sources and compare the sources of our good to the sources of someone else's good. It is common, and the root of much conflict in human society, that we derive value from different kinds of goods and activities, although there is often a fair bit of overlap across individuals. Alternatively, we can assess a person's well-being in terms of its duration as when we say of someone that he lived a very long and happy life. We can also compare different individuals' welfare in terms of this dimension of well-being. Thus we might say that from the perspective of duration, a very good life of 70 years is much better than one of 40 years. Likewise we can compare the value of two individuals' lives from the perspective of the quality or depth of their well-being. When Mill argued that it would be better to be Socrates dissatisfied than a pig satisfied, he was making a judgment about the relative quality of the two lives.

Apart from these (and other) dimensions, we can also judge and compare self-interest in terms of its breadth. This type of judgment and comparison is rather underrepresented in the literature on ethics, but it assumes an interesting and important role in the debate about the practical justification of morality. Whereas assessments of the depth of self-interest measure how rich the value of someone's life is—how far down it goes—assessments of the breadth of self-interest measure how wide or how far out it extends (in terms of other people). Extreme Psychological Egoists assume an unusual, simple, and very narrow understanding of self-interest. According to the Extreme Psychological Egoist, our self-interest is determined entirely independently of the self-interest of others. For the Extreme Psychological Egoist, an advance or a diminishing of the good of another has no direct effect on one's own good. Egoists can admit that effects on others can have indirect effects on oneself, but they deny that one's own welfare is dependent and directly connected to the welfare of another.

Consider an extreme example to illustrate this point. A slave owner might be upset about the death of his slave, and the slave's death might indirectly affect his good. In this sort of case, the slave owner cares not for the effects of the loss of life to the slave, or for the losses experienced by those who care about the slave. Rather, the slave owner is upset because the passing of a good worker may inconvenience him or because the slave's death imposes an economic cost on him. Although the slave owner might otherwise have somewhat broad self-interest (imagine that he does care about his family, friends, and fellow citizens), his good does not include the good of the slave. Whereas the owner does not grieve for the slave or his family because he did not care about the slave for his own sake, someone who loved the dead man would. Although this example is unusual, most people would agree that their own self-interest is dependent on the well-being of others. Thus most of us would count the loss of a loved one as not only a terrible loss to the loved one but also as a loss to ourself too. When we grieve the death of someone we love, we grieve both for the person we love and for ourself. We experience loss. Conversely, we derive satisfaction from the achievements, successes, and good fortune of those we care about. To the dear friend who has just realized some significant achievement we might say "I'm so happy for you," but this achievement typically makes us happy too.

Arguably, one test of whether you truly care about someone else for his sake is whether you experience to some degree gains and losses to the other person's welfare in this way. We doubt the sincerity of the person who claims to love someone deeply but who feels indifference—or even worse—profound sorrow upon learning of the "loved" one's negative results for cancer. Likewise, we call the person who secretly revels in his "friend's" setbacks a false friend. Furthermore, there appears to be at least a rough correlation between the intensity of this sort of experiencing and the strength of the bond between the two individuals. Whereas you might be indifferent to the animal who gave its life for your snack, and you might be saddened to learn of the death of a respected public figure, you might be devastated by the suffering and untimely death of your child, as was the woman in Hume's example.

Once we recognize that there is this dimension of breadth to self-interest, we can appreciate the difference in the breadth of our self-interest. Some of us care only a little for many people but a lot for the select members of our intimate circle of family and friends. Other people seem to care deeply for a cause or for many others. Sociopaths care only for themselves and thus seem to have very narrow self-interest. To help compare ourselves along this dimension of welfare, we can conceive of the idea of a spectrum of self-interest in terms of breadth. So, for example, we just noted that sociopaths care not for others and therefore seem to have very narrow self-interest. But we might wonder whether their lives would in fact go better if they could cultivate a wider self-interest. Likewise, we might ask this about ourselves. Would our lives go better if we extended our self-interest in some ways or respects? Perhaps some people would do well to narrow their self-interest?

With the help of this idea, we can represent the Deep Skeptical Challenge to Ethics by asking how it can ever be in anyone's self-interest to care for someone else for her sake. To meet this challenge, we must show how life goes better by having wider, as opposed to very narrow, self-interest. Notice that regardless of what we think about this, if the extreme psychological egoist's account of our self-interest as being very narrow is right, then there would be little prospect of responding to the Deep Skeptical Challenge to Ethics since it could not advance anyone's good to care for anyone else for his sake. If X's well-being is entirely independent of Y's, then what self-interested and rational reason could X have for caring about or acting for Y for Y's sake?

One problem with the extreme psychological egoist's account of self-interest is that it is assumed to be correct rather than defended as such. So while it is possible that the Extreme Egoist has it right, he gives us little reason beyond this for thinking this. More generally it is possible that we do not have free will and that every time we say we act for the sake of someone else, we are deceiving others or ourselves. However, in the absence of some more convincing reason or reasons for thinking that the Extreme Psychological Egoist is correct about these matters (beyond the mere possibility that the view is correct), we are wise to look for alternative explanations of our behaviour.

7.8 Ethical Egoism

In our discussion of the breadth of self-interest, we noted that we can situate people along the spectrum of this dimension of well-being from the very narrow to the very wide. We also noted that while someone might claim to have rather wide self-interest, it is a further question whether her life might go better if she limited her caring. More broadly, we noted that since the Deep Skeptical Challenge to Ethics asks how it could ever be rational to act or care for someone else for her sake, it raises the question whether anyone's self-interest really is wide. To meet the challenge, then, we need to show not only that people do care about others but also that it is good for them to be this way.

Ethical Egoism, at least on some of its interpretations, argues that the Deep Skeptical Challenge to Ethics cannot be met. Whereas Psychological Egoism purports to be a descriptive account of human motivation, **Ethical Egoism** is the normative theory according to which everyone should be motivated only by his own good. Thus, the Ethical Egoist stands opposed to many Psychological Egoists by recognizing that people can and do act contrary to their own best interests. However, many Ethical Egoists insist that it is never in one's own self-interest to act out of a concern for someone else for her sake. On the other hand, they argue that it sometimes can be in our self-interest to act in ways that benefit others (even if we don't act out of a concern for them). In other words, many Ethical Egoists argue that we can meet the Weak Skeptical Challenge to Ethics.

Unlike its descriptive counterpart, Ethical Egoism is both plausible and subtle. Acting out of a concern for one's own interests is consistent with acting in ways that help others. Philosophers have referred to this as an individual's **enlightened self-interest.** The idea of enlightened self-interest refers to what is in a person's long-term best interests and, as we have observed, it can be in someone's enlightened self-interest to act in a way that benefits others. Since it embraces the idea of enlightened self-interest in this way, Ethical Egoism should not be seen as recommending selfishness. Whereas selfish behaviour implies indifference toward or outright disregard for others, many versions of Ethical Egoism do not. Furthermore, we can also distinguish Egoism from altruism. Whereas Egoism refers to acting out of self-interest, altruism refers to acting for the sake of others. Ethical Egoists argue that we should not act altruistically, but since many use the idea of enlightened self-interest, they are not also committed to recommending that we act selfishly either.

Ethical Egoists maintain that one serious flaw in many traditional moral outlooks, political theories, and political movements is the subsuming of the good of the individual to the benefit of the group. They remind us that each of us count too and that we should not assume that the moral life is or need be equivalent to a life of altruistic self-sacrifice. So, for example, Ethical Egoists point in the 20th century to the danger of movements like Nazism and Communism as examples of movements that led to the formation of immoral states where individual well-being was sacrificed for the supposed higher good of the group. Ethical Egoists also draw on the work of people like the Russian-born American writer and philosopher Ayn Rand (1905–82) and her philosophy of "Objectivism" for support. Best known for her novels *The Fountainhead* and *Atlas Shrugged,* Rand defended her view that morality requires of each of us that we not sacrifice ourselves for others, but instead morally pursue our own well-being and, above all, respect ourselves.

> **Ethical Egoism** is the normative theory according to which humans should be motivated only by their own self-interest.

> **Enlightened self-interest** is an individual's actual good.

Ethical Egoism and the Breadth of Self-interest

Although many Ethical Egoists appeal to the notion of enlightened self-interest, they vary in their opinion of how broad our self-interest should be. Ethical Egoists who conceive of our self-interest as being fairly wide admit the possibility that the Deep Skeptical Challenge to Ethics can be met. If so, we can see these versions of the theory emphasizing that morality does not require of individuals that they sacrifice their happiness for the sake of others. In contrast to this group, however, are those Ethical Egoists who embrace narrow accounts of the breadth of self-interest. According to these versions of the theory, the Deep Skeptical Challenge to Ethics cannot be met since such views leave no room for recognizing the possibility that one person's good could be advanced by acting out of a concern for someone else for his sake.

7.9 The Force of the Deep Skeptical Challenge

The question for us is whether we can meet the challenge. Can we offer good grounds for conceiving of self-interest more broadly? How can it be in anyone's self-interest to act for the sake of someone else? Although we might be able to argue that such behaviour is moral, although the Ethical Egoist might dispute this, our question is whether it could be prudentially rational. Consider again the problem with respect to our original example involving the old man. If you discovered the wallet, you might be able to offer ethical reasons for returning the wallet: doing so would be good for the old man, good for society, and so on. You might also be able to offer some more obviously self-interested reasons of the sort (1–9) that we noted earlier. But if you do not have these self-interested reasons for returning it, why should you do so? Why should you care about the old man?

You might argue that you can gain the benefits of co-operation in society without caring about others very much, and caring about the old man is just a weak and stupid way to be. So, for example, if it looks like you won't get caught, why shouldn't you keep his wallet? Imagine you look around and you don't see any cameras or other people. You could just reach down and scoop it up. Why shouldn't you, prudentially speaking? Surely you can use whatever money you find. But, you might say:

1. I will feel guilty and ashamed of myself for doing such a bad thing.

In response we might argue that you need to break out of your old way of simply accepting what you were taught to think and feel. Your new goal should be to live a good life for you, admitting morality into that life insofar as it fits. Arguably, keeping the wallet would be a morally bad thing to do, but it would be prudentially good for you. When you consider the matter more carefully, you might see that you experience these feelings of guilt and shame because of the way you were raised. But you can now see that your conditioning isn't in your best interests. Rather than feel guilt and shame, perhaps you should take pride in your intelligent self-promotion. Perhaps you should resolve to feel good about yourself only when you actually advance your self-interest, not when you unquestioningly do what you were raised to do. Taking this wallet thus might become a kind of liberation for you, a defiant act of enlightenment, freeing you from the influence of the mushy, soft-headed propaganda your parents and teachers filled your formerly impressionable head with.

2. What about the Golden Rule? Wouldn't you want the old man to return your wallet if you dropped it?

Yes, but I am very careful not to drop my wallet. The Golden Rule, one might argue, is for suckers anyway. Fortunately, we live in a world with a lot of suckers. So, you could reason, the chances are good that if you ever did drop your wallet, some good-intentioned sucker would give it back to you. In the meantime, you can enjoy spending the old man's money.

The Deeper Skeptical Challenge to Ethics strikes at the very heart of our rationale for being moral. What can we say on behalf of the rationality of being ethical? How can it be rational to promote your welfare by caring for others for their sakes? Why should you be moral? Why should you have wide self-interest? We take up this Deep Skeptical Challenge to Ethics in Chapter 8.

7.10 Review

We began this chapter by distinguishing between two skeptical challenges to ethics. According to the Weak Skeptical Challenge to Ethics, it is not rational to act in ways that benefit others. On this view, the best way to promote your own good is to aim directly for it. Although we have already responded to this in Chapter 2, our consideration of the Weak Skeptical Challenge to Ethics led us to consider the Deep Skeptical Challenge to Ethics. This view asks how it can ever be rational to act primarily out of a concern for someone else for her or his sake. A response to this challenge presupposes that we can and do sometimes act for the sake of others, but we next considered a theory that claims that this is false. Psychological Egoism is a theory about human motivation according to which humans are motivated by a concern for their self-interest. In its extreme form, it is the view that humans always only aim to advance their self-interest, where an individual's self-interest is understood narrowly to be independent of the self-interest of others.

In the course of examining the case for extreme versions of Psychological Egoism, we noted that the theory interprets all human behaviour in terms of the advancing of self-interest. It thus excludes the possibility of being disconfirmed by counterevidence. As such, Psychological Egoism, we noted, is unfalsifiable and, rather than being a scientific theory, is what Karl Popper called a theory in pseudo-science. Once we recognized this, we raised the question whether Psychological Egoism, at least in its extreme forms, presents a convincing interpretation of human behaviour, and we observed that although the Extreme Psychological Egoist presents us with a possible interpretation of our behaviour, he offers little support for his view.

After considering the idea of the breadth of self-interest we moved on to examine Ethical Egoism, the theory that humans should be motivated only by their own self-interest. We noted that Ethical Egoists who conceive of self-interest as being very narrow deny that we can meet the Deep Skeptical Challenge to Ethics. Finally, in

the last part of the chapter, we considered the force of this challenge, which cleared the way for us to address it in Chapter 8.

Notes

1. Hume (1777), Appendix II, p. 143.

Exercises

Progress Check

1. What point does the example involving the old man illustrate?

2. Distinguish between the Weak and the Deep Skeptical Challenges to Ethics.

3. What is Psychological Egoism? Distinguish between deterministic and non-deterministic versions of the view. Distinguish between extreme and moderate versions.

4. How does the Extreme Psychological Egoist respond to the claim that we often act for selfless reasons?

5. What is Popper's distinction between science and pseudo-science?

6. Why is Extreme Psychological Egoism a pseudo-scientific theory?

7. What does it mean to say that someone has wide self-interest? What point does the example involving the slave owner illustrate?

8. What is Ethical Egoism?

9. Outline the strongest case you can for the view that it is not rational to return the old man's wallet.

Questions for Further Reflection

1. If you return the wallet to the old man because you want his praise and gratitude, is this proof that you really do care about him for his sake? Why or why not?

2. Our motivations for acting can be complex. We can act for both other-regarding reasons and for narrowly self-interested reasons. How can we judge our moral motivations as being "mainly" moral? What problems are there in interpreting one's own motivations?

3. Explain and critically evaluate one of the extreme versions of Psychological Egoism.

4. To what extent, if any, is the breadth of our self-interest subject to change and within our control? Defend your view.

5. Explain and critically discuss the strongest version of Ethical Egoism.

Group Work Activity:

The Breadth of Our Concern for Others

In this chapter we considered self-interest in terms of its breadth. We noted that we differ in the extent to which we care about others. People like Gandhi, Martin Luther King Jr., and Nelson Mandela have devoted much of their lives to improving the lives of many thousands of other people. In contrast, most of us seem to care mostly about our own relatively small circle of friends and family. Thus we seem to differ in terms of how wide our self-interest is. In your groups, consider the following questions:

1. Prudentially speaking, how wide should your self-interest be? In other words, how many other beings should you care about to live the life highest in prudential welfare? Can you go too far? Can you care about too many others at the expense of your own happiness? Are we all alike or are we different in this respect? Do you think people like Gandhi, King, and Mandela have lived happy lives? Why or why not? Discuss.

2. Is the goal of living a life high in prudential value compatible with being a morally good person? What tensions can you detect between achieving these goals? Discuss.

Group Work Activity:

The Depth of Our Concern for Others

In this chapter we compared differences in the breadth of our concern for others. We noted that some people seem to have fairly narrow self-interest, whereas others seem to have very wide self-interest. Though it is useful to distinguish in these ways, our account is incomplete in a number of respects. For example, we also differ in terms of the depths of our concerns for others. Some care about others only a little bit; others care passionately. Some care about others only enough to call the fire department if they are in trouble. Others care enough to run into the burning building. Your task is to try to develop an account of how we might judge and compare differences in the depths of our concerns for others. Try to develop your view as much as possible.

Weblinks

Lawrence Hinman has an excellent Web site on Egoism with numerous references to related literature at **ethics.acusd.edu/theories/Egoism/index.html**

For more on Egoism, go to **The Internet Encyclopedia of Philosophy** entry on the topic at **www.utm.edu/research/iep/e/egoism.htm**

To begin investigating the ideas of Ayn Rand, a famous defender of Ethical Egoism, go to **www.aynrand.org**

For an interesting Web site on the Golden Rule in world scriptures, go to **members.aol.com/ porchfour/religion/golden.htm**

8 A Practical Justification of Morality: Love, Friendship, and Welfare

Learning Outcomes

In this chapter we continue our work from Chapter 7. We take up the Deep Skeptical Challenge to Ethics by considering why it can be prudentially good for someone to care about others for their sakes. To present this view, we consider three examples that lead us into an examination of the nature and value of love and friendship. The chapter thus presents a challenge to some versions of Ethical Egoism. We also consider a feminist objection to the argument advanced by Nel Noddings, according to which the traditional focus on rationally justifying morality distorts our experience of the moral life. Finally, we point ahead to Chapter 12 where we consider a holist argument in Environmental Philosophy that is friendly to Noddings's objection.

Upon the successful completion of this chapter you will be able to

1. appreciate the Deeper Skeptical Challenge to Ethics;

2. understand the value of having wide self-interest;

3. explain the perspective of the exclusively narrowly self-interested person in three cases;

4. identify the nature of true love and friendship;

5. explicate the problem of loving true friends and loved ones unconditionally;

6. say why money can't buy you love;

7. have some awareness of why true friendships are not necessarily moral;

8. outline the value to society of having ethical citizens, and;

9. summarize Noddings' ethic of care and the criticism her view presents to the traditional philosophical project of trying to justify morality.

8.1 Introduction

As we noted in Section 7.3, the Deep Skeptical Challenge to Ethics forces us to explain why we should, prudentially speaking, act out of a concern for another person for his sake. In other words, is there a connection between promoting the prudential welfare of another person for her sake and thereby promoting one's own prudential welfare? Why should we cultivate having wide self-interest? In reaching this understanding of this skeptical challenge, we have distinguished it from the Weak Skeptical Challenge to Ethics. As we noted, we can act in ways that benefit others without being motivated by a concern for whom we benefit, according to which it is not rational to act in ways that benefit others. As we noted in Section 7.3, the skeptic advancing the Weak Skeptical Challenge to Ethics wonders about the rationality of returning the wallet to the old man for any reason. In contrast, the skeptic advancing the Deep Skeptical Challenge to Ethics wonders about the rationality of returning the wallet to the old man out of a concern for him.

A failure to mark the distinction between the two challenges leads to the overly easy dismissal of the Deep Skeptical Challenge to Ethics. We saw that there is much to be said for co-operation, and if the skeptical doubts about the value of morality could be met merely by pointing to the benefits of co-operating with others, there would be little to wonder and worry about. But the Deep Skeptical Challenge to Ethics doesn't question the wisdom of engaging in co-operative behaviour; it questions the wisdom of caring for others for their sakes, of having wide self-interest. Our task now is to try to meet this challenge.

This might seem a rather odd or perhaps even useless undertaking. After all, most of us have wide self-interest; there are very few sociopaths. Why bother defending a perspective most of us already take, especially since we feel that this is the way we should be? The reason is that wide self-interest is not simply an all-or-nothing concept. Although we can contrast the idea of having narrow self-interest with the notion of having wide self-interest, we can also think about how wide our self-interest should be. Should we care for many others or only for our own small circle of family and friends? Should we embrace the great social causes of our day, the causes that significantly impact the lives of thousands or even millions of others? Should our concern stretch even further to encompass caring for all the sentient creatures of our planet?

We also differ in terms of the depth of our concerns. Should we care a little or a lot? Should we care just enough to not directly harm others, or should we care as passionately as we can? Should we reserve our greatest concerns for our family and friends and just a little for everyone else, or should we try to distribute our caring more equally? Part of the value of addressing the Deep Skeptical Challenge to Ethics is that doing so forces us to appreciate how wide and deep our self-interest is, and to reflect upon how wide and deep it should become. So although it is true that we already care about others for their sakes, we differ greatly in terms of the breadth and depth of our caring.

Of course the depth and breadth of our caring for others for their sakes is not fixed and unchangeable; they vary both in terms of their scope and their intensity. Because we can exercise a great deal of control over both, we can modify our caring by coming to understand reasons for changing. These reasons are the subject of our enquiry.

In this chapter we will consider the argument that generally life goes better having wide self-interest. To appreciate this, we will need to examine the nature of love and friendship, and how having these can contribute to living a prudentially good life. We will discover why money can't buy us love, and we will broach the topic of the moral limits of loving another person. Most people simply take it for granted that love and friendship are prudentially good, but understanding the contribution love and friendship make to meeting the Deep Skeptical Challenge to Ethics helps us better appreciate the nature and value of these basic human goods.

Most textbooks on ethics devote very little space to these topics, which is odd. Perhaps their exclusion is due to an overemphasis on traditional moral theory, or at least on traditional moral theories that focus on duty, obligation, and right conduct. This lack of emphasis is inversely proportional to the importance of love and friendship in our lives, or at least the lives of most of us. Perhaps this partly accounts for why the philosophical study of ethics has been as disconnected from life as it has been. Rather than regard the study of ethics as being academic in the pejorative sense, answering the question "Why be moral?" leads us to considering important practical issues at the heart of most people's lives.

8.2 Three Cases

Let's begin our enquiry into the Deep Skeptical Challenge to Ethics by considering three cases. Rather than worry about trying to prudentially justify being moral, perhaps we should set our cares aside and embrace the rationality of merely acting co-operatively without caring for others for their sakes. After all, we have clearly shown the benefits of acting co-operatively, of acting in ways that benefit both others and ourselves, and this amply meets the Weak Skeptical Challenge to Ethics. As for the deeper concern about the prudential value of having wide self-interest, perhaps the best response is to join the skeptics.

Before we do so, however, we should consider the argument for the rationality of caring for others for their sakes. To make this argument, it will be useful to first consider some cases designed to test our intuitions. The first two cases involve situations where there is no obvious co-operative benefit from helping a friend or loved one and the challenge thus becomes to try to explain why we, prudentially speaking, should act to help them. The third case involves an idea for a friendship store that encourages us to explain why friendship cannot be purchased.

1. The Case of the Dying Friend

Imagine that your best friend, gravely ill, is in the hospital. You know that visiting her will make her happy because she is rather depressed and you always know how to cheer her up. As a result of some incontrovertible evidence, you reasonably believe that, sadly, she will likely die very soon, perhaps before the night is out. However, hospitals give you the creeps, and you always find visiting people there makes you depressed. Even worse, since you promised your sick friend that you would visit her, another friend has acquired a couple of tickets to an entertainment spectacular that you are dying to see. Tonight, as it turns out, is your last chance because the show's run is ending with this evening's final performance.

Prudentially speaking, what should you do? Should you keep your promise to your dying friend, swallow your aversion to visiting hospitals, and help make her final moments good ones? Imagine further that she has no other friends or family and that if you don't visit her, she will spend her last hours in the company of strangers or, even worse, alone. Also assume that no one else will ever find out about your promise so that if you don't visit her, you won't have to explain your behaviour to anyone. Should you instead go to the show and enjoy what is quite likely to be a once-in-a-lifetime entertainment experience? Your friend is going to die anyway, and there is nothing you can do about that. *C'est la vie!*

2. The Case of Arranging the Murder of a Loved One for Profit

Here is an even more outlandish scenario. Think about the person that you love most in the world. Let's say, for argument's sake, that it is your mother. What is the prudential value of your relationship with her to you? One could argue that most of what you receive from her can be identified as various goods and services. Maybe she makes things for you and always remembers you on your birthday. She offers you support and encouragement, and she helps you when you need advice or when you are down. Isn't it true that most of what she offers you can be purchased on an open market? We could pay people to buy us things, send us birthday cards, offer us advice and encouragement, and so on.

Next, imagine a mysterious and strangely powerful spirit convinces you that he can reliably quantify the total remaining goods and services that your mother will give you for the rest of her life. Imagine, just for argument's sake, that the spirit predicts accurately, and he says that it would cost about $100 000 to buy all the goods and services that your mother will provide you with until she dies. Furthermore, he says he will give you $200 000 if you let him kill her now. You just need to give the word. Imagine there is no chance that anyone will find out about your connection to your mother's death, so you needn't worry about going to prison. Prudentially speaking, should you accept his offer?

3. The Friendship Store

Consider my idea of "The Friendship Store." It is really a service where, for a monthly fee, I provide people with friends. My concept goes beyond offering my customers short-term companionship, and it isn't some sort of cover for purchasing sex. It is an ongoing payment-for-friendship business. People in need of friendship select a promising potential friend from my huge computer directory of contract employees. I carefully screen my employees and provide extensive friendship training for them. I also help match potential friends according to backgrounds, interests, political and religious beliefs and values, and so on. To ensure a high rate of friendship uptake, I provide my customers with personality testing and advice from my staff of expert psychologists. I then arrange an initial meeting and offer ongoing support.

Typically, the friendships start slowly, the way friendships do. At first, my customers spend only a few hours with their new friend, but as the relationships develop, they spend more and more time together. My customers often find they need to see my employees more often and for longer stretches. My staff keeps time sheets and because monthly fees are based on the length of time and nature of the goods and services provided by the hired friends, and because contact increases as time passes, I get richer and richer.

Moreover, I feel good about myself because I provide the public with a valuable service. I'm really a humanitarian. I help make people happier. There are many lonely, busy people out there with plenty of disposable income, and I set them up on their way to enjoying the benefits of true friendship. We all know how important it is to have true friends. If I can make the world a better place and make a buck in the process, what's wrong with that? Win-win.

The rationale behind my business is sound, too. Friendship is wonderful, but when you think about it, what do we really receive from our friends? Sometimes they buy us things like dinner and presents. They also effectively provide us with services. When we are sad, lonely, or frustrated, our friends listen sympathetically, support us, and sometimes offer us useful advice. They act as confidantes and amateur counsellors and therapists. They share in our good times. We also talk and spend time together. As the years roll by, we develop a history, and our identities become more closely and deeply connected.

All of these goods and services, everything our friends give us, can, in principle, be purchased on an open market for a price. It is true that you cannot buy memories of a shared history (yet), but I am not running The Old Friendship Store. All of the friendships I administer start from scratch. Though my business has the disadvantage of not being able to instantly offer long-time, developed friendship, it has the advantage of allowing customers to choose their friends more carefully than most of us currently do. Let's face it, our friends are not perfect. And although Friendship Store friends are not perfect either, quite likely they are superior to the friends you have now. The Friendship Store offers you the opportunity of exchanging or gradually replacing your present, flawed friends with some new ones from my team of professionals. The potential market for my business is huge. The Friendship Store should appeal not only to the lonely and busy but also to people looking for a change. All you need is money.

Is there a flaw in The Friendship Store idea? Can money buy you friendship? Why or why not?

8.3 The Cases Considered from the Perspective of Someone with Narrow Self-interest

Before we refocus our attention on taking up the Deep Skeptical Challenge to Ethics, let's consider the examples again from the perspective of a defender of narrow self-interest, say an Ethical Egoist with narrow self-interest (see 7.8 for an explanation of this view). This will help us appreciate the strength of this position.

Regarding the Case of the Dying Friend

The task here is to explain why we should, prudentially speaking, go visit our sick friend. Someone with narrow self-interest would say that we should go to the show instead. Recall from Section 2.9 that, provided there is a reasonable guarantee that co-operation can be enforced, it is rational to co-operate with others because there are benefits available to individuals acting together that are not available to individuals acting on their own. This applies to your relationship with your friend. Until now, you have co-operated with each other because you each appreciated the mutual benefits of doing so. Having friends is prudentially good. During the course of your relationship, you have helped your friend and she has helped you. As a result, you gained many benefits that otherwise you would not have enjoyed. Your friendship has enriched both lives.

However, the question is, Why should you co-operate with her now? Perhaps you think you should visit her because you owe it to her. But, as someone with narrow self-interest, you don't care about her for her sake, and given your reasonable expectation of her imminent demise, there is no reason to think that if you go to the hospital you will receive in return any compensating co-operative benefit. For you two, there is no tomorrow. It might sound cold, but she will likely be dead by morning and incapable of offering anything to you to prudentially justify your visiting her tonight. It would be different if she calls and tells you to get over to the hospital right away or else she will cut you out of her will, at least if she has a decent-sized estate. That would give you an incentive to go. The money you would receive from her estate would enable you to buy things that outweigh the disvalue of missing the show. For that, too, you could swallow the bad experience of going to the hospital tonight. But she doesn't call and tell you this.

You might think that only a cold and immoral person would think these thoughts, but so what? You are just being sensible. The experience of going to the show would be much better than going to the hospital. The show will be fun and exciting; the hospital, creepy and depressing. What could prudentially justify going to the hospital instead? Why should you care about your friend for her sake? Going to the show best advances your welfare, and if you want to live a prudentially good life, you should do things that best promote your well-being.

Remember, too, that as Ethical Egoists, we can't say we should go to the hospital because we will feel guilty, ashamed, or bad if we don't, or alternatively, that we will feel good about ourselves if we do, because we are consciously trying to choose what's prudentially best for us and base our feelings on that. If, on reflection, you think that you have been brainwashed or somehow manipulated into making this promise and doing this prudentially bad thing, why should you feel guilty about not doing it? On the other hand, why would you feel good about acting stupidly, once you see the folly of your promise? It is everyone for himself or herself. Indeed, if the situation were reversed, you would expect your friend to go to the show too, and you would marvel at her foolishness if she decided to visit you instead, wouldn't you?

Regarding the Case of Arranging the Murder of a Loved One for Profit

Many of the considerations that apply in the analysis of the first example apply here, too. Speaking again as someone with narrow self-interest, we can see that plainly you should take up the spirit's offer and accept the $200 000. How could anyone prudentially justify not doing this? With the money, you can purchase almost everything your mother would have provided you with, and on top of that, you can use the extra $100 000 to buy things that will further enhance your welfare. If you want to, you can pay someone some of the extra money to supply you with even more services. Instead of mom, you could have Supermom! This is much better for you than letting your mother live. Again, if the roles were reversed, wouldn't she take up the offer? If you refused, wouldn't she shake her head at having raised such a dumb child?

In response, someone might point out that we noted that *most* of what your mother offers you could be purchased on an open market. What about the things that can't be so purchased? What are these things, and would their loss tip the balance in favour of not taking the offer? Although another person might be able to provide you with many of the goods and services that your mother will offer you over the course of the rest of her life, *something will be missing.* But what exactly? And why should you care? People say that anyone can give you things and do things for you, but you have only one mother. This is true, but so what? What is so special about her giving you things and doing things for you?

Some might say that money can't buy emotion. But this is both vague and false. When we pay to go to the movies or to be entertained, aren't we effectively buying emotional experiences? When we go to the movies, we experience excitement, joy, sadness, anger, melancholy, frustration, and a whole range of other emotions. If there is a special, irreplaceable feeling that contributes to your happiness, which you get from your mother and could not pay someone else to give you, and the risk of losing this feeling makes it reasonable for you to not take up the spirit's offer, what is this feeling?

Likewise, in this vein, people sometimes say that money isn't everything. What are "the kinds of things that money just can't buy"? Are they the feelings that go with love and friendship? You can't buy love at the movies. The Beatles said they don't care too much for money, because money can't buy them love. But they don't tell us why. What is love, anyway? And why is it so prudentially valuable?

Consider this: Because she loves you, your mother's giving is genuine and sincere. She gives out of her love for you, someone might suggest, and not out of an expectation of receiving anything in return. Supermom might also give, but her giving won't be genuine. It is this genuineness that you would lose by having your mother killed. Even if this is true, so what? How would this loss of love and genuineness cancel out the prudential value of the extra $100 000 for you? Sincere as her giving may be, your mother still gives you only the finite amount that she gives, and now you are being offered twice as much. Why isn't it in your prudential interest to take the greater amount over the lesser? Shouldn't you jump at this chance and be grateful for having such a fabulous opportunity?

In light of what we have seen so far, you also might doubt whether your mom's giving is so genuine. Why are you so sure that she loves you? She says she does, but perhaps she is deceiving herself. It is easy to misinterpret her behaviour, as we have observed in connection with the example of returning the old man's wallet from Chapter 7. You know that she has performed actions that have been good for you many times, but why should you think that she cares about you for your sake? Why would that be rational? Some might say that you should not have your mother killed because you owe her for having given you life. But what if you have worked off your debt to her? Certainly this is possible, isn't it? Maybe you saved her life, and did many things that have benefited her over the years, so now you are even. Perhaps all those times you thought she was acting out of love for you, she was merely acting in her own narrow self-interest by performing actions that benefited her. Again, it's just like the example of returning the old man's wallet.

Your relationship with your mother has been a co-operative one. She has helped you and you have helped her. As a result of your co-operation, you each have enjoyed benefits that you otherwise wouldn't have enjoyed. Now, however, things have changed. Now you are presented with an opportunity to benefit by harming her. Since she cannot offer you anything of equal or greater value by co-operating with her and not having her killed, you have no reason to do so. The rational thing is to accept the spirit's offer.

As far as you can see from a narrow self-interest, the only thing that your mother offers of value that Supermom doesn't is her ability to give based on your shared past, and her extensive knowledge of you. This perhaps is irreplaceable. You have many happy memories of your past co-operative activities, and your mother's knowledge of your character and preferences specially advantages her when you co-operate. Still, how could this cancel out the extra $100 000? It is worth something, but not that much. It would also be a mistake to think that because something is irreplaceable, it is therefore very valuable. I'll never get another pair of shoes exactly like the ones I'm wearing now, so they too are, in a sense, irreplaceable. But that doesn't make them worth $100 000.

It is true that you and Supermom will be starting from scratch, but so what? When your mother dies, you will still have your memories of your good times together. Maybe over time you can teach Supermom to give you superior goods and services than your mom ever could. That extra $100 000 can make up for a lot, and besides, only fools are sentimental.

Regarding The Friendship Store

From a narrow self-interested perspective, there seems to be nothing wrong with the idea of The Friendship Store, either. The underlying premise of the business is that true friends offer each other goods and services that promote each other's happiness, and that these goods and services can, in principle, be purchased on a market. This premise seems sound. If your friends didn't contribute to your well-being by giving you things and doing things for you, why would you want them as friends? They would be of no use

to you. Thus, when you go to The Friendship Store, you are looking to buy what friends offer each other. Since this is something of value, it makes sense that you will have to pay for it. Nothing good in life is free.

8.4 Reason and Passion

The defender of narrow self-interest accepts the wisdom of living one's life guided by reason. However, we might reply to the logic of the arguments presented by the narrowly self-interested person by saying that there is more to life than logic. The problem with you, we might say, is that you are too cold. Your dispassionate obsession with being rational is your undoing. If you want to be really happy, you need to care, to feel for others. By obsessively searching for a rational justification for ethics, your effort to be happy is doomed from the start. It is a mistake to try to rationally justify caring for others.

The flaw in this response is that it is based on a false dichotomy. We do not have to choose between either being rational or being caring. The example of the apparently reasonable but uncaring narrowly self-interested person leads us astray. Feeling strongly that we should visit our dying friend and that we should not have our mother killed, we are tempted to reject rationality rather than our loved ones. But we can have our cake and eat it too. The life of passion and reason are not mutually exclusive, and the example of the cool, uncaring, narrowly self-interested person provides us with no good reason for thinking otherwise. We can live examined lives and care for each other. We need only look to a good argument for being compassionate to affirm this belief.

8.5 Distinguishing Ethics from Altruism

The examples we have been considering in this chapter are useful because they help focus our thoughts on the Deep Skeptical Challenge to

Ethics. They press us to explain why we should care about others for their sakes. As we have seen, when we are faced with cases where the challenge is to prudentially justify acting co-operatively, we can often defend our behaviour. However, these first two cases are different because, as the defender of narrow self-interest observes, it is not so obvious that acting co-operatively here would be wise. Yet unquestionably, most of us would not abandon our terminally ill best friend or have a loved one killed even for a great amount of money. Moreover, we think that this makes sense too. These are not just the right things to do; they are also the rational things to do. How can we explain this?

The defender of narrow self-interest thinks that when we act in these ways, we operate on autopilot. We don't think, we just do. Since it so often happens that caring for others makes prudential sense, we overlook those times when it does not, and we act irrationally by acting for the sake of another when we will not receive any decent compensating benefit in return. The defender of narrow self-interest would say that what we need to do is stop and think. Perhaps if we see that co-operating with others is often justified, but caring for them for their sakes is not, when we are faced with a situation where we are required to act for another's sake, we will act more intelligently and look out for our interests. By all means be willing to co-operate, but do so only when there is something in it for you. This sort of reasoning might also appeal to people who think that ethics always requires sacrifice, and that to be ethical one must be altruistic. This, some believe, is idealistic and something we will grow out of. It might sound selfish but, if you want to make it in the real world, they say, you have to look out for number one.

The error in this can again be traced to a false dichotomy. The idea that promoting the prudential good of someone else for her sake can thereby make your life better off will seem ridiculous if you assume that your self-interest is not dependent on how others fare. If you equate self-interest with narrow self-interest, then acting for the sake of another may indeed appear altruistic and self-sacrificing. But why should we think that we must choose between acting to promote our own prudential good or acting altruistically to promote the prudential good of others? The notion that our prudential good can overlap with the prudential good of others is certainly possible. Once we accept it as a possibility, we are presented with an alternative to the narrow conception of self-interest. And once we reach this point, we need reasons for thinking that having narrow self-interest is prudentially superior to having wide self-interest. Although this might be true for some people, we should not just assume that it is true for everyone. Here we need to look and see. Our challenge, then, is becoming clearer. We must explain and defend the account of wide self-interest introduced in Chapter 7.

8.6 Lessons the Cases Teach Us about Love, Friendship, and the Prudential Value of Caring for Others

We can begin by re-examining the three cases. Let's start with the concept of The Friendship Store. This is perhaps the easiest one. What's wrong with the idea of a Friendship Store? When presented with this story, many people say that Friendship Store "friends" are not really friends. If they were true friends, they would not take money for doing the things they do. Are Friendship Store "friends" only conditionally friends, that is, are they "friends" only on the condition that the client pays his account each month?

Imagine that you hired one of these "friends" and that everything has been going smoothly until you call your hired "friend" early one morning. Someone dear to you has just passed away, and you ask your Friendship Store "friend" to come over to be with you. Imagine, further, that your account at The Friendship Store is overdue, and your hired "friend" knows this. What would she do? If she were a true friend, she would want to be with you. As a Friendship

Store "friend," however, she is not getting paid, and it is against company policy to go. If she does come over, then that shows she has now become a true friend, and she is no longer acting as a hired "friend." Hired friends are in it for the money and therefore can never be true friends. This shows that the whole concept of a friendship store is nonsense.

So we consider so-called Friendship Store "friendships" conditional, whereas true friendship is unconditional. In this case, the condition of friendship is that one friend pays the other each month to continue with the relationship. But this analysis is still flawed. The problem is with the idea that true friendship is unconditional. This sounds impressive, but it is an exaggeration. We sometimes say that we love our friends, children, parents, brothers, sisters "no matter what," that is, unconditionally. But arguably, this should not be the case. The idea of unconditional love is odd; it is the kind of love that some people think God has for us. Thus some say that God loves us no matter what, regardless of what we do. As Neera Kapur Badhwar has pointed out, however, unconditional love is impersonal.[1] If I love you no matter what, then regardless of what you do and who you become, I will love you. If this is the case, then in what sense do I love *you*, the unique, irreplaceable individual? We love our friends for who they are. We don't think that anyone could be substituted for them. Yet if you love someone unconditionally, then you are in effect saying they could be substituted.

Imagine your best friend, someone you have known for years, has always been sweet and considerate. Lately, however, he's started to change. There's a harder edge to his attitude and demeanour. At first, you attribute this personality change to some hardship he has experienced. But over time it becomes more and more evident that his change is not temporary. His formerly charming veneer of gruffness gradually gives way to a disconcerting and then a disturbing new ruthlessness. He starts getting into fights in public. Before you know it, he has taken up axe murdering.

Admittedly, the transformation from Boy Scout to axe murderer is outrageous. But the likelihood of something like this occurring isn't relevant. The point is, if you are truly committed to your avowal that you love him unconditionally, then you would have to say you love him just as much now as you ever did. After all, you love him no matter what, for better or worse. This is so even if *he* no longer respects the person he has become. When you tell him through the prison bars that you love him as much as you always did, and he realizes you are being sincere, he might rightly wonder whom it was you thought you loved in the past. Your admission might lead him to negatively reassess his view of your feelings for him, especially given his new sense of self-loathing. Ironically, your expression of everlasting love for your friend in his darkest moment depresses him, as it should. Rather than feeling that he was at least well-loved by you in the past, he now realizes that it wasn't him you loved in particular. He was merely a placeholder for anyone because if he was loved unconditionally, he wasn't loved for his own unique qualities and style.

Our desire to express our commitment to our loved ones by proclaiming that we love them no matter what confuses steadfastness with unqualified loving. We want to be steadfast, and not fair-weather friends, and stand by our loved ones through hard times. But this can be carried too far. People grow, and our love for others is not static. Relationships evolve in many different ways, and our identities don't usually undergo dramatic transformations overnight. Personal conditional loving must make allowances for these facts. Furthermore, as the axe murderer example shows, the nature of the change counts too. There is a rightful limit to the kind of changes that we can accommodate.

The flaw in the concept of The Friendship Store is not that Friendship Store "friendships" are conditional. The problem is with the nature of the conditions of the "friendship." As Aristotle argued, **true friendship,** or what he referred to as character friendship, involves mutually recognized and mutually reciprocated well-wishing

True friendship involves mutually recognized and reciprocated well-wishing for the sake of one's friend.

for the sake of one's friend. The problem with Friendship Store "friends" is that their primary motivation is financial. They are not mainly acting out of a concern for their "friends"; they are working for their own financial gain. The test of this is that once their customers cannot pay, the hired "friends" will not be there for them. This is the way fair-weather "friends" behave. In contrast, if you really love someone, you will be there for her because you care about her for her own sake, even if it is unpleasant or difficult.

The main problem with the narrow self-interested analysis of the examples is that this perspective asks only what our friends and loved ones can directly give or do for us. Regarded in this way, perhaps the rational thing to do is to abandon our sick friends and our loved ones. But this measure of the value of our relationships is incomplete. It overlooks the value of caring about another person for his sake. Of course, if your well-being is independent of the well-being of others, you will not experience this sort of good. You cannot, according to Aristotle's sensible account, even be a true friend because true friends care about each other for the other person's sake. Relations between friends and loved ones, like other morally motivated behaviours, share the quality of demonstrated concern for another person for her sake.

We can appreciate the prudential value of caring for another person for his sake only by expanding our understanding of the nature of our own prudential welfare. If we consider the possibility that our well-being depends upon how other people fare in life, then we can see why it is rational for us to visit our sick friend and not sell our mother for $200 000. If you have self-interest wide enough to include the well-being of your friend, then visiting her for her sake makes prudential sense for you because your good is dependent on her good. You don't help her in order to feel better about yourself. Rather, as a result of helping her, you feel better. Once you feel this way about her, prudentially speaking, you should go to the hospital because you care more that she not suffer than that you have fun at the show. Indeed, given your wide self-interest, you could not enjoy your time at the show know-

ing that she is suffering and that you could be doing something to relieve that suffering. It is not that you wouldn't enjoy the show under better circumstances. You would. It is also not that the hospital environment is creepy and depressing. It is. But given your deep regard for your friend, for her sake, you would rightly feel awful at the thought of her spending her last moments in a state of miserable abandonment. The thought of this would make you sick. A similar analysis applies in the case of your mother. You would not sell her for $200 000 because your good is dependent on hers to a great extent. Given your deep attachment to and love for your mother, whatever of value you could purchase with the extra money cannot cancel out the disvalue to you of her death. The loss of the value of her life to her would greatly diminish your happiness. This is very much like the example we considered in Chapter 7 from Hume of the woman who dies of grief at the loss of her child.

8.7 Why Money Can't Buy You Love

The goods of love and friendship can be fully experienced only by those with wide self-interest, by those who can be motivated by concern for another person for her sake. People with narrow self-interest cannot experience these goods, and so we should approach narrow self-interested analyses of the value of love and friendship with caution. Since these goods cannot really be purchased, they are not easily compared to goods and services we can buy on a market. Money can't buy us love because love is the state and experience of caring for another being for that being's sake. Such caring doesn't materialize instantly or come with a money-back guarantee. The value of your love for your mother cannot be replaced, let alone augmented, by Supermom. You don't wish her ill, but you don't much care about Supermom, either. You love your mother.

The examples in this chapter hardly do justice to the value we derive from caring about others. Our love for those we care about is not usually a burden; it is the source of much of our happiness. We take delight in our loved ones' happiness, as they do in ours, and this delight compounds our own joy in a way that someone with narrow self-interest cannot appreciate. This mutuality adds richness and meaning to our lives.

This is also not to say that everyone should have wide self-interest. Some people are happier with narrow self-interest. Rather, many of us can and do have wide self-interest, and for most of us, life goes better being this way. Not only can it be moral to care about others for their sakes; it can be rational, too. Each of us must discover for himself or herself when and to what extent we, prudentially speaking, should care about others, but our analysis of the value of having wide self-interest meets the Deep Skeptical Challenge to Ethics.

8.8 The Moral Limits of Loving Another

Establishing the rationality of having wide self-interest is one thing; specifying how wide it should be is another. Both prudentially and ethically speaking, how much should we care about others? Many views in ethics dispute this issue. We have also noted the similarity between friendship, love, and morality. But there are puzzles here, too. Friends care about each other for each others' sakes, but is all loving ethical? One problem is that there is some competition for our concern. There are many beings out there who make claims on our affections, and there is much potential for conflict. For example, it may be rational of you to prefer that your mother not be killed to receiving $200 000. But here we have been assuming that the extra money would be used for your own narrow self-interested ends, say, to buy things that will make your own life easier. Things get more complicated, however, when you weigh the value of your loved one's life not against extra goods for yourself but against vital goods for others.

Imagine you had to choose between your mother continuing to live or receiving $100 million from the mysterious spirit. Although you might be able to make some case for the view that it would be rational of you still to prefer that

your mother live, it would be considerably more difficult for you to defend the view that this would be the ethical choice. You could do a lot of good for many suffering people in the world with $100 million. Imagine that if you don't take up this offer, the spirit would otherwise not distribute the equivalent of $100 million worth of goods and services. Arguably, the value of your mother's life doesn't outweigh this. So if the choice is between your mother living and many other people not suffering and perhaps surviving, then arguably, you should morally choose the good of the many.

This variation on our original example raises difficult questions, some of which we will begin to address in the next chapter. As we shall see, problems like these in ethics are not as hopeless as they sometimes might appear.

8.9 The Value to Society of Having Ethical Citizens

Throughout our discussion in this chapter and Chapter 7, we have focused our attention on answering the question, Why be moral? The case we have considered for having wide self-interest is good, but we can expand our account of the prudential value of being moral by widening our focus. Thus far, the argument for the rationality of caring for others for their sakes has centred on the prudential value of love and deep friendship. But we can add to our case by thinking more carefully about the prudential benefits of caring for other people in society for their sakes.

The argument about the value of love and friendship is instructive, but it doesn't address a question lingering from Chapter 7. Although we can see why prudentially we should care about our close friends and loved family members, why should we care about strangers for their sakes? How can promoting the good of strangers for their sakes advance our own well-being? The benefits alluded to in the examples of helping one's closest friend and mother rested on the depth of our relationships. But there is no such depth when one talks about helping strangers or casual acquaintances. Perhaps the Deep Skeptical

Challenge to Ethics still applies here? Reconsider the example from Chapter 7 of the old man dropping his wallet. Although we might now see a reason for returning wallets dropped by our dearest friends and loved ones, why, prudentially speaking, should you return the wallet to the old man? To what extent can you take delight in returning his property, given that he is a stranger you are likely never to meet again? More to the point, doesn't the prudential value of keeping his wallet outweigh whatever benefit you receive by helping him for his sake? Here, of course, we are assuming the situation is such that you needn't worry about being seen or getting caught by any-one else if you keep the wallet.

This worry is not one that has typically been carefully considered. Some have noted that the likelihood of such situations arising is so low that we needn't worry about them. Others have ventured that the mental effort needed to deter-mine when one should take advantage of another person's hardship in this way without being detected is so great that we shouldn't bother. It is easier to just habitually do what's right. Returning the wallet is simpler, easier to learn, easier to teach, and easier to do. Though there is some merit in these responses, they are incom-plete. There is more to be said on behalf of the prudential value of caring for others than we have so far noted. To see this, let's revisit another point from Chapter 2.

We saw there that there are two ways by which we achieve co-operation in society, through the coercive power of law or extra-legal threats and through being motivated out of a concern for others for their sakes. We also noted that we can enjoy the benefits of co-operation without being motivated by a concern for others for their sakes; narrowly self-interested people can co-operate for their mutual advantage. One might think that this is all we need. Even further, we might be tempted to think that, with a rea-sonable guarantee that co-operation will be enforced, it would be redundant for people to care about each other, at least with respect to the kinds of benefits we documented in the water shortage and taxation examples from Section 2.9.

Consider a variation of an example by the

nineteenth-century English jurist John Austin (1790–1859), and discussed by H.L.A. Hart. A gunman approaches you in an alley late one night. Pointing his gun at you, he informs you that he wants to be your friend. In the spirit of your new friendship, he adds, he wants you to hand over your money and your watch. If you believe that he will act on his threat if you don't co-operate, why should you be concerned about him for his sake? It seems like some kind of joke. More generally, why should we in society encourage people to care about each other to facilitate co-operation if we have a legal system in place that already reasonably guarantees com-pliance with the law? Why should we care about our fellow citizens for their sakes?

To begin to answer this question, we can note the difference between ensuring that you co-operate with the gunman and ensuring that people in society co-operate generally. The gun-man's threat is difficult to avoid. In contrast, ensuring co-operation in a complex modern society where a system of law applies to perhaps millions of people is much more difficult. In society it is easier to be a parasite or a free rider. People beat the system all the time. Not all income is reported and taxed, and we can't have everyone audited or a police officer on every cor-ner. Even in totalitarian and authoritarian states where high rates of compliance with the law are achieved mainly through coercive threats, people need to care about each other too. As Hart has noted, all humans are vulnerable. Even the most powerful and murderous dictators must sleep, and so must rely on the help of some supporters.

In response, some say that although it might not be feasible to have police on every corner, we can greatly minimize incidents of lawbreaking by having a powerful and extensive security force, as they do in some repressive states. This is true, but it points to some advantages to society of having cit-izens who genuinely care about each other. As an illustration, consider the following story. Once when I was staying with relatives in downtown Toronto, I tried to rent a video at a corner store. The man behind the counter wanted me to show him two pieces of identification and sign a blank credit card voucher in the amount of $300 as a security deposit to rent one video. Compare that experience to one I had in a small holiday cottage community. When I enquired about renting a video at a store there, the woman behind the counter said that it would be no trouble. She just wanted to know the last four digits of the phone number of the cottage where I was staying so she could call to remind me to return the rental if I forgot to do so on time. What accounts for the differences in policy between the two businesses? They were both there to make money, but only the lady at the cottage-country store seemed to welcome my business. As it turns out, since I was so suspicious and anxious about leaving the security deposit, I ended up not renting a video at the store in Toronto.

No doubt the owner of that store would have preferred to have a more trusting policy, but past experience probably taught him otherwise. Probably as a result of people not returning movies, he needed to implement a strong coercive threat to encourage potential customers to co-operate. In contrast, the proprietor of the small-town store likely didn't experience much theft, so there was no need for a heavy-handed policy. Looking a little deeper, we can see that there were other relevant differences too. The store in Toronto was located in a busy, impersonal neighbourhood where people were strangers. The country store was located in an environment where, despite the temporary summer inhabitants, people mostly knew and trusted each other. They were a lot friendlier, too. This suggests that people were more likely to care about each other in the small town than in the big city.

What do the stories teach us about the benefits of having citizens who care about each other for each others' sakes? Apart from the fact that the country store was more welcoming, the rentals were cheaper. The owner of that store didn't have to purchase an elaborate and expensive security system, so those savings could be passed along to her customers. In contrast, the owner of the store in Toronto needed such a system, in addition to the other strict policies, to protect his investment. Not surprisingly, these costs were also passed onto his customers.

We can see more evidence of the advantages in the respective communities of the two stores.

The condominium complex I was staying at in the city was like an armed camp. Guards screened visitors behind thick Plexiglas windows. In the small town, people didn't even bother locking their doors at night or when they went out. Applying this lesson to society in general, we can see that states populated by citizens who genuinely care about each other achieve their co-operation more efficiently and with less expense. Since they don't have to spend so much on things like law enforcement, correctional institutions, and the justice system to achieve compliance, such states can devote more resources to other goods, like public health and education. Furthermore, there is much to be said for the contribution that friendliness makes to living a good life. People genuinely motivated by goodwill toward their fellow citizens in turn generally enjoy life in their communities and share in the good fortune and lives of those around them. These feelings are extensions of some of the benefits of a life filled with love and good friendship. Such people are also less burdened by the sort of ever-present anxiety that marks life in an armed camp, however well fortified.

Does this co-operating attitude give us a decisive reason for returning the old man's wallet when we can get away with keeping it? It gives us some reason, but whether that is enough is something we must each decide for ourselves. Although there are good reasons for caring about others for their sakes, this doesn't mean that, prudentially speaking, we should always be so motivated. We need to determine for ourselves when it is appropriate. For example, although it might be moral of me to run into a burning building to save my neighbour's cat, it is not something that is in my wide self-interest. I care about many beings, including the cat to some extent, but there is a limit to my caring too, as there should be.

8.10 Noddings's Feminine Approach to Ethics

Some who welcome the idea that we should cultivate wide self-interest might still wonder about some of the assumptions that drive the project of responding to the Deep Skeptical Challenge to Ethics in the first place. These commentators have argued that in the history of Philosophical Ethics, there has been a decidedly male-dominated preoccupation with attempts to rationally justify morality. This focus on the question of the rationality of morality, they maintain, falsely subsumes the role that caring and compassion plays in our lives to the role that reason plays. The criticism is not that the ethical life is irrational or non-rational; rather, the charge is that the focus on the question about the rationality of being moral distorts the true picture of the moral life.

One notable proponent of this criticism has been Nel Noddings who, in her influential book *Caring: A Feminine Approach to Ethics and Moral Education,* has argued for the priority of the caring relation in moral life.[2] Although she describes her work as "feminine" as opposed to "feminist," Noddings's critique of traditional male-dominated Philosophical Ethics is often categorized as feminist, and it shares with many other feminist critiques an insistence upon the importance of recognizing the uniqueness of the subjective experiences of particular caring relations.

Rejecting what she refers to as the traditional "ethic of principle," Noddings instead outlines her "ethic of caring." She argues that moral conduct is rooted in caring. Since for Noddings the caring relation, for example, the love a mother has for her child, is ethically basic, and since caring is essentially non-rational, she sees herself as providing a coherent account of morality that does not rest on the establishing of moral truth or moral facts.

Noddings begins her discussion of caring by noting that relations are ontologically basic. By this, she means that we should recognize that human encounters and affective response are basic facts of our existence. All caring, moreover, involves a relation between a "one-caring" (the person doing the caring) and a "cared-for." *Engrossment* is a process whereby a one-caring receives or in some sense feels the suffering of a cared-for. Receiving another in this way, Noddings argues, involves not projection but reception. One does not ask, "How would I feel in such a situation?" So, for example, in deciding whether we should lie to protect a loved one, we should judge the particular circumstances rather than simply act according to some general rule that prohibits lying. Rather, one opens up to the feelings of the other and this receiving is affective. Noddings uses the phrase "displacement of motivation" to describe what happens once engrossment occurs. She argues that in caring, one not only feels for the cared-for but also becomes motivated to relieve the suffering of the cared-for. Whether the one-caring acts to aid the cared-for depends on whether the one-caring thinks such action would be prudent. It is only at this stage of the process that reasoning comes in.

Noddings believes it is vital that, in considering how to help the cared-for, we keep our objective thinking anchored in the caring relation. By tying our thinking to the concrete situation, she argues that we can do what is best for the cared-for. Noddings claims to be describing the nature of the basic caring relation. She thinks, for example, that mothers receive their babies rather than try to imagine what it is like to be a baby when they first react to their baby's cry. It is, moreover, the cared-for who inevitably suffers when we attempt to impose general rules and principles on unique situations. It is the uniqueness of human encounters, the uniqueness of the subjective experiences of particular caring relations, then, which makes applying general principles a dangerous business. This uniqueness is also what Noddings's method of ethics strives to recognize and preserve.

Noddings, then, argues that our interest in moral behaviour arises out of our natural impulse to care, a natural impulse that is good. An ethic of caring builds on this sentiment. She writes that

> . . . we might say that moral statements come out of the moral view or attitude, which, as I have described it, is the rational attitude built upon natural caring. When we put it this way, we see that there can be no justification for taking the moral viewpoint—that in truth, the moral viewpoint is prior to any notion of justification.[3]

On Noddings's analysis, the goal of responding to the Deep Skeptical Challenge to Ethics is an academic one disconnected from real moral relations and experience.

This critique of the project of responding to the Deep Skeptical Challenge to Ethics rests on a conception of morality that eschews the individualistic perspective that characterizes both the viewpoint with which we began Part 2 and the viewpoint taken by the Ethical Egoist. However, Noddings's position has itself been subject to criticism from other feminists. Some feminists hold that Noddings's traditional "feminine" emphasis on caring serves to further stereotype women as caregivers.[4] Others insist that caring is not inherently moral, but it becomes virtuous only when it is morally appropriate. This suggests that we need both caring and justice.[5]

In Chapter 12 we will return to the idea that compassion and feeling constitute the foundation of ethics when we consider an argument for Holism in Environmental Philosophy. Whereas Noddings emphasizes the priority of feeling in our caring relations, Holists argue that morality must be based on feeling first and foremost, or else we would not have survived as a species and evolved the advanced thinking and communication skills upon which some moral theories, like Kant's, for instance, rest.

8.11 Review

After presenting and beginning to consider the Deep Skeptical Challenge to Ethics in Chapter 7, in this chapter we turned our attention to further explaining the challenge and to meeting it. The skeptic demands to know why, prudentially speaking, we should care about others for their sakes. The cases of the dying friend and the murder of a loved one for profit are ones in which caring for others for their sakes is not clearly beneficial from the perspective of narrow self-interest. Indeed, as the narrow self-interested analyses show, the wise thing to do in these cases is to act immorally.

To show the prudential value of being widely self-interested, we needed to explain why it would be prudentially good to visit one's friend and not have one's mother killed. To do this we had to appeal to the idea of our wide self-interest and

show the prudential value of love and being a true friend. In the course of doing this, we examined the nature of friendship and unconditional love, and we saw why money can't buy us love. We also raised the question of the moral limits of loving another. Furthermore, in addition to seeing the case for having one's wide self-interest extend at least as far as the good of one's loved ones and closest friends, we considered some reasons for extending it to include others in society, like the old man. This led us to note that, although there are prudential reasons for caring for strangers and our fellow citizens, there also are prudential reasons for limiting the extending of our concern in this way.

In the final part of the chapter, we considered an objection to the whole project of trying to rationally justify morality. According to Nel Noddings's account of ethics, the male-dominated traditional focus on justifying morality distorts our experience of ethics by subsuming the central role played by caring to the role played by reason. As we noted, Noddings argues that in order to gain a clearer picture of the moral life, we need to carefully attend to our actual experiences and appreciate the central importance of the caring relation. For Noddings, relations are ontologically basic in morality. She thus firmly rejects the individualistic focus typical of much moral philosophy and represented, for example, by Ethical Egoism.

Notes

1. See Badhwar (1987).

2. Noddings (1984).

3. Noddings (1984), pp. 94–95.

4. See Card (1996).

5. See Friedman (1993).

Exercises

Progress Check

1. What is the Deep Skeptical Challenge to Ethics?

2. What is the value of defending having wide self-interest, especially considering that most of us already have a wide self-interest and think we should?

3. What responses to the cases involving the dying friend and the murder of one's loved one would the person with only narrow self-interest have?

4. Why is the dichotomy between self-interest and altruism false?

5. Explain the flaw in the concept of The Friendship Store.

6. What does it mean to say that you love someone unconditionally? What is the error in loving your closest friends and loved ones in this way?

7. What is the main problem with the narrowly self-interested analyses of the cases involving the dying friend and the murder for profit?

8. Why is it rational for people with wide self-interest to visit their dying friend and not sell their mother for $200 000?

9. Why can't money buy you love?

10. Why are not all true friendships moral?

11. What is the value to society of having ethical citizens?

12. Outline Noddings's account of the caring relation and the role it plays in ethics.

Questions for Further Reflection

1. Are the examples involving the dying friend and the murder of one's loved one different from the case involving the old man and his wallet? Why or why not?

2. Imagine you could pick up the old man's wallet without him or anyone else noticing. Would it be in your self-interest to do so? Why or why not?

3. (a) Is the goal of living a happy life compatible with the goal of living a morally good life? If not, why not? If so, to what extent? Why?
   (b) If you think the goals are compatible, to what extent do you think you would have to compromise your happiness to be ethical? Why? Can you adjust your goal to be happy to perfectly match your goal to be moral? Why or why not?

4. Most of us care for our friends and loved ones conditionally, that is, subject to certain conditions. Under what conditions would you end a

relationship with a loved one or a friend? Are there some actions or character traits that you could not tolerate in a friend? How is this connected to your own self-respect and identity? Explain.

5. What is the value to you of having true love and friendship?

6. What are the moral limits of loving someone? Under what conditions, if any, are friendships immoral? Explain.

7. Explain and critically evaluate Noddings' critique of the project of trying to respond to the Deep Skeptical Challenge to Ethics.

Suggested Further Reading

An excellent place to begin to further explore the idea of friendship is with Aristotle's classic treatment in Books 8 and 9 of his *Nicomachean Ethics*, and with Book 1 of his *Politics* (see Aristotle [1984]). In recent times in philosophy, there has been a renewed interest in the study of friendship and love. John Cooper commented on Aristotle's account in two interesting and much discussed papers (see Cooper [1977] and [1980]). See also the papers by Kahn (1981), Sherman (1987), and Badhwar (1987). Badhwar also edited a collection of readings on friendship (see Badhwar, ed. [1993]). For more on this topic see, too, the paper by Lawrence Thomas and his books (Thomas [1987] and [1989]).

Lawrence Blum, in his book (Blum [1980]), discusses friendship and altruism, and Thomas Nagel examines the possibility of altruism in his book of the same name (Nagel [1970]). Badhwar has an excellent discussion of the distinction between altruism and self-interest in her 1993 paper, and there are other fine papers on this and related topics in that quarter's edition of *Social Philosophy & Policy*. The question of the connection between ethics and friendship is also examined by Railton (1984), Badhwar (1991), and Cocking and Kennett (2000). Susan Wolf's 1982 paper "Moral Saints" discusses some related issues. For a feminist analysis, see Friedman (1993).

Apart from Noddings's treatment of caring and the related commentaries mentioned above, see also Mike W. Martin's chapters on caring relationships in his book, *Everyday Morality*, Part 5 (Martin [2001]).

Weblinks

A good place to begin your Web investigations into Aristotle's philosophy is with **The Internet Encyclopedia of Philosophy** entry on Aristotle at www.utm.edu/research/iep/a/aristotl.htm

You can also examine the specific entry on Aristotle's ethics at www.utm.edu/research/iep/a/aristotl.htm

For an online version of Aristotle's *Nichomachean Ethics and Politics*, visit MIT's **Internet Classic Archive** at classics.mit.edu/index.html

For an online version of the *Politics*, visit the archive at members.tripod.com/~batesca/aristotle.html

There are also various links to papers on Aristotle's account of friendship at Clifford Bates, Jr.'s **Aristotle's Political Philosophy Page** at members.tripod.com/~batesca/aristotle.html

9 Weighing the Value of Life I: The Case for Equality

Overview

Learning Outcomes

In this chapter and the next, we explore some difficult ethical questions of social policy and law, questions concerning the problem of weighing and comparing the value of human life, both to other lives and to other sorts of goods. Our main aim in this chapter is to explain and evaluate the view that in allocating scarce resources, we should give all those vying for them an equal chance of receiving them. Underlying this approach is the view that all people deserve equal consideration, and in turn, we consider one basis for this claim, the Kantian sentiment that human life is priceless and should not be traded off for other sorts of goods. In the course of challenging these claims, we uncover a tension in our values between desiring a long life and desiring one that is high in quality. The appreciation of this tension clears the way for us to approach our problem from another perspective in Chapter 10.

Upon the successful completion of this chapter, you will be able to

1. outline some of the main methods for resolving ethical problems of allocating scarce resources;
2. explain and critically evaluate some influential arguments for the lottery method;
3. provide an account of the Kantian distinction between subjects and objects and between dignity and price;
4. connect these Kantian ideas to an argument for the view that all human life is both priceless and equally valuable;
5. explicate the idea of a cost/benefit analysis; and
6. contrast the tensions that arise from our commitments to the values of living a long life and living a life high in quality.

9.1 Introduction

Turning away from the perspective of ethics in relationships, in this chapter and the next one we take up a question for society at large: What is the value of human life? We focus on two answers. The first is that all human life is equally valuable and should be regarded as such; the second is that human life is differently valuable and should be treated as such. The question whether humans should receive equal or unequal consideration in society is a pressing concern for social policy developers and analysts, and legislators and decision-makers in various fields. If we can make some progress on this basic ethical question, then perhaps we might be able to make some useful ethical progress in the areas of law and social policy.

With an eye to determining how much consideration we should give people for the purposes of creating law and social policy, we will explore two main positions:

1. Give all people equal consideration.
2. Give people unequal consideration depending on their qualities and circumstances.

Different moral frameworks support these different positions, and in the course of exploring arguments for each, we will examine these different theoretical bases. To get us started, we need a way of conceiving of the differences between the two sorts of positions. What is the basis of their disagreement such that they reach opposing viewpoints? Although there may be more than one difference between them, we will focus only on their differing views over the value of life. The question "How much is human life worth?" is a basic question for ethics, but one that surprisingly has been largely neglected in the history of philosophy in the West. One rationale for according equal consideration to people is on the grounds that their lives are equally valuable. Likewise, a reason for giving unequal consideration to individuals is because their lives are unequal in value.

In this chapter we will examine the view that human lives are equally valuable and that we all should receive equal consideration. In Chapter 10 we will examine the opposing view: that lives are differently valuable and that we should receive different amounts of consideration. To further focus our attention, we will concentrate on trying to solve the science fictional problem case, the Crisis in Space, described in the next section. The dilemma posed by the crisis is to choose from a small group of survivors an even smaller number who will continue living. As a result of an explosion, a shuttle carrying a dozen survivors is stranded far from Earth. Unfortunately, there are enough supplies for only six people to survive until help arrives. The question is, Who should live and who should die?

Although obviously far-fetched in many respects, the scenario raises difficult and pointed questions about justice, with useful implications for a wide range of practical issues. Essentially, our task is to fairly allocate life-saving resources in a situation where not all those who want them can receive them. This problem of distributive justice is acute in two ways: it is a matter of life or death, and it is a matter of all or nothing. In other words, either a beneficiary receives sufficient goods to survive, or does not and dies. The problem also helps clarify a possible misunderstanding of the notion of giving someone equal consideration. One might say that in order to give someone equal consideration with another person for a scarce resource, one must give each an equal chance to *compete* for the resource. In this sense, all minimally qualified applicants for a limited number of spaces to enter a law school receive equal consideration if each application is judged fairly on its own merits. Here giving equal consideration translates into a commitment to a weak principle of equal opportunity.

This, however, is not the sense of "equal consideration" we are talking about. In our sense, to give someone equal consideration is to give her an equal *claim to*, or *share of*, whatever is to be distributed. Thus, if the problem is to distribute five apples to five claimants, we give each person equal consideration by giving each one apple. In situations of all or nothing, that is, in situations where the goods to be distributed cannot be divided up in this way because not everyone can receive something, this won't work. The view that all lives are equally valuable recommends one method of solving the problem. It says that we should conduct a fair lottery that gives each person an equal chance to survive. This method, which we will dub the lottery method, generally involves resolving allocation or distribution problems of justice by according equal consideration to all those vying for whatever is to be distributed. The other method, which we will dub the ranking method, and which we will examine in Chapter 10, consists of ranking people according to their qualities. Underlying this approach is skepticism about the idea that all lives are equally valuable and that we all have an equal right to life.

9.2 A Problem Case: Crisis in Space

Background

The setting is 60 years in the future. As a result of considerable scientific advances and discoveries, we have started to colonize Olympia, a planet in a nearby star system. The planet is uninhabited by humans or human-like creatures, but it boasts a thriving and complex chain of life of both flora and fauna. In the past few years, great progress has been made creating a diverse, permanent settlement of several thousand humans.

Despite impressive advances in transportation technology, the trip to Olympia still takes about 10 months. As a representative of the international organization planning the Olympia settlement, you, together with your colleagues, are ultimately responsible for all aspects of interplanetary travel. You are in charge of the maintenance and functioning of the four shuttles that have been regularly travelling back and forth between Earth and Olympia, and for the wellbeing of the human passengers on board.

The Crisis

Last night, you received word of a disaster aboard one of your shuttles. Due to a catastrophic explosion and fire, many people have been killed, and there has also been a loss of supplies and damage to the ship. The ship is disabled and slowly drifting roughly halfway between Earth and Olympia. The good news is that life support systems are operating and 12 people have survived the disaster. You are in regular contact with them and you know that some sense of order has been restored. However, they are anxious about their future and are looking to you for information and guidance. The bad news is that there are enough supplies for only six people to survive until the rescue shuttle arrives in about four months. There is no way to save all 12 survivors, and you must decide what to do.

The Challenge

With your colleagues, you must plan a course of action. First, you must decide what to do about the surviving passengers. As a moral person, you want to do what is right and fair, and your rescue operation will focus on doing what is best for them. You can, of course, let them decide what to do until the rescue shuttle arrives, but as a mission leader, you are ultimately responsible for their safe passage. Imagine that through surgically implanted monitoring equipment, you have the technical means of killing any passenger or group of passengers, so one obvious option is to select the six survivors who will remain to be rescued by killing those who you deem to be unworthy of rescuing. The question is, What should you do?

To help you with your choice, you have biographical information about the 12 survivors. Though nationals of many different countries, most are associated in one way or another with various United Nations organizations. Some other relevant details of their lives are summarized below. You could undertake a more extensive analysis of the 12 passengers' lives, but you must decide reasonably quickly. Finally, keep in mind that you might very well be held accountable for whatever decisions you reach, so be prepared to publicly defend your plan.

The 12 Survivors

1. Dr. Anil Sharma, 40, is a former resident in thoracic surgery at a New York teaching

hospital. Originally from Northern India, Dr. Sharma is travelling to Olympia to work with her husband, who is also a surgeon. They are childless.

2. Don Richards, a marathon runner, is a senior administrator and judge with expertise in international law and relations. He has worked for the United Nations in a variety of humanitarian capacities for over 30 years and is travelling to the Olympia settlement to work as a senior official in the new settlement government. Mr. Richards, a widower with 10 grandchildren, is multilingual. He just turned 67.

3. Yoshiki Yamamoto, 29, has various skills in the building trades. A reformed drug addict, Mr. Yamamoto has been clean for five years. His half-brother is the director of the space agency and your boss's boss.

4. Sarah Moore, five, is the daughter of the new chief of medicine at the settlement's medical facility. A beautiful girl with a sunny disposition, Sarah has a mild form of Down syndrome.

5. Susan Moore, 34, is a kindergarten teacher and Sarah Moore's mother. She is almost eight months pregnant and travelling to join her husband, who left for Olympia six months ago to take up his position.

6. Ming Chen, 16, is a quiet but passionate student with a keen interest in, and aptitude for, mathematics. She is also a talented cellist. Since the disaster, she has been withdrawn and depressed, often weeping quietly and avoiding contact with the other survivors. Her parents—both research scientists—were killed in the fire. Unilingual, Ming speaks only Mandarin.

7. Otto Schmidt, 48, is an ordained Lutheran minister, and former international soccer star and captain of Germany's national soccer team. In addition to leading his own ministry on Olympia, he will also be regularly reporting on life there for a large European television network. Due to his great popularity and friendly and outgoing nature, he's been hired by your organization to help promote the settlement project back on Earth. He's scheduled to make his next broadcast in two days. Mr. Schmidt is fluent in German, French, and English.

8. Izzy Weinstein, 22, is a mining engineering student. His parents are geologists on Olympia, and he plans to continue his studies at the settlement. His fiancée was killed in the fire.

9. Dr. Gabriella Garcia is a professor of immunology at a large university medical school in Brazil. An expert in infectious diseases, Dr. Garcia has a background in microbiology. Single with no children, she is 44. Dr. Garcia speaks English and Portuguese.

10. Dr. Abdullah Mohammed, 53, is a pedologist with a Ph.D. in agricultural science. A native of Pakistan and a devout Muslim, Dr. Mohammed is an expert in soil physics and chemistry. His wife will be joining him on a future shuttle mission and he has two adolescent daughters. He is fluent in Urdu and English.

11. Michelle Simard, 75, is a celebrated poet and visual artist who has lately been a roving cultural ambassador for the United Nations. Opinionated and assertive, Ms Simard was appointed as the settlement's first poet laureate. She will be working on various cultural projects at the new settlement. Multilingual, Ms Simard has also been commissioned to paint a series of paintings on her impressions of life on Olympia.

12. Jung Ho Kim, 28, is a computer programmer and systems analyst. Formerly he worked for the Korean government at the United Nations in New York. He recently signed a seven-year contract to assist with the expansion and maintenance of Olympia's computer network. Fluent in Korean and English, Mr. Kim is single and has no children, but he provides financial support for his widowed mother and disabled younger sister.

Tasks and Questions

1. Draw up your own plan and decide how you would deal with this crisis, including whether you think that you and your colleagues should decide who would live and die.

2. What is the fairest method to use for deciding what to do?

3. Briefly explain the ethical argument for your method.

4. Explain how you applied your method in this case.

5. Who should live and who should die?

Take some time to think about and respond to these questions before proceeding with your reading.

9.3 Deciding Who Should Decide

Though obviously hypothetical, the Crisis in Space poses a difficult ethical problem for those who would try to justly distribute the life-saving resources that each survivor needs. Typically, those who have tried to answer these questions and perform these tasks, whether alone or together with their classmates, have tended to react in two ways. Either they recommend that a fair lottery be conducted, to give each survivor an equal chance or, more commonly, they take up the challenge of ranking the survivors according to some quality or qualities they possess, with an eye to subsequently killing those who don't make the grade. Upon reflection, however, we can see some issues that require our attention before we advance to the level of either employing a lottery or otherwise selecting among the people on the list.

One might begin by wondering whether the moral course is to make and implement a plan on behalf of the survivors at all. Although you are a "mission leader" (in the comfort of your surroundings on Earth) charged with the responsibility of the passengers' safe passage,

what right do you have to decide who lives and who dies? Many argue that the whole exercise is a non-starter because no one has the right to "play God" and dictate for others whether they will live or die in this crisis. Giving the argument a Kantian spin, some hold that by choosing life or death for others, we would fail to respect the autonomy of the survivors. According to this argument, the ethical option is to treat the survivors with the respect they deserve and to clearly explain their situation, leaving the responsibility of deciding what to do up to them. Although you and others back on Earth can offer advice and information, it would be immoral to decide for them what should happen, especially given the paltry information you have on which to base your decisions and the fact that you are withholding information from them about their plight. Since killing anyone in this way would be immoral, on this view the ethical course is to refuse to take up the task.

In response, some argue that although the sketchy biographical information does show up the artificial nature of the example, and although one can sympathize with concerns about failing to respect autonomy, the dire circumstances force you to choose. As a leader your duty is to lead, to make the hard decisions, and to be accountable for what happens next. This means you must ensure that the fairest method of selection is fairly employed and that the survivors remain safe until they are rescued. Appealing to a consequentialist justification, the argument is that one must be guided first and foremost by what will lead to the best overall outcome for all involved. If you disable the devices that allow you to kill, then you would give up power you might need to enforce your authority.

The argument that you must reserve the power to make a final decision can go some way to meeting the objections from those who say the decision is not yours to make in the first place. Defenders of this position argue that you can show your respect for the autonomy of the survivors by explaining to them, honestly and candidly, their situation and by listening to their recommendations. Ultimately, however, there is a limit to this. The situation on board is not a democracy. To ensure order, you must make the final decisions. By giving up the power to kill, you risk having the survivors somehow corrupt a fair selection process, say through rigging the outcome, or of choosing a selection method that is unjust. For example, they might decide on the basis of each according to his threat advantage. Even worse, you must guard against the possibility of anarchy, violence, and further tragedy if you renounce your power to choose. In response to those who say that you underestimate the character and commitments to justice among those on the ship by making these suggestions, you could reply that these are not normal circumstances. We are not talking about fairly dividing up a pie when there is not enough to go around. Indeed, given the extremely stressful circumstances, and considering the state of shock, confusion, fear, and depression the survivors are experiencing, it would be immoral for you not to choose.

By way of a counter-reply to these points, defenders of the approach that we should let the survivors have the final say could insist that this argument remains flawed because it still fails to adequately respect their autonomy. Yes, the situation is stressful, even dire, but it is a mistake to presume to know how they might react. Speculating that this or that bad result might occur if you let them choose treats them like children incapable of deciding what is best for themselves. The argument that you should make the decision is also flawed because it is based on the questionable assumption that as a result of your position, you must know what is best. It is arrogant to assume that by virtue of your status as a "mission leader," you know what is right or best. What training or education did you receive that positions you to make these decisions? This is the other part of the point of the original objection that one should not choose on behalf of the survivors because in doing so one is "playing God."

These reasons and arguments provide us with a glimpse of the debate over the question of who should decide. In formulating your response to the situation, you will have to work out your view about this.

9.4 Selection Methods and Their Rationales

Regardless of who decides, something has to be done. So, setting aside this question, let's assume, just for the sake of argument and to keep our analysis moving, that you decide that you should make the ultimate decision. To identify those who will live and those who will be killed, you need to select and then use a method or some methods for choosing. Following are three options:

1. Solicit Volunteers

Although this option is unlikely to resolve the problem entirely, one can argue that soliciting volunteers among the adult survivors may alleviate it somewhat by reducing the number of hard choices you will ultimately have to make. The ethical justification for employing this method is that, as adults, we should be free to do as we please as long as in doing so we don't unjustly harm others. This option thus expresses respect for the adult survivors as autonomous individuals with a right to make their own choices regarding their death. This view is reflected in Common Sense Morality, according to which it is right that adults should be allowed to act heroically, for example, by sacrificing their lives for the sake of a cause or for the good of others, in circumstances where we would not require them to act in this way. Although a professional firefighter has an obligation to enter a burning building to try to save someone trapped inside, we do not think that passersby do, although we also think that they may if they wish. So it could be argued that the inclusion of this method conforms to our common sense views about ethics.[1]

In response, someone else might argue that although using this method may sometimes be unobjectionable, we shouldn't assume that it would always be so. Minimally, we might require that those who do volunteer first pass a test to prove that their choice is informed and uncoerced, and that they are competent to make such a decision. More interestingly, one could argue that even those who are competent and freely choose to give their informed consent to die should not be permitted to do so. Such might be the case if the loss or threat of loss to the other survivors from the volunteer's death is so great as to cancel out the volunteer's right to choose to die. This obviously very controversial line of reasoning appeals to a consequentialist or perhaps a utilitarian justification. Thus, some might say that Dr. Sharma, as the only qualified medical doctor and surgeon, should not be allowed to volunteer for suicide because her loss could endanger the others. Moreover, she has a professional obligation to tend to the ill and oversee the care of the survivors until help arrives.

2. Conduct a Fair Lottery

Many will maintain that the only fair way of deciding who should live and who should die is by conducting a fair lottery that gives each survivor an equal chance of living. Underlying the **lottery method** or **fair lottery method** is the view that we all deserve equal respect and consideration and that, as humans, we have an equal right to life. We will explore this view in a moment.

3. Rank on the Basis of Some Quality or Qualities

Finally, the most popular method of selecting is the **ranking method**—to choose on the basis of a ranking that appeals to some quality or qualities of the survivors. Underlying this method is the conviction that the claim that we all have an equal right to life is unconvincing and that, as a matter of fact, our lives are differently valuable both to ourselves and to others. Defenders of this approach appeal to examples like the following to help sway the skeptics. They point to the supposed extremist nature of the argument for a fair lottery and note that although the idea that we have an equal right to life sounds noble in principle, in practice it would commit us to counterintuitive and blatantly unjust choices. They observe, for example, that a commitment to a lottery would mean that in order to choose between saving the life of a 107-year-old blind, deaf, and immobile man in the advanced stages of senile dementia and a healthy young mother of three, we would have to flip a coin.

Although the above methods can be combined in various ways, we will concentrate on considering justifications for the lottery method in this chapter, and the ranking method in the next.

9.5 The Case for a Fair Lottery

A number of reasons support the view that the fairest method of choosing among the survivors is to hold a lottery that gives each one an equal chance. In our discussion, we will have space only for a selective treatment of some of these reasons. We can roughly classify them as being either positive or negative in character. We will call arguments that emphasize the strength of the case that a lottery is best because of the strong moral rationale for giving each survivor an equal chance "positive arguments." They are positive because they recommend a lottery on its own merits. We will call arguments that challenge the method of ranking people on the basis of some quality or qualities they have "negative arguments." These arguments are negative because they question the fairness of any ranking method, and they purport to show that a fair lottery is a superior alternative.

Negative Arguments

Defenders of the lottery method express several concerns about the project of ranking people by their qualities. One involves the daunting complexity of any sophisticated ranking method. How, first of all, does one identify relevant qualities? What is the basis of this kind of decision?

> The **lottery method** or **fair lottery method** involves resolving allocation or distribution problems of justice by according equal consideration to all who are vying for whatever is to be distributed.
>
> The **ranking method** resolves allocation or distribution problems of justice by ranking people who are vying for a good or resource according to one or more of their qualities.

For instance, some might intuitively think that an individual's age is a relevant criterion. Why? If age is relevant, then at what point does discrimination on the basis of age become ageism (unjust age discrimination)?

Once we begin to rank people according to their qualities, where do we stop? If age is relevant, then perhaps marital status, how many dependants one has, intelligence, and a whole host of other factors are relevant, too. Assuming that we could compile a complete list of all the relevant factors, there is the further problem of assigning weights to them. Is age more important than dependant status? Why? If so, when? Always? Sometimes? If some factors are not always more important than others, our task will become immensely more complicated. The Crisis in Space example includes only a few people to select from, but choosing among them on the basis of their qualities looks like an impossibly difficult task.

In light of the complexity and sheer number of the judgments it seems we are committed to making if we decide to rank individuals by their qualities, critics also argue that we need some confidence that our judgments are both impartial and justified. They worry that any ranking procedure will be riddled with subjective prejudice, that decision-makers will be "playing God" with other people's lives on the basis of their own biases. We know we have unconscious biases. How will our ranking procedure filter these out? Could any procedure filter out all such biases? At best, it seems that the method will be useful only in rare cases where there are obvious extreme differences between people, like in the example of the 107-year-old man above. Typically the differences will not be so pronounced. How, for example, are we to choose between Izzy Weinstein, the 22-year-old mining engineering student, and Jung Ho Kim, the 28-year-old computer programmer? Although there are differences between them, what reason is there for judging the differences to be sufficiently great to justify saving one and killing the other? No, defenders of the lottery method assert, the only non-arbitrary method is to draw straws. Moreover, unlike the complex method of ranking by qualities, the lottery method is simple to use.

Positive Arguments

We observed earlier that proponents of a lottery method argue for their selection procedure on the grounds that all the survivors should be given an equal chance to survive because they all have an equal right to life. The idea that we have equal rights has a powerful hold in our society. Equality rights are enshrined in our *Charter of Rights and Freedoms*. We teach our children to assert and defend their equal rights. We also regard the historical development of democratic states founded on equality rights as great improvements over past forms of government. But what arguments support the idea that we have an equal right to life?

One such argument appeals to the idea that since we all have a soul, in the eyes of God we are all equal, and from this the notion that we have an equal right to life is derived. However, since we have already ruled out appeals to metaphysical assumptions based on religious matters of faith to support the arguments of this book, we cannot appeal to this idea.

Perhaps the most influential secular argument for the idea that we have an equal right to life is Immanuel Kant's. In his *Foundations of the Metaphysics of Morals,* Kant appeals to a distinction between price and dignity to help try to show that the lives of rational beings, including humans, are incomparably and infinitely valuable. He claims that as rational beings we have dignity that is "infinitely beyond any price" and that dignity has "unconditional and incomparable worth."[2] According to this Kantian line of reasoning, anyone who insists on comparing the value of life to other sorts of goods, or who puts a price on life, degrades its value. That person fails to appreciate the logical difference between subjects and mere objects. As rational agents with (apparently) free will, Kant believes we can set our own laws to live by. In contrast, mere objects do not act, but are merely subject to the laws of nature. Moreover, since all rational beings can choose and act, all are equally deserving of respect in what Kant calls the "kingdom of ends." Therefore, all subjects have dignity as ends in themselves. In contrast, objects have a price.

Kant's argument that there is a fundamental difference in kind between subjects and objects has intuitive appeal. For example, it seems to help explain the immorality of the practice of slavery. The idea of using someone exclusively as a tool or instrument for the good of someone else is immoral because such regarding fails to accord the slave the necessary dignity to which he is entitled. The idea that one can buy a slave is a confusion based on treating subjects with dignity as if they were objects with a price. On Kant's outlook, it is both a conceptual confusion to act in this way and a moral mistake. His argument also helps provide a moral justification for democratic forms of government. On his view, all mature rational beings are equally responsible for determining the laws under which they collectively live. It is their equal status as ends in themselves that explains why all have both equal rights and responsibilities as citizens.

The idea that human life is infinitely valuable suggests that we can compare the value of one human life to another, and that because each is infinitely valuable, they are equal in value. Furthermore, Kant's distinction between subjects with dignity and objects with a price suggests that we cannot compare the value of a human life to other non-rational beings' lives or to mere things. Human life is incomparably valuable. Although Kantian scholars disagree about the correct interpretation of Kant's views, the idea that human life is infinitely valuable and that it should not be compared to the value of mere objects rings true in the ears of many people. For this reason, people often claim that human life is "priceless."

To test your own intuitions about the appeal of Kant's argument, consider the following example. Imagine the owner of a small business discovers that one of his products, which meets government specifications for safety, in fact poses an appreciable risk to the lives of innocent users, a risk that only he knows about. Imagine, further, that the businessman will suffer a loss of profits on the sale of his product if he recalls them to replace them with products with a safer design. What should he do? He could ignore his

concerns and continue to sell, hoping for the best, and then blame the government specifications if someone dies. Most of us, however, would agree that the ethical choice would be to suffer the loss in income so as not to jeopardize the lives of innocent people.

The interesting question is why this is the right thing to do. Why is the option of continuing to produce the product morally objectionable? Is the objection that there is too little value placed on human life? In other words, is the claim that not enough profit would be made to justify the risk? On this approach the moral course to follow is determined by something like a utilitarian cost/benefit analysis that gives roughly equal weight to the interests of all involved. The cost/benefit analysis consists of forecasting the likely costs and benefits to everyone of continuing to sell the product. Essentially, the main issue is whether the likely benefits to the owner would outweigh the potential risks to the users. Based on this calculation, and the other ones germane to this situation, the ethical choice is to stop production and redesign the product.

Alternatively, could we claim that since human life is incomparably valuable, it is unethical to even consider comparing the value of human life to profits? Following the Kantian argument we just examined, many say the businessman should not continue to produce the product in its present form because it is immoral to place a dollar value on a person's head. We should not trade lives for profits. Notice that in this instance, both methods for determining what the owner should do lead to the same conclusion. Under different circumstances, though, the methods could recommend incompatible solutions. This is because the justifications appeal to different moral theories with some different moral assumptions.

9.6 The Killing Machine

The following thought experiment is designed to help challenge the Kantian argument for according humans an equal right to life. It also helps us appreciate that the reason why the businessman should not continue to produce the product is not because it is immoral to trade lives for profits or to place a dollar value on a person's head. Rather, the businessman should have the product redesigned because, in this case, the potential losses cancel out the likely benefits of continuing to sell.

Imagine that you are offered the opportunity to be a potential beneficiary of some new technology. The technology is a device, illustrated below (see Figure 9.1), that enables us to acquire various goods. A person is locked into one chamber. A button is pushed, and then various goods are created and placed into the second chamber. Unfortunately, to create the goods, the person in the first chamber is killed. The inventor of the device has asked me to represent his interests. He has also decided that the fairest way of benefiting from the technology is to enlist the support of volunteers. The volunteers will, by volunteering, acquire both an equal risk of being selected by a fair lottery to be locked into the chamber, and an equal share of the benefits. Under which conditions, if any, would you agree to participate?

First scenario: You are offered the opportunity to be a member of a group of 100 people, one of whom will be selected to die in the chamber. Everyone else wins $50.

Second scenario: You are offered the opportunity to be a member of a group of 500 people, one of whom will be selected to die in the chamber. Everyone else wins $1000.

Third scenario: You are offered the opportunity to be a member of a group of 5000 people, one of whom will be selected to die in the chamber. Everyone else wins $1000, a new car every other year for the rest of her or his life, and a free luxury vacation anywhere in the world every year for the rest of her or his life.

In subsequent scenarios we can increase both the number of people who might participate (2500, 5000, and so on) and the potential benefits. We can also imagine that the process is set up such that if your number is called, there is no escaping, so you cannot enjoy the benefits without assuming the risks.

At what point would you agree to participate? When I ask people this question, although more and more say they would volunteer as the benefits increase and the risk decreases, a significant number do not. When I ask, "Who finds the whole idea of this device and its use morally repugnant, and thinks that it should be outlawed?" or "Does anyone think that the idea of

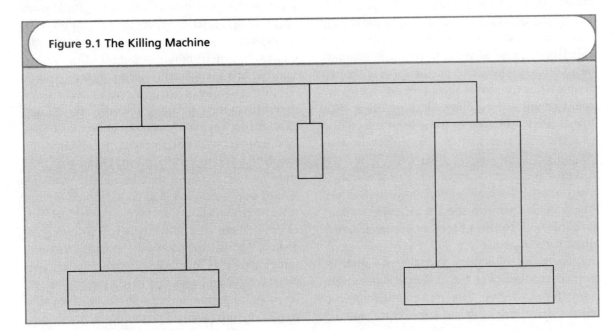

Figure 9.1 The Killing Machine

placing a dollar value on life is offensive?" many say that they do. Certainly the idea of killing people for things, even if the people volunteer to assume the risk that they will die in the machine, sounds immoral to many. However, if you think this way, consider the idea that the practice of using the Killing Machine is in relevant ethical respects like the practice of using the automobile.

Thousands of people, including careful drivers, die every year in car accidents in Canada. We know that many deaths could be avoided if automobile manufacturers built tanks instead of cars, or if we reduced the speed limit on our highways to, say, 10 kilometres per hour. Yet we do not lobby the government to force manufacturers to build more expensive but significantly safer vehicles, nor do we lobby for a great reduction in speed limits. We value having the opportunity to purchase reasonably affordable cars and we value convenient travel over the risk of dying on the road. In other words, we place a greater value on these other goods than we do on human life. So effectively, not only do we compare the value of human life to other goods; we commonly rank those other values above the value of life. Although we regret the loss of life and serious injuries on our roads and highways, and although we downplay the risks to us, most of us think that these tradeoffs are acceptable.

We could set the risk of dying in the Killing Machine so that it approximates the risk of being killed in a car accident; a risk we can estimate based on past experience. Furthermore, although people value the use of their cars differently, we could envision the Killing Machine being such that it gives a benefit to those who use it that roughly compares to the average benefit that people get from driving their cars. While the machine is unlike the automobile in some obvious respects, the basic ethical point is that the practices that involve the use of each kind of machine both consist of trading human lives for other sorts of goods.

For those who think that the two sorts of practices are different, the challenge is to explain why. If you cannot, then to be consistent you must either revise your attitude toward ranking

the value of life or cease driving cars. A common objection is that in the Killing Machine lottery, we aim at killing someone to acquire the benefits, whereas we do not intend to kill anyone on the roads to enjoy the benefits of driving. In each case, however, we can regard the deaths involved as an unfortunate but practically unavoidable effect of gaining the respective goods acquired through each practice. In each case our intention is to gain some benefit, not to kill someone. We participate in the Killing Machine lottery in order to receive a chance to obtain desired goods, not to commit suicide.

Another objection is that the Killing Machine is guaranteed to kill, whereas there is no certainty that people will die in car accidents in the future. In response we can concede that although it is possible that no one will die in car accidents, it is very unlikely, and this remote possibility should not affect the behaviour of a reasonable person. To see this, consider the following variation on our experiment. Imagine a randomizing device is attached to the Killing Machine and set so that it reflects the odds that no one will die on our streets in the future. Say, for argument's sake, that there is a one in 10 billion chance that when the button is pushed, goods are produced but no one is killed. This variation would not induce a reasonable person to change her attitude from prohibiting the device to permitting it. By analogy, a reasonable person should not take comfort from a one-in-10-billion possibility that no one may die in a car accident in the future.

Although we perhaps discount the risk of dying in cars as a coping measure, the Killing Machine lottery forces us to be conscious of the risk involved. In the experiment, the risk must be weighed prior to participation. Given this, and since in both scenarios we take a life-threatening risk to gain a non-essential good, should we not react by changing our car-driving behaviour? This would be required if one accepted the price/dignity distinction, which makes a *very* strong claim— some values (life, for example) should not be compared with other goods that have a mere price. Yet, when we are forced to confront our practices with respect to our claimed theoretical convictions, most of us say that, upon reflection, we are justi-fied in making comparisons.[3]

To help see this, consider the following. The comparison between the Killing Machine and the car is based on the assumption that both machines offer us goods that we don't need to survive. This highlights the voluntary nature of the choices we make in putting our lives at risk in each case. However, the consequences of choosing to destroy the Killing Machine and forsake the car are greater than we have noted so far. If we choose to make these machines illegal, then to be consistent we must also criminalize the use of any thing or activity that poses a risk to human life for the sake of enhancing the quality of life. Effectively, this is what the Killing Machine and the car do for us, but when we look around, it is evident that these tradeoffs pervade our lives. Life is risky. In addition to dying in obviously risky activities like skydiving and mountain climbing, people die each year from a multitude of apparently safe activities including playing golf (lightning strikes) and obtaining soft drinks from vending machines (tipping leads to crushing). If we really tried to live according to the idea that life is infinitely valuable, then, for the sake of our quality of life, we could not justify taking any risks.

When we reflect carefully upon these issues, we see that we value not only life but also quality of life, and in order to secure this we must take risks with our lives. The Killing Machine example helps us to see the error of thinking that we truly believe, or should believe, that life is infinitely valuable. This view is often expressed by saying that life, or any other similarly regarded value, is priceless. By maintaining that life is priceless, we hope to prevent attempts to trade off lives for other goods, and many of us find it especially unethical to trade lives for money or profits. However, as the Killing Machine experiment reveals, our wish to express our high regard for life by claiming that it is priceless is inconsistent both with our behaviour and with our considered views. Although we think life and other highly regarded values are very valuable, it is an exaggeration to claim that such values are infinitely great.

Those who despair at explaining a morally relevant difference between the risks we take by participating in the Killing Machine lottery and the risks we take in any number of ways in our daily lives might wonder whether there is any positive lesson to be learned from the experiment. The important lesson is this: Before we can think seriously about fairly weighing and comparing values we rate highly, and before we can appreciate the ethical limits of such comparisons, we must divest ourselves of the notions that some values are either incomparable or infinitely great.

Once we recognize that we think we are justified in comparing the value of our life to other sorts of goods, we can ask how much human life is worth. Once we see that we do not really think our lives are priceless, we can begin to seriously consider when they can be risked for the sake of goods to ourselves and to others. This is a necessary step to take before we can begin to answer many important questions in ethics, public policy, and various fields of Applied Ethics. Furthermore, once we see that it is an exaggeration to say that life is infinitely valuable, the case for thinking that all lives are equally valuable is greatly weakened. If human lives are not all infinitely valuable, then what reason do we have for thinking that they are or should be regarded as being equally valuable?

The Kantian argument for equality is just one positive argument that could be advanced in support of the lottery method. Likewise, the thought experiment involving the Killing Machine gives us some reason for doubting the claims that human life is infinitely and incomparably valuable, but our brief discussion is not the last word in this debate. There are other arguments that can be advanced in support of the lottery Method, so our discussion is far from comprehensive. Still, in light of these doubts and to provide some breadth to our investigation, we should also devote some space to considering the argument for using a method that involves selecting survivors by ranking them according to their qualities and circumstances. We turn to this task in Chapter 10.

9.7 Review

In this chapter we began to address the question of the value of human life. To help direct our discussion, we considered the Crisis in Space, which models in relevant ways many of the problems we are examining. As a first step forward in developing an ethical response to our problem, we considered the lottery method, which responds to the problem by according equal shares to all those vying for consideration. It rests on the view that all humans have lives that are equally valuable and that we all have an equal right to life. As a result, it recommends that we resolve the Crisis in Space by conducting a fair lottery, giving each of the survivors an equal chance of being selected to live.

In the course of evaluating the ethical justification for this method, we surveyed some arguments attributable to Immanuel Kant. The arguments can be used to support the widespread belief that humans have an equal right to life due to their equal standing as beings with dignity capable of formulating and following their own plans in life. We noted how Kant's distinctions between subjects and objects, and between dignity and price, help support some of our common moral beliefs. Putting these beliefs to the test, we considered an example involving a businessman and a moral dilemma involving the question of trading innocent lives for profits. Examining our views about this led us to the Killing Machine thought experiment, where we tested our intuitions about the idea that it is immoral to compare the value of life to other sorts of goods and things. Our analysis of this example showed that the very strong claims about the immorality of comparing the value of life to the value of mere objects, and about the infinite value of human lives, are false. Appreciating this clears the way for us to address the difficult question of how to we can fairly measure the value of life, both to the person who is the subject of the life and to others affected by it. We take up this challenge in Chapter 10.

Notes

1. See Slote (1985).

2. Kant (1785), p. 54.

3. As James Griffin observes, "It is easy here to move imperceptibly from Kant to cant." (Griffin [1986], p. 82).

Exercises

Progress Check

1. What can it mean to say that two individuals deserve equal consideration for a scarce resource? What sense are we using in our discussion?

2. Briefly explain the debate over the question of who should decide who should live and who should die.

3. Outline the main methods for solving problems like the Crisis in Space.

4. Outline the main negative arguments advanced on behalf of the lottery method.

5. Outline the main positive argument in support of the lottery method.

6. Explain Kant's distinction between price and dignity. How does it support the idea that all humans have an equal right to life?

7. Explain the two kinds of ethical arguments for not continuing to sell the product in the example involving the small-business owner.

8. Which moral theory or theories support these arguments?

9. What is the main point of the Killing Machine example?

10. Explain how the analysis of the Killing Machine example shows there is a tension in our unreflective commitments to both living a long life and to living a life high in quality.

11. How does the argument against the idea that life is infinitely valuable also threaten the idea that human lives are equally valuable?

Questions for Further Reflection

1. Explain and critically evaluate the best argument for the view that the survivors in the Crisis in Space example should decide what to do amongst themselves.

2. Explain and critically evaluate the view that there should be a limit to letting people volunteer to die in the example.

3. Does Dr. Sharma have a duty to stay that cancels out any wish she might have to volunteer? Does anyone else? What about those survivors with dependants both on board and in general? Defend your position.

4. If the decision was made to hold a lottery to resolve the crisis, should Susan Moore, the woman who is almost eight months pregnant, be given one chance or two? Alternatively, can you think of another better option? Explain and defend your view.

5. What is the best response that the defender of the lottery method can make in response to the counter-example of the 107-year-old blind, deaf, immobile, and senile man?

6. What good options are there for combining the use of the methods? Support your answer.

7. What does it mean to say that something is priceless? What kinds of things can you think of that are regarded as being priceless? What, if anything, do they have in common?

8. We have limited our discussion to considering the amount of moral consideration we should give to humans. Imagine now that we broadened our focus to consider the amount of consideration that we should give to all sentient non-human animals too. Should this change in our focus alter the case for considering the lottery method? Why or why not? Defend your view.

9. What other arguments are there for using the lottery method in the Crisis in Space example? Are any of these decisive? Explain and defend your view.

Weblinks

There is an interesting discussion of risk analysis and risk management at the Web site of the Ontario Ministry of Agriculture and Food at **www.gov.on.ca/omafra/english/research/risk/frameworks/asum1b.html#RISK ANALYSIS**

The American Risk Assessment & Policy Association's Web site contains various risk assessment links at **www.fplc.edu/risk/Rapa.HTM**

You can also investigate the Web site of the American Society for Risk Analysis at **www.sra.org**

Group Work Activity:

The Ethics of Setting Safety Standards

As we have noted in this chapter, we value quality of life and length of life, and often our commitments to these values are in conflict. For example, we want vehicles that are both reasonably inexpensive and reasonably safe. We also know that there are many factors contributing to traffic fatalities, and that one of these is speed. So we know that one way to minimize accidents that cause death, injury, and property loss would be to reduce the speed limits on our highways.

Imagine that you and the other members of your group have been empowered to set the speed limits on our highways. You can leave them as they are, increase them, decrease them, or follow some combination of possibilities (for example, raise them for daytime and lower them at night, alter them based on traffic conditions, and so on).

1. What information would you like to have to make the best ethical decision about what to do?

2. What ethical principle or principles should guide your decision-making?

10 Weighing the Value of Life II: Ranking by Qualities

Learning Outcomes

In this chapter we continue the work from Chapter 9 of answering the important public policy question about how to assess and compare the value of individuals' lives. We will continue to use the Crisis in Space example as our test case. In this chapter, we focus on the issues and problems of a ranking method.

Upon the successful completion of this chapter, you will be able to

1. present and assess some arguments for determining which factors are morally relevant in ranking people for receiving shares of scarce public goods in situations like the Crisis in Space example;

2. distinguish between different senses of the expression "life is priceless";

3. recount the important events in the Latimer case and relate relevant ethical issues of the case to the issues of this chapter;

4. explain the idea of a minimally prudentially valuable life; and

5. identify some problems with determining the prudential value of a person's life, with making comparisons of prudential value between different people, with assessing the value of the impact of people on society, and with comparing the values of these impacts.

10.1 Introduction

In Chapter 9 we began the task of answering the question about the value of human life. Specifically, from the perspective of formulating law and public policy, we wanted to know how public officials should apportion consideration to people in society. When the consideration takes the form of allocating goods like education and health care, the problem becomes one of distributive justice. More narrowly, we considered a specific problem, the Crisis in Space, which highlights two aspects of these cases that force us to make especially difficult moral choices.[1] In our test case, the goods to be distributed are the necessities of life itself, so those who do not receive the goods will die. As well, the problem in this case is acute: half of those vying for survival will be denied.

To resolve cases like the Crisis in Space, we outlined two main approaches. The lottery method gives all an equal chance to acquire the scarce goods. In contrast, the ranking method allocates the goods according to rankings based on judgments about the qualities and circumstances of those desiring help. One basis of the lottery method is the belief that since all lives are priceless, all people deserve an equal chance at survival. Although there may be other bases for the lottery method, and although our assessment of this approach was rather brief, we saw that there is reason for doubting the idea that all lives are equally valuable and that all should receive an equal chance to survive the crisis. In this chapter we further consider arguments for the lottery method, but our principle focus will be on considering arguments for the other sort of approach to determining who should live and who should die.

A ranking method refers to any method that ranks potential beneficiaries and that is based on skepticism of the idea that all lives are equally valuable and that people therefore deserve equal consideration.[2] Unfortunately, the question "which ranking method is best for the Crisis in Space dilemma?" is one that we cannot answer here. More modestly, our aim will be to begin to methodically develop a reasonable ranking method and consider some of the many issues and problems that would need to be sorted out to answer this question. More generally, we are interested in the ethical issues connected to the whole project of ranking people for consideration on the basis of their qualities and circumstances. To help draw this out and to illustrate some of the issues and problems associated with defending a ranking method, we consider the case of Robert Latimer, the Saskatchewan farmer convicted of murdering his 12-year-old severely disabled daughter Tracy in 1993. This groundbreaking case in Canadian legal history raises two questions especially pressing for us:

1. How do we assess the value of someone's life to her? and

2. What are the wider implications for society of endorsing a ranking method in cases of distributive justice like the Crisis in Space example?

Although we will address each of these questions and some others in some detail, we do not have the space to carefully develop our method and the argument for it at great length. We can, however, at least gain a good sense of how the method might work and what support there is for it and for other methods like it. Despite the apparent modesty of our ambitions, even these few steps will prove useful and interesting. Many people new to the study of philosophy believe that all the work that can be done in philosophy has been done, and, likewise, that in ethics there is little left for us to do. One of the main benefits of developing our ranking method is that it will point to much work that remains to be done in this important area of ethical enquiry.

10.2 Selecting by Qualities

As with the argument for the lottery method, the argument for the ranking method can be seen as having both negative and positive dimensions. We can regard the arguments that are critical of the lottery method as being negative and arguments that support the ranking method on its own independent merits as positive in character.

Negative Arguments

Our discussion of the Killing Machine thought experiment in Chapter 9 is an example of an argument that undermines the ethical rationale for the lottery method. As such, it is a negative argument that advances the case for the use of a ranking method. Apart from this line of criticism, defenders of the ranking method also question the assertion that choosing randomly is not "playing God." Recall that proponents of the lottery method argue that ranking methods are based on subjective biases and that decision-makers who use the methods will be "playing God" with other people's well-being and lives. In effect, then, the critics charge that ranking methods are arbitrary and involve the objectionable imposition of the wishes of some on others. In response, defenders of the ranking method raise this same charge against the lottery method.

Defenders of the lottery method assume that since the method involves random selection, where each person is given an equal chance, that it is therefore not arbitrary. However, this is true only if it is fair that each person *receive* an equal chance. The fact that the method assigns resources equally is unfair and arbitrary if some should be given more consideration than others should. Proponents of the ranking method argue that we need reasons for thinking that everyone should be given an equal share. Indeed, if the so-called "fair" lottery method assigns equal chances to persons with unequal claims, then users of this method would be the ones "playing God" with other people's well-being and lives. We should not assume that just because the lottery is not rigged, and because it gives an equal chance to all, that it is therefore fair. We need to look and see what is fair.

Positive Arguments

In addition to the arguments against the lottery method, defenders of the ranking method argue that often justice demands we weigh the interests of people disproportionately according to various factors. The ranking method rests on skepticism of the idea that all people deserve equal consideration. According to it, we need to determine how much consideration to give people based on relevant criteria. These criteria can be determined by the qualities of and facts about the people vying for consideration. They can also be influenced by the nature of the allocation problem and by the circumstances of the choice situation. Once the relevant criteria are set, a selection procedure ranks potential recipients according to the criteria and then a distribution decision is made.

To get a better sense of this, let's consider how we might begin to methodically develop and apply a ranking method to the Crisis in Space example. The survivors of the crisis are distinguished by the following differentia: age, sex, race, education, contributions to society, burdens on society, dependant status, marital status, emotional state, religious affiliation, intellectual capacity, medical condition, professional responsibilities, occupation, life skills, linguistic skills, public profile, criminal record, character traits, and nationality.

From this list, we need to consider which of these differences and qualities would be relevant for weighting the claims of the survivors. How do we do this? What makes a quality morally relevant in determining whether it should count toward a survivor's claim to further survival? We have an intuitive sense about this, but we need the best principled and grounded argument we can develop to undercut charges that our ranking criteria are arbitrary and unjust. We feel, for instance, that deciding who should live based on the colour of their hair or on the day of the week on which they were born would be wrong because these differences are morally irrelevant. Likewise it is difficult to see the relevancy of an individual's sex, race, or nationality. On the other hand, many feel that whether a person has dependants or professional responsibilities is relevant. The challenge, then, is to develop a method for first identifying what counts as a relevant quality or factor.

What counts will be determined differently by different ethical theories, but we do not have space to work through this process for all of them. Ideally, we should base our argument on theoretical foundations that leave us as much flexibility as possible so our account can evolve in different ways depending upon the ethical framework we ultimately settle upon. Given this, let's develop our argument on some welfarist assumptions. Recall that **Welfarism** is the foundational view in ethics according to which the purpose of morality is to promote the good of those beings that have a good of their own. On the welfarist view, only the welfare of sentient and potentially sentient beings matters for ethics.[3] Therefore, a ranking procedure that is consistent with Welfarism would be one that accords weight to whatever promotes the good of sentient beings. For the survivors, this means that what is relevant to weigh is what would promote their good (what we have referred to as their prudential good) and the welfare of others affected by what happens as a result of the decisions we make.

Roughly, then, we need to identify factors that influence the good of the individual survivors and the good of others that are affected. Since the survivors are all sentient beings, their well-being is morally relevant; therefore, one respect in which the survivors can be ranked is according to (1) the value to them of surviving. Furthermore, since others in society who have a good of their own are also affected by who lives and who dies, another morally relevant respect in which the survivors can be ranked is according to (2) the effect on society of them surviving.

10.3 The Value to the Survivors of Surviving

One way we can rank the survivors is purely in terms of the likely effects on them of surviving. What would the likely losses and benefits to them be? Our analysis of the Killing Machine thought experiment calls into serious doubt the notion that all lives are equally valuable because they are infinitely valuable. Even so, many people might still insist that life *is* priceless. The idea that we all have an equal right to life, as we noted, has a powerful hold on our society, and proponents of this view might appeal to their convic-

tion that life is priceless to try to support this belief. In response, we can note that there is a sense in which life is priceless, but this sense is not the one on which we can base an equal right to life. You can say that your life is priceless because no amount of money can restore your life once it is gone. In this sense your life is beyond any price. But it is another sense of the idea that your life is priceless that is relevant for us: the idea that your life is infinitely valuable, and this is false. We can very greatly value our lives without thinking they are priceless in this second sense. So, for example, although my life is very valuable to me, I don't think its value cancels out the value of everything else in the world. Looked at in this way, the idea that a life is infinitely valuable is preposterous. The challenge, as we noted, is to express the high regard we have for our lives without exaggerating.[4] Beyond this, defenders of a ranking method must fairly compare the values of the lives of different people in cases of distributive justice.

> **Welfarism** is the foundational view in ethics according to which the purpose of morality is to promote the good of those beings that have a good of their own. According to the Welfarist, only welfare matters for ethics.

The reason why the second sense of the word "priceless" is the one that is relevant for us is because our concern with problems of distributive justice involves making moral comparisons between potential outcome distributions. This in turn involves comparing the effects of these outcomes on different people, and one factor involved in this is ranking the relative benefits of these outcomes for these people. In other words, we are interested in the second sense of the word "priceless" because the ranking method commits us to comparing values, including the values of the lives of different individuals.[5]

Part of the problem with comparing the value of lives is that determining the value of a person's life varies depending on one's perspective. Thus, whereas some might regard someone else's life as being of little value even to him, others might disagree and hold that it is greatly valuable. Who is right? This issue is central in the ethical debate over the Latimer case.

10.4 The Latimer Case

The Latimers—Robert, his wife Laura, and their three children—lived on their farm in Wilkie, Saskatchewan. On October 24, 1993, Robert placed his 12-year-old daughter Tracy into his pickup. He ran a hose from the truck's exhaust pipe to its cab and while he sat watching from the box of the pickup, Tracy died of carbon monoxide poisoning. Tracy suffered from a severe form of cerebral palsy. A quadriplegic who weighed 40 pounds at the time of her death, she had undergone numerous surgeries in her short life, with the prospect of more ahead of her. She could not talk or feed herself, and she was said to have the mental capacity of an infant. In his confession to the RCMP, Mr. Latimer said he killed his daughter out of love for her because her life was one of unremitting suffering and severe pain with no prospects for improvement.

Charged with first-degree murder, Mr. Latimer was convicted of murder in the second degree by a jury on November 16, 1994. As is customary, the judge did not inform the jurors that conviction on this charge brings with it a minimum 10-year sentence. The jury recommended a one-year sentence.[6] Mr. Latimer appealed, and on July 18, 1995, the Saskatchewan Court of Appeal decided 2–1 against him. Upon further appeal to the Supreme Court, a new trial was ordered on the grounds of jury interference. Prior to the original trial, the RCMP, acting on orders from the Crown, had questioned jurors about their beliefs on topics such as euthanasia, abortion, and religion. The second trial began on November 5, 1997. The Crown contested Mr. Latimer's claim about the quality of his daughter's life, asserting in a brief submitted to the court that Tracy enjoyed visits from her family and that she "enjoyed outings, one of which was to the circus, where she smiled when the horses went by."

Once again, the jury convicted Mr. Latimer of second-degree murder. However, in view of the circumstances, they recommended that he be eligible for parole after a year. On December 1, 1997, the judge in this case, Justice Ted Noble, handed down his sentence. He granted Mr. Latimer an extraordinary constitutional exemption from the 10-year minimum sentence on the grounds that such a punishment in this case would be cruel and unusual. Instead he imposed a punishment of two years less a day. The first year would be served in jail, the remainder at Mr. Latimer's farm. In his decision Justice Noble argued that the law "recognizes that the moral culpability or moral blameworthiness of murder can vary from one convicted offender to another," and he described Tracy's murder as a case of "compassionate homicide." He found that Mr. Latimer was a loving father who acted out of a concern for his daughter in murdering her. He also acknowledged Tracy's suffering and the adverse effects her severe disabilities had on her enjoyment of life. Nevertheless, Justice Noble stated that Mr. Latimer wrongly took her life. He argued that Tracy's suffering "was not unremitting, and her life had value and quality."

The Crown appealed Justice Noble's sentence, and on November 23, 1998, the Saskatchewan Court of Appeal overturned Mr. Latimer's constitutional exemption and imposed the 10-year minimum sentence. This time Mr. Latimer appealed, again to the Supreme Court. On January 18, 2001, the court announced a unanimous decision against him, upholding the life sentence with no chance of parole for 10 years. Mr. Latimer is currently serving his sentence. With his legal options exhausted, his only chance for a reduced sentence is if the federal cabinet grants him one.

10.5 Second-Class Citizenship?

What are we to make of this tragic case? Two issues are especially relevant for our discussion: the idea that all life is equally valuable and the question of how to measure the value of other people's lives both to them and to others. Advocates for the disabled feared that a reduction in Mr. Latimer's minimum sentence would send a message to Canadian society that, according to our law and government, disabled citizens' lives are less valuable than able-bodied people's lives. One worry was that Canadians would generally not distinguish between Tracy Latimer's very severe disabilities and others who live with much more moderate ones. They would instead lump all people who face the challenges of disabilities into the same category. Advocates feared, in other words, that a decision for Mr. Latimer would sentence all Canadians who live with disabilities to "second-class citizenship." There was also a concern that such a decision could open the door for other similar cases where people would seek an exemption from the minimum sentence for murder.[7] In response to the Supreme Court's final ruling, Cheryl Gulliver of the Canadian Association for Community Living remarked, "It means that when people who are vulnerable, that their life is as valuable as everybody else. It's true equality."[8]

We have surveyed some reasons for doubting the claim that everyone's life is equally valuable to them because all lives are infinitely valuable. What other ethical justification is there for this view? It is true that Tracy Latimer's life was priceless in the sense that no amount of money could restore her life to her after it was taken. But the idea that her life was as valuable to her as everyone else's is to them needs to be supported. Thus we need to examine the moral claim to an equal right to life more carefully.

In our treatment of the question of how much consideration we should give to individuals, we have so far confined our discussion to the implications the arguments have for cases of distributive justice like the Crisis in Space example. However, the Latimer case raises wider possible implications. If one favours the ranking method over the lottery method, does that also commit one to saying that some people deserve fewer or inferior rights than others in the wide range of situations covered by the law? Mr. Latimer's case rested on his claim that he was helping Tracy when he killed her, which suggests that he believed that her life was less valuable to her than the lives of most people are to them. If we agree with him, are we committed to re-evaluating our commitment to according every Canadian equal rights? If so, what implications would this have for the setting of policy and law besides the sorts of cases of distributive justice that we are focusing on? Practically speaking, how could we re-evaluate anyway? Those who defend the ranking method over the lottery method will have to come to terms with these other implications and the questions to which they give rise.

10.6 Determining the Value of Life

Before we can address the question whether all lives are equally valuable to the subjects of the lives, we need a way of at least roughly comparing the value of the lives of different people. This is a difficult problem that we will not be able to resolve here. However, we can at least identify some of the issues and questions that need to be resolved in order to answer this question. One way to proceed is to identify the minimum conditions one must meet in order to enjoy life at all. We could then reject those who fail to meet these conditions as living lives that are not valuable to their bearers, let alone as valuable as everyone else's lives. We could then try to rank those who meet the minimum conditions in terms of the value of their life beyond these minimal levels by attaching at least rough measures to the value of their experiences and likely future experiences.

This modest proposal faces a number of criticisms and hurdles. Some argue, for instance, that since all (usually human) life is sacred, all life is equally valuable and should be regarded as such. On this view, even those who experience their life as a never-ending misery and hardship have a duty to prize life because God regards their life as holy. As we have noted, however, arguments that appeal to metaphysical beliefs that rest on faith do not carry weight in our discussion. What can we say to those who do not believe, as a matter of faith, that life is sacred? In a secular society, we must write laws and public policies that are open to the critical scrutiny of all regardless of our own religious convictions. Divested of its religious associations, the idea that all life is valuable, let alone equally valuable, becomes an empirical claim that stands in need of support. In the face of people who experience their lives as disvaluable, it seems the burden of proof is on those who insist that all life is valuable, and should thus be regarded as such, to make their case.

So what are the minimum conditions one must meet to enjoy life at all? One must have a life of some duration, be capable of experiencing, and experience or have the potential to experience life positively. These first two conditions touch on ground we will cover in Chapter 11. The first condition excludes dead beings and inanimate things. The second condition excludes all non-sentient beings, and those lacking the potential for sentience. It is this third condition, the idea that for life to be valuable one must experience, or have the potential for experiencing, life positively that we need to address. What does this mean? To fill out an account of the idea of a positive life value, we need a better appreciation of the contributors to, or ingredients of, a good life. The following list is reasonably comprehensive and gives us some sense of the variety of goods that contribute to living a prudentially good life, that is, a life good for the person whose life it is. Here, then, are seven overlapping components of good lives in no particular order:

1. the goods of pursuing knowledge, education, understanding, contemplation, spiritual reflection, intellectual challenge and stimulation

2. the goods of appreciating beauty and experiencing aesthetic pleasure, including creating art (music, dance, painting, writing, sculpture, film, photography, theatre, etc.)

3. the goods of solidarity, friendship, fellowship, love, co-operation, and social interaction generally

4. the goods of autonomy, achievement, accomplishment, self-realization, the joys of competition, and purposeful activity

5. the goods of the pleasures, including leisure activities and exercise

6. the satisfaction of all other course-of-life needs, including freedom from anxiety, harassment, and relief from pain, anguish, sickness, and injury

7. self-respect

These sources of welfare give us some indication of the complexity of the idea of living a life that is prudentially valuable. Since we recognize many potential contributors to a good life, our account is not simplistic. For example, it does not simply reduce to the idea that for a life to be good it must be pleasurable, because pleasure is not our only source of welfare. So we can make sense of the idea that even though people endure chronic pain, their lives are still prudentially valuable because of the satisfaction they draw from their relationships, work, or accomplishments. Minimally, we can at least say that lives that lack the above sources of welfare are not prudentially valuable.

There is also the question of time. Typically, sentient beings experience some of these values in some combination for some duration of life. How much is enough? There is also the question of quantity (How much is enough?), and the problems of combining the two factors (How much for how long?). Beyond this, we would have to weigh the value of these goods against the disvalue of negative states and experiences and determine how to factor into our judgments the potential for the experience of future goods and future disvalues in a life.

These points are relevant for settling one of the main disputes in the Latimer case, namely, the question of the value of Tracy Latimer's life to her. At Mr. Latimer's trials, the defence and prosecution disagreed over the answer to this question; prosecutors argued that her life was valuable. Justice Noble ruled that her life had "value and quality." Furthermore, advocates for people with disabilities argued that Mr. Latimer underestimated the value of Tracy's life to her, and that most people tend to judge the value of other's lives by their own standard of what makes life worth living. In contrast, Mr. Latimer argued that his daughter's life was a misery to her with no realistic prospects for improvement.

In reflecting upon this case, it seems that if it could be shown that Tracy would have wanted to continue living because her life was valuable enough to her, that would establish that Mr. Latimer was mistaken in his judgment and guilty of murdering his daughter. In that case, the wrong would have been depriving Tracy of the good of life. From the perspective of the person who is killed, this is the main reason why murder is immoral; it deprives one of the good of life. Therefore, it seems to follow that if continued life is prudentially bad, that is, if life offers mostly misery and meaningless suffering, then at least from the perspective of the person who is killed, killing that person may not be prudentially bad. Thus, even if this is not true of the Latimer case, it raises the possibility that there may be other cases where the person killed both could not express his wishes and was living a life that was not even minimally prudentially valuable. It would seem that in these sorts of cases that from the perspective of the person who is killed, the killing would not be immoral.

The Latimer case is unlike typical cases of murder in at least two respects. In most cases, people are able to express their preference not to die, and we assume that the loss of the victim's life is a bad thing for her. In this case, however, not only was Tracy Latimer unable to express her wishes about preferring to live or die but also, due to her condition, it was not clear whether the loss of her life from her perspective was bad. In light of this uncertainty it was necessary on the prosecution's side to show that her death was bad for her and necessary for the defence to claim that the loss of her life was a good thing from her perspective. Therefore, the question whether her life was even minimally prudentially valuable, including whether it had the potential for reaching this level, was crucial.

So how can we judge who was right? Obviously, this is another difficult question, but we can at least note that whether Tracy Latimer's life was even minimally prudentially valuable to her does not depend merely on whether she ever enjoyed or derived satisfaction from anything. Since the standard of judging a life to be minimally prudentially valuable requires judging a life over time, and judging the balance of value and disvalue in the life, it is possible to enjoy some moments in the course of an otherwise unbearably prudentially poor existence. Thus, establishing that Tracy Latimer seemed to enjoy a visit to the circus and that she seemed to enjoy visits from her relatives is not sufficient for showing that, overall, her life was even minimally prudentially valuable.

This assumes that the moral badness of murder from the victim's perspective is that it deprives the victim of the good of life. However, those arguing against Mr. Latimer might hold that the badness of his action was not in depriving his daughter of the good of life, it was taking her life at all. On this view, murder seems to be wrong because life is sacred but, as we noted earlier, the burden of proof here is on those espousing this view to show that it is reasonable. At first glance, at least, it seems that life is not always overall prudentially good.

Exercises 10.1

Progress Check

1. Explain the distinction between the lottery method and the ranking method.

2. How can defenders of ranking methods respond to the criticism that such approaches involve "playing God" with people's lives and well-being?

3. How do ranking methods of distributing scarce resources work? Briefly explain.

4. Outline the argument for determining what makes a person's qualities relevant for deciding whether to give them consideration in the Crisis in Space example.

5. Why is a person's hair colour morally irrelevant for fairly allocating resources in situations like the Crisis in Space?

6. What is Welfarism?

7. What does it mean to say that "life is priceless"?

8. What was the concern regarding "second-class citizenship" sparked by the Latimer case?

9. Why did some fear that a finding in favour of Mr. Latimer would sentence Canadians with disabilities to second-class citizenship?

10. What are the minimum conditions of enjoying life at all?

11. Why does a sophisticated account of a prudentially good life not simply state that for a life to be good it must be pleasurable?

12. Briefly outline the notion of a minimally prudentially valuable life.

13. Explain the debate over the question of the value of Tracy Latimer's life. What is the ethical significance of this question?

Questions for Further Reflection

1. Explain and critically evaluate the view that the following factors are relevant criteria for allocating scarce public goods:
   a) dependant status
   b) professional responsibilities

2. Under what circumstances, if any, would a person's
   a) sex,
   b) race, or
   c) nationality
   be a relevant factor for allocating scarce public goods? Defend your view.

3. Briefly outline the problems in determining the prudential value of someone's life.

4. Under what circumstances, if any, is a person's life disvaluable? Explain and support your view.

5. Under what circumstances, if any, is someone justified in killing someone else whose life is disvaluable? Defend your view.

6. What problems do you see with the idea of describing an account of a minimally prudentially valuable life that would be applicable to all people?

7. What would one need to know to have answered the question of whether Tracy Latimer's life was minimally prudentially valuable? Explain and defend your view.

10.7 The Problems of Making Interpersonal Comparisons of Prudential Value

Imagine that we achieved our reasonably modest goal of explaining the conditions necessary for living a life that is at least minimally prudentially valuable. To complete our project of ranking people by the prudential value of their lives, we would also need to contend with the problems of comparing the prudential value of one life to another one. These are the problems of making intersubjective comparisons, or comparisons of value between different people. What could be the basis for these comparisons of welfare? One possibility is that we could rely on the self-reports of the people involved. Generally, we could conclude that those who say they are well off are living lives higher in prudential value than those who say that life is only poor to fair. Although it seems that a convincing story about the basis for intersubjective comparisons will likely factor in the self-reports and judgments of the people involved somehow, there are obvious limitations and difficulties with relying exclusively on these. For instance, in cases where we

Group Work Activity:

The Latimer Case

Your Task

Imagine that you and the members of your group are Supreme Court justices on the Canadian Supreme Court of Ethics. Your task is to outline the cases for and against Robert Latimer on the charge of wrongfully killing his daughter. Whether you find him innocent or guilty, you must explain and justify your judgment. Also, if you find him guilty you should also make a determination of just punishment, and defend your sentence. If you reach a unanimous decision, then you can jointly write it. If your decision is split, you must write two judgments. However you decide, be prepared to defend your decision(s) in class. Your decision(s) will be judged on the basis of the quality of the arguments you advance in support of it (or them).

Since you are not legal experts, you are not being asked to make legal judgments. Rather, you should focus on the moral issues in the case and base your judgments on them.

Note: This chapter contains a brief outline of the facts of the case. To further inform your decision, you are encouraged to further research the case. Good places to start are the references at the end of this chapter, the library, and the Internet.

have no self-reports to go on (fetuses, the severely autistic), or only non-verbal ones (babies, very young children), our method would be useless or severely limited. There are also questions about the reliability of our self-reports of our state of well-being. Not including those who simply lie about how life is for them, we would need to contend with cases where people seem to have an unreasonably rosy or gloomy picture of their life. For one thing, our skewed judgments of our own state can be caused by misinformation ("yes, that bloodletting was just what I needed") or by a lack of information ("it sure looked safe to eat"). Alternatively, they may be caused by faulty judgment. Amartya Sen has identified the problem of people who misdescribe their state of well-being as a result of being oppressed or exploited:

> The hopeless beggar, the precarious landless labourer, the dominated housewife, the hardened unemployed or the over-exhausted coolie may all take pleasures in small mercies, and manage to suppress intense suffering for the necessity of continuing survival, but it would be ethically deeply mistaken to attach a correspondingly small value to the loss of their well-being because of this survival strategy.[9]

Any account of intersubjective welfare comparisons that rested on individual self-reporting would have to resolve these problems.

Another option is to completely exclude any judgments or self-reports from the people involved when one makes intersubjective comparisons of well-being. On this approach, we do not even consult them and instead judge how well different people's lives are going for them according to an objective measure like, for example, their share of the basic goods and opportunities that people need to live prudentially good lives. A flaw in this approach, though, is one we discuss in greater length in Chapter 12. Arguably, a necessary condition of someone's life going well for him is that he has a positive attitude toward it. We all know of people who by external or objective measures would be judged to be faring very well in life but who genuinely seem to be unhappy. A method of making intersubjective comparisons that did not even consult people's attitudes about their own well-being would be in

danger of completely overlooking the very thing it was supposed to be determining.

This sort of method of making intersubjective comparisons of value between people rests on another flawed assumption: the idea that the value of life experiences is the same for different people. If determining an individual's well-being was a simple function of calculating the amount and number of goods and opportunities she received, then we could simply estimate the total value of life experiences for each person and then make our comparisons. But we are different, and we derive satisfaction in different ways from different things. We also value similar kinds of experiences differently. So, for instance, the value of the experience of reading this sentence might differ very much between someone who has been literate for many years and someone who is just becoming literate very late in life.

In making judgments about the value of life to others we need to try to take their perspective into account. On the other hand, we should not overvalue their assessments. Someone's claim that his experience of life really is more valuable than the lives of everyone else is unreasonable. The challenge for developing a good account of the basis or bases upon which we can make intersubjective comparisons of value is to strike some sort of reasonable balance between these competing demands and perspectives.

In the absence of having a fully worked-out account that solves these problems, should we abandon all ranking methods? Does the fair use of a ranking method depend upon the resolution of these issues? A defender of ranking methods could argue that it does not for several reasons. On this outlook, the problems perhaps limit the usefulness of any method, but do not require that we simply dump it. First, even without a resolution for all the problems we noted, we can still rightly make at least rough intersubjective comparisons for a range of cases where there are great differences between the prudential life values of the people being compared. On this view, the problems with intersubjective comparisons of prudential value apply to cases where the differences are less pronounced.

Where we can make rough comparisons, we can say that lives of very low quality, by the measure of our sources of welfare, are less valuable to their bearers than lives high in quality. In addition to the dimension of quality or degree of welfare, we can also factor in likely future length of life. A life very high in quality but that will probably last only for five more minutes is less prudentially valuable than a life of marginally lower quality that will likely last for fifty more years. Generally speaking, when it comes to comparing at least some minimum standard of quality of life, more is better.

These regrettably very vague remarks about length and quality of life provide us with some basis for developing our ranking criteria. However, to add greater precision to our ranking method, we would need to address the many questions that arise in the course of thinking about these issues. Despite this, we now have grounds for identifying some of the differentia from our original list as relevant for informing our ranking judgments. So, for example, an individual's age is arguably a potentially morally relevant factor since there is a connection between a person's age and the length of life she likely still has to live. To take our earlier example from Chapter 9, you can argue that the 107-year-old man's life is less prudentially valuable than the young mother's life in part because he probably has much less time to experience the good of life than she does. Thus, even if he was living a comparable quality of life to the young woman, prudentially speaking his life is less valuable.

In addition to age, what other differentia from our list are relevant for ranking the survivors according to the prudential value of their lives? When it comes to making judgments about quality of life, we would have to make a connection between the quality identified and the sources of welfare. To use the quality in our ranking, we would have to apply it to the survivors and then defend our application.

In response to concerns that our ranking method is looking rather vague, defenders of ranking methods also argue that the issue is not whether a ranking method is perfect, it is whether it is superior to alternative options. Thus, supporters of a ranking method could try to argue that their approach should be used because, despite its limitations, it remains fairer than other ranking methods and the lottery method. We need to continue to develop the method and simultaneously develop strategies for dealing with its shortcomings. For example, defenders of this view might argue that we should use their ranking method where we can fairly do so and perhaps resort to a lottery method in situations where ranking would be unfair. So if we had to choose between two people born days or weeks apart, distinguishing them on the basis of the time they will likely enjoy whatever we are distributing would be arbitrary. Instead, in cases like these we should flip a coin.

Another possible response to concerns about the limitations of our method for making intersubjective comparisons of value is to hold that there is another relevant kind of consideration for judging someone's ranking, namely, the effects on others who are involved. Rather than pursue the arguments regarding the shortcomings of the method for ranking people on the basis of intersubjective comparisons of value, let's turn to consider how one might go about ranking people by this other criterion.

10.8 Effects on Society

In turning away from the problems of ranking the survivors according to the costs and benefits to them of surviving to considering the effects on others affected, we might just be jumping out of the frying pan into the fire. As complicated as the task of ranking individual lives according to their prudential value is, our task is made much more complicated by raising this next issue because ranking the survivors according to the effects on others raises many puzzling questions. Again, our best hope here is to make some progress and introduce more questions to ponder.

As a first step at sketching out how a ranking method might weigh the effects on others of saving some group of the survivors, we can simplify our task by categorizing those affected and dealing with the effects on them separately. Specifically, we can examine the effects on

1. the survivors' friends, family, dependants, and others to whom they have special obligations,

2. the other survivors, and

3. society in general.

1. The effects on the survivors' friends, family, dependants, and others to whom they have special obligations

The survivors are distinguished by their marital status, their dependant status, and their professional responsibilities. Arguably all of these factors are ethically relevant for ranking them because of the connection between these factors and this first set of wider effects. Our society is organized such that we have special obligations to some individuals as a result of our relations with them. We have special obligations to our friends, family, and dependants. For example, a father has responsibilities to his children that other people in society who are not so related to the children do not have. Due to these responsibilities and the attendant expectations of the children, it follows that the children have claims against their father that they do not have against others. Therefore, the death of their father would impact these children in ways that the death of someone without his responsibilities would not. So we have some reason for thinking that an individual's dependant status is a relevant factor to consider when creating a fair ranking method.

In response, some dispute the relevance of this sort of reason because admitting it would unfairly discriminate against those who voluntarily choose not to have children and those who cannot have them. Furthermore, one might question the fairness of a society that is organized such that we have these special responsibilities. Alternatively, some concede that whereas this sort of reason may be relevant sometimes,

because the strength of the reason will always be weak, it should never make the difference in deciding whether someone should live or die. We should similarly classify obligations people have to their spouses and to other adult dependants.

The case of professionals who have special obligations as a result of their position in society or as a result of their occupation also needs to be considered here. Although the obligations are not typically to family or friends, the obligation is a special one that others in society do not have, so there is a connection to the issue of dependant status. Psychiatrists, lawyers, physicians, and many other professionals have obligations to their clients that no one else has. Moreover, these obligations can greatly impact their clients' well-being. In Chapter 9 we considered the argument that sometimes those with these special obligations should not be free to voluntarily choose to die. Specifically, we considered whether Dr. Sharma should be allowed to volunteer to leave. If we argue that she should not, it seems that to be consistent, she should also receive more consideration for staying as a result of her professional obligation to care for those in need of medical attention.

2. The effects on the other survivors

Underlying the ethical rationale for using a ranking method in the first place is a commitment to some principle of utility over a commitment to equality. The basic idea is that fairness requires that we strive to do as much good as we can, or more carefully that we do more good rather than less. Given this, some might argue that in addition to considering the effects on the survivors to them of surviving, one must also take into account the effects on the group of our selections. If, for example, there was someone who was likely to murder the others, this probable effect gives us a reason for excluding the likely murderer. Of course, in our scenario there is nothing so dramatic, so the question becomes whether the likely effects on group survival and welfare are enough to make a difference in deciding who should live and who should die.

3. The effects on society in general

Finally, many people argue that we should also weigh the probable effects on wider society when determining who should be selected. However, there are many questions and potential pitfalls down this road. The first one is making a case that such effects are relevant, that sentient beings are affected by the decision. Once the case for possible relevancy is established, we must show that the difference to society is likely great enough to justify making a difference in selecting the final six survivors. To take another dramatic example, imagine that one of the survivors was needed so that she could save the lives of everyone on Olympia, and there was no one else who could accomplish this. In this case, arguably not only would this be a relevant reason to consider this person but it would also outweigh any other consideration for anyone else. So it seems that at least sometimes the effects on others is relevant.

Of course, when we are faced with more common and less extreme examples, like the Crisis in Space situation, the task of fairly factoring in effects on society becomes much more difficult. All of the survivors will likely have some effect on the society of Olympia, and beyond that perhaps back on Earth. However, no one seems to be either vital to the survival of the inhabitants of the colony or so dangerous that we should say that he must stay or go. The problem then is to try to determine the extent of the effects that each person's survival will have and then determine how much weight to give to this. For example, people are sometimes inclined to give the reformed drug addict, Mr. Yamamoto, less consideration because of the potential threat he poses. But to justify this judgment, wouldn't one have to clearly demonstrate the threat and then present a convincing case that it is fair that his chances be discounted because of his past addiction? Obviously, this in turn raises a number of questions about the moral badness of his addiction, his culpability for having it, the likelihood of him relapsing, the probability of him then harming others, and so on.

In response to concerns like these, many argue that we should simply disregard all such considerations and instead either abandon the ranking approach or focus exclusively on likely benefits to dependants and to the survivors themselves. Although this may or may not be a good idea for this situation, the idea that effects on society are never relevant is, as we just showed, false. So always ignoring this factor is a mistake unless we can advance another reason or reasons that would convince us. If such a case cannot be made, we need to address the difficult question of determining when a person's influence is likely to be great enough to make a difference to our rankings. If we don't want to accord incremental weight to someone's probable effects, whether likely good or bad, because to do so is impracticable or because it leads to arbitrariness, then we must set some threshold that would need to be crossed for this sort of reason to count.

We will also need a better idea of what counts as having a relevant effect on society. Although we cannot examine this issue in great detail, we can at least present some points to ponder. First, if what is relevant is what affects the sentient beings involved, we should consider both positive and negative effects. Therefore, we should examine both contributions to society and detractions from it. But how should we consider both? Are they equally important, or is one kind of effect more important than the other kind? More likely whether one is more important will depend on the specific circumstances. If so, then what sorts of circumstances justify weighting one more than the other one and why?

Also, to avoid unjust age discrimination, it seems that we should regard these effects both prospectively and retrospectively. That is, we should weigh both likely future effects on society and consider past effects. Many argue that what counts is what people are likely to do for society in the future. But why shouldn't we also factor into our deliberations what people have done for society in the past? Isn't it a simple matter of justice that we owe more to those who have given more than others have? Imagine there are two women competing for some scarce resource. They started from similar points in society with similar opportunities and skills. One woman devoted her life to helping the disadvantaged while the other concentrated on having a good time. Shouldn't we give the resource to the person who gave so much more to make life better for others?

If we accept that we should consider both forward-looking and backward-looking effects, we will also have to contend with the difficulties of ranking them against each other. How do we fairly compare a person's probability of contributing to society against someone else's actual past contributions? If we favour actual contributions, aren't we unfairly discriminating against younger people? On the other hand, some argue that we should be directed by what will benefit sentient beings in the future so we should discount past contributions and give greater weight to likely future contributions. But doesn't this unfairly discriminate against older people? Also, wouldn't this sort of policy tend to discourage people from helping others?

Apart from determining what counts as having a relevant effect on society, we will also need to somehow measure these effects and rank them against each other. We have so far been taking this for granted, but apart from a range of extreme examples, this task is fraught with difficult evaluative judgments. One problem is fairly determining what counts as contributing to society. Some argue that economic measurements of productivity could help us here, but others reject such measurements insofar as they are tied to the production and consumption of goods and services. In the eyes of these people, those who contribute to the endless pursuit of economic growth and consumption inflict harm on the environment and therefore generally take away from the collective good.

To take a different kind of example, do artists and philosophers who question our received attitudes and values contribute to society? James Joyce's work was censored, and he was a scandal to the Church and conservative Irish society before he was later more widely embraced for his literary genius. In philosophy, Socrates was famously put to death on the charges of heresy and corrupting the youth of Athens. Did these men contribute to society? Most of us would say now that they did, but we have the benefit of hindsight. The challenge is to make fair judgments as we go along. So, for instance, do graffiti artists who protest against dominant power structures in our society contribute to society or are they just a bunch of criminals with no respect for private property? Often, graffiti artists create works that challenge prevailing attitudes. Indeed, one might argue that one purpose of graffiti art is to foment dissent. However, in both its form and content, graffiti offends many. It is also illegal and, arguably, for it to retain its effect it must remain so, much like acts of civil disobedience. In other words, much of the power of graffiti art comes from the illegal circumstances of its creation and the connected message of the work. As such, how can a society even recognize the contributions that graffiti artists make to society without thereby co-opting them or undermining the social value of their work? Could there be an official showing of graffiti in a national art gallery?

The Problems of Comparing Different Effects

Just as we differently value things and pursuits in life we also disagree about what counts as contributing to and taking away from society. In other words, any method of making comparative judgments would have to address worries about "playing God." Whose value system should be used? What counts as bias? This problem actually runs deeper than just finding the right value system to use to make comparisons. It raises the question whether there is a single right value system. Of course, people disagree about these basic value judgments. Whereas we might be inclined to favour value systems that reflect the *status quo,* what justification is there for them apart from the fact that they are dominant? Should this be a matter of which values are most popular, or not? For example, in our society we seem to tend to value in many different ways those who have entrepreneurial skills and competitive instincts over those who are more nurturing and co-operative. Do business people and deal-makers contribute more to society than child-care and social workers? Judged by standard measures like their wealth and the status we accord them, the answer seems to be "yes," but of course this is debatable.

Likewise it is debatable whether they should be so regarded. Any attempt to rank people according to their contributions to and detractions from society will have to contend with these thorny problems and construct some sort of ranking procedure that fairly measures and compares these judgments.

We have surveyed just a few of the issues and questions that need to be addressed to fairly implement a ranking method that factored in the effects on society of those who are vying for consideration. In addition to identifying what counts as contributing to or taking away from society, and in addition to devising an account that would allow us to fairly measure and compare these effects, we would also have to apply our method to particular cases like the Crisis in Space. Unfortunately, we do not have the space to discuss the actual survivors in our example at any length and make a case for selecting some group of them. However, in Chapter 13 we will apply some of the conclusions and lessons we have drawn to a real-life problem, the question of the just allocation of scarce health care resources.

The Difficulty of Comparing Prudential Value and the Effects on Society

Apart from all of the other questions we have noted, a ranking method that included both consideration of the value to the survivors of surviving and the effects on society would also need to give relative weightings to these different values. Should the effects on those vying for consideration be weighted more heavily than the effects on others in society who would be affected by our distribution decisions? If so, how much more? Does this depend on the particular circumstances of the allocation situation? If so, does this mean that we would have to adjust our weightings depending on the nature of the specific problem we are examining? How would we do this?

We noted in Part One that Utilitarians argue that we should weight the interests of all persons equally, so it seems that at least one moral theory provides us with an apparently straightforward response to our difficulty. However, in

order to accept the Utilitarian perspective, we would need an argument for giving each person equal consideration in the first place, and as we have already noted, this argument is not obviously forthcoming.

10.9 Review

In this chapter we further pursued answering our question about the value of human life. We addressed this question from the perspective of formulating public policy and law, and we narrowed our focus to consider how we should adjudicate competing claims for scarce resources among humans in situations like the Crisis in Space example. However, whereas in Chapter 9 we focused on explaining and evaluating arguments for giving all humans equal claims to these scarce resources, here we concentrated on the issues raised by allocating resources according to the qualities of the people vying for consideration and the circumstances of their situations. Typically, this involves granting unequal claims to and shares of the resources.

After briefly further examining some reasons for not giving equal claims, the remainder of the chapter was devoted to developing a fair ranking method and considering some of the problems and issues to which this project gives rise. The method that we began to develop rests on the welfarist assumption that any ranking procedure must distribute resources on the basis of what would promote the good of the sentient beings involved. Thus, the morally relevant factors of a fair ranking method are those that influence the good of these beings. In the case of the Crisis in Space example, we classified these factors according to their influence on the survivors themselves and to the other sentient beings affected by our allocation decisions.

To help illustrate some of the problems with this first issue of fairly assessing the value of someone's life to her, we discussed the well-known case of Robert and Tracy Latimer. A central point of dispute in this case was the question of the value of Tracy Latimer's life to her, that is, the prudential value of her life. In the course of considering this question, we discussed the idea that life may not always be prudentially valuable overall, and we explored the notion of what it is for a life to be even minimally prudentially valuable. Apart from assessing the prudential value of people's lives to develop our ranking method, we also need to make comparisons between people of the prudential value of their lives. In exploring some challenges with making these interpersonal comparisons of prudential value, we considered the role that a person's self-evaluation of his well-being might play in our method.

Finally, we considered some ethical issues concerning identifying and judging the value of a person's life to others, including society in general. In weighing the effects on others, we examined the moral claims that they have on us as a result of our special connections to them. These include obligations we have in virtue of our parental and family responsibilities and our professional responsibilities. We then examined some problems with trying to measure an individual's contributions to society, comparing the different kinds of contributions that different people make, and identifying a single perspective to make these judgments.

Notes

1. The Crisis in Space case is presented in Section 9.2. Since a number of references are made to this case, you should read it over if you have not already done so.

2. For an explanation of what is meant by giving someone "equal consideration," see Section 9.1.

3. See Sumner (1996), chapters 6 and 7.

4. Philosophers have been prone to make exaggerations of this sort in their work. One famous example is John Rawls's claim in *A Theory of Justice* that "Each person possesses an inviolability founded on justice that even the welfare of society as a whole cannot override." See Rawls (1971), p. 3.

5. The question of the ethical legitimacy and limits of making these kinds of comparisons is the problem of the commensurability of value. For an excellent discussion of this problem, see Griffin (1986), Chapter 5.

6. As reported on the CBC's *The National* on November 13, 1997, three jurors—Carolyn

Huber, Kelly Keyko, and Maggie Nogue—told CBC reporter Eric Sorensen that this information likely would have made a difference to their original finding of guilt.

7. The imposition of a minimum mandatory sentence for second-degree murder was passed into law in Canada in 1976. It was part of a compromise measure for abolishing capital punishment. At the final appeal hearing, lawyers for the federal government argued that a decision in favour of Latimer would jeopardize the values underlying the imposition of a minimum sentence. Some have argued too that such a decision would have opened the door for other convicted murderers to appeal their sentences on the grounds that they constituted cruel and unusual punishment.

8. From the CBC's *The National*, January 18, 2001.

9. Sen (1987), pp. 45–46.

Exercises 10.2

Progress Check

1. What are intersubjective comparisons of prudential life-values?

2. What difficulties are there with basing intersubjective comparisons of prudential life-values on the self-reports of the people being compared?

3. Why would intersubjective comparisons of prudential value between people be "in danger of completely overlooking the very thing they are supposed to be determining" if they make no mention at all of the self-reports and attitudes of the people being compared?

4. Why is it true that when it comes to comparing at least some minimum standard of quality of life, more is better?

5. Outline an argument for considering a person's dependant status when developing a fair ranking method.

6. Imagine you were faced with choosing who should receive the only life-saving dose of medicine: a young and otherwise healthy mother of three or a 107-year-old blind, deaf, and immobile man in the advanced stages of senile dementia. What ethical principle supports the case for giving the medicine to the young mother?

7. For the purposes of allocating consideration in examples like the Crisis in Space, and assuming

that we should weigh the effects on society, what counts as having an effect on society?

8. What is the argument for considering both prospective and retrospective effects?

9. Briefly outline the problems mentioned above with determining what contributing to society consists of.

Questions for Further Reflection

1. What suggestions do you have for contending with the problems of relying on the self-reports of people of their own well-being that are due to
   a) misinformation,
   b) a lack of information, and
   c) faulty judgment?

2. Explain and critically evaluate the view that intersubjective comparisons of prudential life-values need not make any reference to the views of the people being compared.

3. Why isn't the task of comparing the value of life between different people a simple matter of adding up and comparing their share of the basic goods and opportunities that one needs to live a prudentially good life?

4. Outline how you think we should go about both respecting people's accounts of the prudential value of their life and not overvaluing their views.

5. Do people who (a) choose not to have children and (b) cannot have children deserve less consideration in situations like the Crisis in Space than those who do have children? Why or why not? What morally relevant difference, if any, is there between situations (a) and (b)?

6. Explain and critically evaluate the view that people convicted of crimes deserve less consideration for scarce public goods than people who have not been convicted. Under what conditions, if any, is a person's criminal record a relevant factor in these cases?

7. How does one fairly compare a person's likelihood of contributing to society to someone else's actual past contributions?

Weblinks

I have benefited greatly from the wealth of information on the Latimer case on the CBC's Web site. The transcripts from *The National* have been especially useful. To read this information, go to **www.cbc.ca** and enter "Latimer" in the search engine.

The Scope of Morality I: Anthropocentrism and Welfarism

Learning Outcomes

In this chapter we consider and contrast two positions on the question of the proper scope of ethics. Anthropocentrism is the view that only humans can and should be given moral consideration. Welfarism endorses the view that all beings have a prudential good; all sentient beings can and should be given moral consideration. In the course of our discussion we consider the basic arguments for these positions and some of the debate over accepting them.

Upon the successful completion of this chapter, you will be able to

1. identify the anthropocentrist account of the proper scope of morality;
2. explain the distinction between the nature of value and its instances;
3. distinguish between the concepts of instrumental value and intrinsic value;
4. appreciate the distinction between subjects and objects as this bears on the welfarist view;
5. explicate what it means to say that the experiencing subjects of lives are valuers;
6. describe the welfarist view of the scope of morality and appreciate the role that consciousness plays in this;
7. outline some of the implications that accepting Welfarism has for animal liberation;
8. articulate the case for including those with the potential for gaining consciousness among those for whom Welfarists can have a moral concern; and
9. explain and evaluate the argument that Welfarism is flawed because it admits the possibility that the practice of necrophilia may be ethical.

11.1 Introduction

Our concern in Part Two is with examining moral issues and questions from various perspectives. Thus far, we have considered some issues that pertain to ethics and the individual, ethics in relationships, and ethics in society. However, in all of these discussions we have limited our focus to the ways ethics bears on humans. In the final two chapters of this part of the book, we turn our attention to some moral issues that concern non-human animals and the environment. There are many issues worthy of our attention in these areas, but since so much of ethics has presupposed that ethics is for man and, more recently, for humans, a logical theme for our investigation is the question of the scope of morality.

This question asks, Who can be given moral consideration? We will examine four competing answers to this question, the first two in this chapter, and the final two in Chapter 12. Moving from the narrowest to the widest view, we begin with the anthropocentric outlook that humans are the only types of beings that can (and should) be given moral consideration. In contrast, Welfarists argue that all beings that have a good of their own are logically capable of receiving consideration, and although this category includes many humans, it includes many non-human animals, too. Since Welfarists believe that all sentient and potentially sentient creatures are logically capable of receiving moral consideration, and since not all living beings are sentient or potentially sentient, Welfarists argue that many living beings are not the kind of beings that can be given consideration for their own sake. In contrast, the biocentric view holds that all living and potentially living beings can and should be given consideration. On this outlook, whether one is alive or not is morally important, and we should demonstrate our respect for life.

Defenders of Anthropocentrism, Welfarism, and Biocentrism all adopt individualistic perspectives. For each of these perspectives, what matters is the individual, although they disagree about which individuals are morally considerable. In contrast, Holism or Deep Ecology represents a different kind of ethic, where the goal is not to promote the good of individuals except insofar as doing so promotes the integrity, stability, and beauty of particular ecosystems and the environment as a whole. Since many aspects of ecosystems are non-living, Holism is an even more inclusive moral view than biocentrism.

Much of the discussion of these issues involves conceptual matters and, after a brief survey of the anthropocentric outlook, we will examine many of the philosophical issues in the debate over the scope of ethics. Particularly we need to clarify our understanding of several issues in **Axiology,** or Value Theory. The question of who can be given moral consideration involves an appreciation of who is morally considerable or morally valuable. We also need to appreciate what it means to say that a being has a good of its own. Moreover, since Welfarists distinguish between subjects and objects in terms of consciousness or sentience, we need to clarify our understanding of these concepts and categories.

Apart from our interest in determining who can be given moral consideration, we need to fill out our own moral outlook. We should be able to explain why we draw the line of moral standing where we do, and we should be able to defend our choice. Depending on which stand we take, this investigation will also help us better address many practical questions. The best answers to the questions "To whom can one have moral obligations?" and "Why?" give us insight into an assortment of puzzling ethical issues including, for example

- the morality of abortion;

- the ethics of cloning and using stem cells in research;

- the moral standing of non-human animals;

- the ethics of using non-human animals in scientific research that benefits humans;

- the ethics of raising and consuming non-human animals;

- our moral obligations to future generations; and

- the morally proper attitude to take toward the environment and the Earth as a whole.

By developing our understanding of the proper scope of morality, and specifically by addressing our two questions, we will be well-positioned to approach these other particular issues with some confidence and insight.

11.2 Anthropocentrism

According to **Anthropocentrism,** only humans can and should be given moral consideration. In the history of ethics, although there have been notable exceptions, most ethical theorists have simply presupposed an anthropocentric perspective.[1] Natural Law defenders, Kantians, Rights Theorists, Contractarians, Ethical Egoists, and Consequentialists all have tended to be anthropocentric on the question of the proper scope of morality. They have paid little attention to the idea that non-human animals can and should be subjects of our moral concern.

As we saw in Chapter 2, the classical version of Natural Law Theory is based on an Aristotelian metaphysical view according to which all beings have their own particular *telos*, end, or function. Our *telos* is to live in accordance with reason. According to the defender of classical Natural Law Theory, since other species of animals in the world lack reason and free will, they are bound not by natural laws but by eternal laws, or the laws of science. St. Thomas Aquinas believed that we should not be cruel to animals so as not to develop a habit of being cruel to men. The idea that animals can and should be given moral consideration for their own sakes was foreign to him. Similarly, Immanuel Kant argued that we have no direct duties to animals, only indirect ones, because animals are not ends in themselves. As we noted in Chapter 5, Kant argues that only beings capable of living by their own reasoned choices are ends in themselves and deserving of respect. Since animals fall outside this boundary, they do not directly count, ethically speaking.

These appeals to rationality and free will to mark the supposed significant difference between humans and non-human animals also help explain why many traditional Rights Theorists, Contractarians, and Ethical Egoists have adopted an anthropocentric perspective. Some Rights Theorists have grounded natural rights in Natural Law; some have based them on our status as beings with free will. Likewise, Contractarians like Hobbes have come out of the Natural Law tradition and equate moral standing with moral agency. Finally, insofar as Ethical Egoism is a theory about moral agency ("One should always act to promote one's own good"), Egoists, too, have tended to assume an anthropocentric outlook.

Although Consequentialists like Jeremy Bentham have sometimes recognized that non-human animals deserve moral consideration, their theories usually have focused on humans and human affairs. So while Bentham recognized the moral standing of non-human animals capable of suffering, his commitment to a principle of equal respect and consideration was mostly understood and expressed in terms of its effect on humans. This is true of many Utilitarians and Consequentialists who followed Bentham. Only relatively recently have Utilitarians and Consequentialists thought seriously about what their commitment to equality means as regards non-human animals.

> **Anthropocentrism** in ethics is the view that only humans can and should be given moral consideration.

11.3 Welfarism and Value

In contrast to an anthropocentric outlook, Welfarists maintain that all beings with a good of their own can be given moral consideration, and since many non-human animals have a good of their own, many animals besides humans count morally.

To appreciate the welfarist view on the question of the proper scope of morality, we need to make sense of the claim that every being with a good of its own can be given consideration. In turn, to appreci-

> **Axiology,** or Value Theory, is the study of the nature of value.

ate this view, we need to examine some ideas in Axiology.

The word "good" is a synonym for "value." If we can develop our understanding of value, then we can explain what Welfarists mean when they say that one has a good of one's own. The study of Value Theory, what philosophers call Axiology, is quite complex and multi-dimensional. First, let's distinguish between the *nature* of value and its *instances*. To define "value" is difficult, but we might try by drawing up a diverse list of valuable things, or instances of value, and then determining what properties all the things on the list share. In order for our method to be successful, our investigation must identify the set of essential properties of valuable things such that the term "valuable" applies to all those things having these properties and to nothing else.

Whatever else it contains, our account of the nature of value must recognize that there are different *dimensions* of value. We measure a thing's value along different scales reflecting these different dimensions. For example, in Chapter 2 we noted that the prudential value of something refers to the value for the being with a good of her own. Contrast this with the idea of the moral value of something. Since they measure different dimensions of value, a particular act, for example, can score differently on different scales. It can be morally bad but prudentially good for the person performing the act. So, for example, the act of a man resigning from a position in government might be prudentially good because his job was harming his health and adversely affecting his well-being, but morally bad because he had done much good for others and his replacement is inept. Since things can be good or bad, we should also note that the scale we use to measure admits positive, neutral, and negative values. To represent this idea, think of a simple whole number line:

$$\ldots\ 4\ \ 3\ \ 2\ \ 1\ \ 0\ \ -1\ \ -2\ \ -3\ \ -4\ \ldots$$

> **Instrumental value** refers to the value of something as an instrument or tool for achieving some purpose.
> **Intrinsic value** refers to the value of something as an end in itself.

Now imagine we could roughly estimate how valuable something was by assigning it a numerical value. To do justice to our concept of value, we would have to acknowledge that a thing's value (or in this case its disvalue) could be negative.

11.4 Instrumental Value and Intrinsic Value

Within each dimension of value, we can refer to things as being valuable in different ways. Something has **instrumental value** if it is useful as an instrument or tool for achieving some purpose. For example, a pen has some instrumental (prudential) value as a tool for writing and expressing one's thoughts. Different objects can be instrumentally valuable in different ways, depending on what exactly we are measuring. Thus, with respect to being a tool for writing on delicate surfaces, my pen has more instrumental (prudential) value than, say, a sharp rock.

In contrast, something has **intrinsic value** if it is somehow valuable as an end in itself. Typically, when we discuss the intrinsic value of objects, we are interested in making aesthetic value judgments. So, for example, we can assess the intrinsic (aesthetic) value of a painting by judging the value of the experience of the painting itself. Again, different objects can be intrinsically valuable in different ways, depending on what we are assessing. For instance, when it comes to gaining insights into the human condition, the intrinsic value of the experience of a Rembrandt self-portrait is greater than the intrinsic value of a typical black velvet painting of a crying clown.

Instrumental and intrinsic value assessments are distinct but not mutually exclusive. This means some things can possess both kinds of value. Although the painting of the clown is not very intrinsically (aesthetically) valuable, it might be quite instrumentally (prudentially) valuable as a doorstop. Or, to take another example, we can appreciate a first-edition copy of a great novel for both its intrinsic and its instrumental value. If you value the experience of reading the novel, then you value it intrinsically. You can also value it instrumentally, however, by taking advantage of its financial worth as collateral for a loan.

11.5 Subjects and Objects

In addition to these distinctions, in order to explain the welfarist view, we must also distinguish between subjects and objects. The subject/object distinction can be a slippery one, so we need to take care here to specify exactly what we mean. For instance, in grammar we distinguish between the subject and the object of a sentence. We also speak of the subject of a study or investigation, and the object of a game. For our purposes, however, **subject** means "the possessor or bearer of a life." Thus, we talk about someone being the subject of a life. In contrast, **object** means "a dead being or inanimate thing."

In the earlier examples used to illustrate the instrumental value/intrinsic value distinction we referred to objects. Pens, rocks, paintings, and novels are inanimate things, but the value distinction applies equally to subjects too. Living beings also have instrumental and intrinsic value. For example, we refer to both the instrumental and intrinsic value of trees. Trees are subjects of lives and when we hang children's swings from their branches, we value or use them instrumentally. We also value them intrinsically when we admire their beauty. In this case, our appreciation of the tree itself provides us with value, namely aesthetic value.

11.6 Consciousness

Within the class of living beings or subjects, we also need to distinguish between those possessing consciousness and those that are not conscious. **Consciousness** refers to the state of being sentient or aware of one's external surroundings.[2] Our understanding of consciousness, or the experience of life, is based on the possession of some sort of mental life. Thus, subjects possessing functioning brains and nervous systems are prime examples of conscious beings. The experience or awareness of one's life registers in a number of forms including perceptions, pleasures, pains, and thoughts. External stimuli cause us to perceive, feel, and think. Subjects that are lacking the apparatus necessary for experiencing life are not conscious. We do not say they are unconscious because this implies they are only currently in a non-conscious state but may at some time become conscious. Since they lack the necessary apparatus, they have no potential for becoming conscious. Thus, we reserve the term "unconscious" for beings with both the necessary apparatus for becoming conscious and the potential to do so.

Most humans are conscious beings and we can speak of both the instrumental and intrinsic value of these people. My dentist, for example, has instrumental (prudential) value as a tool for improving my oral health. Although, as we noted in Chapter 5, it is arguably immoral to value a conscious being merely as a tool or instrument, it is acceptable to value him in this way. It is moral for me to visit my dentist and avail myself of his services.

We can also speak of the intrinsic value of conscious beings, again as when we make an aesthetic judgment and say of someone that he is attractive. Uncontroversially, we say that conscious beings possess both instrumental and intrinsic value. The intrinsic value *shared by* objects and subjects, both conscious and not, is of the aesthetic variety.

> A **subject** is the possessor or bearer of a life.
> An **object** is a dead being or inanimate thing.

> **Consciousness** refers to the state of being sentient or aware of one's external surroundings.

11.7 Valuers and the Valued

In our brief survey of Value Theory, we have so far limited ourselves to a consideration of the bearers of value, what we can refer to as the valued or the valuable. Pens, paintings, rocks, novels, my dentist, and the beautiful man are all members of the class of valuable things. Good, whether instrumental or intrinsic, prudential or aesthetic, inheres in them. They are, or potentially can be, valued.

To make sense of the idea of having a good of one's own, however, we need to explain how, with respect to value, subjects are unlike objects. To do this we must expand our analysis to include the category of **valuer** to account for someone who appreciates or realizes value. We noted that valuations can be positive, neutral, or negative, and to evaluate something in these ways, you must take an attitude toward it. You must regard or evaluate it as good, bad, or indifferent. Consider the statements, "I *really like* ice cream," "Pat *hates* cell phones." Taking an attitude, regarding, appreciating, and evaluating are all mental events of conscious experiencing creatures. Thus, logically, according to the Welfarist, only beings that experience can be valuers. And assuming that one must be alive to experience, only experiencing subjects can be valuers.

As both bearers of value and valuers, conscious subjects stand in an interesting relation to themselves. Unlike all other things that are merely bearers of value, conscious subjects can appreciate or realize their own value. They have value for themselves or for their own sake. To borrow Kant's terminology, they are *ends in themselves.* Whereas for Kant the idea of being an end in yourself was based on the possession of rationality, here the sense of being an end in yourself is based instead on being a valuer capable of valuing yourself and your experiences. Thus, in addition to appreciating or realizing the value in other things, as both valuers and bearers of value, we can appreciate our own value for ourselves, that is, our prudential value. When we make a *prudential value assessment* of something for someone, we are assessing the value for her from her perspective. Since only beings that can be both bearers of value and valuers qualify, and since a moral concern is a concern for someone for her sake, only conscious subjects can be given moral

> A **valuer** is someone who appreciates or realizes value.

consideration. This is the welfarist account of the scope of morality.[3]

11.8 The Animal Liberation Movement: Singer and Regan

This welfarist analysis of the scope of morality has been advanced and defended by some of the leaders of the animal liberation movement in environmental philosophy and ethics. Both Peter Singer, author of *Animal Liberation,* and Tom Regan, author of *The Case for Animal Rights,* advance welfarist defences for including non-human, sentient animals within the scope of morality.

Singer argues from a consequentialist perspective for the welfarist notion that the idea of having a good of one's own presupposes, minimally, sentience. He writes, "The capacity for suffering and enjoyment is *a prerequisite for having interests at all,* a condition that must be satisfied before we can speak of interests in a meaningful way."[4] Singer argues that beings lacking consciousness or the potential for it logically do not fall into the category of those who can be given consideration for their own sake. Furthermore, once we recognize that non-human animals count, then we should change our practices in significant ways to reflect this appreciation. A stubborn refusal to respect and consider the interests of all sentient beings, and to restrict our concern to humans, is pure *speciesism,* he asserts, akin to racism and sexism. It is morally indefensible.

In contrast, Regan argues from a welfarist base for the view that conscious non-human animals are inherently valuable, and this forms the conceptual basis for according them moral rights. Regan is critical of grounding the case for giving non-human animals moral consideration on Utilitarianism for a reason we noted in Chapter 4. Like Rawls, he is critical of the classical utilitarian commitment to a principle of aggregation, the idea that utility should be maximized regardless of who benefits (recall that Rawls argues that this principle does not show adequate respect for persons as distinct individuals and it is, therefore, unjust). Rather, Regan maintains that conscious non-human animals, as experiencing subjects of lives, as valuers capable of appreciating their own value, are inherently valuable. Furthermore, we have a duty to respect this.[5]

11.9 Potentiality

Our account of the welfarist view of the scope of morality is not quite complete. So far, we have asserted that Welfarists think only conscious subjects are the kinds of beings that deserve moral consideration. However, we need to revise this account to contend with the issue of potentiality.

Consider the problem: So far we have noted that according to the Welfarist, all conscious beings deserve moral consideration but that all those who are either subjects of lives but non-conscious, or objects, deserve no moral consideration. This means that in addition to those persons whom we would typically categorize as deserving of moral consideration, we must also include all conscious fetuses. We know that human fetuses acquire consciousness at around 20 weeks gestation on average—roughly halfway through a normal pregnancy. According to our present account, all those fetuses who have organized brain activity such that they can experience deserve consideration, whereas those who are not yet capable of experiencing deserve none whatsoever. This seems arbitrary and overly harsh. Why should we give consideration to fetuses who have the most rudimentary experiences, but give none whatsoever to those who are even the briefest of moments away from this stage of their existence? Why draw the line at consciousness, and not at potential for consciousness?

In response, we could argue that potential is just that—potential. Unconscious fetuses are not currently experiencing subjects of lives and therefore they cannot experience harm or loss. Of course, in those cases where we are not sure if a fetus is conscious, we should err on the side of caution and accord the fetus moral standing. So, although there will be a range of grey-area cases, there will be many more cases where we have no

doubts. Although it may be true that all these other beings have the potential for gaining consciousness, there is always the possibility that they will not realize their potential. Why, then, should they gain entry into the circle of beings that can be given moral consideration along with all those beings that are valuers? Why *not* draw the line at consciousness?

The flaw in this argument is the assumption that we must accord equal recognition to the moral standing of all those beings that have the potential for consciousness if we admit them into our circle. By admitting potential valuers into the welfarist circle, we are not committing them to the idea that these beings deserve equal consideration with all other members of the group. We are merely recognizing that in virtue of their potential for becoming conscious, they can be given moral consideration. They are fundamentally different in kind from objects like pens and rocks, and from non-conscious subjects like weeds and fungi.

11.10 The Dispute between Anthropocentrism and Welfarism

Both Anthropocentrists and Welfarists maintain that individuals are the kinds of beings toward whom one could have a moral obligation. However, they differ over how to limit their circle of moral concern. Anthropocentrists point to the possession of qualities such as reason and free will as what distinguishes those who can be given moral consideration from those who cannot. Applying this criterion, they then argue that among the creatures of our planet, only humans possess the relevant criteria.

In response, Welfarists argue for a different view. They hold that all beings that are conscious bearers of lives—all valuers—are, logically speaking, the kinds of beings that can be given consideration. Before we consider the dispute between the two outlooks more carefully, it will be useful to note one important respect in which they agree.

The Moral Standing of Amoral and Evil Beings

Someone might criticize both Anthropocentrism and Welfarism for being too inclusive. When we ask the question, "Who deserves moral consideration?" a common answer is, "All moral beings." Many argue that you must show consideration to others in order to deserve it yourself. "Remember the Golden Rule," they say: "*Do unto others as you would have others do unto you.*" According to this view, those who are considerate of others deserve consideration in return. By extension, those who act amorally toward others, that is, those who act without ethical regard for others, don't deserve to be treated with respect themselves. Even more strongly, many argue that those who are evil, who wilfully harm others, should not be accorded any moral consideration. To give heinous criminals moral consideration is not only weak, according to this view, it is immoral.

By admitting all manner of morally depraved and evil persons into their circle, do Anthropocentrists and Welfarists exhibit a regrettable moral failing? No. To see that neither view is committed to any ethically questionable position, here we need to reconsider the question we are posing. Specifically, we need to distinguish the logical or conceptual question, "To whom can one give moral consideration?" from the ethical question, "Who deserves some moral consideration?" These are entirely different kinds of questions. By saying that only humans or only valuers are the kinds of beings to whom we can have moral obligations, Anthropocentrists and Welfarists are not prejudging the second moral question. Whether we should care for the amoral and the evil is a separate question—one we are not trying to settle now. Even if an individual qualifies and enters one of the circles, the Anthropocentrist or the Welfarist could still choose to give him very little consideration or none at all.

A Dispute over What is Morally Relevant

Whereas Anthropocentrists believe that only beings with free will or rationality are the kinds of beings for whom it even makes sense to say that one could have a moral obligation toward, Welfarists argue that all conscious beings count.[6] Welfarists argue that the point of morality is to promote prudential value, that is, to promote the good of those beings that have a good of their own. Secondly, Welfarists hold that a moral concern for someone is a feeling for him. When you feel for another, you care that she not experience prudential disvalue. This means she does not possess rationality or the capacity to choose, but simply the capacity to suffer. Thus, for example, using our example from Chapter 3, one reason we don't want the boys to set the cat on fire is because the cat will suffer excruciating pain, and from its perspective, this would be a horrifying experience.

Although our experience of our lives is very different (indeed, there is perhaps a limit to which we can even imagine what a cat's life is like), according to the Welfarist, there is a critical way in which we are alike. Minimally, we can both suffer. Therefore, it is because the cat, like you and me, is a sentient creature that it is the kind of being for which we can have concern. Because we care that creatures that can experience do not experience gratuitous suffering, and because the cat is among the class of valuers, all of whom experience their lives, the cat qualifies as a being that can be given moral consideration. This is also true for all other conscious subjects. Whether the cat is capable of choosing its own course in life, or whether the cat is a member of our species is simply not relevant, according to the welfarist view. What matters, they insist, is that the cat can suffer.

Welfarists argue that Anthropocentrists who exclude non-human animals from their circle of moral concern must meet three challenges. They must argue for a criterion other than sentience or consciousness as relevant, and then must show that only humans meet whatever criterion is selected. Finally, and most importantly, they must either show that only humans are sentient—a hopeless undertaking—or they must show that the criterion of sentience is irrelevant. This final challenge is the hardest one for the non-Welfarist to meet.[7] Welfarists can recognize the relevance of other qualities for determining the amount of consideration owed to individuals. They can accept the view that some lives are more prudentially valuable for the sorts of reasons we considered in Chapter 10 and for other reasons besides. Moreover, they can admit that many non-humans score lower than many humans with respect to these relevant criteria. So, for example, some argue that although many non-human animals are sentient, they lack self-consciousness, the capacity to plan for the future, rationality, free will, or the capacity to use language abstractly. The Welfarist can, although need not, concede all of this. The case for Anthropocentrism, however, depends on showing that sentience is irrelevant-and showing that other qualities are relevant does not establish this. In the absence of a persuasive argument for the view that sentience is irrelevant, the argument for Anthropocentrism is unconvincing.

11.11 The Value of Objects and Non-conscious Subjects

This argument places the burden on the Anthropocentrist to argue for his view. But many criticize both Anthropocentrism and Welfarism, noting that these two are not the only possible views regarding the question of the scope of morality.

Setting aside the case for Anthropocentrism, let's consider some objections to Welfarism. Critics who take issue with the Welfarist view that only conscious beings have a good of their own note that it *does* make sense to say that objects and non-conscious subjects have a good of their own. For example, we might say that it is not good for your computer monitor to have a hard object bashed into it. If this is correct, then the computer monitor, too, deserves moral consideration, according to the welfarist analysis.

In response, Welfarists distinguish between the harm that conscious beings experience and the damage to which objects are subject. When we say that bashing the monitor is not good for it, Welfarists argue that we mean that the monitor will be damaged by the blow, not that the monitor will experience the harm that a sentient creature would. Since objects and non-conscious subjects are not conscious, they have no experiences. Thus they cannot experience harm.

Welfarists suggest that it might be helpful to reserve the term "damage" to refer to losses inflicted on objects and non-conscious subjects, and to use the term "harm" to refer to losses experienced by conscious subjects. Typically, when people say that they must treat some object "gently" or that we should be "kind" to our cars, they are speaking metaphorically, not literally.

Logically, then, according to the Welfarist, we can have moral obligations only toward the right kinds of beings. Therefore, although you should take care not to damage things, your moral obligation to do so is an obligation only to those who rely upon the objects or own them. These beings are the only ones who could experience harm as a result of the damaging of an object or non-conscious life. When your computer monitor is smashed, you, as the owner, are the one who experiences harm, in this case in the form of a costly financial loss. Generally, and assuming no unusual conditions, others have a moral obligation to you to not damage your personal property. This distinction between damaging and harming helps clarify the welfarist position.

Regardless of the distinction between harming and damaging, someone might still insist that objects and non-conscious subjects do possess a good of their own. As the bearers of values, they have a good of their own, a sake. Therefore, based on the welfarist analysis, they deserve moral consideration. To dispel the confusion in this reasoning, Welfarists say we need to disambiguate between two meanings of the expression "has a good of its own." If you mean, by using this expression, that something is a bearer of value, then the claim is acceptable. Your computer monitor in this sense has a good of its own if we mean that it is a bearer of some positive value. Likewise, when we say that an object with intrinsic (aesthetic) value is valued as an end in itself, we mean that it is a bearer of value, in this case intrinsic value. It is valued just for the experience of it itself and not as a means to some other good. If, on the other hand, by using the expression "has a good of its own," you mean that your monitor has a good of its own *for itself*, a good that it can appreciate, then the Welfarist would disagree. Since only things that are valuers, things that can appreciate value, can have a good for themselves, computer monitors don't qualify. So, too, objects that are intrinsically valuable are not valuable for themselves since they are not valuers and thus don't have a good of their own. Moreover, since the meaning of the phrase "has a good of its own" is relevant here in the second sense, then only conscious subjects can be given moral consideration on the welfarist analysis.

11.12 Welfarism and the Ethics of Necrophilia

According to Welfarism, only conscious living beings or those who have the potential for life and consciousness are the kinds of beings to whom we can have a moral obligation. We noted that leaders of the animal liberation movement have showed how accepting this view requires that most of us greatly alter our lives. In addition to the other ethical theories that have embraced Anthropocentrism, defenders of animal liberation argue that most of us simply assume an anthropocentric ethical outlook. If we are to take seriously the welfarist argument, then we must stop treating many non-human animals as things worthy of no concern for their own sakes. This means we will need to seriously consider adopting vegetarianism for moral reasons, and we will need to re-think our use of non-human animals in scientific research that exclusively, or primarily, benefits humans. Along with these two sorts of changes, we will need to alter all of our practices that fail to accord conscious, non-human animals the respect and consideration to which they are entitled.

These are some dramatic ways in which a serious commitment to Welfarism might lead to changes in our lives. Critics of Welfarism note that, apart from these changes, a commitment to

Welfarism would commit us to tolerating some other practices that many of us find offensive. Moreover, they argue that since the practices are immoral, the welfarist perspective must be flawed. Take, for example, the practice of necrophilia. Necrophilia refers to the condition of being erotically attracted to corpses. The idea that anyone would want to engage in sex with a dead body is one that most people find disgusting and incredible. Certainly it is not typical for people to publicly proclaim their endorsement of necrophilia. Indeed, necrophiles are publicly scorned and dismissed as deviants in need of psychiatric help, if they can be helped at all.

But critics argue that if we take seriously the welfarist idea that we can have moral obligations only to either conscious subjects or those with the potential for consciousness, then we will also need to reconsider whether necrophilia is immoral or, more carefully, under what conditions it is immoral. At this stage in the discussion, no doubt many will be tempted to skip this part of our investigation. But we will press on.

One consequence of Welfarism is that, just as we have no obligations to the dead because the dead cannot be harmed, it follows that we have no obligations to the dead not to have sex with them. Thus, according to the welfarist analysis, whatever is immoral about necrophilia cannot be explained in terms of our obligations to the corpses not to harm them. Of course, others can be harmed but they must be conscious. The idea that necrophilia cannot be unethical on the grounds that it harms the dead is far removed from the revulsion that most people have for the practice. It also leads us to the notion that, under some conditions, Welfarists would have to admit that perhaps necrophilia is not immoral. For some appreciation of this notion, consider the following scenario.

The Necrophilia Society

Imagine that a group of necrophiles entered into a society to engage in their passion for necrophilia. To ensure that their society is ethical, they adhere to the rule that they will have sex only with the dead bodies of people who, as adults and while alive, gave their free and informed consent to have their bodies used in this way in the future. Members of the society sign consent forms of their own, and they achieve some success getting others to sign, too. There are various other restrictions that they support, including some having to do with ensuring that their practices are physically healthful.

Assuming that they follow their own rules, are they guilty of immoral behaviour?

What are we to make of this unusual society? Critics charge that Welfarists might be able to imagine many circumstances under which necrophilia is unethical, but it is not at all clear that they include the circumstances of the society described in the above scenario. For example, we can imagine people who find disturbing the thought that their own bodies might be used in this way when they are dead. Arguably, it would be immoral to disregard someone's wishes in this matter. But here the harm would be to the person while they are alive, and more to the point, the Necrophilia Society respects people's wishes in this matter. So it seems that the society's practices are not immoral for the reason that they use only the bodies of people who give free and informed consent.

What about harms to society in general? Could the Welfarist not argue that since the practice is disgusting it should be legally prohibited? What about the bad effects on children who might become aware of the existence of the Necrophilia Society? Would this awareness not harm them? Because these questions raise issues that we cannot adequately address here, let us leave these questions open and merely repeat the critic's main point: insofar as necrophilia is an immoral practice, it is so not because of any obligations we have to corpses not to harm them. In circumstances where this is the only harm, the Welfarist will have to admit, contrary to common sense, that necrophilia is not an immoral practice. We pursue the question whether there are harms to society, and whether we are justified in legally prohibiting actions that cause such harms in our discussion of Legal Moralism in Chapter 16.

In reply to the charge that Welfarism might sometimes sanction the practice of necrophilia, Welfarists can argue that what needs changing is not a commitment to Welfarism, but our common sense beliefs about necrophilia. As with the changes we need to make regarding our treatment of sentient, non-human animals, Welfarism will require that we revise some of our other common sense beliefs about ethics, however uncomfortable we might be about this. But that is the price one pays for adopting a consistent ethical outlook. Loath as we might be to admit it, we should perhaps accept that there really is nothing immoral about the practice of necrophilia, at least under certain conditions. Finally, Welfarists can add that tolerating a practice is not the same as endorsing it.

11.13 Conclusion

We have only briefly considered some of the debates about whether one should accept an anthropocentric or welfarist response to the question about the proper scope of morality. Many will be quick to point out that our discussion is far from complete and that there are other questions between Anthropocentrists and Welfarists that need further study. Furthermore, we need to consider some other positions too. Why should we accept a view that excludes many living beings from receiving moral consideration, as Anthropocentrism and Welfarism do? What are we to make of the moral significance of life? Alternatively, some might wonder how our feelings and beliefs that we should respect nature could possibly fit into an anthropocentrist or welfarist ethical outlook. Should we not have more respect for the environment than would be supported by Anthropocentrism and Welfarism? Do either of these views take environmental ethical concerns seriously enough?

In the next chapter, we begin to consider these questions and issues and take some steps toward remedying the regrettable brevity of our discussion thus far.

11.14 Review

We set out to answer the question, "To whom can one have a moral obligation?" or, "For whom can one have a moral concern?" from the anthropocentrist and welfarist perspectives.

According to Anthropocentrism, only humans can and should be given moral concern. Different Anthropocentrists advance different reasons for why this is so. Some common reasons include the assertion that only humans are rational, have free will, or are moral agents.

In contrast, according to Welfarism, only beings that have a good of their own can be given consideration. In the course of explaining the welfarist view, we used and explained some distinctions taken from Value Theory. Specifically, we distinguished between instances, dimensions, and kinds of values and valuers. To explain the idea of a valuer, that is, the idea of someone who appreciates or realizes value, we distinguished between bearers of lives, or subjects, and dead beings and things, or objects. Furthermore, within the class of all subjects, we distinguished between conscious beings and non-conscious ones. Consciousness, we noted, refers to the state of being sentient or aware of one's external surroundings.

Welfarists argue that conscious beings are both bearers of value and valuers. As such, they can appreciate their own value and the value of other things. This capacity for appreciating, or more generally, for having a mental life, explains the concept of having a perspective, which in turn explains the idea of having a good of one's own, or prudential value. According to the Welfarist, only beings that have a perspective on life can experience their lives as being good or bad for them. In other words, only beings that value, whose lives can go well or poorly, are the kinds of beings for whom it makes sense to say we can have a concern.

Having a concern for another for that being's sake refers to his unique perspective on, and experience of, the world. More specifically, it refers to the prudential value for that being. Since a moral concern is a concern for someone for her sake, it follows that only conscious sub-jects can be given moral consideration in the welfarist analysis because only conscious subjects have a good of their own. This is the welfarist account of the scope of morality.

With the basic outline of the welfarist view in hand, we then clarified and extended our discussion. We observed that the welfarist views about the scope of morality have been taken up by some leaders of the animal liberation movement, including Peter Singer and Tom Regan. Briefly, we also noted some implications that taking a serious welfarist stance would have for our practices regarding the treatment of sentient, non-human animals. We then examined an argument for including beings with the potential for consciousness and potential future conscious beings among those for whom the Welfarist can show moral concern.

In the final part of the chapter, we discussed what the debate between Anthropocentrists and Welfarist amounts to. First, we clarified our question by distinguishing between the logical or conceptual question, "For whom can one have a moral obligation?" and the moral question "Who deserves moral consideration?" We saw that identifying someone as being among those to whom we can give moral consideration does not commit either the Anthropocentrist or the Welfarist to giving moral consideration to that being.

As for what separates the Anthropocentrist from the Welfarist, we proposed that the case for choosing between Anthropocentrism and Welfarism boils down to a dispute over what is logically relevant. Welfarists insist that the fact of sentience is relevant and argue that Anthropocentrists must persuade us otherwise to make their case for their view that we have direct obligations only to humans. Finally, we ended by considering an objection to Welfarism; namely that accepting the view would commit us to accepting beliefs that defy common sense. Specifically, for example, the Welfarist must accept, in theory at least and perhaps also in practice, that sometimes necrophilia would be ethically acceptable. We concluded by considering possible responses a Welfarist might make to this charge, and we also noted some of the limitations of our brief discussion in this chapter.

Notes

1. Baxter (1974) and Norton (1988) are two exceptions where an anthropocentric viewpoint is defended.

2. Consciousness is different than self-consciousness. Whereas consciousness refers to the state of being sentient or aware of one's external surroundings, self-consciousness refers to the state of being aware of oneself as distinct from others. Not all beings who are conscious are also self-conscious. Human infants, for example, are conscious but not self-conscious.

3. What is referred to as "Welfarism" here has alternatively been called "Experientialism" by Mark Bernstein:

   > Roughly, experientialism proclaims that an individual's well-being is exhaustively constituted by how well or poorly she is faring "from the inside." Welfare is purely and totally subjective: to the extent that the individual feels good, his life is going well, and to the extent that he feels poorly, his life is going badly. (Bernstein [1998], pp. 22–23.)

   More precisely, the account of Welfarism described here follows the account explained and defended by Sumner in Sumner (1995) and Sumner (1996), where a necessary but not sufficient condition of a life going well is that the bearer of the life has a positive attitude toward it. For more on this debate, see Chapter 12.

4. Singer (1990), p. 7.

5. See Regan (1983).

6. There is an exception worth noting here. Anthropocentrists who believe that what counts is being a valuer and who believe, further, that only humans are valuers, are mistaken about this second point. Of these Anthropocentrists, the Welfarist would say that they have identified the right criterion for determining who, logically speaking, can receive moral consideration, but they have misidentified the members in this group of beings who can receive moral consideration.

7. A good example of someone coming to appreciate this argument is Michael A. Fox, who initially argued in his book *The Case for Animal Experimentation* that non-human animals are not members of the moral community. See Fox (1986a). However, within a year Fox repudiated this view and maintained instead that the suffering of non-human animals is relevant. See Fox (1986b, 1987).

Exercises

Progress Check

1. What is Anthropocentrism in ethics? What reasons have been cited in support of it?

2. Explain the distinction between the nature of value and its instances.

3. Explain the distinction between instrumental value and intrinsic value.

4. Explain what is meant by the claim that instrumental and intrinsic assessments of things are "distinct but not mutually exclusive."

5. Explain the distinction between subjects and objects, as these terms are used by the Welfarist.

6. Explain the distinction between the intrinsic value of objects or subjects and the intrinsic value of valuers.

7. What is consciousness?

8. What does appreciating or realizing value involve?

9. Why do Welfarists think that logically only experiencing subjects can be valuers?

10. Why do Welfarists think that only conscious subjects deserve moral consideration?

11. Explain the distinction between the logical or conceptual question "To whom can one have a moral obligation?" and the moral question "Who should receive moral consideration?"

12. Explain the argument for considering a being's potential for gaining consciousness as relevant for determining whether one can give the being moral consideration.

13. Explain the debate between Welfarists and their critics over the question of whether Welfarism must regard the practice of necrophilia as being ethically acceptable, at least sometimes.

Questions for Further Reflection

1. Outline the strongest case you can make for an anthropocentrist approach to the question of the scope of morality. Is such a position speciesist? Why or why not?

2. How many different dimensions of value can you identify? How are they different, exactly?

3. How is consciousness different from self-consciousness?

4. According to the welfarist view, only valuers can be given moral consideration because only valuers have a good of their own. We noted that this excludes many non-conscious subjects. Yet many people think we have moral obligations to all living creatures, conscious or not. This view endorses respect for life.

   a) Since this view conflicts with the welfarist view of the scope of morality, does it follow that Welfarists don't show proper respect for life? Defend your answer.

   b) What does it mean to say that we should have respect for life?

   c) How might Welfarists respond to this sort of criticism?

5. Under what conditions, if any, should society promote the interests of non-human animals over humans? Defend your view.

6. Welfarists accord moral standing to beings that have the potential for acquiring consciousness, however low that potential may be. According to this definition, male sperm and female ova deserve some moral consideration by virtue of their potential for becoming part of a conscious being. Is this absurd? Does it follow that ovulating women have moral obligations to have as many children as possible, and that fertile men ought not to masturbate or have sex where conception is prevented? What response to this apparent absurdity can you make?

Suggested Further Reading

We have already noted sources for the main ethical theories discussed earlier in the book and there you will find some support for Anthropocentrism.

For Kant's view regarding our obligations toward non-human animals, see his "Duties Towards Animals and Spirits," in *Lectures on Ethics*, trans. L. Linfield (New York: Harper & Row, 1963). James Sterba discusses the general challenge to traditional ethics posed by Environmentalism in his book, *Three Challenges to Ethics: Environmentalism, Feminism, and Multiculturalism* (New York: Oxford University Press, 2001).

The case for Welfarism has been advanced by a number of philosophers working in Environmental Philosophy and ethics especially. Apart from the works referred to earlier by Singer, Regan, and Sumner, for more discussion of these issues, see also Singer and Regan's *Animal Rights and Human Obligation*, 2nd ed., Tom Regan and Peter Singer, eds. (Englewood Cliffs, NJ: Prentice-Hall, 1989). Singer has also edited another collection of papers on this topic (Peter Singer, ed., *In Defense of Animals*. New York: Basil Blackwell, 1986.)

R.G. Frey has been a notable critic of the welfarist account and he presents his position in his books *Interests and Rights: The Case Against Animals* (Oxford: Clarendon Press, 1980), and *Rights, Killing and Suffering: Moral Vegetarianism and Applied Ethics* (New York: Basil Blackwell, 1983).

Group Work Activity:

The Sources of Prudential Value

Prudential value is drawn from a number of different sources. In other words, there are many contributors to a prudentially good life. For example, the goods of friendship and education promote individual happiness or well-being. On your own, try to identify as many different sources or contributors to individual well-being as possible. Next, in your group, create a comprehensive list of these sources of prudential value. Try to classify these different sources and contributors into distinct classes. Finally, try to answer the following questions:

1. Which sources of value can all experiencing subjects enjoy? Why?

2. Are there any sources of value that all experiencing subjects need to realize in order to survive?

3. Are there any sources of value that some experiencing subjects are incapable of enjoying? If so, what are these? Why are these valuers incapable of appreciating these values?

4. Are there any sources of value that only humans can enjoy? Defend your answer.

5. Are there any sources of value that only non-humans can enjoy? Defend your answer.

Group Work Activity:

The Necrophilia Society

1. Many people find the idea of necrophilia repugnant and immoral. Consider again the idea of the example of the Necrophilia Society. On your own, try to identify what, if anything, is immoral about this society. Next, as a group, see if you can reach some consensus among the members of your group as to what is immoral about the Necrophilia Society and try to draft an explanation of your collective moral judgment of this society.

   a) If you and your colleagues argued that the Necrophilia Society, properly regulated, is not immoral, how will you respond to the objection that the presence of the society poses a public threat to our larger Canadian society? How can you respond to the criticism that the mere existence of the Necrophilia Society poses a danger to children, minimally, because it sets a bad example and sends children immoral or dangerous views about human sexuality?

   b) If you argued that the Necrophilia Society is immoral, try to explain why. Defenders of the right of the society to operate can argue that finding a practice disgusting is insufficient reason for legally banning it. It is also insufficient reason for depriving those who practice necrophilia under the circumstances outlined in the scenario of their freedom. It would be like outlawing hand-holding among people from different races in public just because most other people in the society thought it was disgusting or "unnatural." How do you respond to the charge that opposition to the Necrophilia Society is unsupportable and intolerant prejudice?

Weblinks

There are numerous Web sites concerning the issues in environmental ethics and philosophy that we have begun to raise in this chapter. A good place to begin your search of these sites is at the Web site created by The Center for Environmental Philosophy at the University of North Texas. You can find this rich resource at **www.cep.unt.edu**

Among the many points of interest at this site is the specific site of the journal **Environmental Ethics**, which is located at **www.cep.unt.edu/enethics.html**

The Centre for Applied Ethics at the University of British Columbia contains many resources on environmental ethics at **www.ethics.ubc.ca/resources/environmental/**

People for the Ethical Treatment of Animals (PETA) is an international non-profit organization. Their Web site is at **www.peta.org**

12 The Scope of Morality II: The Biocentric Outlook and Holism

Learning Outcomes

In this chapter we continue the investigation we began in Chapter 11. Specifically, we will examine Biocentrism and Holism and consider these views on the question of the proper scope of ethics. In the course of this examination, we will also further develop the argument for Welfarism.

Upon the successful completion of this chapter, you will be able to

1. provide a biologically sound account of the nature of life;
2. explain and critically evaluate the arguments for Biocentrism and Holism on the question of the proper scope of ethics;
3. distinguish between perfectionist and prudential value; and
4. define "ecology" and outline the role it plays in the defence of the Land Ethic.

12.1 Introduction

In his book *Sea of Slaughter*, Farley Mowat documents the fishing industry's "biocidal" activities. Among the victims is the herring fish. Mowat relates the story of a herring seiner, or fishing vessel, that in the spring of 1953 in the Gulf of the St. Lawrence caught in its net a million herring. This apparently was an unremarkable event for its time. Mowat explains, however, that due to prolonged, intensive fishing the herring began to disappear by the early 1970s.[1]

The sad story of the herring is depressingly familiar. It is one of many that have as their common theme two ideas: (1) the natural world is being destroyed, and (2) we are responsible for its destruction.

Many of us think, for various reasons, that we should care about and for the environment. We worry about our increasing abilities to despoil and destroy the environment, and we worry that our consumer society values consumption and growth at the expense of nature. We also worry about the world our children will inherit. From within this environmental consciousness, we might look to moral philosophy for some clarity and guidance. Which ethical outlook makes the best sense of our concerns about the environment? What kinds of concerns should we have? Should we be directly concerned only about humans, about all sentient creatures, all living ones, or about ecosystems as wholes? Once we have settled the issue of the proper scope for our concerns, we also want some guidance about how to rank them and assess our actions with respect to the environment.

In Chapter 11 we examined two responses to our questions about the scope of ethics, Anthropocentrism and Welfarism. Each view identifies beings that can be given moral consideration and justifies its particular reasons for doing so. However, many critics from within Environmental Philosophy maintain that these two outlooks are too narrow. By focusing on humans and sentient beings respectively, these outlooks fail to adequately capture the moral responsibilities we have to other parts of nature, both living and non-living. These critics insist that part of our failing is theoretical: the old ways of conceiving of ethics and its scope are insufficient for contending with the frightening and looming environmental crises on the horizon. Part of the problem, in other words, is that our old ethics are not capable of guiding us in the ways we should be guided with respect to the environment. We need broader and fairer ways of conceiving of the moral attitude we should take toward the greater natural world.

In this chapter we consider two such outlooks, Biocentrism and Holism, and address the question of their fitness as accounts of the proper scope of ethics.

12.2 What Is Life?

Many people feel that there is something morally significant about life and that the divide between the living and the non-living marks the line between those beings that can be given consideration and those things that cannot. To spell out this view we first need to say more carefully what life is.

How can we distinguish between the living and the non-living? Although we all have some appreciation of the difference between these two, the question "What is life?" has proven to be surprisingly controversial and difficult to answer. The challenge is not with identifying clear examples of living beings, but with avoiding arbitrariness in distinguishing between the living and the non-living in borderline cases. While it is beyond our scope to try to settle this debate, to help us on our way it will be useful to refer to a more detailed account of the nature of life.

According to biologists Neil Campbell, Jane Reece, and Lawrence Mitchell, there are at least seven properties common to all living beings.[2] They are

1. *Order:* All the other characteristics of life emerge from the complex organization that marks all living organisms.

2. *Reproduction:* Living beings reproduce. Life comes from life.

3. *Growth and Development:* Living beings grow and develop according to programs encoded in inherited DNA.

4. *Energy Utilization:* Living beings take in energy that is transformed to do work.

5. *Response to the Environment:* Living beings respond to their environment.

6. *Homeostasis:* Homeostasis refers to the processes by which a living being's regulatory mechanisms maintain its internal environment within a tolerable range.

7. *Evolutionary Adaptation:* Living beings evolve as a result of the interaction between them and their environment.

According to Campbell, Reece, and Mitchell's account, beings must possess all of these qualities to be alive. Since Campbell, Reece, and Mitchell are biologists, and since their account is defended in a biology textbook, it is not surprising that it is based on a cell theory of life that includes specifically biological references to things like cells and

DNA. A critic might charge, however, that although we are most familiar with life through biology, the idea of a living being can be given a functional explanation, for example, anything that functions as a living being is one. It need not have the physical manifestations of things like cells and DNA provided it functions as a living being does. This more neutral or abstract understanding of life opens up the possibility that, for example, machines might some day properly be regarded as living, even if they do not possess cells and DNA in the ways that we do. If they possessed the seven characteristics they would qualify on Campbell, Reece, and Mitchell's account.

12.3 The Biocentric Outlook

Biocentrism is a view in ethics within which the class of all beings that can be given moral consideration includes and is limited to all living beings. The challenge for the Biocentrist is to identify a relevant quality shared by all living beings by virtue of which they qualify as beings capable of receiving moral consideration.

The three main defenders of the biocentric outlook, Kenneth Goodpaster, Robin Attfield, and Paul Taylor, each argue that living beings can be given moral consideration because they have a good of their own, or a welfare. The idea is that, since all living beings are possessors of a good of their own, they can be considered for their own sake. This feature, if it can be shown to be part of all living beings, would correspond to Campbell, Reece, and Mitchell's criterion that living beings grow and develop and that we can determine the difference between a being's life going well and its going poorly. Let's consider the three biocentric views more carefully.

> **Biocentrism** is the ethical view according to which the class of all beings that can be given moral consideration includes and is limited to all living beings.

1. Goodpaster

Kenneth Goodpaster argues, "Nothing short of the condition of *being alive* seems to me to be a plausible and nonarbitrary criterion" for determining who or what can be given moral consideration.[3] Goodpaster asserts that, although the idea that a being is sentient is a sufficient condition for being given consideration, it is not a necessary condition. In support of this assertion, he advances two interesting points. He argues that like sentient life, insentient life has features that model the biologic function of sentience. Sentience, he explains, can be understood as an adaptive feature of some organisms that allows them to identify and respond to potential threats. According to this analysis, our capacity for experiencing pain is merely one mechanism we happen to have for responding to our environment and for maintaining homeostasis. In other words, our capacity for sentience helps us to survive.

But just as we have capacities that help sustain our lives, insentient living beings have also evolved capacities for dealing with threats to their existence. For example, plants adapt to changing weather conditions to maintain their survival, trees grow bark to repel pests, and insects have evolved to blend into their environment to escape predators. The point is that homeostasis and responding to one's environment are present in all life, so, according to Goodpaster's argument, there are no essential biological differences between sentient and insentient living beings.

Secondly, Goodpaster argues that like sentient life, insentient life also has interests. It makes perfect sense to say that trees need sunlight and water to survive and that if they do not receive these sources of energy and nourishment, they will be harmed. Although an insentient life may not have desires because it has no mental life, having desires, he holds, is not necessary for having interests. Insentient living beings are unlike mere things in that they can grow and develop, be harmed and benefited, and we can at least roughly tell the difference even if they cannot represent and express their interests.

2. Attfield

Like Goodpaster, Robin Attfield also argues that all living beings have a good of their own. Unlike objects such as cars, living beings grow and develop independently of the influence of humans.

Furthermore, just as both sentient and insentient life forms grow and develop, they also reproduce and preserve themselves. These are all qualities that distinguish living beings from non-living ones. Moreover, since sentient beings have moral standing, and since insentient life shares these distinguishing features with sentient life, this is an argument for according moral standing to all living beings. Attfield refers to this as "an analogical argument for holding that all the organisms concerned not only can but also do have moral standing."[4]

A criticism of Attfield's analogical argument is that we must also consider the matter of the difference between sentient and insentient life. What are we to make of this difference? What is the moral importance of sentience? Attfield explains that in considering this question we must remember the distinction between moral standing and moral significance. The question of the moral standing of a being asks whether that being can be given *any* moral consideration at all. In contrast, the question of the moral significance of a being asks *how much* consideration is owed to the being. Since insentient living beings have a good of their own, a good that can be harmed or benefited, Attfield concludes that they have moral standing. At most, the disanalogy between sentient and insentient life shows that sentient beings should receive greater moral consideration than insentient ones, not that insentient living beings should receive none at all. Indeed, he concedes, it may be true that insentient living beings have only a very slight moral significance.

To help illustrate his point, Attfield refers to an example from one of his earlier papers.[5] Imagine that there has been a nuclear war and there is one remaining sentient survivor. Imagine, furthermore, that there is one healthy remaining elm tree, a tree that if left untouched could go on to propagate its species. Would it be immoral for the survivor to chop down the tree? Attfield argues that it would be and that most of the people who consider this example would agree with him. Moreover, the immorality is partly due to the wrong done to the tree itself. In other words, he concludes, it would be wrong to kill the tree because it has its own intrinsic value.

3. Taylor

The idea that all living beings have a good of their own sits at the basis of another influential defence of the biocentric outlook advanced by Paul Taylor. Taylor explains and defends his account in a series of papers and in his book, *Respect for Nature*.

Before we consider Taylor's view more carefully, note first a point about terminology. Taylor actually coined the expression "the biocentric outlook" to describe his respect-for-life ethic.[6] Although we have adopted his term to describe the view that all living beings can be given moral consideration, there are differences between the positions held by the various proponents of what we are calling "the biocentric outlook." For example, Attfield defends the notion that sentient beings' lives are more morally significant than non-sentient beings' lives. So, for example, according to Attfield, humans are more important than onions. In contrast, Taylor is a "biocentric egalitarian" who believes that from the perspective of ethics, all lives, regardless of species membership, are equally morally important.[7] Thus, on Taylor's outlook, humans aren't more morally important than plants.

Since they defend specifically different views, one might wonder why we are referring to each as adopting Biocentrism. The reason is that we are concerned with outlining and distinguishing various answers to the question of who or what can be given moral consideration. At this level of the discussion, Goodpaster, Attfield, and Taylor all share the same perspective. So although it is true that Attfield and Taylor defend different views within the biocentric outlook, they share, along with Goodpaster, the conviction that all living beings can be given moral consideration because all living beings have a good of their own. This is the point of referring to them as Biocentrists, although they disagree over the answer to the question, Which is the best version of Biocentrism?

Whereas Attfield supports the idea that all living beings have a good of their own by arguing that all living beings have their own intrinsic value, Taylor asserts that each living being has "inherent worth." For Taylor, the concept of inherent worth is not dependent on an entity being valued by a conscious valuer. Rather, he holds that every living being is a "teleological (goal-oriented) center of life" that pursues its own unique good. Moreover, according to Taylor, "a living thing is conceived as a unified system of organized activity, the constant tendency of which is to preserve its existence by protecting and promoting its well-being."[8] For Taylor, all living beings have a well-being or welfare that they seek to promote, consciously or not. This explains why they all have inherent worth: They have a good of their own as living beings independently of how they are valued by others (whether we think the oak tree is valuable is irrelevant; since by being an oak tree, it is valuable). Taylor's account of inherent value seeks to capture what it is about life that gives moral agents a reason for demonstrating respect in their actions toward other living entities. As he puts it, if some entity has inherent worth, then "all moral agents have a *prima facie* duty to promote or preserve the entity's good as an end in itself and for the sake of the entity whose good it is."[9]

12.4 A Welfarist Criticism of Biocentrism

Defenders of Biocentrism hold that all living beings have a good of their own, or a welfare, by virtue of which they can be given moral consideration. The logical idea is that since all living beings are possessors of a good of their own, they can be considered for their own sake. In response to the question "Who can be given moral consideration?" Biocentrists disagree with Welfarists. They maintain that all living beings, and not merely all sentient beings, can be included. However, Biocentrists agree with Welfarists that having a welfare, or a good of one's own, means one can receive consideration. Nevertheless, Welfarists question Biocentrists' attribution of a welfare to all living beings.

In Chapter 11 we outlined the welfarist argument for the view that to have a well-being one must be a conscious valuer. We noted the Welfarist's argument that a necessary condition of making a prudential welfare assessment of someone's life is that it be possible to assess it from that being's perspective. We also observed that, according to the Welfarist, having a perspective presupposes having consciousness, or being a valuer; the idea that in order for a being to have a good of its own for itself that it can appreciate, it must logically be the sort of being that is able to appreciate. It must, in other words, be conscious. On this point Peter Singer, for example, argues that non-conscious life does not qualify. Singer draws the line of moral considerability at sentience and criticizes the view of another defender of Biocentrism, the famous German doctor and missionary Albert Schweitzer (1875–1965), who argued that all living beings demonstrate a "will to live" which we should respect.[10] Schweitzer's view is echoed in the positions of Goodpaster, Attfield, and Taylor, which we have just examined. Schweitzer's notion of a "will to live" suggests that along with these other theorists, he too believes living beings have the qualities of growing and developing and maintaining homeostasis, and that this distinguishes the living from non-living things and dead subjects. Singer, however, challenges the intelligibility of the notion of a will to live that does not imply having a conscious desire to live. At best, he argues, the idea of insentient life having a will to live is a metaphorical way of speaking, since insentient living beings literally do not *will* anything; they have no desires. Once we recognize that the insentient living being's "will to live" is not a conscious willing, Singer asks whether we should respect it. Is it wrong, for example, to kill a weed? Is there any intrinsic value in its life? More precisely, does the weed's life offer it any value? Singer writes:

> Suppose that we apply the test of imagining living the life of the weed I am about to pull out of my garden. I then have to imagine living a life with no conscious experiences at all. Such a life is a complete blank; I would not in the least regret the shortening of this subjectively barren form of existence.[11]

From this he concludes that the lives of insentient beings have no prudential value. Therefore, there is no immorality to the weed and other such non-conscious living beings in killing them.

12.5 Sumner's Argument against Biocentrism

Whereas Singer argues that insentient living beings do not have a prudential good, the Biocentrists, as we have noted, maintain otherwise. They insist all living beings have a welfare that can be harmed or benefited. Although insentient beings cannot have desires, they add, they do have needs.

To take Goodpaster's example, we know that trees need water and sunlight to survive and flourish. According to Taylor's analysis, all living beings have interests, even if they do not all take an interest (a conscious attitude) in having their interests met. Every living being is a "teleological (goal-oriented) center of life." Although they do not consciously strive to promote and protect their interests, they nonetheless do so non-consciously. Furthermore, since all living beings display order, homeostasis, and grow and develop, we can identify their interests and distinguish them from mere objects. And since they are the bearers of these needs, they are the ones who are benefited or harmed when their needs are either met or not met. As Attfield argues, since all living beings have a good of their own, they can all be given consideration for their own sake. How could the Welfarist dispute this?

In response to this sort of argument L.W. Sumner claims that the Biocentrists conflate two different dimensions of value, *perfectionist value* with *prudential value*. On the basis of the possession of one sort of value (perfectionist value) they ascribe to insentient living beings the other sort of value (prudential value). Although the Biocentrists are right to insist that it is the possession of prudential value that is relevant for being given moral consideration, Sumner argues that they are mistaken in ascribing this sort of value to insentient life. He defends the view that only sentient beings can take the subjective per-

spective necessary for having a prudential good and therefore only they can be given moral consideration. Let's consider his argument more carefully.

1. Insentient Beings Possess Perfectionist Value

In Section 11.3 we noted that there are different ways in which something can be good or bad. We spoke of the act of a man resigning from his job as scoring high on the prudential value scale—because doing so is good for him—but low on the ethical value scale—because his resignation is bad for others. Apart from the dimensions of prudential and ethical value, Sumner notes that we also make aesthetic and perfectionist value judgments. Aesthetic value judgments are typically made about works of art, where we say of something that it is good and mean that it is beautiful, provides insight into the human condition, and so on. In contrast, something has perfectionist value if "it is a good instance or specimen of its kind."[12] Thus, perfectionist value judgments are made relative to standards for whatever it is that is being measured. For example, a watch that scores high on the perfectionist value scale is one that keeps accurate time.

Sumner agrees that insentient living beings do have perfectionist value and that each life is the possessor of its perfectionist value. So, for example, the tree that receives water and sunlight will likely score higher on the perfectionist value scale for trees than trees that do not receive these resources. In this sense, when we say that a tree is good, we mean that it has perfectionist value—it is a good specimen of its kind—and since it is the bearer of this value, this perfectionist value belongs to or inheres in the tree itself. In this sense, insentient living beings have a good of their own. However, Sumner argues, it is a fallacy to slide from saying that a living being has perfectionist value to saying that it has prudential value.[13] He charges that this is the source of the Biocentrists' error. They conflate the truth that insentient life has perfectionist value with the false belief that such beings therefore have a prudential good.

2. The Distinction between Prudential Value and Perfectionist Value

As a first step in appreciating Sumner's argument, we must see that perfectionist and prudential value judgments are different. Prudential value assessments, Sumner claims, are subject-relative:

> Welfare assessments concern the prudential value of a life, namely, how well it is going for the individual whose life it is. This relativization of prudential evaluation to the proprietor of the life is one of the deepest features of the language of welfare: however valuable something may be in itself, it can promote my well-being only if it is also good or beneficial for me.[14]

In contrast, Sumner explains that perfectionist value judgments lack this subject-relativity. A judgment of something's perfectionist value is made not relative to the thing being judged, but relative to the standards of excellence or goodness for things of that kind. In other words, in making a perfectionist value judgment about a tree, we are saying something about how that tree compares to the standard of a good tree of that species, not something about how well the tree's life is going for it.

Sumner argues that in the case of a tree, there is no prudential good to consider to contrast with the perfectionist value to see the difference between the two. But when we turn to an example of a being that can possess both sorts of values, we can clearly see the difference between them. Consider, then, the distinction between the perfectionist value of the life of a typical adult human and its prudential value. However we measure the perfectionist value of a human life, we can imagine someone scoring very high in that regard, but still reasonably believing that her life was nonetheless a disappointment to her. Her well-being is lower than it might have been.

We all know examples of people who have, for instance, accomplished much but who have sincerely judged their life to be less satisfying or happy than it might have been. We can explain the conceptual distance between these two sorts of value judgments of a life by noting that the perfectionist value judgment is made against a standard that is independent of the judgment one makes of one's own welfare. Of course, these two sorts of judgments can assess equal levels of perfectionist and prudential value—many humans who score high in perfectionist value can be equally satisfied with their lives—but the point is that we are making two logically different kinds of judgments.

3. The Subjectivity of Welfare

Even if it is conceded that perfectionist value judgments are different in kind from prudential value judgments, the Biocentrist might still insist that we can make prudential value judgments of all living beings' lives. Why does the Welfarist restrict such judgments to sentient beings? Sumner argues that a descriptively adequate theory about the nature of welfare is one that will accurately describe our experience and corresponding concept of welfare. He divides all potential accounts into two categories: objective theories and subjective theories. Briefly and most importantly, subjective theories treat the having of a positive attitude toward something as a necessary but not sufficient condition of the thing being beneficial. Sumner claims it makes no sense to say that a person's life is really going well for him if he sincerely believes that it is not. This is not to say that believing your life is going well makes it happen: having the positive attitude is not enough. Simply, the point is that one's life cannot be prudentially good unless one has a positive attitude toward it. Objective theories deny this.

4. The Objectivity of Welfare

If it is true that a necessary condition of one's life going well for oneself (that is, one's life scoring high in prudential value) is that one must have a positive attitude toward it, then one must minimally be a conscious valuer to be a bearer of this sort of good. According to this analysis, in other words, a necessary condition of even having a good of one's own for oneself—a welfare—is that one be sentient. Sumner explains it this way:

> It follows on this sort of account that a welfare subject in the merely grammatical sense—an individual with a distinct welfare—must also be a subject in a more robust sense—the locus of a reasonably unified and continuous mental life. Prudential value is therefore perspectival because it literally takes the point of view of the subject. Welfare is subject-relative because it is subjective.[15]

According to Sumner's analysis, then, insentient living beings cannot be given consideration for their own sake because they have no mental life, and therefore cannot take an attitude toward their own life. Since they are not conscious, they have no well-being. Since they have no well-being, we cannot give them consideration for their own sake. They cannot experience either harm or benefit because they cannot *experience*. Their lives, as Singer puts it, are "complete blanks." The welfarist argument against Biocentrism purports to show only that insentient living beings cannot be given moral consideration. This is not to say that we do not have any reason for respecting insentient life. On the welfarist analysis, however, since only beings that are valuers count, all decisions regarding morality should consider only valuers. In other words, insofar as living beings' lives are valuable, they can logically be valuable only for experiencing subjects of lives. Thus, only sentient beings can be given consideration for their own sake.

This is not to say that living beings' lives are not valuable, or even that they have no value of their own. The idea that an insentient being can flourish points to the notion that it can be a locus of perfectionist value, value it possesses intrinsically. If we want to say that an insentient being has a *sake*, this is fine provided we do not imply that an insentient living being has a prudential good. Since having a good of one's own for oneself implies that one be an experiencing subject, insentient beings do not qualify. So, according to Welfarists, although such living beings may be good specimens of their kind, they cannot logically be bearers of prudential value because they lack the requisite perspective of beings with a welfare.

12.6 Holism

> That land is a community is the basic concept of ecology, but that land is to be loved and respected is an extension of ethics.
>
> *Aldo Leopold*
> Foreword to *A Sand County Almanac*

Whereas Welfarists criticize Biocentrists for trying to extend the idea of moral consideration too far to include all living beings, defenders of the Land Ethic criticize Biocentrism for not being inclusive enough. They argue that we should extend our circle of moral concern to include entire ecosystems, and even more widely, the Earth as a whole biotic community.

Defenders of the **Land Ethic**, or **Holism**, believe that we should extend our conception of our moral community to embrace all the interdependent elements of the environment, including not only humans or other sentient creatures but all living beings, waters, and soils. Once we take this holistic perspective in ethics, our focus should shift from demonstrating concern only for individuals to acting for the benefit of biotic communities as a whole. What does this involve? As architect of the Land Ethic Aldo Leopold (1887–1948) puts it, from the holist ethical perspective,

> The **Land Ethic**, or **Holism**, is the view in ethics that the moral community includes all the interdependent parts of entire ecosystems, including the Earth as a biotic community as a whole. Eschewing an individualistic perspective in ethics for a holistic perspective, and grounding ethics on ecology, Holists believe that acts are right insofar as they promote the integrity, stability, and beauty of the biotic community. Acts are wrong otherwise.

> A thing is right when it tends to preserve the integrity, stability, and beauty of the biotic comunity. It is wrong when it tends otherwise.[16]

Leopold's Land Ethic begins with the idea that we should understand ethics from the perspective of ecology. **Ecology** is the biological study of organisms' relations to each other and to their surroundings. Looked at from an ecological perspective, Leopold argues, ethics is

> **Ecology** is the biological study of organisms' relations to each other and to their surroundings.

nothing more than the tendency of interdependent individuals to develop modes of co-operation. Beginning from the association of small groups of humans and extending to an increasingly wider circle of moral concern, humans have evolved wider and wider associations of co-operation. The next logical step in this evolution is to include the land within the moral community. In other words, according to Leopold, Holism is the next logical development in ethics.

12.7 The Conceptual Foundations of the Land Ethic

Leopold was a conservationist, a forester, a writer, and an expert in wildlife management. He was not a professional philosopher. Until relatively recently, many philosophers ignored or dismissed his views as being out of hand.[17] Some, however, have taken up his position and advanced more philosophically sophisticated support for it. One such thinker is J. Baird Callicott, who argues that Leopold's Holism rests on five conceptual foundations.[18]

1. A Humean-Smithian Moral Psychology

Callicott asserts that the moral sense theories defended by David Hume and Adam Smith (1723–90) are the most ecologically sound. The natural law idea that God could be the source of morality is inconsistent with a natural explanation of ethics, since it appeals to a supernatural source. Also, moral theories like Kant's, which appeal to reason as the basis for ethics, are incompatible with the fact that as a species, humans must have developed means of co-operating prior to the development of advanced thinking skills. Thus, he concludes, only Hume and Smith's view that morality essentially involves feelings or sentiments is consistent with a natural history of ethics. Callicott adds that this view of ethics leads to Holism. As Leopold claims, the next step in the evolution of our ethics should be to extend our concern to biotic communities as wholes.

2. A Darwinian Protosociobiological Natural History of Ethics

As we noted in Chapter 3, a sociobiological explanation of ethics explains ethics from the perspective of the study of the biological foundations of human social behaviour. Since "proto" means "original," a protosociobiological explanation of ethics explains how ethics could have developed among our species from the beginning. Augmenting the Humean-Smithian moral psychology, Callicott maintains that if you consider how our species managed to survive and flourish by being ethical, you are again led to Holism.

A Darwinian protosociobiological natural history of ethics attempts to explain the history of ethics from the perspective of survival, and to show how ethical behaviour could have promoted our success as a species. Callicott argues that our social natures led us to care for each other and the benefits of our co-operating helps to explain our evolutionary success. Furthermore, if we have flourished to this point through the gradual widening of our circle of moral concern, then to continue to flourish we must continue to extend our circle of moral concern to include the Earth as a whole.

3. Darwinian Ties of Kinship among All Forms of Life on Earth

Callicott argues that the widening of our circle of moral concern can be understood in terms of Darwinian ties of kinship. As our ethical sensibilities have grown, so have those whom we identify as kin. The logical extension of this process is to extend our kinship ties to include the entire planet.

4. An Eltonian Model of the Structure of Biocoenoses

In his book *Animal Ecology*, published in 1927, Charles Elton developed the idea of a biotic community as a working model for ecology.[19] Within this model, organisms effectively play various interconnected roles in their environment such that they form a biocoenosis or biotic community. Callicott argues that this model helps explain Holism. In this model, humans too have a role, one that is connected to our ability to behave morally. We are part of the Earth and we have evolved to care about each other. Looked at from a global perspective, arguably our role is to behave ethically toward the Earth as a whole, to promote the integrity and stability of the global biotic community.

5. A Copernican Cosmology

Finally, Callicott explains that the shift to a Copernican worldview challenged the idea that humans occupy a central place in the universe. The idea that God somehow privileges our species was more difficult to defend once Copernicus showed that the Earth revolves around the sun as opposed to the Ptolemaic view that the Earth is at the centre of the universe. Furthermore, the idea that our planet is just one among many encourages us to identify ourselves as earthlings. Holists endorse this shared identity as equal members of the Earth's community. As Leopold writes, "In short, a land ethic changes the role of *Homo Sapiens* from conqueror of the land-community to plain member and citizen of it."[20]

12.8 In Support Of Holism

In our discussion of Biocentrism, we noted that the Biocentrist tries to show that all living beings have a prudential good. Holists reject this approach and argue, instead, that the restriction of ethical considerability to individuals is arbitrary and ecologically ignorant. They maintain that once you gain an awareness of the multiple interdependent relations of individuals in ecosystems, interrelations that involve all aspects of the environment, then you will be ready to extend ethics to such wholes. Doing so requires that we promote the values appropriate for ecosystems, as opposed to only those values appropriate for individuals. This means, in addition to acting ethically toward sentient beings, we also have duties to promote the integrity, stability, and diversity of ecosystems. The traditional ethical failure to extend ethics to embrace these values has rested on a failing of perspective. An awareness of ecology can help us overcome this.

The Land Pyramid

Although Leopold accepted Elton's model of a biotic community, he conceived of it as extending to the land. In his analysis, biotic communities include soils because soils are part of the flow of energy through the whole system. He explains the complex interrelatedness of thriving biotic communities with the help of his image of a land pyramid. At the base of the pyramid are the soils in which plants grow and through which energy is directed upward through the various overlapping and interconnected food chains. The food chains wind their way from the soils to the plants, insects, and successively larger animals up to the apex. Whereas energy flows upward through the food chains, it moves downward via various means through death and decay.

The height of the pyramid depends on the amount of speciation in the ecosystem, with elements at lower levels of the pyramid greatly outnumbering those at successively higher levels. Furthermore, the pyramid is built upward over time, with those levels existing lower down being older. In this model, the creatures like us near the apex of the pyramid are the products of the workings of lower levels. Indeed, the individuals who are accorded moral consideration on traditional ethical outlooks arrive relatively late on the scene and depend for their presence on the older and vastly more numerous lower levels. Edward Wilson remarks that among animals, invertebrates "rule the Earth" because they have existed for at least 100 million years longer than vertebrates and "by virtue of their sheer body mass."[21] He observes, for example, that each hectare in the tropical rain forest in the Amazon basin contains a few dozen birds and well over 1 billion invertebrates. Measured by body mass, 93 percent of the dry weight of animal biomass is made up of invertebrates, with ants and termites combined taking up one-third. In turn, when the biomass measurement includes all plants and vegetation, animals make up only a small percentage (less than 0.1 percent). Not only are levels below us older and greater in mass, but also we depend on their continued healthy existence for our survival. Wilson argues that whereas the rest of the world would scarcely notice our extinction, if the invertebrate species died out, we would likely not survive for more than a few months.

Duties to Ecosystems

In support of Leopold's Land Ethic, Holmes Rolston III argues that it is a mistake to judge ecosystems as morally inconsiderable on the grounds that they fail to meet the criteria found in morally considerable organisms. Rather, we need to appreciate that ecosystems should be measured in terms of their own values and processes. These values, which he refers to as "systemic values," are the values of speciation, selection pressure, adaptive fit, and life support. These systemic processes are both "prior to and productive of" individuals.[22] Individuals "are *what* they are because of *where* they are."[23]

Rolston argues that animals near the apex of the pyramid have evolved to be what they are as a result of survival pressures lower down. "Complexity," he explains, "is an organism-in-environment phenomenon."[24] He notes that when lions are caged, their brains degenerate within a decade. Therefore, looked at from the perspective of ecology, the reductionist individualist perspective of traditional ethics is arbitrary. It is also shortsighted. In addition to valuing ecosystems for their own peculiar values, we should also support them because our own survival depends on our ecosystems' continued functioning.

The Need for Holism

> "Nature, Mr. Alnut, is what we were put in the world to rise above."
>
> Dialogue from the movie *African Queen*

Unlike the churchy arrogance toward and disdain of nature portrayed by Katherine Hepburn's character in the *African Queen*, Holists warn that our continued survival depends on our recognizing that we must live with the Earth. Leopold argues that given our increasing ability to destroy the integrity, diversity, and stability of the biosphere, Holism is now a moral imperative. We must move beyond our traditional ethical outlooks and extend our moral concern to include the land. Given that our individualistic ethical theories have failed to stem the threat to the environment, it is clear that we need to embrace a wider, holistic ethic. Furthermore, the benefits of such a shift are evident. Since it is based on an understanding of ecology, and since it promotes a sensitive and sensible environmental consciousness, and, moreover, since much of the threat to the environment and to our own future is based on ignorance of ecology, Holism represents hope for the future.

12.9 The Debate over Holism

> Help save the earth. Commit suicide.
>
> *Bumper sticker message*

Critics of the Land Ethic note that this perspective endorses moral directives that are repugnant and contrary to the basic assumptions of our present ethical outlooks. The Holist's worry is that our lives pose the greatest threat to the stability and integrity of the environment. Since Holism urges us to counteract this threat, it seems to follow logically that this "ethic" requires of us that we kill ourselves, and that we do so on a massive scale. According to this line of criticism, any so-called "ethic" that requires copious human "diebacks" must be fundamentally flawed.[25]

Response

Defenders of the Land Ethic argue that the interpretation of Holism that generates this repugnant view is uncharitable and a caricature of a serious ethic. Leopold encourages us to extend morality to embrace the land; not to replace our present moral concerns, but to add concern for the land to them. Thus, we need a new approach that reconciles our existing commitments with ones to ecosystems as wholes. In the literature there has been much discussion of the prospects of this, with some defenders insisting that the viewpoints are fundamentally at odds and some claiming that a reconciliation is viable.[26] Callicott, however, maintains that we can embrace holist concerns consistent with our regard for those we care about now by enlarging our circle. The model for this is the Humean-Smithian view outlined in Section 12.7. Callicott suggests that our moral concerns can be ranked, with those we care about most comprising our highest-ranked interests and so on down the line:

> Family obligations in general come before nationalistic duties and humanitarian obligations in general come before environmental duties. The land ethic, therefore, is not draconian or fascist. It does not cancel human morality.[27]

On this model, then, Holists are merely arguing that we should add one set of concerns for the land at the lowest level of our hierarchy of moral concern. Most importantly, we should recognize that we can and should give moral consideration to ecosystems. Defenders of the Land Ethic assert their theory does not require that we kill ourselves; it requires only that we change the way we live our lives to incorporate concern for the land into our practices. This can mean that we limit both our own future growth and our future economic expansion plans if doing so will promote the integrity and the stability of local ecosystems and the Earth as a whole.

Counterresponse

Even if the first objection (killing ourselves) was overstated, critics note that adopting a more holistic approach in ethics will still create conflicts that are at odds with individualistic ethical outlooks. The problem is that adopting Holism either must make a difference to our practices or not. Since Holists reject this latter idea—that Holism makes no difference—then it must have some impact. As a result, when sometimes there are conflicts between promoting the good of individuals or sacrificing that good to promote the integrity and stability of the environment, we

should help the environment. But why? More precisely, what motivates a moral commitment to Holism at the expense of the good of individuals in the first place?

Since the case for Holism rests partly on the notion that ecosystems are prior to, productive of, and supportive of the lives of individuals, defenders of the Land Ethic might argue that there will be no conflicts between the two sets of values. To defend this approach, however, we must show that the moral values that support the good of individuals are entirely consistent with the moral values supporting the integrity and stability of ecosystems.

In fact, Holists typically recognize that there will be conflicts. Rather than argue that there will be none, they argue instead for the view that the two outlooks can be reconciled with a minimum of tension. Thus, they hold that sometimes we should act on the values of the Land Ethic at the expense of the good of individuals.

At this point, though, critics wonder why we should do this. What is the moral argument for choosing the values of the whole at the expense of the individual? Consider an illustration of the problem. Holmes Rolston III tells the story of the dilemma faced by park officials in an American national park, Yellowstone National Park, when an outbreak of pink eye threatened a herd of bighorn sheep.[28] Should the officials intercede on behalf of the sheep and treat the disease with antibiotics, or should they leave the sheep to fend for themselves against this threat? The officials opted not to intervene, partly on the grounds that humans should not interfere in the ecosystem where the battle between sheep and one of their natural parasites, the *Chlamydia* microbe, is a part of the natural order. As a consequence of this decision, half of the herd was blinded and died from starvation.

Rolston, appealing to the values of the Land Ethic, cites approvingly of the officials' decision, but a Welfarist might wonder whether they did the right thing; and if they did the right thing, whether they did so for the right sorts of reasons. Setting aside worries about Rolston's appeal to the idea of the parasite being natural and implying that park officials' interceding would be unnatural and therefore wrong,[29] a Welfarist can accept choosing not to intervene in a situation like this one. For example, a Welfarist could accept not intervening because we cannot confidently do so without also imperiling the well-being of many other sentient creatures. The concern is not for the *Chlamydia* microbe (an insentient being) but for the possible future consequences of such intervention for other individual sentient beings, such as other sheep. But this is not the Holist's justification. The proponent of the Land Ethic argues that in this sort of conflict between promoting the good of some sentient individuals or maintaining the integrity and stability of the environment, we should do the latter. Why?

Callicott appeals once again to the holistic interpretation of the Humean-Smithian moral psychology to justify this kind of decision. He notes that in our various circles of moral concern, we include non-human animals. These mixed communities include various domestic animals that by virtue of their membership are entitled to greater concern from us than wild animals. Wild animals stand outside our most immediate circles of concern. He explains that they are

> . . . by definition, not members of the mixed community and therefore should not lie in the same spectrum of graded moral standing as family members, neighbors, fellow citizens, fellow human beings, pets, and other domestic animals.[30]

According to Callicott, since wild animals fall outside our immediate concern and occupy only the furthest reaches of our circle, they should be subject to the demands of the Land Ethic. In this case, it means the park officials should let them go blind and starve to death since this seems the best course for promoting the integrity and stability of the ecosystem of which they are a part.

Welfarists might wonder why the demands of the Land Ethic should count at all. Setting aside the notion that perhaps we should care more for the sheep and less for the ecosystem, the question is, What motivates a moral concern for the ecosystem in the first place? Notice the question is not whether we should act in a way that is environmentally sensible. Like Holists, Welfarists, too, can learn the lessons of ecology

and recognize the importance from their own moral outlook, of acting in ways that preserve the environing conditions that support the lives of sentient beings. Indeed, for insisting on the point about the interrelatedness of life and for detailing the threat our behaviour has posed to the environment, the Welfarist can thank the Holist. But why, the Welfarist may ask, do we have duties to ecosystems?

By asking this question the Welfarist is raising a conceptual point about the scope of morality that is connected to our original question. Throughout this chapter and in Chapter 11, we have been examining answers to the questions "Who can be given moral consideration?" and "Why?" If we are to embrace the holist answer to this first question, then we need an answer to the second one. The Welfarist can wonder why the Holist thinks we have duties to ecosystems that do not simply reduce to promoting the good of the individual sentient beings in those ecosystems. Here there are two possibilities. Either (1) we have direct duties to ecosystems that entail that we promote their integrity and stability, or (2) we have duties only to sentient beings that we indirectly satisfy by promoting the Holist's values.

This second possibility does not give us the holist answer to our questions, because it points to a reason that rests on a welfarist outlook, which recommends that we follow ecologically informed practices. In this case, however, our goal is ultimately welfarist. The Holist must opt instead for the first possibility to defend his case for an alternative moral perspective. The Holist claims that the welfarist focus on individuals is arbitrary given the interconnectedness of life in biotic communities. But the Welfarist draws this distinction because, as we have seen, a moral concern is a concern for someone for her sake, and among all the various elements of ecosystems, only sentient beings have a prudential good. Thus, there is a point for singling out such individuals. This is not arbitrary or stipulation. This approach provides a reason for thinking that Welfarism supplies the correct answer to our question.

It is also a fallacy to think that just because our circle of moral concern has expanded in the past, that it must continue to do so to improve into the future. The Welfarist argues that we have finally reached our destination. In contrast, and more to the point, the Welfarist insists that the Holist offers no relevant reason for accepting the view that whole ecosystems can be given moral consideration. This is not to say that the park officials in the example involving the sheep should have interceded. However, in the absence of a reason for thinking that Holism is the right account of the proper scope of ethics, they should not have refrained from helping simply because they had a duty to the ecosystem not to do so. To act in this way is to act without reason. In the absence of a reason for thinking that Holism supplies us with the correct account of the story of the scope of ethics, the Welfarist concludes that Holism, just like Biocentrism, remains an unmotivated ethical outlook. The challenge the Welfarist thus presents to the Holist is to supply the missing reason.

12.10 Review

In this chapter we continued our investigation into the questions we raised in Chapter 11 about the proper scope of ethics. Specifically, we explained and examined arguments concerning two views, Biocentrism and Holism. After first outlining an account of the nature of life, we considered arguments for Biocentrism, the view that the class of all beings that can be given moral consideration includes and is limited to all living beings. Kenneth Goodpaster, Robin Attfield, and Paul Taylor each defend the biocentric outlook on the grounds that all living beings, sentient and insentient, have a good of their own, a welfare.

In response to these arguments, we considered some counter-arguments from Welfarists who agree with Biocentrists that all beings that have a prudential good can be given moral consideration, but who dispute the notion that insentient living beings fall into this class. Singer argues against another Biocentrist, Albert Schweitzer, that the apparent will to live exhibited by living beings is not a conscious willing and that insentient living beings have no well-being. In response to the

biocentrist insistence that all living beings do have a welfare because they can be harmed and benefited, L.W. Sumner claims that the Biocentrists conflate two different dimensions of value, perfectionist value with prudential value. On the basis of the possession of one sort of value (perfectionist value), they ascribe to insentient living beings the other sort of value (prudential value). Sumner argues that the Biocentrists are mistaken in ascribing prudential value to insentient life. He defends the view that only sentient beings can take the subjective perspective necessary for having a prudential good and therefore only they can be given moral consideration.

In the second part of the chapter we considered the argument for the Land Ethic, or Holism, the view in ethics that the moral community includes all the interdependent parts of entire ecosystems, including the Earth as a biotic community as a whole. Eschewing an individualistic perspective, and grounding ethics in ecology, Holists believe that acts are right insofar as they promote the integrity, stability, and beauty of the biotic community. Acts are wrong otherwise. In support of Holism, we noted both Callicott's discussion of the theoretical foundations of the position and Leopold's explanatory model of the land pyramid. Leopold believes that this model displays the essential interconnectedness of biotic communities, communities that include soils. This model also shows how humans are products of the environment and dependent on the functioning of ecosystems for their survival.

Finally, we considered the Holists' belief that ecosystems as wholes can be given moral consideration. We distinguished between supporting holist values for instrumental reasons, namely because doing so is best for sentient beings, and supporting Holism on its own terms. It is on this last point that the Welfarist challenges the holist view of the scope of morality. When there is a conflict between promoting holist values and the good of sentient individuals, why, asks the Welfarist, should we consider supporting holist values? To answer this question, the defender of the Land Ethic must explain and defend the idea that ecosystems can be given moral consideration. In the absence of such a defence, Holism is unsupported.

Notes

1. See Mowat (1984), pp. 176–178.

2. See Campbell, Reece, and Mitchell (1999), pp. 2–9.

3. Goodpaster (1978).

4. Attfield (1983), p. 153.

5. See Attfield (1981).

6. See Taylor (1982).

7. James Sterba uses this phrase to describe Taylor's version of the biocentric outlook. See Sterba (1994), p. 229.

8. Taylor (1986), p. 45.

9. Taylor (1986), p. 75. Taylor distinguishes his idea of inherent worth from what he calls "intrinsic value" and "inherent value" on pp. 73–75.

10. Schweitzer (1926), pp. 246–247.

11. Singer (1979), p. 92.

12. Sumner (1995), p. 772.

13. Sumner (1995), p. 789.

14. Sumner (1995), pp. 769–770.

15. Sumner (1996), p. 43.

16. Leopold (1949), pp. 224–225.

17. Callicott notes several examples of this. See Callicott (1987), pp. 186–187.

18. See Callicott (1987), pp. 187–195.

19. See Elton (1927).

20. Leopold (1949), p. 204.

21. Wilson (1987), p. 84.

22. Rolston (1987), p. 272.

23. Rolston (1987), p. 249.

24. Rolston (1987), p. 254.

25. For more on this line of criticism, see Aiken (1984), p. 269; Regan (1983), p. 262; and Sober (1986), especially the section "Granting Wholes Autonomous Value." "Diebacks" is Aiken's term.

26. On this debate, see Callicott (1980, 1987, and 1989), Sagoff (1984), Warren (1983), and Sterba (1994, 2001).

27. Callicott (1987), p. 208.

28. See Rolston (1987), p. 265.

29. For more on this sort of concern, see Sober (1986).

30. Callicott (1989), Chapter 3.

31. Peacock (1996), p. 440.

32. See Lovelock and Margulis (1974).

33. I owe these recommendations to Peacock.

Exercises

Progress Check

1. Outline Campbell, Reece, and Mitchell's account of the properties common to all living beings.

2. What is Biocentrism?

3. Briefly explain Goodpaster, Attfield, and Taylor's defences of Biocentrism.

4. What is Singer's criticism of Schweitzer's view? Explain his example involving the weed.

5. What is perfectionist value? What does it mean to say that a tree has perfectionist value?

6. How does Sumner distinguish perfectionist value from prudential value?

7. How does Sumner distinguish objective from subjective theories of prudential value?

8. Why does the argument that insentient living beings do not have a prudential good not also show that we should not respect life? What reasons would a Welfarist have for respecting the lives of insentient living beings?

9. What is the Land Ethic, or Holism?

10. What is ecology?

11. According to Leopold, what is ethics from an ecological perspective?

12. What are the conceptual foundations of the Land Ethic, according to Callicott? Explain.

13. Explain Leopold's idea of a land pyramid. In what sense, or what senses, are we dependent on those below us on this pyramid, according to the Holist?

14. Explain Holmes's view that complexity and individuality are "organism-in-environment" phenomena.

15. From the perspective of the Holist, why are traditional ethical perspectives reductionist?

16. Why do Holists believe that entire ecosystems can be given moral consideration?

Group Work Activity:

The Gaia Hypothesis

Canadian philosopher Kent Peacock offers the following more abstract definition of life than the one we outlined in Section 12.2. According to Peacock, "a living being is a dissipative physical system that maintains by active cybernetic processes a high degree of internal order in spite of surrounding thermodynamic gradients."[31]

Notice that Peacock's definition includes many—but not all—of the features of the one advanced by Campbell, Reece, and Mitchell and that it is more abstract. Peacock's definition makes no specific references to cells or DNA. Even the reference to cybernetics is more neutral since cybernetics is the science of systems of control and communication in animals and machines.

One interesting feature of Peacock's definition is that it admits the possibility that the Earth itself is a living being. This notion is known as the *Gaia hypothesis*. Gaia is a term from ancient Greek meaning "Earth Goddess." The originators of the Gaia hypothesis are James Lovelock and Lynn Margulis.[32]

The *Gaia hypothesis* is a hypothesis in science that the entire planet is itself a living being. James Lovelock and Lynn Margulis advanced this hypothesis. The Gaia hypothesis is controversial and the subject of much debate. Even more controversial is the suggestion that the Earth is a *sentient* living being. According to this interpretation of the Gaia hypothesis, humans collectively form the consciousness of our planet. If this view can be defended, then within the welfarist analysis, the Earth itself can be given moral consideration.

Your Task

Explain and critically assess this controversial idea that, as a sentient living being, the Earth itself can be given moral consideration for its own sake.

1. Explanation

For this first part of your task, you will need to research the Gaia hypothesis. First, research informed discussion of the hypothesis and with the other members of your group, craft a one-page summary explaining the hypothesis. In this part of your project, you should aim to expand on and clarify the view without judging it. As a place to start in your research, you might consider locating one or more of the references in the notes to this chapter or the suggestions contained in the Suggested Further Reading and Weblinks sections below.

2. Assessment

For the second part of your task, critically evaluate the argument for the view that the Gaia hypothesis provides us with a reason or some reasons for giving the Earth moral consideration. In constructing your assessment, you might want to consider the following questions:

a) In what respects would the Earth as a conscious living being be like you or me?

b) To what extent do these similarities support the view that we should give the planet itself moral consideration? Explain.

c) To what extent, or in what respects, is the Earth understood as a conscious living being unlike you or me? What impact, if any, does this have on the argument for giving the Earth moral consideration for itself?

Questions for Further Reflection

1. Explain and critically evaluate Attfield's analogical argument for the view that all living beings can be given moral consideration.

2. Explain and critically evaluate Sumner's view that perfectionist and prudential value judgments of people's lives assess different dimensions of value. Can you think of any examples to support his position? Can you think of any counter-examples? Explain.

3. Explain and critically assess Sumner's argument for the subjectivity of welfare.

4. Holists argue that only the Humean-Smithian moral theory is ecologically sound. Explain and

critically evaluate their criticisms of Natural Law and Kantian moral theory.

5. Explain and critically evaluate the holist argument that since humanity's circle of moral concern has generally been growing wider over time, that it follows logically that to further improve we should extend our concern to include the land.

6. Why do Holists argue that the traditional restriction of the scope of morality to individuals is arbitrary and ecologically ignorant? How does the Welfarist respond?

7. According to Holmes, what are the systemic values of ecosystems? Can you explain and connect these values to Leopold's land ethic values? Explain.

8. Explain and assess the "dieback" objection to the Land Ethic.

9. a. What motivates a moral commitment to Holism at the expense of the good of individuals?
   b. Under what conditions, if any, do you think we would be ethically justified in so acting? Explain and defend your view.

10. Did the park officials act ethically by refusing to help the bighorn sheep suffering from pink eye? What sorts of reasons would count as a moral defence of their decision? Why?

11. Outline and assess the strongest argument for Holism on the question of the proper scope of ethics.

Suggested Further Reading

The journal *Environmental Ethics* is a good source for discussions on the topics of this chapter.

Leopold's view is presented in his *A Sand County Almanac* (Leopold [1949]). For some excellent commentary and discussion of this from a number of experts in a variety of fields, see *Companion to A Sand County Almanac: Interpretive and Critical Essays*, edited by J. Baird Callicott (Callicott [1987]).

For a good introduction to the Gaia hypothesis, see Chapter 8 of Kent Peacock's book (Peacock [1996]). Apart from the original paper with Lynn Margulis (Lovelock and Margulis [1974]), James Lovelock has published much on the Gaia hypothesis, including two books (Lovelock [1979] and [1988]). The notion that the Earth can be conceived as a conscious creature and that humans can be the Earth's consciousness is raised in "The Quest for Gaia," by Lovelock and Sidney Epton (Lovelock and Epton [1986]). For an overview of the hypothesis, see Joseph (1990), and for the proceedings of a scientific conference on the hypothesis, see Schneider and Boston (1991).[33]

Weblinks

For a number of relevant links, including one to the journal *Environmental Ethics*, see the Weblinks in Chapter 11.

The Aldo Leopold foundation has an informative Web site with a good set of links on topics related to Holism at **www.aldoleopold.org**

EcoTopia/USA's Ecology Hall of Fame has an entry on Aldo Leopold with related links at **ecotopia.org/ehof/leopold/links.html**

Part 3

Issues

Whereas in Part Two we examined a number of practical questions and issues from various perspectives, in this final part of the book, we consider a set of current issues in Bioethics, Business Ethics, and ethics and the law. There are of course many other areas within Applied Ethics. For example, there is Environmental Ethics, an area we treated at some length in Part Two. But the main areas are the ones we select from here. Our aim is not to comprehensively discuss the many applied issues one could consider. Rather, we focus on a few select issues to extend our analysis of ethics to some practical problems. The topics have been chosen for their interest, currency, and range.

Bioethics

The field of Bioethics has grown enormously over the past 30 years or so. Standard topics in this area include questions about the ethics of abortion, euthanasia, reproductive technology, the patient-healthcare provider relationship,

and Research Ethics. Some of our work earlier in the book can help us make progress on these issues. For example, our lengthy discussion of the scope of morality in Chapter 11 bears directly on the debates over abortion, euthanasia, and the ethics of using non-human animals in research that mostly benefits humans.

Instead of further pursuing discussions of these issues, we consider two other pressing ethical problems of our time: the problem of the just allocation of scarce medical resources and a number of problems in the field of ethics and genetics. Chapter 13 picks up our work from chapters 9 and 10 on the question of how much consideration should be given to individuals. Specifically, we examine the practical problem of how to fairly allocate scarce resources among patients. We focus on developing a fair policy. In Chapter 14 we analyze several ethical questions related to emerging research advances in genetics. With an eye to developing ethical law and policy, we consider questions concerning the ethics of research into cloning, stem cells, germ-line genetic alteration, and ectogenesis.

In addition to surveying some of the background science, we see how law and policy might develop in different and somewhat conflicting ways, depending upon our basic underlying moral assumptions. Thus, we draw some connections between our meta-ethical and theoretical moral beliefs and some topical ethical problems.

Business Ethics

There are a host of interesting topics within the expanding area of Business Ethics. In Chapter 15, we look at one such topic. The debate over affirmative action has for many years been a divisive topic within the field of employee-employer relations. Focusing on affirmative action as it applies to initial hiring and advancement decisions, we consider this topic from various justice perspectives. In addition to considering the ethics of affirmative action from the perspectives of compensatory and distributive justice, we also examine it from the much-neglected perspective of intergenerational justice. Furthermore, whereas the issue of affirmative action in the philosophical debates has traditionally focused on discrimination on the basis of sex and race, in Canada nowadays debates about employment equity and affirmative action extend to our treatment of persons with disabilities and Aboriginal peoples. Our treatment of the topic includes consideration of persons from these groups too.

Ethics and the Law

The large area of ethics and the law ranges over a number of issues and topics, including some we have already surveyed. In Chapter 2, for example, we considered the question of the relationship between law and morality from the perspective of Natural Law Theory and some current debates in the philosophy of law. Furthermore, in addition to considering the question of the necessary moral content of law, we also considered how we achieve co-operation in society through law and morality. In Chapter 16, we turn our attention to the question of the rightful limit of the use of power by the state against the individual. Specifically, we focus on the question of the value of freedom and the pressing practical problem facing our Supreme Court of how to set limits to our *Charter* rights. To make progress on these questions, we examine John Stuart Mill's position in his treatise *On Liberty*. We also discuss the related topics of Legal Moralism and paternalism.

Issues in Bioethics I: The Just Allocation of Scarce Medical Resources

Learning Outcomes

In this chapter we address the problem of fairly allocating scarce health care resources. We focus on the microallocative question of how to distribute resources among patients, and we consider the case for giving them equal consideration.

Upon the successful completion of this chapter, you will be able to

1. distinguish between the three ways of classifying problems regarding the scope of justly allocating scarce health care resources and the two kinds of scarcity;

2. explain the issues of procedural justice that the problem raises;

3. contrast some competing arguments regarding the proper role of doctors in allocating resources;

4. identify and evaluate some important arguments for giving patients equal consideration;

5. note the various moral intuitions and principles that underlie and guide our ethical judgments on this question; and

6. outline some of the challenges that still must be met to develop fairer policies.

13.1 Introduction

In 2000, 147 Canadians died while waiting for transplantable organs. Less dramatic are the cases in which people experience a diminished quality of life as a result of being denied access to resources, or in being delayed in accessing them. Many assume that the challenge of fairly allocating scarce resources is simply one of execution and increasing supply; that what we need to do is fairly apply our already worked out and just policies and strive toward reducing the number of cases of unfulfilled need in the future. The argument of this chapter, together with those from chapters 9 and 10, questions our complacent trust in the policies that currently govern us.

Alternatively, some people avoid addressing the issues we will examine out of apathy or ignorance. They just don't care or don't know and leave the burden of creating just laws and policies to the experts. In the spirit of enlightenment, we should wonder about this attitude. As responsible citizens and consumers, all mature Canadians have a duty to intelligently participate (or at least be ready to participate) in debates about the creation of laws and policies that have the potential to fundamentally affect our lives. By exchanging ignorance, apathy, and complacency for a basic awareness of the main issues and an appreciation of the ethical work that remains to be done, we will take some useful steps toward promoting an informed and thoughtful discussion of these important matters.

We begin by distinguishing between some of the different problems with fairly allocating scarce health care resources, and we narrow our focus to considering the problems of the just microallocation of resources, that is, allocation that selects between patients vying for the resources. After reviewing the debate over the question of who should be responsible for fairly allocating public health care resources, we consider the role of doctors in our system from two opposing viewpoints. We then face the challenge of devising fair policies. Since versions of policies that give patients equal consideration for resources are most popular, we examine the case for this first. However, these policies exclude the full range of moral intuitions and principles that play a role in our deliberations on this topic. To do better justice to this range of principles, we briefly consider the prospects of developing a more sophisticated policy that gives some role to allocating resources on the basis of a ranking method. We conclude by raising some problems with this initiative.

Much of the work of this chapter builds on our discussion from chapters 9 and 10. Thus, you are encouraged to review our progress there before proceeding.

13.2 The Just Microallocation of Scarce Health Care Resources

There are many problems with justly allocating scarce health care resources in our society. Our focus will be on one set of these concerns, namely, the allocation of resources among individual patients. We commonly refer to the *macroallocation* of resources to describe what governments at all levels do in setting their health care budgets. At the macroallocative level, questions of justice include questions about what amount of resources should be devoted to health care. A typical question is how we should balance devoting resources to health care against devoting resources to other areas of public concern, like education, transportation infrastructure, foreign aid, recreation, and so on.

Once these budgets are set and the available resources are apportioned to various regional health authorities and health care institutions, problems of *mesoallocation* arise. These problems concern the just distribution of health care resources at the institutional level. For example, the question, "What proportion of the available health care resources should be allocated to various departments and programs, like neonatal care, community health programs, and emergency care?" is a question of the just mesoallocation of scarce health care resources.

Beyond these sorts of decisions, we also face *microallocative* decisions that involve deciding among particular individuals for scarce resources. Although there are connections between the three sorts of problems, our concern is with examining problems of the just microallocation of scarce health care resources.

This threefold classification of the problems of distributive justice in health care suggests one way in which health care resources can be scarce at the microallocative level. They can be scarce simply because insufficient financial resources were allocated at a higher level to enable us to give health care resources to all who want them. This sort of shortfall can be called *financial scarcity.* In instances of financial scarcity, there simply isn't enough to go around so we need to decide how to fairly distribute what we have. There may be insufficient medicines, treatments, medical supplies, trained personnel, physical facilities (for example, a shortage of chronic care beds, acute care beds, or operating rooms), or technology. In each case, however, one possible solution is to devote more societal resources to increasing the supply of whatever is needed.

A different kind of scarcity occurs when there is an inadequate supply of something that cannot be rectified in any straightforward way by allocating more money to the shortage. Such is the case with the scarcity of transplantable organs and human tissue in Canada. We will call this sort of shortfall *organic scarcity.*[1] In the case of organic scarcity, we can devote more resources to try to increase the supply of organs and tissue for transplant by, for example, funding research into stem cells and xeno-transplantation (transplanting from one species to another). We could also look at ways of financially compensating donors to try to improve our current rate of less than 14 per million Canadians. But, currently, for various reasons, the available demand for transplantable organs and tissue far outstrips supply. Moreover, since supply has been steady the last few years and demand is increasing, it looks in the short term that this sort of scarcity will also increase. We will assume that these problems will persist for the foreseeable future and that we need to deal with the issues of microallocative justice to which they give rise.[2]

Obviously we cannot engage in a comprehensive discussion of all of the problems of microallocative justice in health care. But we can apply some of the points we have made in chapters 9 and 10 to some of the problems and issues in this area. Moreover, to widen our scope somewhat, we can consider problems due to both types of scarcity.

To illustrate some problems resulting from financial scarcity, we will take the example of the just microallocation of resources on Intensive Care Units (ICUs). Since hospital ICUs face shortages of equipment and staff, those charged with distributing available resources have to make allocation decisions between patients.

To illustrate some of the problems resulting from organic scarcity, we will take the example of the issue of the just microallocation of transplantable organs.

By applying some of the lessons that we have learned to these two serious problems, we can further illustrate some of the ethical issues that we have been considering. We can also raise some questions and advance some arguments that challenge the ways in which we currently allocate our health care resources, and suggest ethical concerns that need to be addressed further.

13.3 The Question of Perspective

Before we examine the problems of the just microallocative distribution of resources in health care that we have outlined, we should first determine which perspective we should take. Should the patients decide among themselves who should receive the resources? Should their doctors decide? Alternatively, is the burden on the health care institutions, as representatives of wider society, to take responsibility for fairly allocating the resources? Should the responsibility be shared? If so, how? In our discussion of the Crisis in Space (in Section 9.2) we noted a similar debate over who should make decisions about who lives and who dies. As the mission leader, you represented your organization. If we assumed that the organization was both public and non-profit (the United Nations Space Agency, for example) we have an analogy to this situation.

We should not press this too far, however, since there are also some important dissimilarities. On the shuttle there is no one who has the role and responsibilities that physicians do in the health care case. Also, on the shuttle it is much simpler for the potential survivors to organize and plan their solution to the dilemma. In the health care case, this is much more difficult, for one thing, because there are potentially many more patients competing for resources than there are potential survivors on the shuttle. For example, according to Health Canada, there are nearly 3700 Canadians waiting for transplants.[3]

This decision is also more difficult in the health care dilemma because there are differences between the kinds of health care cases that we are considering. For instance, we know who is on the waiting lists for organ transplants when these resources are allocated, but often we do not know who will need ICU resources when these are distributed. In the case of ICUs, we often need to make decisions about whom to admit before other patients, who arrive later, need the resources.[4] So the idea of holding a meeting among those competing for the resources and letting them decide, as we might think of doing on the shuttle, is not so easily accomplished in the ICU example.

Although we might seek input from the patients and potential patients, in our earlier discussion, we also noted that a primary reason for not giving them the final word is to try to ensure fairness through impartiality. Likewise in the health care situations, arguably we should try to avoid decisions based on personal biases. It seems to be one of our settled ethical intuitions that in situations where some sort of public good is being distributed, it would be unfair to allocate on the basis of some biased personal interest. For instance, in the Crisis in Space example, many think that it would be unjust to include the fact that Mr. Yamamoto is your boss's boss's half-brother in your deliberations simply because you might want to curry favour with the agency director. Even if you ultimately weight the claims of the passengers differently, you should begin by giving each equal concern and attention so that your decision is based on the relevant merits of their case. According to this line of reasoning, we rule out favouring Mr. Yamamoto for your own personal benefit. Since your responsibility is to promote the welfare of all the passengers as best you can, essentially any personal interest you might have in helping Mr. Yamamoto is morally irrelevant.

In explaining the moral basis for adopting a societal perspective on the problem, we should appreciate the difference between giving each passenger equal concern and attention and giving each equal consideration.[5] We must distinguish the reasons for giving each person equal concern and attention from the reasons that determine who should ultimately get the consideration, in this case the life-saving goods. As we just noted, one reason for giving each person your equal concern and attention at the start is that you have a responsibility to all. Each passenger is a potential beneficiary of the goods to be distributed. Furthermore, each is accorded an equal claim to them at the outset of the trip when there is plenty for everyone. Therefore, you have a responsibility to approach the Crisis by giving each one your equal attention and concern. You must, in other words, be impartial in your treatment of the passengers.

To move from the view that you must be impartial in your treatment of the passengers to the view that you should give each equal consideration in the form of an equal chance to win a lottery to stay, we need to advance further argument. Agreeing to give each person an equal opportunity in the weak sense of giving each one an equal chance to compete for a future place on the shuttle is different from agreeing to give each one an equal opportunity in the stronger sense of giving each person an equal share of the goods (in this case in the form of an equal chance in the lottery). Perhaps we can best see this difference by noting that we could decide that after fairly and equally considering each passenger's case for staying, we should rank them differently based on the merits of their case. Should all potential patients in Canada begin with an equal claim to the concern and attention of the system for the resources to be distributed? Some argue that since Canadians fund the public health care system, a person must at least be a Canadian to be among the pool of those eligible for the resources, at least in the case of expensive resources. According to this view, we can give non-residents health care resources on humanitarian grounds, but out of fairness to those who pay, we should place limits on how much to give. Although there are ethical issues we might consider here too, let's bypass these and accept for the sake of argument that, minimally, to be considered for a transplantable organ or for ICU treatment in Canada, one must be a Canadian.

A further question is how we should regard the claims of all those in the pool of potential beneficiaries. Again, for the sake of argument, let's accept that a feature of our system is that all Canadians by virtue of being citizens of this country have at least an equal claim to compete for the health care resources in the system. Although all might not have an equal claim to receive them (think of the controversy involving the case of the 107-year-old-man from Section 9.4), all are entitled to the equal concern and attention of those who distribute the resources to be considered for them.

13.4 The Role of Physicians in Allocating Scarce Health Care Resources

If we accept that procedural impartiality is a feature of any fair microallocative decision process in health care, how do we ensure this? Ideally, we would have a system that enables the impartial application of whatever system of allocation that we judged to be fair. Each patient's interests would receive the equal concern and attention of the distribution system so that each patient's claim to the resources was fairly heard. What is the best way of achieving this?

Currently in Canada, doctors play an important role in the distribution of health care resources. Physicians determine whom to admit

to ICUs and also help determine who gets wait-listed for organ transplants. For this method to be consistent with the impartial processing of claims to scarce resources, doctors would need to be like the ideal judge who adopts a strictly impartial outlook in the conduct of a trial. However, although there is considerable pressure on doctors to be the guardians of scarce medical resources and weigh competing claims impartially, they are also bound by their often-conflicting duties to particular patients. Not surprisingly, physicians' culture emphasizes the traditional duty to act on behalf of one's own patients.

This is evident in the guidelines that doctors' professional associations have set out. Both the Canadian Medical Association and the American Medical Association have adopted guidelines to help doctors make just microallocation decisions (see Table 13.1). Although these associations emphasize that resources should be distributed fairly and efficiently, each set of guidelines downplays the responsibility to fairly allocate resources while stressing the doctor's traditional fiduciary duty to her patient. Indeed, the guidelines hardly mention concerns of microallocative justice.

Similarly the emphasis on duty to one's patient is also reflected in physicians' practices. According to a survey of critical care doctors conducted by the Society of Critical Care Medicine, four factors are important in determining whether to admit a patient to an ICU:

1. quality of life from the patient's perspective;
2. likelihood of survival;

Table 13.1 Professional Association Guidelines for Making Just Microallocative Health Care Decisions[6]

Recommended Factors for Doctors to Consider when Allocating Organs and Human Tissue

Canadian Medical Association	Probability of benefit to the patient	Severity of medical need	Length of time on the waiting list		
American Medical Association	Probability of benefit to the patient	Severity of medical need	The impact of treatment in the quality of the patient's life	The duration of benefit	The amount of resources required for successful treatment

3. potential for reversibility of the disorder; and

4. the nature of the disorder.[7]

The emphasis on fulfilling one's duty to one's patient may be consistent with allocating scarce resources fairly for some range of cases. However, it could be argued that in cases where there is a conflict between acting for the sake of one's patient and giving the scarce resource to another more deserving patient, it is unfair to expect doctors to choose.

Consider an illustration of the difficult position in which doctors may be placed by the present setup. Imagine that there was a scarce course of treatment that offered a potential life-saving benefit to some newborns who needed it. After two weeks of treatment, more than 99 percent of the babies who will survive can be weaned off the treatment with excellent chances of a full recovery. For the remaining babies who have not been sufficiently benefiting from the treatment, further treatment offers only a very slim chance of recovery. Imagine furthermore that you are a doctor who puts a baby on the treatment. Two weeks pass, and it is clear that he has not been benefiting and that the prospects of his benefiting from the treatment enough to make a difference to his recovery are slight, say less than 10 percent. You also know that another premature baby now needs these resources and that the chances are much greater that this treatment will save this other baby's life. If she does not receive it, she will soon die. There are no other hospitals that can provide the treatment to the baby in need. What should you do?

Arguably this is an unfair question to ask. If you believe your duty is to respect the first baby's parents' wishes to continue the treatment, then you may be seen as acting in fulfillment of your duty to your patient but contrary to the demands of justice. If you encourage the parents to discontinue the treatment then you might be regarded as acting in accordance with what is fair but contrary to your duty to your patient. A better system is one that administers policy impartially on the basis of just ethical principles. Under such a system, the question would not be "What should you as the doctor do about this?" because you would not have the power to deter-

mine the outcome. The question would be, What is a fair policy to govern situations like these? Once we answer this question, it would then be a matter of implementing our policy, which might require, for example, that parents be forewarned that their baby may be taken off the treatment after a set period of time if the treatment is not working sufficiently well.

This example, by the way, is not a bit of fiction. It is based on Dr. Robert D. Truog's account of the use of extracorporeal membrane oxygenation (ECMO), a form of cardiopulmonary bypass useful for many newborns with life-threatening respiratory failure.[8] Truog explains that this treatment is truly scarce because it is not available everywhere, and it requires the services of highly trained professionals around the clock. He wonders about the ethics of our present culture in which we think it wrong to end the possible life-saving treatment of one patient to make way for another patient.

Response

In response you might note that Truog's point about the questionable ethics of continuing treatment for patients with slight chances while denying access to those with much better prospects is separate from the question of how to organize a fair system of resource allocation. Although the ECMO example seems to point to a problem with a system that empowers doctors to make microallocative resource decisions, it could just as well be a failing in a system that does not place this power into doctors' hands. The main issue is whether our system, which allows physicians wide powers in determining who should receive what, is best or not.

Defenders of the present process might argue that there are both substantial benefits with the present setup and potentially serious shortcomings with one that would place decision-making power elsewhere. First, they could argue, we do a disservice to the professionalism of doctors to suggest that they should not be empowered to make allocation decisions because of worries about potential conflicts of interest. With their experience in medicine and with making difficult life-and-death decisions, they are generally capable of making the fair allocation decisions they are trained to make. They are also in the best position to do so. Also, worries about conflicts between duties to one's patients and duties to society are overstated since doctors do not think that patients are entitled to unlimited resources no matter what. Replacing our process with one that is designed to be more impartial would also likely require adding another level of bureaucracy to the system. Following the model of the judicial system would involve something like requiring that allocation decisions be made by a judge or some impartial hospital panel or committee that would consider allocation requests from patients. It might also add the duties of the lawyer to the duties of the physician. Arguably, a system that was designed to free doctors from deciding between conflicting demands would come at the price of inefficiency.

For a similar reason, we should also resist efforts to codify a set of rules that doctors should follow in determining who should receive scarce resources. Many argue that a feature of any fair system is that it must indicate to users how decisions will be made and that the problem with the CMA and AMA guidelines in Table 13.1 is that they are too vague. However, given the complex nature of health care allocation decisions, any workable set of rules that tried to anticipate all the possible situations they would need to contend with would be unduly restrictive and doomed to be unjust. Instead, our system provides guidelines to doctors, but relies ultimately on their judgment and sensitivity to the particular circumstances of the case before them. What this system loses in transparency and predictability, it gains in flexibility, and this best serves the interests of justice.

Finally, proponents of our process might caution us not to throw the baby out with the bath water in our efforts to weed out unfairness in the microallocation of health care resources. We need to distinguish between changing our process of allocating resources, where doctors hold much power, from changing our ideas regarding what counts as a fair distribution of resources in particular cases. The example of ECMO in ICUs above is perhaps a good example of where we need to alter or refine our views about what fairness requires. However, these changes need not entail changes to our process of allocating resources.

Counterresponse

As a counterresponse, advocates of reform might accept that any reforms should avoid as much as possible the pitfalls of inefficiency noted above. However, they might also insist that in situations where doctors do face conflicts, we would be better off devising methods of decision-making that eliminate as much as possible the tendencies of physicians to act on behalf of their own patients at the expense of the rightful claims of others to the scarce resources. Yes, doctors do recognize limits in their duties to their patients regarding claims to health care resources. But the present issue is whether doctors' culture sets those limits too far in favour of their own patients at the expense of other patients. The worry, in other words, is that our system, which places so much responsibility into physicians' hands, is out of balance. Obviously this is a complex issue, but we need to strike a better balance between ensuring fairness in our process and ensuring efficiency. Just as it would be a mistake to leave the task of fair microallocation solely to doctors, it would also be a mistake to adopt a process that was rigid and bureaucratic.

13.5 The Challenge of Devising Fair Allocation Policies

In addition to addressing the question of the fairest system for implementing policies governing the microallocation of scarce medical resources, we also need to determine the policies themselves. This demanding and complex task raises many questions and issues. Although there are limits as to how much progress we can make, we can draw on our work from Chapters 9 and 10 to help us along. Our aim will be to selectively discuss microallocation policy issues with one eye to making some substantive progress and the other to identifying some problems that remain to be considered.

13.6 The Case for Giving Equal Consideration

We have surveyed a number of reasons for giving people equal consideration for scarce resources. People argue that equal consideration is best because it is fair as well as being simple to implement and explain. Let's reconsider each of these reasons in turn.

Fairness

Defenders of policies that give everyone equal consideration argue that their view is fair for some different reasons. In chapters 5 and 9 we noted the Kantian argument that states that all humans who (apparently) have free will and are capable or potentially capable of reasoning are subjects equally deserving of respect in the kingdom of ends. Within this account, all such beings' lives are infinitely, and thus equally, valuable.

However, through the use of the Killing Machine thought experiment, we saw that this Kantian idea accords neither with our practices nor with our considered views. Although we want to express our conviction that life is generally very valuable, the notion that it is infinitely valuable seems an exaggeration. Furthermore, once we draw back from the claim that life is not infinitely valuable, then we need another reason for thinking that different lives are equally valuable and that we all have an equal right to life. It seems that if we are to locate support for giving all persons equal consideration in the microallocation of scarce medical resources, we will have to look elsewhere.

Another reason policies giving equal consideration are said to be fair is that they avoid the arbitrariness of ranking methods. If the choice is between giving two people in roughly equal circumstances with roughly similar qualities either equal consideration for some resource or making very fine discriminations, then the fairest option

is to give equal consideration. If we have to choose between giving a transplantable liver to one of two people who are distinguished only by a slight difference in age or intellectual capacity, then to avoid arbitrariness we should flip a coin. This does indeed seem fair. But this does not help the case for a wide-ranging policy of giving equal consideration because it rests on the assumption that the people being considered for the resource are *already* roughly equal in terms of the prudential value of their lives or their likely effects on society or both. Therefore, although giving equal consideration makes sense in situations where there are only slight differences between people, we cannot appeal to this argument to ground a far-reaching policy of giving equal consideration.

A third reason policies of giving equal consideration are said to be fair is that they do not penalize people for factors and circumstances that are beyond their control. Underlying this notion is an appeal to a principle according to which people should be treated in ways consistent with what they deserve. Policies of giving equal consideration, like the lottery method discussed in chapters 9 and 10, counterbalance the tendency of ranking methods to favour individuals for qualities over which they can take little or no credit. For instance, in the Crisis in Space example, many people will argue that Sarah Moore should be killed because, sad as it is, her life is less valuable to herself and to society than at least six other survivors' lives are. Setting aside the issue of whether this is true, some argue for a policy of equal consideration because it would be unfair to penalize Sarah for something she had no control over, specifically the disaster itself and her Down syndrome. A similar sentiment underlies the view that it is unfair to favour people who have dependant children over people who, through no fault of their own, are unable to conceive.

Many argue that the moral intuition that resources should be allocated on the basis of desert (of who deserves what) works both ways. Just as many think it wrong to penalize people for things that are beyond their control, many also agree that it is acceptable to penalize those who are responsible for their situations. So, for example, some would argue that people who choose to break the law and harm society are rightly considered less deserving of public benefits as a result of their actions. According to this view, we would be justified in selecting a law-abiding citizen for a transplant over a criminal guilty of serious crimes like sexual assault and murder. Likewise, imagine we had to choose between two candidates for a heart transplant. The first person has lived a very healthy life, but he suffers from a worsening life-long congenital heart defect. The second person's heart was failing as a result of a very unhealthy lifestyle that included smoking, a poor diet, and little exercise. All other things being roughly equal, many argue that we should choose the first person because he was not responsible for his need, whereas the second person largely was.

This reasoning appeals to the principle of desert and it does have some influence on us. It seems unfair to penalize people for things over which they have little or no control just as we think people should be rewarded for their efforts. However, many philosophers have debated the extent to which we are responsible for what we have and what we do.[9] Even if we accept some principle of desert, sometimes there is still a question of how far we should extend this. If the principle of desert at work here is supposed to help support a principle of equal consideration, then why stop at giving equal consideration to humans? Laboratory rats are not responsible for being rats. Should they not receive equal consideration with humans for the same reason?

Much the same case can be made for many other non-human animals, yet we think we are justified in using them to benefit us. Why? As we noted in Chapter 11, philosophers such as Peter Singer argue that our actions can be explained by our speciesist attitudes. We are simply unduly prejudiced against non-human animals. Although this may be true to some extent, it does not fully account for our behaviour. We also think that the principle of desert is sometimes trumped by a principle of utility according to which we are justified in favouring those with more valuable lives. So, if you had to choose between saving a laboratory rat or a healthy young child, we think you are justified in selecting the child for reasons of utility. (Whether this reasoning justifies the use of non-human animals in research that primarily benefits humans is, of course, a related but still separate question.) If this is so in cases like the rat and the child, the question arises as to when it is also true in cases where we have to choose between two or more people.

Building on the work of Kant and others, and leaning on this principle of desert, John Rawls has articulated and defended an influential argument for equality. Specifically, Rawls defends a version of Liberal Egalitarianism that is based on a belief that we are autonomous beings capable of forming and acting on our own individual plans of life. We are also generally moral beings interested in respecting the claims of others to follow their life plans. Given our similar status as autonomous beings, and given that basic rights and liberties are necessary for living prudentially good lives, we think it rational to organize society so that all humans are given the greatest set of equal liberties and rights possible.

Since according to Rawls's view, we intuitively accept the idea that all humans deserve equal rights, his argument for equality need not be seen as resting on any claims about human life being infinitely, and therefore equally, valuable. Furthermore, many people find Rawls's claims about equality appealing. We could argue that given the point about the principle of desert and Rawls's appeal to our autonomous natures, we should organize society such that the basic necessities of life are shared, at least to some extent. So we might be able to make an argument for the idea that we think that all Canadians deserve at least a claim to a minimum standard of health care in order to have a chance to live a minimally decent life. This sentiment certainly seems consistent with our settled views about equality and fairness.

There is, however, a further question regarding how far this sort of reasoning will take us in the debate over the just microallocation of scarce medical resources. The problem once again is that our intuitions and beliefs about equality are not the only ethical beliefs that come into play here. A thoroughgoing and exclusive appeal to equality would commit us to giving equal consideration to all who could benefit from scarce resources, and as we have noted, this too runs counter to our intuitions and settled judgments. By examining the other supposed merit of giving equal consideration, its supposed simplicity to use and explain, we can perhaps see this from another perspective.

Simplicity

In our test case, the Crisis in Space from Section 9.2, the option of giving each survivor equal consideration was quite straightforward. We would conduct a lottery that would give each survivor an equal chance of being selected to remain.[10] Indeed, one of the chief advantages of using the lottery method is that it seems simple to use and explain, especially in comparison to more complex methods of choosing individuals based on their qualities and circumstances. Similarly, some might think that these merits extend to giving everyone equal consideration for the distribution of scarce health care resources. In principle, giving everyone equal consideration does seem simple enough. In the case of those waiting for transplantable organs, we would rank everyone's claim equally and then award resources based on the results of fair lotteries. In situations where we need to allocate the resources sequentially, as in the case of an ICU, we could approximate the lottery method by perhaps adopting a First Come, First Served policy that gives all an equal claim to the resources.

A thoroughgoing and exclusive commitment to giving equal consideration would require that we give all those who have *any chance* of benefiting *in any way* from the resources an equal claim to them. Earlier, we said that we would limit the potential pool of beneficiaries to Canadians, but if we were to exclusively appeal to an ideal of equality to justify allocation decisions, then it seems that we would have to abandon this limitation. If the only relevant consideration is that all humans receive equal consideration, then all who could

use the resources should be given an equal claim to them.

As appealing as a commitment to equality is, in practice people do not usually rely on it exclusively for determining how to fairly allocate scarce resources. Typically, other competing ethical principles are also invoked to help determine some range of distribution decisions. Sometimes the other competing principles enter allocation decision-making covertly, and they are not explicitly regarded as such. For example, some argue that to identify a suitable pool of potential candidates for scarce resources, we first need to set eligibility criteria. As we noted earlier, these can be based on factors like citizenship. Commonly they are also based on factors like "likelihood of benefit" or "prospects of success." In other words, potential candidates for a scarce resource must not just have any chance at all of benefiting from the resources but must meet some likely threshold of benefit.

Although the justification for having the selection criterion (or criteria) can be couched in terms of scientific probabilities and details about the patient's illness or disease, the decision to limit access to the pool is based on a value judgment. Furthermore, although this sort of eligibility criterion seems reasonable enough, it is based on a different value judgment than simply giving everyone equal consideration. This justification for limiting which people are eligible for a scarce resource is based on an appeal to a moral principle of utility. The basic idea is that we should set eligibility limits in this way because it would be wasteful to give everyone an equal chance to receive the resources, given that many who would receive them will likely benefit very much less than others would. Once we appreciate why the eligibility criteria are set as they are, we must determine the fairest balance of equality and utility.

Moving away from a pure commitment to giving everyone equal consideration also complicates our process. In addition to simply holding a lottery that gives everyone an equal chance, and explaining to everyone why we are doing this, we now have to set our eligibility criterion or criteria, and explain them. Our policies, in other words, must reflect the complexity of our ethical beliefs and feelings.

We could also argue that the motivation to do this actually comes from unpacking our commitment to equality. In other words, we could argue that our original intuitions and settled beliefs about equality never justified giving anyone who could benefit in any way at all equal consideration for the scarce resources. For example, Rawls's argument appeals to the view that all those capable of forming and acting on individual life plans should be given an equal claim. Kant argues that all rational beings with (apparently) free will deserve equal consideration. But these groups of individuals are arguably not co-extensive with all living humans. Some comatose persons and people with little or no higher brain functioning who nonetheless exist on life support are examples of people who would not meet Rawls's or Kant's criteria.

Why isn't a commitment to giving all equal consideration the same as the commitment to equality that Kant, Rawls, and others argue for? The disparity here is the result of a point we noted earlier, in our discussion of the Killing Machine thought experiment from Chapter 9. There we noted that we do not simply value life itself, but life lived at some minimal level of quality. Giving all who might benefit in any way at all from scarce resources access to them violates this conviction. Therefore, egalitarians such as Rawls can appeal to their egalitarian ideals to explain why we should not, for example, give scarce resources to people who have very limited higher brain functioning with no prospects for recovery. The commitment to equality is a commitment to life lived at some minimum level of quality, not just life *per se.*

Thus, the commitment to giving equal consideration turns out to be both more restrictive and more complicated than it seemed at first glance. Indeed, it is no longer clear what it means to give someone equal consideration for a particular resource. Once we appreciate that we value both longer life and adding value to life, then even proponents of a lottery method must contend with allocation problems where these competing goals conflict. Here we can see a number

of challenges. What balance should we seek to strike between extending life and enhancing quality of life? What counts as living life at a minimally decent level of quality? Notice that these are questions that you can ask of yourself. In response to the first question, some people write living wills that specify conditions under which their life as judged by them would drop below an acceptable level of quality. Below this level, they choose not to receive any further treatment that is simply intended to extend their life. In determining this, they would have to answer this second question.[11]

13.7 Problems with Ranking Methods

Our look into the case for giving potential patients equal consideration for scarce health care resources reveals a number of complications in developing fair policies. We noted that although our ethical intuitions and principles can usefully help us along, they also conflict. Once we carefully consider what committing to a policy of equal consideration would entail, and once we back away from trying to rely exclusively on this, we see that the task of fairly allocating resources is both incomplete and quite challenging.

Unfortunately, the alternative of mixing policies that sometimes give equal consideration and sometimes rank patients according to some ranking method raises many questions. Since we have already surveyed many of the philosophical problems with developing these sorts of policies in Chapter 10, we will not re-examine them here. We will, however, summarize our account of the challenges that must be met on this front.

Whereas the lottery method is based generally on a commitment to equality, ranking methods rest generally on a commitment to a principle of utility. As with the case for the lottery method, defenders of ranking methods also argue that their approach is fairest. However, we have already noted that there are four kinds of problems that must be addressed to develop a fair ranking method; we need to explain how we can fairly

1. determine the prudential value of someone's life to him;

2. compare the prudential values of the lives of different people;

3. determine the value or disvalue of a person's effects on society; and

4. compare the values or disvalues of different people's effects on society.

It should be stressed that these represent only a sampling of the problems, but solving them would greatly advance our efforts at devising fair ranking methods.

13.8 Review

In this chapter we built upon some of our discussion from chapters 9 and 10. Those chapters addressed the question of how much consideration we should give to those who deserve it. More specifically, we focused on examining this question from the perspective of society, and we narrowed our treatment to the consideration we should give to humans.

Even more narrowly, in this chapter we addressed a variation on our original question by asking how we should fairly allocate scarce medical resources among patients. Thus, we applied some of our progress to a pressing practical question for our society.

Since the question of how to fairly allocate scarce resources is so complex and multi-faceted, and since our concern has been with distinguishing between what is owed to individuals, we concentrated here on the problem of just microallocation. Thus, we posed the question, What is the fairest way of best meeting the needs of patients vying for scarce health care resources?

We first developed our discussion of some issues of procedural justice, which followed up on the more abstract discussion of the same topic from Section 9.3. In this chapter we were especially concerned with examining competing views regarding the proper place of doctors in the allocation system. After considering some arguments on both sides of this debate we left this issue unresolved.

In the final part of the chapter, we took up the challenge of devising a fair policy. Since many policies rest on a commitment to some principle of equality, and since they recommend some variation of a First Come, First Served approach, we devoted most of our attention to re-examining the arguments for this. We observed that there does indeed seem to be a place for respect for equality in our settled moral feelings and beliefs. However, the project of fairly allocating scarce health care resources is complicated because we recognize other relevant moral principles and beliefs that we think should play some role in justifying our policies too.

Complications arise when our settled moral feelings and beliefs come into conflict as, for example, when we feel pulled by both a principle of equality and a principle of utility. To better accommodate the full range of principles we think should be respected, we turned to briefly examine the prospects of developing a more sophisticated policy that gives some role to allocating resources on the basis of a ranking method. We concluded by raising some challenges that still need to be met to complete this task.

Notes

1. We will refer to this as *organic* as opposed to *organ* scarcity, since the resources in short supply include not just organs, like kidneys, livers, pancreas, hearts, lungs, and the small bowel, but also human blood products and tissues including bone marrow, heart valves, corneas, bones, joints, and muscle tissue.

2. Although, in Chapter 14 we consider the ethics of pursuing one solution that involves increasing the supply of organs and tissue through stem cell research and research into cloning.

3. Health Canada's National Organ and Tissue Information Site, Facts and FAQs at **www.hcsc.gc.ca/ english/organandtissue/facts_faqs/index.html**

4. I owe this point to Robert Truog (see Truog [1992]).

5. For an explanation of what "giving someone equal consideration" means for us, see Section 9.1.

6. For the CMA statement, see the Canadian Medical Association Policy Statement entitled

Organ and tissue donation and transplantation (Update 2000). For the AMA statement, see the Council on Ethical and Judicial Affairs, American Medical Association, "Ethical Considerations in the Allocation of Organs and Other Scarce Medical Resources Among Patients," *Archives of Internal Medicine* 155 (1995), pp. 29–39.

7. The Society of Critical Care Medicine Ethics Committee, "Attitudes of Critical Care Medicine Professionals Concerning Distribution of Intensive Care Resources," *Critical Care Medicine*, 22 (1994), pp. 358–362.

8. See Truog (1992).

9. Questions about free will, responsibility, and desert have been much debated both in ethics and social and political philosophy. A relatively recent debate was sparked by John Rawls's argument for his view, justice as fairness, which was in turn challenged by Robert Nozick in his influential book *Anarchy, State, and Utopia.* See John Rawls, *A Theory of Justice* (Cambridge MA.: Harvard University Press, 1971), Chapter 2; and Robert Nozick, *Anarchy, State, and Utopia* (New York: Basic Books, 1974), Part II.

10. Although, even in this rather simple case there was the complication of deciding whether to give an equal chance to both the pregnant mother, Susan Moore, and her fetus, and the resultant challenge of determining what to do if the fetus was selected but Susan Moore was not.

11. Although determining even for oneself how to weigh the values of length of life and quality of life is difficult, it becomes much more complicated when we must make comparisons across different people's lives, and differing numbers of people's lives. This, however, takes into account problems with the just mesoallocation of scarce health care resources.

Exercises

Progress Check

1. Identify and distinguish between the three ways of classifying problems about the scope of justly allocating scarce health care resources.

2. Identify and distinguish between the two kinds of scarcity of health care resources.

3. Why do some people think that any fair system of distribution must be impartial in its treatment of patients?

4. Explain the distinction between giving patients equal concern and attention and giving them equal consideration.

5. When determining who should receive scarce resources, why must we defend moving from accepting that patients deserve equal concern and attention to the view that they deserve an equal share of the resources? What other alternative is there?

6. Explain the distinction between the weak and strong senses of giving someone an equal opportunity.

7. What factors do the Canadian Medical Association and the American Medical Association recommend doctors consider when making allocation decisions?

8. Briefly outline the arguments for giving patients equal consideration when allocating scarce health care resources.

9. Why can't the argument from avoiding arbitrariness ground an all-encompassing policy of giving patients equal consideration?

10. What problems are there with basing an allocation policy exclusively on giving all equal consideration?

11. What does it mean when we claim that some eligibility criteria for allocating scarce health care resources are really based on value judgments?

12. Why do Rawls's and Kant's arguments for equality not justify giving all beings equal consideration?

Questions for Further Reflection

1. Explain and critically evaluate the view that only Canadians should be eligible to receive health care resources through Canadian public institutions like hospitals and clinics.

2. Should non-Canadians ever be given free treatment in Canada for humanitarian reasons? If so, outline and defend both the circumstances and underlying principle(s) that support(s) your view. If not, explain why not.

3. Explain and critically discuss the debate over the appropriate role of doctors in the just microallocation of scarce health care resources.

4. What suggestions do you have for developing a system of determining who makes allocation decisions that best balances fairness and efficiency?

Group Work Activity:

Developing an Allocation Policy

You and the other members of your group are medical ethics consultants for a large hospital. Until now, the hospital has always had a First Come, First Served policy with regard to patients wanting access to medical resources. However, in light of recent cutbacks, there has been some pressure to formulate a new policy.

Some people have been complaining that some resources that traditionally have been scarce (for example, organs for transplant), and some that are becoming scarce due to the cutbacks, are not being distributed fairly. In the face of this criticism, a committee has been organized to determine whether to recommend that a new policy be formulated and, if so, to provide one to the hospital's senior administrators for their consideration.

Other members of the committee are looking to your group of medical ethics consultants for guidance. Specifically they are wondering what role, if any, the following factors should play in a new policy:

1. the potential patient's age;

2. the potential patient's degree of intellectual functioning;

3. the potential patient's contributions to society (viewed prospectively and/or retrospectively);

4. the potential patient's ability to pay for the resource (or resources); and

5. the extent to which the patient is likely to benefit from the resource (or resources) in the long term.

The committee is especially interested in knowing whether you think any of these factors should be included in the new policy.

If you think these factors should not be included, explain why not. For example, if you think a potential patient's age is not a morally relevant consideration for a policy for distributing scarce medical resources, explain why. If you think one of the factors is relevant, explain why, and specify as best you can how potential patients should be ranked according to the factor. Alternatively, if you believe that a First Come, First Served policy is still the best one, argue your case.

---

5. Critically assess the factors that the Canadian Medical Association and the American Medical Association recommend doctors consider when making allocation decisions.

6. Explain and defend your solution to the problem of fairly allocating ECMO treatment.

7. Briefly outline and defend your view of the role that a principle of desert should play in determining fair microallocation policies.

8. Eligibility criteria that limit the possible pool of potential beneficiaries of a health care resource can be based either on value judgments or not. Give an example of each sort of criterion and explain and defend your examples.

Suggested Further Reading

Council on Ethical and Judicial Affairs, American Medical Association, "Ethical Considerations in the Allocation of Organs and Other Scarce Medical Resources Among Patients," *Archives of Internal Medicine* 155 (1995), pp. 29–39.

Canadian Medical Association, *Organ and tissue donation and transplantation (Update 2000)*, Canadian Medical Association Policy Statement.

Robert Nozick, *Anarchy, State, and Utopia* (New York: Basic Books, 1974), Part II.

John Rawls, *A Theory of Justice* (Cambridge Mass.: Harvard University Press, 1971), Chapter 2.

Robert Truog, "Triage in the ICU," *Hastings Center Report* 22 (1992), pp. 13–17.

The Society of Critical Care Medicine Ethics Committee, "Attitudes of Critical Care Medicine Professionals Concerning Distribution of Intensive Care Resources," *Critical Care Medicine* 22 (1994), pp. 358–362.

For more on Rawls's view, you might also consult John Rawls, *Political Liberalism* (Rawls [1993]) and his paper, "Kantian Constructivism in Moral Theory," (Rawls [1980]).

Weblinks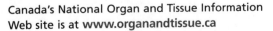

Canada's National Organ and Tissue Information Web site is at **www.organandtissue.ca**

14 Issues in Bioethics II: Genetics

Overview

Learning Outcomes

In this chapter we survey some pressing concerns in the emerging area of the ethics of genetic research. Specifically, we work toward developing just law and policy in this area by examining moral questions arising from research into somatic cell and germ-line genetic alteration, stem cells, ectogenesis, and cloning. Before addressing these moral questions, we first consider some of the related background science. Still, our investigation demonstrates how our starting moral assumptions help determine our responses to ethical questions, and how different ethical outlooks lead us to different, and sometimes conflicting, moral conclusions.

Upon the successful completion of this chapter, you will be able to

1. outline the basic ideas and issues in genetics to make reasonably informed judgments about the ethical questions concerning somatic cell and germ-line genetic alteration;

2. explain the basic background science of stem cells and cloning to make reasonably informed judgments about the ethical questions concerning the ethics of stem cell research and research into cloning;

3. distinguish between the main policy positions in Canada and some other countries on these topics; and

4. assess the ethical questions concerning stem cell research, ectogenesis, and research into cloning from two different moral perspectives, and compare the responses generated by these outlooks on these issues.

14.1 Introduction

In this chapter we examine some ethical issues in genetics. While researchers have made impressive advances both in our understanding of this field of study and in related technology, many countries, including Canada, have been working to fill in the legal and policy vacuum left by the rapid advances in science. As we search for just laws and policies, we need to sort out the many ethical issues and concerns raised by the new possibilities that research into genetics presents us with. Although the number and complexity of the issues prevents us from comprehensively examining each one, we can at least make some useful ethical progress in investigating two of the more promising and controversial fields within genetic research: stem cell research and cloning.

Stem cells are cells that renew tissue. They can divide much more than all the other cells in our bodies and they can differentiate into various kinds of cells. By harnessing the potential of stem cells to become literally any other kind of cell, and by growing these cells in cultures, scientists hope to be able to use stem cells to treat an impressive variety of illnesses, diseases, and disabilities.

Although the great promise of stem cell research is appealing, optimism is tempered by numerous ethical worries. For example, one particularly promising branch of research involves using embryonic stem cells. Extracting the stem cells needed for research and potential therapeutic purposes kills the embryo, so one obvious question is whether this is ever morally justified. There are also other concerns about the possible sources of the stem cells that we could use. For example, one especially controversial practice involves creating embryos specifically for the purpose of deriving their stem cells. Should we create life to kill it and use it for our own ends? As with the concerns with the ethics of stem cell research, there are also concerns about the practice of cloning.

We will begin our examination of these issues in Bioethics by outlining some of the background science and filling out our account of some of various controversial practices. After we take a closer look at the two issues, we will survey some of the policies and laws that govern this research in Canada and elsewhere. We will then consider the main ethical issues more carefully.

14.2 Basic Genetics

Why do some people have brown eyes and some blue? More generally, why do individual plants and animals possess particular characteristics? These are questions in *genetics,* the study of heredity. Specifically, genetics is the study of the inheritance patterns of particular traits in animals and plants. Since at least 1953, molecular biology has been a field of science within genetics. In that year, James Watson and Francis Crick described the "double helix" structure of deoxyribonucleic acid, or DNA.[1] To appreciate the importance of DNA in the story of genetics, consider that we are all composed of cells. DNA is the chemically encoded information in every cell that is responsible for directing that cell to its end or function. A *genome* is the complete set of all DNA for a particular organism, and except for mature red blood cells, every cell in our bodies contains the complete genome.

Although we each have the complete genome of members of our species, we are different because of variations in our DNA sequences. Our DNA consists of two intertwined strands of repeating subunits called *nucleotides* (see Figure 14.1). Nucleotides consist of one sugar unit, one phosphate unit, and a nitrogenous base. There are four different nitrogenous bases in DNA: A, T, C, and G.[2] The two strands of DNA wrap together such that each base bonds with a base on the other strand. The identity and order of these base pairs along our particular DNA determines our individual DNA sequences. In short, this is what makes us unique. The nucleotides occur along macromolecules of DNA sequences known as chromosomes. Humans have 24 chromosomes: 22 autosomes plus an X or Y sex chromosome. All somatic cells (cells that are not sex cells) contain 46 chromosomes; two sets of 23 chromosomes given by each parent. A normal female has two X chromosomes and a male has an X and a Y. The cells that contain only 23 chromosomes are *haploid.* They are germ cells or sex cells. In the male the germ cell is a sperm; in the female it is an

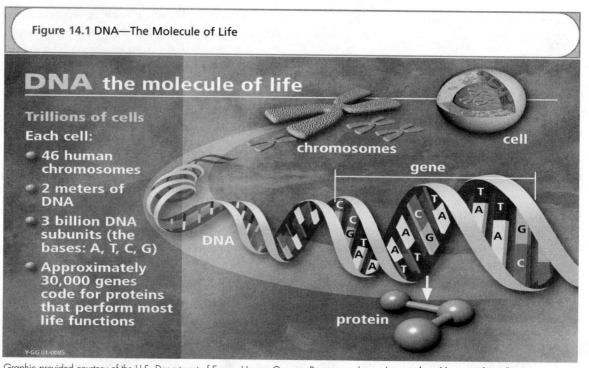

Figure 14.1 DNA—The Molecule of Life

DNA the molecule of life

Trillions of cells
Each cell:
- **46 human chromosomes**
- **2 meters of DNA**
- **3 billion DNA subunits (the bases: A, T, C, G)**
- **Approximately 30,000 genes code for proteins that perform most life functions**

Y-GG 01-0085

chromosomes

cell

gene

DNA

protein

Graphic provided courtesy of the U.S. Department of Energy Human Genome Program and its website at: http://www.ornl.gov/hgmis

ovum or egg. Chromosomes vary in size between roughly 50 million and 250 million base pairs.

Although the human genome contains approximately 3 billion base pairs, only a small percentage (less than 3 percent) make up the basic units of heredity, namely, our *genes*. Genes consist of varying numbers of base pairs of nucleotides, and they determine or control all of our inherited characteristics. The Human Genome Project is the massive undertaking of identifying and mapping our complete DNA, including the approximately 30 000 to 40 000 genes in our bodies.[3]

14.3 Some Ethical Issues in Genetic Research: Genetic Alterations

As a result of recent advances in genetics, the possibilities of direct genetic alteration of DNA are growing. Some researchers envision the development and use of genetic alteration techniques on diseases that are caused by a defect in a single gene. There are approximately 4000 such diseases, which cause thousands of deaths and terrible suffering.[4] Among these are Huntington's disease, Tay-Sachs

disease (a degenerative neurological disorder that kills infants), and sickle-cell anemia. Some hope that through the future development of genetic alteration methods, these diseases will be eradicated. We can categorize these possible research initiatives by whether they are somatic cell or germ-line genetic alterations.

Somatic Cell Alteration

Often referred to as somatic gene therapy, somatic cell gene alterations involve changing the subject's genome through the delivery of a missing gene that is needed for normal protein functioning. There is also hope that in the future we might be able to remove a defective gene and replace it with a normal functioning one. Since somatic cell alterations are alterations to a person's non-sex cells, any change that occurs will be limited to that particular patient. However, somatic cell therapies are prohibitively expensive and fraught with danger. The method of delivering the missing cell now envisioned involves sending it via a gene-carrier called a *vector*. The most common vector now being considered is a genetically modified virus. But there are many concerns with this delivery system because viruses can cause immune and inflammatory response problems. A modified vector might, for example, activate cancer-causing genes or be toxic.

Germ-line Genetic Alteration

A *germ line* refers to the cells that pass genetic information from one generation to the next. Germ cells are sex cells, so germ-line genetic alteration refers to the technique of altering the genetic structure of germ cells to effect changes in subsequent generations. The basic idea is that if we can correct genetic defects in people's germ cells, then those defects, and the diseases and disabilities they cause, will not be passed along to the next generation.

As with somatic cell alteration, researchers envision both delivering missing genes to the germ cells and removing defective ones to replace them with normal functioning genes. Since such procedures involve effecting changes in future generations, they are not, properly speaking, forms of therapy.

Concerns

Apart from the great expense and inherent dangers of performing these procedures, genetic alterations of germ lines also carry the risk of harming future generations of people. Many critics of this kind of research argue that it is unnecessary, impracticable, and immoral. Some worries about immorality stem from concerns about "playing God" with our DNA and our gene pool.

Critics also argue that the potential for genetic alterations is not that great since most diseases arise as a result of a complex set of factors, including interaction among many genes and a person's environment. They also worry that there is no clear way to distinguish gene alteration from so-called "gene enhancement." The same techniques that might allow us to alter our genes to wipe out diseases could also allow us to effect other kinds of changes in future generations. For example, pursuit of this research might lead to the creation of so-called "designer" or "super-babies." There are also fears that changes could be made to future generations on the basis of controversial or plainly immoral value judgments.[5]

In response, defenders of genetic alteration research note that the work is at a very early stage.

Germ-line research, at least as regards humans and other large animals, is at only the discussion stage. The question thus is not necessarily whether the research is practicable now, nor whether the procedures are cost efficient now. The question is whether this research holds sufficient promise to warrant our continued pursuit of it. By all means, these defenders argue, if the research turns out to be disappointing and more bad than good, then it should be abandoned. However, at this early stage in its development, we cannot yet answer these questions. Thus, the prudent course of action is to carry on, place strict ethical limits on the limited research now underway, and then see what we discover.

In contrast to work in somatic cell and germ-line genetic alteration, stem cell research and research into cloning is at a more advanced stage and it is arguably more promising.

14.4 The Science of Stem Cells

Just as there is great potential in stem cell research, there are many ethical issues to be addressed. To fully appreciate both the potential benefits of stem cell research and these ethical issues, one first needs some understanding of the background science.[6]

Stem Cells

Stem cells, as we noted earlier, are cells that renew tissue. They consist of three types: totipotent, pluripotent, and multipotent. "Totipotent" means "total potential," thus **totipotent stem cells** have the total potential of developing into an individual human.

A fertilized egg (or *zygote*), consisting of an egg and a sperm, is the totipotent stem cell. It has the total potential to develop into a human. Upon conception, the zygote, which initially consists of this single totipotent stem cell, begins to divide. At the two-cell stage, the zygote becomes an embryo (until approximately six weeks gestation at which time it becomes a fetus). The resulting product of two totipotent stem cells has the total potential to develop into an individual human, and genetically identical twins develop when these two totipotent stem cells grow separately. After about four days of continued division, the totipotent stem cells form into a *blastocyst*—a mostly hollow sphere with an outer lining of cells and a cluster of inner cells called the *inner cell mass*. The outer layer of cells will develop into the placenta and other tissue needed for the fetus to grow and survive inside the womb. The inner cell mass consists of the next type of stem cells, pluripotent stem cells.

Pluripotent stem cells have the potential to develop into most kinds of tissue in the human body. However, since they cannot develop into the tissue that allows a fetus to develop in the womb, they are not totipotent. They are also distinguished by their unusual longevity. Whereas most cells can divide about 50 times before dying, pluripotent stem cells can divide many more times. The inner cell mass of pluripotent stem cells develops and continues to divide for about the next 10 days. About 14 days after conception, the pluripotent stem cells begin to specialize. They become multipotent stem cells.

> **Totipotent stem cells** have the total potential of developing into an individual.
> **Pluripotent stem cells** are stem cells with the potential to develop into most kinds of tissue. However, since they are not totipotent, they cannot develop into a complete individual.
> **Multipotent stem cells** have the potential to develop into many kinds of tissue, but their future possible development is more restricted than pluripotent stem cells.

Multipotent stem cells have the potential to develop into many kinds of tissue, but their future development is more restricted than pluripotent stem cells. As the growing embryo begins to take on more of the distinctive features of a recognizable human, the pluripotent stem cells develop into more specialized cells within the body. For example, after about 14 days, some pluripotent stems cells transform into the beginnings of a nervous system. Multipotent stem cells exist in the developing embryo and in us through all stages of life.

Potential Benefits of Stem Cell Research

Editors of the journal *Science* claimed that stem cell research was the most significant breakthrough in science in 1999. With its potential for curing currently incurable diseases and for treating an amazing variety of life-threatening, disabling, and chronic diseases, illnesses, and physical infirmities, stem cell research offers hope to literally millions of people. Some argue that it represents the most significant advance in medicine since the advent of transplantations. Optimism, even in the short term, is high. Stem cell research and therapies hold out the potential for providing us with a renewable supply of replacement cells and tissues of every type in the human body, including organs. These replacement cells and tissues could help us treat "a myriad of diseases, conditions, and disabilities including Parkinson's and Alzheimer's diseases, spinal cord injury, stroke, burns, heart disease, diabetes, osteoarthritis and rheumatoid arthritis."[7] For example, it was recently reported that German doctors had taken multipotent stem cells from the bone marrow of the pelvis of a 46-year-old man and injected them into arteries near his failing heart. The cells migrated to his heart and became healthy heart muscle cells that improved his heart's functioning. Professor Bodo Eckehard Strauer, who performed the procedure, commented that

> Stem cell therapy could be more successful than all other previous treatments put together. Even patients with the most seriously damaged hearts can be treated with their own stem cells instead of waiting and hoping on a transplant.[8]

Apart from these amazing therapeutic benefits, stem cell research holds out the tantalizing promise of advancing our understanding of basic bodily growth and functioning. For instance, through learning more about how stem cells work, we could solve the mysteries of our development in the early stages of life. We could also learn more about the cellular decision-making process that causes cells to specialize as they do. By learning more about how healthy cells function, we can perhaps gain insight into what causes cell-development breakdowns that lead to cancer and other disabilities and diseases. Finally, stem cell research holds out the promise of improving our drug-testing processes. By testing new drugs on the full array of cell types that can be stimulated to grow from pluripotent stem cells, we can make our drug-testing research methods more effective and efficient.

Stem Cell Sources

There are a number of sources and possible sources of human stem cells. Unfortunately, one of the most promising is also the most ethically troublesome. The pluripotent stem cells found in embryos can be extracted only by killing those embryos. Science presents us with some different options for acquiring these embryonic stem cells. Typically in the course of infertility treatments at *in vitro* fertilization clinics, many more embryos are created than are used. So researchers have obtained informed consent to use these embryonic stem cells in their research. Scientists can also create their own embryos by artificially fertilizing donor eggs with sperm cells. Finally, there is the process known as somatic cell nuclear transfer (SCNT).

Cloning

A clone is an exact copy of biological material. Scientists are interested in cloning different bits of organic matter, and cloning can involve the duplication of DNA sequences, like genes, entire cells, or entire organisms. There are different cloning processes, the most famous of which is *somatic cell nuclear transfer* or *SCNT*, which involves fusing a somatic cell from whomever it is you want to be the donor with an immature egg cell, or *oocyte*, less its nucleus. The nucleus of an egg cell contains the chromosomes, so the somatic cell, once it is fused with the altered egg cell, provides the new cell with its chromosomes. The altered egg cell contains ingredients essential for embryo development. The fused cell has the full potential to develop into an entire animal. It is, in other words, a totipotent stem cell, just as in normal embryo development, and the totipotent stem cell will divide and form into a blastocyst. In turn, the inner cell mass of the blastocyst will itself contain the pluripotent stem cells with the DNA of the somatic cell donor.

The cloning of Dolly the sheep by Scottish scientists working at the Roslin Institute in 1997 provided the famous proof of this.[9] Dolly also provided support for the idea that somatic cell nuclear transfer could be used to clone an entire human being, and this research, cited by *Science* as the greatest breakthrough in science in 1997, sparked a huge public debate about the ethics of cloning. There are questions about whether the process will work for humans, or more precisely, whether it can work without causing serious health problems for the cloned being.

Apart from SCNT, cloning is also achieved through a process called *blastomere separation*, or embryo splitting. In this process, the zygote is split, thereby creating two or more totipotent stem cells, which are in turn grown separately. Essentially the two totipotent stem cells are clones, or identical twins. But unlike SCNT, where the cloned being has the DNA of a single parent, the twins have DNA from two parents.

Adult Stem Cells versus Stem Cells Acquired through Cloning and Killing Embryos

The presence of multipotent stem cells in all of us provides us with a promising source of stem cells for research and therapeutic purposes. For instance, if multipotent stem cells can be taken from someone in need of a transplant, grown outside the body, and then transplanted back in, the chances of rejection would be minimal. Ethically the main advantage of using adult stem cells is that they do not have to be taken from human embryos. However, research on adult multipotent stem cells is still in its early stages. Some recent research, including some done on humans and noted above, suggests that the prospects may be quite good, perhaps even as good as research involving the use of cloned and noncloned embryonic stem cells. But there also appear to be some limitations on research involving adult multipotent stem cells. Multipotent stem cells have not been located in all areas of our bodies and for all tissue types. For example, pancreatic islet stem cells, which might be useful for treating diabetes, have not been detected. Also, despite the recent promising results, researchers are still investigating whether adult multipotent stem cells can change back into pluripotent stem cells.

Another limitation to using our own multipotent stem cells is that they must first be extracted, grown outside the body, and then transplanted back in. Apart from the time involved in growing a culture of cells big enough to be useful, there is also the difficulty of this process. People needing stem cell treatments for brain disorders would either have to have a portion of their brain first removed to acquire the brain stem cells, or other stem cells from elsewhere in the body would need to be coaxed into developing into brain cells. Moreover, for those requiring stem cell therapy for genetic disorders, their own stem cells would suffer from the original defect and thus be an unsuitable source for the treatment. Finally, there are also the technical difficulties of locating, isolating, and purifying adult multipotent stem cells for use.

If there were no ethical concerns, the ideal course to pursue from a purely scientific perspective would be to continue research into all the kinds and sources of stem cells and to use those types and sources that are most promising. Although not enough data has been collected to make an informed judgment about this, it appears at present that this process would sometimes involve using adult multipotent stem cells (and of course children's multipotent stem cells in therapies involving children), and sometimes using cloned and non-cloned embryonic stem cells.

But of course there are ethical concerns. Some researchers who are troubled by these concerns are content to pursue morally unobjectionable lines of stem cell research. Other scientists argue that, despite our present ethical concerns, we need to keep our options open and continue all research so that we will be better informed to make the right decisions in the future. Some argue that the potential benefits are already great enough to justify our proceeding despite our moral reservations. There are also various views between these positions.

Exercises 14.1

Progress Check

1. What is genetics?
2. Briefly outline the basic relationships between the following genetic materials: DNA, chromosomes, genomes, genes, base pairs, nucleotides, somatic cells, and sex cells.
3. Distinguish between somatic cell alteration and germ-line genetic alteration.
4. What are the main practical and ethical concerns regarding germ-line genetic alteration?
5. What are stem cells? Briefly outline the process of stem cell change and development that begins at conception.

6. What are the potential benefits of stem cell research?
7. What is somatic cell nuclear transfer (SCNT)?
8. Why is SCNT a method of cloning?
9. How else can cloning be achieved?
10. Briefly explain the ethical debate over the question of whether we should pursue adult stem cell research rather than research into embryonic stem cells.

Questions for Further Reflection

1. Should we limit research into altering our DNA? Why or why not? Defend your view.
2. If we should place restrictions on researchers altering our DNA, then either we should completely prohibit such changes or we should prohibit only some changes. Explain the strongest argument for completely prohibiting human DNA alteration.
3. Explain and assess the strongest argument for prohibiting only some kinds of changes.
4. Explain the concern of some people, that there is no clear way to distinguish positive gene alteration from worrisome gene alteration.
5. What are the concerns surrounding gene enhancement and the creation of so-called "designer" or "super" babies?

14.5 Stem Cell Law and Policy in Canada

Which policies and laws should we adopt regarding stem cell research and somatic cell nuclear transfer? As of this writing, Canada has no laws that specifically govern these practices. However, there are a number of policy documents and a draft law that speak to some related issues.

1. The Royal Commission on New Reproductive Technologies Report

The Royal Commission on New Reproductive Technologies was formed in 1989 to examine various aspects of research involving reproductive and genetic technologies. The commission issued its report, *Proceed with Care*, in 1993, which recommended that the Canadian government ban all research involving alteration of the DNA of human zygotes.

2. The Tri-Council Policy Statement

The Natural Sciences and Engineering Research Council of Canada (NSERC), the Medical Research Council (MRC), and the Social Sciences and Humanities Research Council of Canada (SSHRCC) jointly published the *Tri-Council Policy Statement: Ethical Conduct for Research Involving Humans* in 1998.[10] Although the councils recommended that we permit some research involving human embryos, they argued against the creation of human embryos for research purposes, any research that involves developing an embryo outside the womb (*ectogenesis*), cloning persons through the use of somatic cell nuclear transfer, and human germ-line genetic alteration.

3. The Voluntary Moratorium

Perhaps as a prelude to introducing it own law, in July 1995, Canada's federal government appealed for a voluntary ban on research into ectogenesis, germ-line genetic alteration, and the cloning of human embryos.

4. Bill C-47

The Canadian government introduced The *Human Reproductive and Genetic Technologies Act*, or *Bill C-47*, into Parliament in 1996. However, due to the federal election in 1997, this law was never passed. It has not been reintroduced during the present government's mandate. In addition to the practices outlined in the 1995 moratorium, the proposed bill also prohibited the creation of human embryos for research purposes only and all research on human embryos later than 14 days gestation.

5. Reproductive Technology Draft Legislation

In May 2001, Health Minister Allan Rock sent a draft bill to a Commons' committee to discuss and report on by the end of January 2002. The bill would prohibit cloning humans, germ-line genetic alteration, choosing a baby's sex, buying or selling human embryos, and creating embryos for research purposes only.[11]

6. House of Commons Standing Committee Report on the Draft Legislation

In December 2001, the Commons' committee recommended tightening the restrictions on new reproductive technology contained in the draft legislation. However, the committee recommended that researchers be permitted to use embryos remaining from fertility treatments in their research.[12]

There is some agreement among the authors of these documents. They all prohibit or recommend the prohibition of human germ-line genetic alteration. The Tri-Council statement and *Bill C-47* would ban ectogenesis, the creation of human embryos for research purposes exclusively, and cloning persons, including embryos, through somatic cell nuclear transfer. A striking fact about these statements is that they make no mention of stem cell research, mostly because that it was not until 1998, after most of these documents had been published or released, that Dr. James Thomson at the University of Wisconsin first extracted and cultured pluripotent stem cells from a human embryo.[13] In other words, all of the major policy documents regarding cloning and stem cell research were drafted prior to the single most important advance in the research. This means those who drafted the major policy documents were likely unaware of the true potential of stem cell research as outlined in Section 14.4 above. In light of the advances in the research, should we alter our stance toward the prohibited practices? What are the main ethical issues and how do these bear on crafting fair laws and policies?

14.6 Stem Cell Law and Policy in Other Countries

We might look for some guidance in writing our laws by examining what other countries have done since the advances in the research. Unfortunately, there are substantial differences in policies and laws among other research nations. The regulatory situations in the United States and the United Kingdom illustrate this.

Stem Cell Policy in the United States

In 1995, the U.S. Congress imposed a ban on federal funding of all research involving the destruction of human embryos. Displaying his sympathy for this position as recently as May 2001, President Bush asserted, "I oppose funding for stem-cell research that involves destroying living human embryos."[14] However, the U.S. National Institutes of Health issued a report in August 2000 recommending that federal funding be made available for research involving currently existing embryonic stem cell lines. In other words, they recommended that research involving stem cell lines that had already been derived and cultured should be funded subject to both careful ethical review and acquiring the informed consent of the parents of the embryos. Funding should be withheld from stem cells derived from embryos created specifically for research purposes. Despite his earlier remarks, this was essentially the position that President Bush endorsed in his announcement in August 2001. Seeking a middle ground, the president limited federal funding to stem cell lines that had been derived as of August 9, 2001.[15]

Stem Cell Policy in the United Kingdom

In contrast to the relatively restrictive position taken in the United States, Britain has a much more liberal law concerning stem cell research and cloning. After originally passing the *Human Fertilization and Embryology Act*, the British government struck a committee in June 1999 to report on whether the original act should be amended in light of the advances in stem cell research. In April 2000, the committee released its recommendation that researchers be permitted to create embryos specifically for use in stem cell research. The committee also permitted cloning through somatic cell nuclear transfer subject to various ethical restrictions. On January 31, 2001, the amended act took effect.[16]

Apart from these positions, a number of others have been taken elsewhere. Germany forbids the derivation of any embryonic stem cells for research. Other countries, like the Netherlands and France, have either limited or are considering limiting embryonic stem cell research to embryos not needed in the course of fertility treatments. Cloning of embryos through somatic cell nuclear transfer is illegal in Japan and Australia. However, the Australian Health Ethics Committee recommended public debate about whether there is a significant ethical difference between cloning some bits of organic material, like tissues and cells, and cloning entire individuals.[17]

14.7 Ethical Issues

For many issues in law, especially criminal law, there is relatively little variation from country to country. There is a general prohibition on acts of murder, assault, arson, theft, and other property crimes, to cite a few examples. Yet, when it comes to the issues of germ-line genetic alteration, stem cell research, and cloning, there are, as we just noted, many differences in the policies and laws of the countries pursuing this sort of research. Why is this? We might contend that these differences are due to the emerging nature of the research. Whereas the acts we agree should be prohibited are not new, much of the research into genetics, like the recent research into stem cells, is very new. So we might argue that this explains the differences. We could argue that as our societies and our legislators and policy-makers become more informed about the recent advances in science, and as the picture in science becomes clearer, we will begin to see a trend toward more uniformity in the laws of different countries on these issues.

Although this probably does account for some of the differences, arguably another contributing factor is the effect that adopting different moral outlooks with different ethical assumptions has on shaping law and public policy. By comparing and contrasting a range of positions in genetics that are supported by two influential ethical outlooks, we can begin to see how one could be led to adopt quite different policies and laws in these fields. Moreover, we can see how these differences are due in large part to fundamentally different judgments of the value of human life.

We will investigate the ethical debate over the genetic issues we have been considering from two perspectives: the perspective of a Welfarist and the perspective of a Deontologist who espouses respect for human life as a fundamental value. These different starting points lead us to different conclusions about what range of policies and laws are ethically acceptable as regards stem cell research and research into cloning. In pursuing this approach, our aim will not be to show that one outlook is best and that some corresponding set of policies and laws are right. Rather, our aim will be to display some of the arguments that can be advanced from these different perspectives and to engage hypothetical proponents of the two views in some debate. From this vantage point, we will perhaps be able to make up our own minds about which assumptions to begin with and which laws and policies are the ones that we should adopt.

You might assume that the task of forming just laws and policies with respect to issues in genetics merely involves examining and drawing out the implications of some shared ethical outlook in view of the facts about the research. On the analysis that we will pursue here, however, this view is too simple. In our pursuit of just genetic research laws and policies we will need to address questions at two different levels. We must settle both the question of the best or right set of presuppositions and the moral framework to adopt, and the question of the laws and policies that should be created from that framework.

14.8 Two Ethical Outlooks

We identify the distinguishing characteristics of a moral theory according to its position with respect to our basic moral categories. Two of these categories are the right and the good. We talk about principles of right and wrong conduct and about actions or states of affairs that are morally good or bad. As we noted in Part One, one way in which ethical theories differ is in terms of their stance regarding these categories.[18] If a moral theory affirms the priority of the good over the right, then it holds that its theory of the good is ethically basic. In other words, the theory of the good presupposes no prior account of what is right or wrong. There are no inherently or intrinsically right acts on such outlooks

because what is right or wrong is determined by the theory's view about moral goodness. Moreover, what is good can change depending on the circumstances. So, for instance, according to such views, lying is not inherently right or wrong. Whether a particular act of lying is right or wrong is determined by whether it sufficiently promotes the good or not. On these views, then, the right is that which promotes the good somehow. Welfarist theories affirm the priority of the good over the right because they regard the promotion of welfare as ethically basic. What is right is what promotes welfare. As we saw in Part One, Welfarism is the foundational view in ethics according to which the purpose of morality is to promote the good of those beings that have a good of their own.[19] According to the Welfarist, only welfare matters for ethics. What is right is what promotes welfare. Not surprisingly, different Welfarists disagree about how we should promote welfare, but they all agree that what is right is determined by what promotes welfare. According to the Welfarist, then, there are no inherently or intrinsically immoral acts.

In contrast, deontological theories assert the priority of the right over the good. According to these theories, what is ethically right is not determined simply by what promotes the good. Rather, the good is defined in reference to the ethically prior category of the right. As we noted in Part One, deontological perspectives in ethics share the conviction that the morality or immorality of all acts is not determined by their consequences. The end does not justify the means because some actions are inherently immoral; that is, they are immoral by their nature.[20] So, for example, many who take this perspective will maintain that regardless of our aims or intentions, we should, morally speaking, never torture another human being.

Another popular deontological belief is that we should have a fundamental respect for life, especially for human life. What we might call Respect for Human Life or simply the Respect for Life Outlook is a deontological moral perspective that holds that we should have respect for the inherent value of human life. Acts that fail to show such respect are simply wrong. Some versions of this view are distinguished by religious metaphysical assumptions like the belief that we should have respect for human life because we are ensouled and created by God. However, as we have noted, in a diverse society such as ours, it would not be fair to make these assumptions in an inclusive public debate. Although the Respect for Life Outlook sometimes includes such assumptions, it need not. Reasons arising from religious convictions are not the only ones we can cite for showing respect for human life. Many people, regardless of their faith, believe that it is inherently wrong to kill a person. Included in this group are various academics and philosophers. For example, Margaret Somerville, the influential bioethics expert and professor of law and medicine at McGill University, has recently articulated and defended a secular version of this view.[21] Somerville asserts, "That which fails to show respect for life, in particular human life, or puts at serious risk or harms the human spirit is wrong."[22]

Given their differing perspectives on the rightness of acts involving a threat to or loss of human life, Welfarists and proponents of the Respect for Life Outlook may disagree about the ethics of various practices in genetic research and therapy. For example, Welfarists have no basic objection to the practice of creating human embryos for the purposes of stem cell research only. Although they might ultimately object to this practice, they also might not—it depends on the effects this practice is likely to have on the welfare of those involved. In contrast, respect for life defenders believe that this practice is inherently wrong because in deriving the stem cells from embryos, researchers must kill the embryos.

14.9 A Debate on the Issues

Although the Welfarist and proponent of the respect for life view represent only two possible moral outlooks, their differences are instructive. Since so many issues in the genetics debates turn on the proper ethical attitude we should take toward human life, it will be useful to contrast these views and consider specific issues and questions from their perspectives. To facilitate

this discussion, imagine the following debate or dialogue taking place between a proponent of the Respect for Life Outlook (RL) and a Welfarist (W). The dialogue is advanced through the questions and comments of a neutral moderator, and the discussion assumes familiarity with the basic scientific terms in the debate. If necessary, you can refer to the Glossary at the end of the book for clarification of these terms.

Moderator: Let's begin with an issue about which you might agree. Since 1995, the federal government has called for a voluntary ban on ectogenesis, that is, research involving growing a human embryo outside the womb. There seems to be widespread support for this ban. Perhaps you could comment on whether you agree with it and why.

RL: I agree with the ban and I believe it should be part of any new legislation in the field of genetic research. In reflecting upon this issue, we should distinguish between possible applications of ectogenesis in the area of genetics research and the area of research into infertility and reproduction. Although there is some overlap, there are important differences, too. Some people argue that the creation of an artificial uterus would alter the dynamics of the debate over the morality of abortion because it would effectively set viability, the time at which a fetus could survive outside her mother's womb, back to the moment of conception. Debating whether this would be a good thing or not, however, takes us away from our focus since the use of an artificial uterus falls into the area of research into reproduction and infertility, not research into genetics. Regardless of what we think about the ethics of ectogenesis in the areas of reproduction and infertility research, the government could prohibit its application in the area of genetic research.

Why should the government do this? Consider this: Why might someone want to create an artificial uterus to use in genetic research and therapy? If the intention was to grow the embryo into a fetus and then deliver the fetus at maturity, then our example would fall into the area of the ethics of research into reproduction, and we just set that aside. There are two remaining possibilities for the application to fall into the area of genetic research and therapy. The aim might be to grow the embryo for some time, possibly into a fetus, and then at some point and for some reason to kill it. Alternatively, the aim might be to use the artificial uterus to grow an animal-human hybrid fetus to maturity.[23] However, both of these possible uses of ectogenesis are inconsistent with what should be the guiding principle of our research endeavours, namely, to always show respect for human life.

W: I agree that in considering whether ectogenesis should be legalized, we need to distinguish between its possible uses in genetic research and research into infertility and reproduction. However, the two areas are practically connected in one important way. One argument against supporting ectogenesis is its cost. Do the possible benefits of developing an artificial uterus justify the expense? Right now it is hard to see how they would. However, if the funding for the research came primarily from research into reproduction, assuming that was ethical and legal, then the method of creating an artificial uterus would be available for use in genetics research, too. Then the question would be whether its use there would be ethically acceptable or not.

On this question, my view is different than my friend's. I see no fundamental moral problem with using artificial wombs in genetic research, since I reject the assertion that we have a basic obligation to respect human life. Whether particular uses of artificial wombs in genetic research is ethical depends entirely on whether the overall likely benefits to sentient and potentially sentient creatures would outweigh the likely overall costs to them. This means it may sometimes be moral to kill humans. Again, it depends on the benefits.

RL: And you think it would also be acceptable to create animal-human hybrids? Don't you find this idea objectionable?

W: It would be odd, I agree. But whether it would be morally objectionable or not turns on whether the overall benefits to all concerned would outweigh the costs and harms. I have no fundamental objection to the possibility, but I'm skeptical about the value of such research. Why should we pursue it? The only benefits I can foresee, apart from gains to our knowledge, are benefits for us. Typically, at least, this kind of research is discussed in the context of benefiting humans. For example, support for research into xenotransplantation is standardly based on the assumption that it would be acceptable if it could sufficiently benefit us. Since the hybrid creatures would be sentient, or potentially sentient, we must consider the effects on them too. And if they are being created for use as a source of transplantable organs for humans, then obviously the costs to them would be very high.

Furthermore, to justify such research we would need to show not only that its potential benefits would likely outweighs the costs to the interests of all involved but also that it would likely achieve these gains better than other methods. Given the great promise of stem cell research in providing us with a source of transplantable organs, I see no compelling reason for pursuing work into xenotransplantation, or more generally, into creating non-human/ human hybrids.

RL: I agree that we should consider the interests of any potential hybrid creature and that stem cell research is a more promising and, I would say, ethical avenue of research. However, I—

Moderator: Perhaps I could interrupt you to ask this question. You agree that stem cell research is promising. Could you each explain your views about stem cell research and discuss the law and policy options you think we should adopt? Let's begin with a very controversial area within stem cell research, namely embryonic stem cell research and cloning. What is your position regarding the use of somatic cell nuclear transfer in embryonic stem cell research?

RL: I am opposed. Again, though, I think we must first distinguish between the question of the ethics of cloning and the ethics of cloning for the purposes of embryonic stem cell research. Most public debate about the ethics of cloning focuses on science fictional ideas like whether it would be moral to create multiple genetic copies of ourselves. These sorts of scenarios are often far-fetched. But using somatic cell nuclear transfer in embryonic stem cell research is not. Recently, there was a news report about an American biotech firm, Applied Cell Technology of Massachusetts, that currently is using a technique like this one.[24]

Using this technique is wrong for a very simple reason. To appreciate the reason, consider what happens during the course of this process. In somatic cell nuclear transfer, the nucleus of a somatic donor cell is fused with an oocyte, less its nucleus. This fused cell becomes a totipotent stem cell with the same DNA as the somatic cell donor. Once the totipotent stem cell forms into a blastocyst, its inner cell mass of pluripotent stem cells is then taken, thereby killing the embryo, to be cultured, most likely for use in the donor of the somatic cell. The cloned totipotent stem cell is a human being with the complete potential for growing into an adult. So cloning through somatic cell nuclear transfer involves creating life to kill it for its stem cells.

Like many people I believe this is simply wrong. A number of people agree that we should show respect for life and that it is immoral to make and use people for our own ends. Surely if anything is wrong, this is. For the same reason, we should prohibit all embryonic stem cell research that involves killing embryos for their pluripotent stem cells.

This is not to say that I'm opposed to all embryonic stem cell research. I'm opposed to embryonic stem cell research that involves killing embryos for their stem cells. However, the embryos are not the only source of embryonic stem cells. Apparently umbilical cords are a source of pluripotent stem cells, and provided informed consent is obtained, I see no ethical problem with using these embryonic stem cells

in research. I appreciate, of course, that permitting only this kind of embryonic stem cell research represents a considerable limitation.

W: Before we assess the ethics of all embryonic stem cell research, let's consider the issue of cloning more carefully. I don't believe that the issue is as clear-cut as you say. Cloning involves creating an exact copy of biological material. Biological material can be anything from an entire person to the basic biochemical building blocks of life. So imagine I somehow created two identical strings of human DNA, say two identical chromosomes. I would have a clone. But I would not have life, and by your account, I could not have violated your principle of respect for human life. Now imagine I keep adding to my achievement by creating copies of successively longer strings of DNA. Suddenly, according to your view, my actions take on moral significance when I get to the point of cloning a sufficiently long string of human DNA, one with at least 46 chromosomes. Why is this?

Surely there's nothing different in my actions between cloning one chromosome to cloning a complete set. Basically, I have been moving more and more tiny bits of chemicals around. When you think about it in this way, you can see that that's all we are—bits of chemicals ordered and arranged in just the right sort of way. What is the moral significance of this? For me, what matters is welfare. What counts morally is sentience and the potential for sentience. Life itself is not morally significant except that at the moment of conception, the potential for sentience increases because for conception to occur, just the right sort of unlikely conditions must be obtained.

So I suppose the main difficulty I have with your view is appreciating your reason for thinking that it's inherently wrong to act in a way that disrespects human life. Why is life so morally important in your view? Sometimes I think your opposition to genetic research is based on your fear of what we might learn through it. Do you think that we show disrespect for human life by uncovering its mysteries? Are you afraid that we will learn too much?

RL: Your question is based on a common mis-understanding. Many people, especially scientists, think that my opposition to some genetic research is grounded on some medieval or ignorant fear of science. I'm not opposed to education, to the advancement of human knowledge, or to helping the ill. I want these things but not at any price, including the price of disrespecting human life. My view is not so extreme or unreasonable. I also suspect that your position is not as far from mine as you would like to think. Just as I value human life, you too admit that zygotes are morally considerable, that they also count. So we agree that human zygotes and embryos deserve moral consideration. We just disagree about how much consideration is owed them. My view is that, as living humans, they deserve equal consideration with us. Your view is that they deserve less because they have not realized their potential for being sentient.

You also claim that embryonic stem cell research is ethical provided the overall gains of such research outweigh the overall costs, including the costs to embryos who are killed for their stem cells. But how do you measure this? How much does potential count for? Since it counts for something, then it is possible that the gains will be outweighed by the costs. Consider this example. According to a recent report, researchers in the United States fertilized 162 human eggs, from which 50 embryos developed. From that group they derived and managed to culture three embryonic stem cell lines.[25] So, now we have three more lines of stem cells to use but at the cost of 162 lives. Do you think this is right? How can you calculate this fairly? I think the researchers' actions were wrong simply because, however well intentioned they were, they failed to respect life.

You ask me, Why draw the line at life? There are many reasons. My view is straight-forward. By demonstrating equal respect for all human life, our path is much clearer than it is within your view. We simply should not use some people for the sake of others. Furthermore, whether we are just a collection of specially arranged chemicals or not, by respecting human life we effectively enhance the value of all of our lives. We commit to the idea that we are all valuable, and by treating each other with respect, we have more respect. There is great symbolism and significance in accepting the principle of respect for life. By embracing it, we announce that we refuse to regard people as if they were objects. This basic belief underlies much of our shared moral outlook. It helps explain why we think slavery is wrong, and it expresses solidarity with all other members of our species. It is also a fair basis from which we can morally determine law and policy in the area of genetic research.

W: I don't see the fairness of which you speak. A tiny collection of cells is not the same as you or me. It is not physically the same, and I don't see why we should treat it as if it was morally the same. I have respect, too. I respect sentient beings and those with the potential for sentience. But my respect is graduated because I think this is fair. I value the suffering and potential loss of life of those who suffer from terrible diseases and disabilities more than the potential losses of non-conscious embryos. Embryonic stem cell research holds out great promise for these people, and I wonder what would be lost to them if we limited or prohibited embryonic stem cell research out of a respect for life. What about having respect for these people?

I agree with the British that we should permit the creation of embryos for use in stem cell research. We need to explore the full potential of this research. The American policy of funding research involving currently existing embryonic stem cell lines, but not funding research into new lines, attempts to steer a middle course through our positions. However, American researchers have already complained that the existing lines are insufficient. Finally, I fear that based on our past policies in Canada, we will place undue restrictions on embryonic stem cell research.

RL: Your concerns about what we might lose if we don't fully explore embryonic stem cell research are speculative and based on a pessimistic assessment of the potential for using adult stem cells in research. As I mentioned before, my view is neither extreme nor unreasonable. I believe that we should pursue stem cell research, but it should be mostly adult stem cell research. I recommend a more balanced approach to creating laws in this area. Since adult stem cell research does not violate our principle of respect for life, we should pursue it, and like the Americans, we should concentrate our research efforts here. Although there appear to be some limits to this research, the results are not all in yet. Early indications of the promise of adult stem cell research are quite promising, so I don't share your pessimistic outlook. However, even if embryonic stem cell research is more promising than adult stem cell research, we should not pursue it if we must kill to do so.

The question whether we should use the lines of embryonic stem cells that have already derived is a difficult question, one that I have not settled, yet, in my own mind. However, I disagree with policies that permit the use of so-called "leftover" embryos created in the course of *in vitro* fertilization, as is done in some countries. Since those embryos are potentially living, they too deserve our respect.

Moderator: I'm afraid we are almost out of time. Would you each like to add a closing word or two?

RL: Basing our research policies on the moral foundation of demonstrating a basic respect for life may come at a price, but we need to conduct our research, as we need to live our lives, guided by ethical principles. The ethical principle of having respect for life promotes equality, dignity, and solidarity. It should be our guide.

W: We must, indeed, be guided by ethical principles as we construct our policies and laws. But before we determine whether we should pay the price of limiting embryonic stem cell research out of a respect for human life, we must be certain that this is the principle that should guide us. I think there is a fairer and better alternative. We need to pursue embry-

onic stem cell research out of consideration for all those who might suffer if we don't pursue it. We fail these people if we blindly hope that research into adult stem cells will be just as good, or good enough. I hope we have the courage to make the hard choices that morality requires of us.

14.10 Review

In this chapter we surveyed some issues in the ethics of genetic research. After considering some basic elements in the molecular biological study of genetics, including the basic roles played by DNA, genes, nucleotides, base pairs, and chromosomes, we examined the ethics of genetic alteration. In particular, we contrasted the ethical issues concerning somatic cell and germ-line genetic alteration. We then surveyed the science of stem cells and we considered the amazing potential that research into stem cells holds. We noted that some of this research, especially that which involves the use of most embryonic stem cells and the cloning process known as somatic cell nuclear transfer, is ethically worrisome. The problem, we observed, is that although embryonic stem cells provide researchers and medical people with a useful source of pluripotent stem cells, they usually can be acquired only by killing the embryo. The ethical question is whether we should as a society pursue this research or instead focus on less troubling research into adult stem cells.

After surveying the various policy and legal directions taken by Canada and other research countries, we examined the ethical issues in the controversy from two fundamentally different moral outlooks or perspectives. The respect for life deontological perspective begins from the belief that our research should be based on a basic respect for human life. In contrast, the welfarist view values the experiences and potential experiences of conscious or sentient creatures. This view asserts that respect for life, including human life, is not ethically basic. We further noted that since these outlooks lead us to different policies and laws, before we can settle the question of which policies and laws we should adopt, we must first sort out the prior question of the best or right outlook from which we should begin our investigation.

The final debate between representatives of the two positions helped serve to focus the ethical issues for us to consider.

Notes

1. Watson and Crick (1953), pp. 737–738.

2. "A" stands for adenine; "T" stands for thymine; "C" stands for cytosine; and "G" stands for guanine.

3. Much of the information in this account of genetics has been drawn from The Human Genome Project Web site at **www.ornl.gov/ hgmis/project/info.html**

4. Munson and Davis (2000), p. 586.

5. For a fuller discussion of some of these points, see Baird (1994). See also The Royal Commission on New Reproductive Technologies (1993), pp. 936–947. I am indebted to both works.

6. The following account of the facts regarding stem cells and stem cell research is mostly drawn from a United States National Institutes of Health basic introductory essay on the topic. See The United States National Institutes of Health, "Stem Cells: A Primer," May 2000, at **www.nih.gov/news/stemcell/primer.htm**

7. The United States National Institutes of Health, "Stem Cells: A Primer," May 2000, at **www. nih.gov/news/stemcell/primer.htm**

8. Hannah Cleaver and David Derbyshire, "Stem Cell Surgery Saves Man's Heart," *The Calgary Herald*, Saturday, August 25, 2001.

9. *Nature* 385, 810–813, 1997.

10. A copy of this paper is available online at **www.nserc.ca/programs/ethics/english/ policy.htm**

11. Jeff Gray and Campbell Clark, "Rock Unveils Anti-cloning Bill," *The Globe and Mail*. Retrieved May 3, 2001, from **www.globeandmail.ca**

12. Allison Lawlor, "Scientists Should Be Banned from Cloning: Report," *The Globe and Mail*. Retrieved December 12, 2001, from **www.globeandmail.ca**.

13. Thomson, et al, (1998).

14. See John Ibbitson, "Bush Backs Limited Stem-cell Research," *The Globe and Mail*, August 10, 2001.

15. See John Ibbitson, "Bush Backs Limited Stem-cell Research," *The Globe and Mail*, August 10, 2001.

16. The Canadian Institutes of Health ad hoc Working Group on Stem Cell Research, "Human Stem Cell Research: Opportunities for Health and Ethical Perspectives," The Canadian Institutes of Health Research, pp. 11–12, available online at **www.cihr-irsc.gc.ca/ publications/ethics/stem_cell/preamble_ stem_cell_e.shtml**

17. The Canadian Institutes of Health ad hoc Working Group on Stem Cell Research, "Human Stem Cell Research: Opportunities for Health and Ethical Perspectives," The Canadian Institutes of Health Research, pp. 13–16.

18. See chapters 4 and 5.

19. See Chapter 4.

20. See Chapter 5.

21. Somerville (2000).

22. Somerville (2000), p. xii.

23. Margaret Somerville suggests and discusses this possibility in Somerville (2000), pp. 81–82.

24. Associated Press, "Human Embryos Created for Research at U.S. Lab," *The Globe and Mail*. Retrieved July 11, 2001, from **www.globeand mail.ca**

25. Associated Press, "Human Embryos Created for Research at U.S. Lab," *The Globe and Mail*. Retrieved July 11, 2001, from **www.globeand mail.ca**

26. Sharon Kirkey, "Technique Boosts Sex Selection's Accuracy," *National Post*. Retrieved July 5, 2001, from **www.nationalpost.com**

Exercises 14.2

Progress Check

1. Outline the main policy positions in Canada, until 1998, on the main topics of the chapter.

2. Why do these policies make no specific reference to stem cell research?

3. What policies and laws have been adopted in the other countries mentioned in the chapter?

4. What is the Respect for Life Outlook? What is Welfarism? How are the two views different?

5. Distinguish between the respect for life and welfarist positions on the issue of creating human embryos for stem cell research purposes only.

6. What is ectogenesis?

7. What are the possible sources of embryonic stem cells discussed in the debate?

8. Why does the defender of the Respect for Life Outlook think that on the question of the respect we should have for life, the welfarist position is not so different than the respect for life one?

9. Why does the Welfarist think that the Respect for Life Outlook is potentially biased against humans who suffer from the diseases and disabilities that could be treated with embryonic stem cell therapies?

10. Explain the Welfarist's "graduated" approach to giving consideration to embryos based on their potential. (If you need help with this, consult Chapter 11.)

Questions for Further Reflection

1. Explain and critically evaluate the view that there is no ethically significant difference between cloning entire persons and cloning smaller bits of organic material like cells.

2. The Tri-Council policy statement called for a prohibition of cloning people through somatic cell nuclear transfer. How can this be understood as not being a policy about stem cell research?

3. What does it mean to say that an act is "inherently" right or wrong?

4. What, if anything, is inherently immoral about the idea of creating an animal-human hybrid? Defend your view.

5. In the debate, the Welfarist asserts that we are no more than "bits of chemicals ordered and arranged in just the right sort of way."
(a) Do you agree? Why or why not?
(b) If you consider this true, what effect, if any, should it have on the idea that human life is inherently valuable? Defend your view.

6. Explain and critically evaluate the respect for life argument that human life is inherently valuable.

7. What is the basis of the welfarist position? (For help, see Chapter 11.) Do you see any problems with it? Explain and defend your view.

8. What is the price of pursuing adult stem cell research instead of fully exploring embryonic stem cell research? Should we pay this price? Why or why not? Defend your position.

9. Why does the respect for life defender think that the Respect for Life Outlook view promotes "equality, dignity, and solidarity"? Does it? Defend your response.

Group Work Activity:

Sex Selection for Non-medical Purposes

Scientists have developed a sperm-sorting technique that greatly increases the chances of selecting the sex of one's child. The technique involves artificial insemination of sorted sperm carrying the desired chromosome. Sorting is based on the fact that sperm that carries the Y chromosome, the chromosome that results in the birth of a male, contains 2.8 percent less DNA than sperm that carries the X chromosome. The technique has so far proven 90 percent successful in producing girls and 73 percent successful in producing boys. Experts note that this technique, which has long been used by ranchers and farmers to select the sex of animal offspring, has some useful applications for humans. For example, some genetic diseases mostly affect boys, so parents who carry genes for these diseases can use the technique to try to conceive girls.[26]

Some people express ethical concerns over the potential widespread use of the technique, although part of the challenge of marshalling a good moral argument against its use is to explain why such use would be wrong. Some people worry that the technology is discriminatory and that this is bad.

Your task as a group is to develop the strongest ethical arguments you can, both for and against limiting the general use of this technique. Remember to focus on the ethical issues. Once you think you have fairly considered the two sides, develop the policy you would recommend that we as a society adopt regarding this issue.

10. Would the respect for life defender be committed to the view that we should not pursue most embryonic stem cell research even if there was no potential in research into adult stem cells? Why or why not? Is this an extreme or unreasonable view, or not? Defend your position.

11. From the respect for life perspective, should we use already derived embryonic stem cell lines in our research efforts or not? Support your answer.

Suggested Further Reading

The Globe and Mail published an informative report on stem cell research on August 18, 2001. Carolyn Abraham authored this piece entitled "Medicine's Holy Grail."

The information on the science of stem cells was mostly drawn from The United States National Institutes of Health paper, "Stem Cells: A Primer," May 2000, located on their Web site at **www.nih.gov/news/ stemcell/primer.htm**

Much of the information on the regulatory situations in various research countries was drawn from The Canadian Institutes of Health ad hoc Working Group on Stem Cell Research discussion paper, "Human Stem Cell Research: Opportunities for Health and Ethical Perspectives," The Canadian Institutes of Health Research, 2000–2001.

See also Associated Press, "Human Embryos Created for Research at U.S. Lab," *The Globe and Mail*, Wednesday, July 11, 2001.

Hannah Cleaver and David Derbyshire, "Stem Cell Surgery Saves Man's Heart," *The Calgary Herald*, Saturday, August 25, 2001.

Sharon Kirkey, "Technique Boosts Sex Selection's Accuracy," *National Post*, July 5, 2001.

John Ibbitson, "Bush Backs Limited Stem-cell Research," *The Globe and Mail*, August 10, 2001.

Allison Lawlor, "Scientists Should Be Banned from Cloning: Report," *The Globe and Mail*, December 12, 2001.

For other references, consult the notes and the Bibliography.

Weblinks

There is a wealth of information on The Human Genome Project at the Project's main Web site at **www.ornl.gov/hgmis**

There are a number of sites with information regarding stem cells and stem cell research. The Canadian Institutes of Health ad hoc Working Group on Stem Cell Research Web site features a discussion paper and many other resources including a useful set of related links. It is located at **www.cihr-irsc.gc.ca/publications/ethics/stem_cell/ preamble_stem_cell_e.shtml**

The three major research granting institutions in Canada, NSERC, SSHRCC, and MRC, have placed their joint paper, entitled *Tri-Council Policy Statement: Ethical Conduct for Research Involving Humans*, online at **www.nserc.ca/programs/ethics/english/policy.htm** The joint paper's section 8, "Human Genetic Research," and section 9, "Research Involving Human Gametes, Embryos or Foetuses," are especially relevant for this chapter.

15 Issues in Business Ethics: Affirmative Action

Learning Outcomes

In this chapter we examine the ethical debate over affirmative action. We consider many of the reasons and arguments advanced by the various sides of the debate, and we outline the main issues. Our focus is primarily on the question of affirmative action as it impacts hiring practices and career advancement.

Upon the successful completion of this chapter, you will be able to

1. outline the issues in the debate over the fairness of affirmative action policies, programs, and laws;

2. distinguish restitution from compensation and show how this bears on the case for the view that affirmative action policies are needed as compensation for the victims of traditional discrimination;

3. explicate and assess the argument for affirmative action policies from the perspective of distributive justice; and

4. explain and evaluate the argument from intergenerational justice for early mandatory retirement.

15.1 Introduction

On December 15, 1995, the federal government passed the *Employment Equity Act*. Most people would agree with the principle set out in the first part of the act's statement of purpose, to "achieve equality in the workplace so that no person shall be denied employment opportunities or benefits for reasons unrelated to ability . . .". Participants in the ethical debate over affirmative action policies and programs are usually united in their convictions that prejudice and discrimination are immoral and that people should be judged on their merits. Rather, it is the next part of the statement of the legislation's purpose that galvanizes public debate:

. . . and, in the fulfillment of that goal, to correct the conditions of disadvantage in employment experienced by women, aboriginal peoples, persons with disabilities and members of visible minorities by giving effect to the principle that employment equity means more than treating persons in the same way but also requires special measures and the accommodation of differences."[1]

Further compounding the controversy over these "special measures" is section 5 of the act, which outlines the employer's duty under the law:

5. Every employer shall implement employment equity by
   (a) identifying and eliminating employment barriers against persons in designated groups that result from the employer's employment systems, policies and practices that are not authorized by law; and
   (b) instituting such positive policies and practices and making such reasonable accommodations as will ensure that persons in designated groups achieve a degree of representation in each occupational group in the employer's workforce that reflects their representation in
       (i) the Canadian workforce, or
       (ii) those segments of the Canadian workforce that are identifiable by qualification, eligibility or geography and from which the employer may reasonably be expected to draw employees.

In light of passages like these two, many Canadians take issue with the act on philosophical grounds.

The main point of contention is also captured in the equality rights section of the *Canadian Charter of Rights and Freedoms*. Section 15, subsection 1 reads as follows:

(1) Every individual is equal before and under the law and has the right to the equal protection and equal benefit of the law without discrimination and, in particular, without discrimination based on race, national or ethnic origin, colour, religion, sex, age or mental or physical disability.

Again, most people endorse these sentiments. In the margin next to subsection 2, however, specific reference is made to affirmative action programs, and it is with these that many people take issue. Here is subsection 2:

(2) Subsection (1) does not preclude any law, program or activity that has as its object the amelioration of conditions of disadvantaged individuals or groups including those that are disadvantaged because of race, national or ethnic origin, colour, religion, sex, age or mental or physical disability.

The main objection levelled against both the act and the account of our section 15 *Charter* rights is that the goal of promoting equality and minimizing discrimination is not best achieved through, and is not consistent with the use of, discrimination. In short, critics charge that affirmative action programs *are* discriminatory, specifically, that they employ **reverse discrimination.** Two wrongs, they maintain, don't make a right. Proponents of affirmative action programs insist that such programs are needed and that they are the fairest way of promoting equality.

The controversy is hardly academic. Both the statement of our equality rights in the *Charter* and in the *Employment Equity Act* affect us in various ways. For example, the federal government is also an employer and, as such, it is bound by its own legislation. To

> **Reverse discrimination** is used in the debate over affirmative action to refer to policies that unfairly impose costs on a targeted group of individuals (e.g., white men), who have traditionally benefited from existing hiring policies and programs.

facilitate compliance with the act, the government created the four-year Employment Equity Positive Measures Program (EEPMP) with an annual budget of up to $10 million. The program ended on March 31, 2002. While many think the EEPMP program funds have been well spent because they agree with both the goals of the legislation and the means recommended for achieving the goals, others regard the program as a waste of public money.

In this chapter we examine the ethical debate over affirmative action with an eye to outlining the main ethical positions and arguments advanced in the debate. We also pay special attention to the reverse discrimination charge. You are invited to critically consider the various views and make up your mind on this divisive and pressing social issue.

15.2 Two Senses of "Discrimination" Distinguished

The word "discriminate" can simply mean "to act on the basis of a difference between." In this neutral sense, the practice of discrimination is morally unobjectionable, as for instance when one might say that women were discriminated against with regard to identifying potential subjects in a research trial investigating different treatments for testicular cancer. More commonly, however, "discriminate" and "discrimination" are used in their traditional evaluative sense to describe immoral acts or practices, as when someone says "discrimination is wrong." Henceforth we will adopt this usage. Unless specifically noted otherwise, we will use "discrimination" to mean "traditional discrimination," the widely criticized immoral sorts of practices with which we are all familiar.

> **Affirmative action** hiring programs and policies are designed to promote the hiring of various groups of individuals who have suffered from traditional discriminatory hiring practices.
> The **equal opportunity view** of affirmative action endorses the remedying of underrepresentation of individuals traditionally discriminated against by past hiring practices through the scrupulous application of a principle of equal opportunity in hiring.

As we just noted, denouncing discrimination provides reasonable and serious-minded participants in the ethical debate over affirmative action with a common point of agreement. We will begin from this point, too. Given that most of us are opposed to discrimination, the question is whether affirmative action laws, policies, and programs provide us with the most efficient and fairest means of overcoming discrimination. To further narrow our focus, we will restrict our enquiry mainly to affirmative action as it most affects the conduct of business, namely through hiring and promotion practices. Thus, our enquiry into the ethics of affirmative action falls squarely into the group of topics typically considered in courses in Business Ethics.

15.3 The Debate between the Equal Opportunity View and the Enhanced Views

We all deplore past discriminatory practices that have greatly contributed to the current underrepresentation of women, Aboriginal peoples, persons with disabilities, and members of visible minorities in many well-paying and status-conferring jobs.[2] The debate over **affirmative action** can be understood in terms of a disagreement over what a just rate of improvement would be and over the best means of realizing this improvement. Toward one end of the spectrum are defenders of affirmative action programs that would remedy the current underrepresentation by scrupulously applying a principle of equal opportunity to govern hiring and promotion decisions. According to this **equal opportunity view,** if competition for positions is open to all persons, and if hiring and promotion decisions are based solely on merit, then those decisions will not be affected by irrelevant facts about a candidate. Proponents of this view argue that as fields of work undergo a normal turnover of positions they will increasingly reflect society's diverse heterogeneous mix. These proponents caution that the pace of change should not be hastened by means that effectively perpetuate discrimination, this time, usually, against able-bodied white men. They decry attempts at "social engineering" designed to achieve "equality of results" that in reality are examples of unjust "reverse discrimination."[3] Moving away from this end of the spectrum, we find a range of views that call for a more forceful approach to rapidly redress the underrepresentation. These views endorse programs employing reverse discriminatory measures to achieve their goals. We call these **enhanced views**.

The task of identifying affirmative action policies that employ reverse discrimination is not as easy as one might suppose. To help see this, we can contrast the equal opportunity view with various enhanced views by reference to perhaps the most controversial affirmative action policy, namely the quota policy. Quota policies in hiring typically set targets for hiring from groups that traditionally have been discriminated against. The hiring is usually achieved by awarding some specified percentage of positions that become available in some specified time period to group members. So, for example, an automobile manufacturer may adopt a quota policy with the long-term aim of achieving a roughly 50 percent complement of female employees in its engineering staff. To achieve this goal, it may choose between quota policies that promise different rates of progress.

Although there are obviously many different possibilities, it is useful to distinguish between a few of these. For example, a **constant quota policy** is one that mirrors the percentage of currently available, minimally qualified job candidates from the targeted group. An **accelerated quota policy** is one that exceeds this percentage. Imagine that in the case of the automaker, women constitute only 10 percent of the company's current staff of engineers, and they number only 20 percent of the available pool of qualified candidates for this occupation. Thus, the automaker adopts a constant quota policy if it initially sets a quota that mirrors the percentage of women in the pool of qualified candidates, in this case 20 percent, for the first stage of the program. It adopts an accelerated policy if it sets a quota in excess of 20 percent for the first stage.

You might think that to achieve its goal, the company must adopt an accelerated quota of 50 percent. But this is the long-term aim of the policy, one that can also be attained through periodic upward revisions of constant quotas. Part of the company's rationale for adopting a constant quota is to encourage women considering various career options to acquire the needed education and training to become engineers. A quota of even 20 percent may help convince these women that a field of work traditionally dominated by men is opening up. The hope is that, as more women join the pool of qualified candidates, subsequent constant quotas will be raised until eventually the 50 percent goal is attained. Provided each subsequent quota accurately reflects the percentage of qualified female candidates in the pool at the moment it is set, the company will have employed a constant quota policy to reach its goal.

Notice that it is a mistake to automatically equate quota policies with reverse discrimination. The idea that all quota policies must employ reverse discrimination is plainly false. Constant quota policies are merely designed to ensure that one's complement of workers from some targeted underrepresented group reflects the percentage of members of that group in the available hiring pool. Hiring according to this sort of policy would not impose any reverse discrimination.

It is also a mistake to simply assume that all accelerated quota policies must be reversely discriminatory. Imagine that an industry adopts an accelerated quota of hiring 10 percent Aboriginal people for positions becoming available in the next seven years. If the present pool of qualified Aboriginal candidates is 5 percent, then to meet the quota it might

Enhanced views endorse imposing costs on individuals (typically white men) who have traditionally benefited from past discriminatory hiring practices.

An **accelerated quota policy** in affirmative action is a hiring policy that sets a target for hiring underrepresented individuals in the workforce that exceeds the percentage of currently available, minimally qualified job candidates from the targeted group.
A **constant quota policy** sets a target for hiring underrepresented individuals in the workforce that equals the percentage of currently available, minimally qualified job candidates from the targeted group.

seem that some under-qualified Aboriginal persons will have to be hired over some qualified non-Aboriginals. However, the notion that the 10 percent quota can be reached only by discriminating against some non-Aboriginals overlooks the possibility that the target can be achieved through purely non-discriminatory measures. For example, perhaps the current proportion of 5 percent qualified Aboriginal candidates can be substantially increased over the seven-year period through the special recruitment of potential Aboriginal candidates. These special recruitment measures might consist of taking extra steps to inform potential Aboriginal candidates of future career possibilities and encouraging them to acquire the necessary education and training to become qualified. Special recruitment measures would be non-discriminatory because they would expand the pool of qualified Aboriginal candidates without reducing the pool of qualified non-Aboriginals.[4] They are unobjectionable because they are designed, in part, to offset the "white pipeline": the recruitment method whereby most jobs are publicized and filled through the personal contacts of Caucasians. As Gertrude Ezorsky notes, since Caucasians for the most part live in separate societies, and since Caucasians are entrenched in most desirable jobs, the "white pipeline," though intrinsically free of bias, effectively perpetuates discrimination.[5]

The idea that an accelerated quota will discriminate against some qualified overrepresented persons also rests on the debatable assumption that the present group of underrepresented candidates is of roughly comparable ability to any random sample from a comparably sized group of overrepresented candidates. But one might argue that to gain the needed training to be recognized as qualified in fields of work long dominated by the dominant group, and to overcome the barriers of past discrimination and unfriendly and even hostile attitudes exhibited by the majority, those candidates from groups that traditionally have been discriminated against have had to be uncommonly able and determined. The example

of Jackie Robinson breaking the "colour barrier" in professional baseball is a dramatic illustration of this phenomenon. According to this argument, then, assuming qualifications of the underrepresented candidates are estimated fairly, an accelerated quota may very well be needed to ensure that hiring is purely merit-based.

The task of fairly judging the qualifications of people from traditionally discriminated against groups is difficult. When doing this, one must try to take into account the effects, not just of past discrimination but also of ongoing overt and especially *covert* prejudices.[6]

These considerations challenge the popular assumption that all accelerated quotas will be reversely discriminatory. They also suggest that constant quotas, while perhaps a step in the right direction, may only perpetuate the *status quo*. Although these brief remarks are hardly conclusive, they suggest that we cannot easily identify reverse discrimination in quota policies simply by shifting our attention from constant to accelerated quota policies. Rather, it seems that for reverse discrimination to appear, one must adopt an accelerated quota policy that passes the reverse discrimination threshold. Let's call an accelerated quota policy that does exceed this threshold point an **enhanced quota policy**. No doubt the threshold points for enhanced quota policies will vary from case to case, and in practice they may be very difficult to identify accurately. However, since our concern will be with the prospects of justifying such policies in principle, this practical problem need not detain us.

15.4 Restitution, Compensation, and Reverse Discrimination

Although the various advocates of accelerated policies employing reverse discriminatory measures have defended different degrees of reverse discrimination, such defences have been of two types: backward-looking justifications that appeal to norms of corrective justice, and forward-looking justifications that appeal to norms of distributive justice.

An **enhanced quota policy** sets the target for hiring underrepresented individuals in the workforce in numbers that exceed the threshold point for employing reverse discrimination.

According to the backward-looking defence, potential candidates for jobs and promotions who might be subjected to discrimination deserve the preferential treatment of affirmative action programs as compensation for past discrimination.[7] To properly consider this argument it will be useful to examine the related ideas of compensation and restitution.

Onora O'Neill distinguishes between these two forms of rectificatory justice.[8] Restitution, she explains, is a response to the ruptured moral relationship between offenders and victims. This means that restitution cannot be vicarious: that which has been lost must be restored to those who suffered the wrong. To make restitution for stealing your car I must return it and apologize. Restitution would not be made if your insurance company bought you another vehicle or if the state awarded you some money for your loss. My apology is offered in recognition that I cannot make complete restitution to you because although I can return your car, I cannot undo having made you a victim of a crime. My apology expresses my regret at having done this to you and it is my attempt at seeking your forgiveness. In contrast, O'Neill notes that since compensation is a response solely to victims, it can be vicarious in two respects. Victims are compensated if someone offers them something for their loss. The wrongdoers need not provide this. As she points out, we sensibly speak of the victims of natural disasters being compensated for their injuries. Furthermore, compensation *must* be vicarious in another respect: since it does not restore that which is lost, it must substitute a vicarious good. I do not offer you compensation when I return your car and apologize; I make (some) restitution. If I do not return it, then your insurance company would compensate you for your loss if it gave you another automobile or the money to purchase one.

Those concerned with rectifying the injustices suffered by the victims of traditional discrimination would prefer, ideally, to see complete restitution made. As O'Neill observes, this is the most profound response to past violations of rights, and since perfect restitution would restore that which was lost, it would wipe out past wrongs. Thus, if complete restitution could be made, there would be no need for affirmative action programs. If all the hiring decisions and subsequent decisions about promotions of the last 50 years or so had been scrupulously merit-based, there would be no significant underrepresentation to remedy. But, of course, literal restoration cannot be made. It would require minimally that we turn back the clock to the moment in each case when a discriminatory decision was reached, have the decision made anew, this time more equitably, and that we carry on from there.

If perfect restitution is not available to us, is incomplete but still satisfactory restitution available? O'Neill argues that the incompleteness in the sort of case we just considered involving the stolen car is typical in cases of restitution, and it is usually the best we can hope for. She adds that although incomplete restitution cannot undo a wrong, it can expunge it. Even given this lowering of our sights, however, overwhelming practical problems dog any efforts we might make to arrange for restitution to be made to the victims of traditional discrimination. To even imperfectly restore that which those who were arbitrarily denied positions and promotions lost would require that we (1) identify the victims and perpetrators of past discriminatory hiring and advancement decisions, (2) locate the victims now, and (3) offer them the jobs and advancement they would have won. Although perhaps in isolated, and probably recent, cases we may be able to do this, for obvious reasons this task is beyond the powers of even the wisest and most diligent agents of justice in most cases. Moreover, even if this imperfect restitution could now be made, it is questionable whether it would be truly satisfactory. For as O'Neill notes, not only does adequate restitution expunge the wrong but also makes compensation redundant, even offensive. In the cases we are considering, however, compensation still seems required. Even if we could now restore the victims of discriminatory decisions to the jobs they would have won in fair competitions, they are owed compensation for the years of lost wages, benefits, and opportunities that they were unjustly denied.

From this brief discussion, we can see why restitution that undoes or expunges past wrongs is not generally available as a response to the harms of traditional discrimination. Often in these cases, that which was lost cannot be restored by the wrongdoer to the victim. However, compensation, which substitutes a vicarious good, can still be made. And, as O'Neill remarks, although compensation cannot undo or even expunge a wrong, it can counter it. Some participants in the debate over the fairness of affirmative action programs have proposed affirmative action policies designed specifically to compensate the main victims of discrimination.

Objections to Affirmative Action Programs

In response, critics concede that justice requires that all those who have suffered from discrimination be fairly compensated for their injuries. They also grant that since the harms of discrimination are group-based, all members of the group have felt them to some extent.[9] However, they challenge the claim that affirmative action programs offer the fairest means of providing the required compensation.

One problem is that such programs award compensation selectively in the form of employment opportunities. But those who were discriminated against and who now are unable or uninterested in entering the job market will not enjoy the offered benefits. Not only are these benefits not comprehensive but also, arguably, they are given disproportionately. Critics claim that the main beneficiaries of the opportunities are those younger persons who have suffered the least. Correlatively, older workers who have suffered the most benefit the least. This disproportion suggests that enhanced policies are, at best, inefficient means of paying compensation. Considering that this inefficiency is coupled with reverse discrimination, critics add, the case for these programs being justified on retrospective grounds is even weaker.

Response

Defenders, however, have noted that since, for example, able-bodied, young, white men have enjoyed the benefits of male, white-skin privilege at the expense of women, visible minorities, and others, it is appropriate that they contribute to the compensation.[10]

Counterresponse

By this token, critics respond, the greatest contribution should be made by those who have most benefited from past discrimination, namely able-bodied, older, white men. Since enhanced quota policies do not exact this cost, the argument for them on these grounds is further weakened.

Response

Some defenders of affirmative action programs have tried to address this inefficiency and unfairness. For instance, Parker English proposes an affirmative action program that subsidizes the costs of training older African-Americans to compete for more senior positions in their place of work.[11] This "upper-level plan" is designed to compensate these older workers for the adverse effects of discrimination. English claims that, unlike most affirmative action programs, his plan would assign the lion's share of the benefits to those older African-Americans who most deserve them. Moreover, it would place most of the costs—in this case, the increased probability of being passed over for promotions they otherwise would have won—onto those older whites who have most benefited from traditional discrimination. Leo Groarke also argues that affirmative action programs should be targeted to assist older workers gain more senior positions. However, he maintains that since such policies will have only limited effects, they should be supplemented with programs that compensate older victims of traditional discrimination in ways that go beyond job allocation. Since older victims have suffered economic losses, he suggests that benefits in the form of pension reforms and tax breaks be made available to them. In keeping with the notion that the costs of affirmative action programs should be borne primarily by those who have most benefited from traditional discrimination, Groarke proposes that these programs be funded by taxing older white men.

Counterresponse

Critics note that it is not clear why all older white men should bear these costs. Furthermore, despite these rejoinders, the basic objection to instituting affirmative action programs and policies employing reverse discrimination as a means of providing compensation to the victims of traditional discrimination remains. The problem, the critics assert, is that such programs are inefficient and unfair.

15.5 Forward-looking Justifications of Affirmative Action Policies Based on Norms of Distributive Justice

Doubtful of obtaining justification by appealing to norms of corrective justice, some defenders of enhanced views employing reverse discriminatory measures have instead presented a forward-looking, consequentialist case for their view that rests on an appeal to norms of distributive justice. The central idea of this sort of prospective justification is that by introducing some reverse discrimination against those overrepresented in the workplace, we can best eliminate traditional discrimination in the future.[12] As more openings are reserved for women, Aboriginal peoples, persons with disabilities, and members of visible minorities, more of these individuals will become successful professionals. This will have at least two beneficial effects. The presence of these role models in fields of work dominated by overrepresented individuals will encourage other members of groups traditionally discriminated against to pursue similar careers.[13] Their competence will also help break down stereotypes in the minds of those who have harboured prejudice against them. Thus, both directly through exercising their own power and indirectly through their effect on the attitudes of others in power, members of groups traditionally discriminated against who are hired and promoted under enhanced programs will eventually come to exert greater influence over future hiring and advancement decisions. This will effectively counteract the forces of overt and covert biases that have been operating, thereby breaking the cycle of traditional discrimination.

Supporters of this view claim that the harms of traditional discrimination are serious enough to warrant employing reverse discrimination. The hope is that as the threat from traditional discrimination fades, then so too will the need for these powerful countermeasures.

Response

In response, defenders of the equal opportunity view assert that their programs promise a satisfactory rate of progress that is fair to all, and they wonder why proponents of enhanced quota policies believe that the gain in the pace of improvement promised by their policies justifies reverse discrimination.

Counterresponse

Proponents reply by claiming that since increased representation from groups who traditionally have been excluded can contribute to the overcoming of damaging stereotypes, enhanced quota policies are more useful in serving this end than equal opportunity ones. They also point to the value of enhanced quota policies in helping to neutralize the chilly climates often experienced by those first hired after affirmative action programs have been established.[14] Furthermore, they note that there is a qualitative difference in the effects of traditional discrimination and the discrimination caused by their policies. Traditional discrimination is unjust not simply because it arbitrarily denies some persons goods and opportunities, but also because it stigmatizes. The pervasive and powerful message sent to all by the practice of traditional discrimination is that those discriminated against are inherently inferior. In contrast, the discrimination engendered by an enhanced quota policy does not convey a similar denigrating message. Since those reversely discriminated against by the policy need not experience any corresponding threat to their self-esteem, reverse discrimination is not so objectionable.[15]

Despite this, some defenders of enhanced views express regret at the need to employ reverse discrimination to advance their affirmative action goals because they acknowledge that these measures will impose costs on some "victims."[16] They are also wary of a backlash by those who oppose such programs. Given their reluctant endorsement, and in light of the concerted criticisms leveled by proponents of the equal opportunity view, one might wonder whether there is any other means of achieving the goals of enhanced quota policies without having to resort to employing reverse discrimination. What alternative is there?

15.6 The Inefficiency of Traditional Discrimination

The strategy of the enhanced views is to increase the workforce complement of those groups who traditionally have been discriminated against by bypassing some suitably qualified candidates from overrepresented groups when positions and opportunities for advancement arise. Thus, these policies place their burdens mainly onto the backs of younger, able-bodied, white men, and they pursue a solution that overlooks the obstacle of the slow turnover of positions, which, arguably, exacerbates the resolution of the very underrepresentation problem with which they are concerned.

In the final part of this chapter, we will explore an argument for expediting the retirements of the beneficiaries of past discriminatory hiring decisions, mostly older, able-bodied, white men, and then replacing them through merit-based competitions. The case for this approach rests not on considerations of compensatory or distributive justice, but on an entirely neglected consideration of intergenerational justice.

We have been concerned with traditional discriminatory practices that have greatly contributed to the underrepresentation of visible minorities, Aboriginal peoples, women, and persons with disabilities in well-paying and status-conferring occupations. In these sorts of cases, the demand is that all be given an equal opportunity to compete for goods that many desire but only some can enjoy. Bernard Williams notes that some of these goods are limited by their nature—so, for example, there can be only one captain on each ship—whereas others are "fortuitously"[17] limited. Many people satisfy the minimum conditions for obtaining fortuitously limited goods, but since demand for them is so great, more stringent conditions for awarding them have to be imposed. Many believe that the best way to award these positions is on the basis of merit: those who will most likely perform best should, all other things being equal, get the job.[18] Although one might challenge the fairness of either this merit principle or a principle of equal opportunity, let's assume for the sake of argument that each is acceptable.[19]

We can begin to see that the issue of justifying a policy that mostly burdens the older, able-bodied, white male beneficiaries of discriminatory hiring and advancement decisions raises a question of intergenerational justice with the help of two ideas. First, note that in the past 50 years or so many members of groups traditionally discriminated against who would have won fair competitions have been the victims of biased hiring and advancement decisions. For a variety of reasons many others were either discouraged from applying or discouraged from seeking the requisite education and training to apply. The net effect of this practice has been to frustrate the fair application of the merit principle. This leads us to conclude that traditional discrimination has been inefficient.[20] Secondly, note that we endorse the view that a right to a full tenure of employment is conditional upon maintaining a satisfactory level of performance.

One might think that only the first of these ideas is needed. Thus, it might be argued that given the inefficiency of traditional discrimination, the beneficiaries of biased hiring decisions do not have a right to a full tenure of employment. On this view, those who would have won fair competitions but were denied an equal opportunity to compete would have been entitled to a full tenure. But those less-than-best beneficiaries of biased decisions are not so entitled because they likely have not performed as well as the person or persons unfairly passed over would have. One shortcoming of this proposal, however, is that it presents us with a formidable practical problem. To implement the policy, we would have to identify those who won their jobs as the result of traditional discrimination. For obvious reasons, this is an onerous challenge.

Another more serious deficiency is that the argument on which this proposal rests will sometimes be self-defeating. To see why, consider the following example. Imagine that due to a biased hiring decision some years ago, Ralph was chosen over Patricia. According to our proposed policy, he must retire early because he likely has not performed as well as Pat would have. The underlying assumption here is that hiring committees that operate free of prejudice will select the best person for the job. But hiring committees make predictions about future performance, and of course their ability to do this well is limited. Sometimes the early promise of a candidate is not realized; on the other hand, some defeated candidates are late bloomers. A policy that would force all beneficiaries of biased decisions to retire early (assuming these persons could be identified) would be self-defeating insofar as it would require those late bloomers who have excelled to be let go. Thus, rather than lessen inefficiency, as was intended, the policy would in many instances contribute to it.

The justification of a policy that appeals to the inefficiency of traditional discrimination must also appeal to our belief that job security should depend upon the maintenance of minimum performance standards. But once we introduce this latter notion to the justification, one might suspect that the former idea is redundant. Once we include reference to the notion of maintaining minimum performance standards, we might question the rationale for supposing there is any need for an early mandatory retirement policy. Thus, someone might embrace the view that job security should be conditional upon satisfactory performance, but they might add that we already recognize this. People are fired for incompetence. Since we already cite the failure to perform satisfactorily as a reason for dismissing staff prior to normal retirement age,

why do we need a special early mandatory retirement policy? And why would one think that the idea of the inefficiency of traditional discrimination does any justificatory work in grounding such a policy?

We have observed that a right to a full tenure of employment is conditional upon maintaining minimum performance standards. However, whether someone is performing satisfactorily or not is a relative judgment; it usually refers to the quality of work being done by others in the field. But consider the effects of the practice of traditional discriminatory hiring on the setting of standards of work performance. If traditional discrimination has been inefficient, because it has frustrated the fair application of the merit principle, then in occupations where women, Aboriginal peoples, visible minorities, and persons with disabilities have been greatly underrepresented, performance standards are lower than they otherwise would have been in the absence of the discrimination. To help see this point, consider an analogy. Although professional baseball and hockey leagues continued to operate during World War II, many of the best players entered the service. This freed up jobs for some less-skilled players who would not have been able to win their spots otherwise. This became evident when the better players returned and won back their places. It was also evident in the reduced quality of play during the war, compared to the level before and after it. Not surprisingly, an average player during the war years was not as good as an average player before or after them.

We can explain this reduction in the quality of play by noting that since many men entered the service, the pool of possible players contracted during the war years. Similarly, we can see that the practice of traditional discriminatory hiring effectively reduced the pool of job candidates by excluding many members of groups that have been traditionally discriminated against. If there had been no widespread traditional discrimination, the pool of candidates for jobs would have greatly expanded, with predictable positive effects on the subsequent quality of work done. Thus, an average worker in one of these occupations would not have performed as well as an average worker drawn from the expanded pool of candidates in, say, a hypothetical world free of traditional discrimination. Similarly, merely satisfactory work done in our world would have been considered unsatisfactory, and therefore grounds for dismissal, in the more efficient hypothetical world.

15.7 Justice between Contemporaneous Birth Cohorts

These reflections raise an issue of injustice that has thus far loosely been characterized as "intergenerational," but to fully appreciate it, we must speak more carefully. Peter Laslett and James Fishkin have noted some inadequacies with using the idea of successive generations of people to describe the order of succession in a population over time.[21] The term "generation," they argue, appeals to the notion of an individual's generative or kin relationships. Using this idea, we can understand the present generation as constituting a "whole societywide order of contemporary persons" and their brothers, sisters, and cousins. Parents and grandparents belong to the two previous generations, children, nephews, and nieces to the next one. Although this way of classifying the procession of people through time has a rough and ready use, as Laslett and Fishkin note, it is inexact and sometimes inconsistent. Aunts and uncles can be younger than their nephews and nieces.[22] Thus, rather than speak of belonging to some generation, we can identify individuals more precisely by age by reference to their **birth cohort.**

A birth cohort includes all of the people born between any two specified dates. So whereas some nephews are younger, and some are older, than their aunts, the birth cohort of those born in 1950 will always be older than the cohort of individuals born in 1951. Although the concept of a birth cohort is flexible, we can restrict our use of the expression to refer to individuals born in the same calendar year. In

> A **birth cohort** is the group of all individuals born between any two specified dates.

addition to distinguishing between generations and birth cohorts, we should also distinguish between birth cohorts and age groups. Following Norman Daniels, let us use the expression *age group* to refer to people who fall within a certain age range.[23] Hence, as Daniels observes, over time an age group will consist of a succession of birth cohorts. Ten years ago, "infants" included all those born between ten and eleven years ago. Now they include those born in the past year. Daniels notes that whereas age groups do not age, birth cohorts do. As they proceed through the stages of life, birth cohorts pass through different age groups.

Just as we might be discriminated against on the basis of our race or sex, we also might be discriminated against on the basis of our age or membership in a particular birth cohort. We might assume that the different treatment of people according to their race, sex, birth cohort, or age will generate inequalities between persons and hence might be unjust. Daniels asserts that this is certainly true for differential treatment by race or sex. For example, institutions that treat African-Americans differently than whites, by giving some opportunities exclusively to whites, and some only to African-Americans, generate inequalities between persons. Since race is a morally irrelevant trait, the inequalities generated are based on a morally irrelevant difference between persons.[24] In contrast, Daniels argues that differential treatment by age, provided it is consistent, does not necessarily generate inequalities because whereas we do not change our race or sex, we all age. Thus, although we may treat the young one way and the old another, since the young will become old, each is treated both ways over time; thus is treated equally.

15.8 A Case for Mandatory Early Retirement

Daniels' point suggests that an argument supporting a policy of early mandatory retirement cannot obviously be grounded on a concern about difference in treatment by age. However, our argument for raising performance standards is founded on a concern about differential treatment by birth cohort. As with one's race or sex, one cannot change one's birth cohort membership. Thus, unlike differential treatment by age, differential treatment by birth cohort membership does generate inequalities in treatment between persons. Due to the inefficiency of traditional discrimination, members of some birth cohorts are working to lower standards than will those of later cohorts, assuming that we do not backslide on our commitment to preventing a re-emergence of forms of traditional discrimination. In response, we might be tempted to argue that far from being evidence of discrimination, the idea that members of later cohorts are working to higher standards than members of earlier cohorts is a sign of progress.

However, although it may be true that in a hypothetical world free of traditional discrimination members of later cohorts would be working to higher standards than those of earlier cohorts, this is beside the point. Our objection focuses on the difference in standards that is a product not of improved technology or education, but of birth cohort discrimination due to the inefficiency of traditional discrimination. This discrimination is unjust because, again, as with one's race or sex, one's birth cohort membership is a morally irrelevant feature of an individual. To help see this, consider a fanciful example. Imagine that on a capricious whim, the owner of a large company decrees that all those born in 1975 will be held to higher standards of performance than everyone else. These unlucky people will have to significantly outperform their competitors to be hired, and subsequently they will have to outperform their colleagues to be promoted. The injustice of this type of arbitrary difference in treatment is similar to our case. However, whereas this injustice is obvious here, because the example emphasizes the contrast between the different performance standards, the difference is obscured in our case because it becomes apparent only as time passes and the practice of traditional discrimination gradually subsides.

In response, it might be objected that this example is unlike our case in an important respect. The claim that our concern is with the difference in performance standards that is a product of birth cohort discrimination implies that someone treated different cohorts differently, that, in other words, someone discriminated against later cohorts. This impression is fostered by the example of the biased owner who consciously discriminates. But, it might be said, there is no such responsibility in our case. How could one think that those who made discriminatory hiring decisions years ago were really also discriminating against individuals who were not only not present and not then involved in the hiring process, but many of whom were not even born yet? Since this makes no sense, it might be inferred, no one is guilty of discriminating against later cohorts. And since there is no discrimination against later cohorts, there is no requirement of intergenerational justice to raise performance standards.

This objection, however, misses the point. The question whether there is a requirement from intergenerational justice to raise performance standards turns on whether members of later cohorts suffered from discriminatory hiring decisions, not whether there was any discrimination, overt or covert, against them. Although the case for this is incomplete, the argument presented here provides us with some grounds for believing that the lingering effects of those original discriminatory hiring decisions have harmed members of later cohorts. It is also a confusion to think that the passage of time in this case somehow explains why there is no requirement to raise standards. We can see this by considering some other objections.

Someone might object that efforts to redress the harms to later cohorts would be unfair because they would harm those who are innocent of any wrongdoing, namely the beneficiaries of the discriminatory hiring decisions who may be forced to prematurely relinquish their jobs. This objection emphasizes the innocence of those who would suffer from a policy of early mandatory retirement, but it too is beside the point. While we need not doubt the innocence of those beneficiaries of biased decisions, the question is whether they had a right to the decisions made in their favour. According to the argument we are considering, they did not have such a right and therefore cannot claim that any redress, which burdens them now, is unfair. To help see this, consider another example. If you stole someone's property, a painting, say, and gave it to your mother, your mother, who may have grown quite fond of it over the years, could not complain that it would be unjust to expect her to hand it over if its true owner reclaimed it.[25]

This example suggests at least that there is a presumption against supposing that any redress against the innocent beneficiaries of wrongful acts is unjust. But we must attend to the special circumstances of our case to show that an early mandatory retirement policy can be justified. We might admit that although someone who originally benefited from a biased decision was not entitled to that decision, now, years later, his claim to the job may have grown. To appreciate this, consider an argument of George Sher's.[26] Sher argues that the compensation an individual ought to receive in a rectified world (Wr) does not always carry over to the claim he can justly make in the actual world (Wa). To support this, he asks us to consider the case of X, a promising law student, who is discriminatorily barred from entering law school. Although X knows that he will be able to gain entry in another year, he becomes discouraged and does not reapply. Furthermore, we can imagine a Wr without discrimination in which X studies diligently and goes on to a successful and rewarding career as a prominent lawyer. Sher argues that the goods to which X is entitled in Wr fall far short of the compensation he is owed in Wa.

There are two reasons for this. X's entitlements in Wa are diminished by his omissions in this world. His failure to persevere partly explains why he did not succeed as a lawyer. Furthermore, Sher argues that insofar as X's entitlements in Wr stem from what X did after the initial wrong in Wa, that is, after X was accepted into law school in Wr, they are not transferable. As Sher notes, these entitlements are not merely inherited by X in Wr, they are created by X's actions in that world and not performed in Wa. To maintain that X is entitled to compensation for what he might have done in Wr is to say that

. . . what a person should have may be determined by certain actions that neither he nor any-

one else has actually performed. We are plainly unwilling to say things like this in other contexts (nobody would say that a person deserves to be punished simply because he would have committed a crime if given the opportunity), and they seem no more supportable here.[27]

These considerations about compensation are helpful in supporting an early mandatory retirement policy. As in Sher's example, we can distinguish between the claims an innocent beneficiary of a biased hiring decision, call him Y, can make both in Wr in which there is no discrimination and in Wa where, contrary to original expectations, Y works very hard and well and is a great success. Although in Wr, Y would not be entitled to his position and could not object to losing the competition for it, in Wa, Y was awarded the position and can claim by analogous reasoning to X's case an entitlement to benefits earned as a result of Y's efforts. Just as X's failure to persevere explains his diminished claim to compensation in Wa, Y's claim to maintaining his position is strengthened by his excellent efforts in Wa. This explains why a policy that required all individuals who benefited from discriminatory hiring decisions to be summarily dismissed would not only be impractical and self-defeating, but also unfair.

Although a policy that held that no beneficiary of a discriminatory hiring decision has a right to a full tenure of employment would be unfair to people like Y, consider the case of Z, who also benefited from a biased decision. Unlike Y, however, Z went on to a thoroughly undistinguished career and would have been judged an unsatisfactory performer by Wr standards. By this reasoning, Z would have no case against an early mandatory retirement policy that required, say, Z's early retirement. Z's claim to his position has not strengthened over time; indeed it has weakened since he has not made anything of his opportunity. Furthermore, since those entering the job market in a climate where traditional discrimination is greatly lessened or eliminated would be held to the standards enforced in Wr, Z's complaint of unfair treatment by an early mandatory retirement policy seems unfounded. These remarks suggest that a policy requiring the raising of performance standards would not be unjust.

A persistent critic might maintain that this is a hasty judgment, that despite this argument, any move to raise performance standards would be unfair because of its *ex post facto* nature.[28] This objection works like the objection against *ex post facto* law. *Ex post facto* law is unjust because it is unfair to punish people for behaving in a way they could not have known was illegal at the time they performed the now-illegal action. One of the functions of law is to provide norms to guide behaviour, and *ex post facto* law is unfair precisely because it fails to do this. By the very same reasoning, we might claim that any early mandatory retirement policy is also *ex post facto* and therefore unjust.

This criticism has some force, but does not seem to show any basic unfairness in the sort of policy we are considering. It seems to show at most that a fair policy should also provide for some probationary period during which workers judged to be performing unsatisfactorily have an opportunity to raise their performance. The purpose of the probationary period is to give workers used to one set of standards a chance to meet fairer ones. This notice meets the *ex post facto* objection, but no doubt some will say that it does not go far enough. On the other hand, many will say that it goes too far because many of those put on notice will raise their performance and will not be required to relinquish their positions. And this, these people will say, fails to undo the wrong of those benefiting from discriminatory hiring decisions holding their jobs for so long. In response, we should note that the case for raising performance standards is not a substitute for compensation programs for those originally discriminated against. Insofar as the lingering worry of unfairness can be traced to the bad effects on those originally unjustly bypassed, an early mandatory retirement policy can be supplemented with compensation programs for those persons.

This case for raising performance standards has rested on an undefended assumption that the failure to implement an early mandatory retirement policy will cause harm. If performance standards are not raised, those who would have failed to meet the higher standards, and thus who would have been dismissed or forced to retire early, will retain their positions and will continue their substandard work. This will effect two sorts of losses or harms. There will be the losses in the form of lost productivity experienced by employers from the difference between the work that would have been done to the higher standard but is instead done below that level. Secondly, there will be losses to those seeking jobs who would have won the competitions for whatever positions that would have opened up by the dismissal of those who failed to meet the higher standards. These losses will take the form of the bad effects resulting from a delayed entry into the workforce. Although it is unlikely that we would classify all of these losses as significant, the notion that no harm would be done by failing to raise performance standards is also improbable. To fully support this claim we must turn to empirical study, and we must clarify our understanding of the harm threshold; nonetheless, the argument justifying the raising of the standards is not easily dismissed.

15.9 Some Final Objections

Although it would be wrong to abandon all attempts to defend a policy of early mandatory retirement because investigations are unlikely to reveal the precise extent of past discrimination, this fact does pose a problem. The case presented here for raising work performance standards rests on a reasonable assumption about inefficient traditional discrimination, but once we move from the issue of justifying a policy to actually constructing one, we need to specify how much performance standards should be raised. To do this fairly, we need at least a rough appreciation of the extent of traditional discrimination. How are we to measure this?

Here is another objection. Assuming that the case for raising performance standards is accepted, why should we support some policy of early mandatory retirement over other possibilities? After all, if our concern is with raising unfair minimum performance standards, then should not subsequent dismissals be at any age? It also remains to be seen how effective an early mandatory retirement policy would be in advancing affirmative action goals. Coupled with a plan to refill positions on the basis of merit, it could redress the underrepresentation at a rate comparable to many enhanced policies without the need to employ reverse discrimination, but this is mere speculation. To accurately ascertain these benefits, further research, including empirical research, would have to be done. One factor influencing the rate of progress will be the policy itself. Different policies would contribute to different rates of redress. Among the other questions that need to be answered are these: (1) How many individuals currently performing merely satisfactorily will raise the quality of their work to the fairer, more demanding standard, assuming all policies will offer employees this opportunity? (2) How many of those positions lost through a failure to meet the new standards will be refilled? Although a skeptic may have doubts about the extent of the contribution that any policy will make to remedying the underrepresentation problem, it is worth emphasizing that the argument presented here is importantly independent of these affirmative action concerns. The case for raising performance standards is a matter of justice between contemporaneous birth cohorts.

15.10 Review

We began by considering the cases for affirmative action policies employing reverse discrimination from the perspective of backward-looking defences appealing to norms of corrective justice and forward-looking justifications appealing to norms of distributive justice. Although a number of points were made on behalf of each sort of defence, various criticisms have been advanced too. The most persistent objection is that such policies are unfair because they needlessly employ reverse discrimination to achieve their goals. In response to this familiar and much discussed objection, we considered an argument for a policy of early mandatory retirement designed to alleviate the need for reverse discriminatory measures. Although the argument for the policy is subject to several objections and is limited in its scope, there are also a number of points to be made on its behalf. It also seems that it is worthy of further study and consideration.

Notes

1. Fishkin and Laslett (1992) p. 8. A copy of the act is online at **laws.justice.gc.ca/en/E-5.401/index.html**

2. Participants in the debate also deplore discrimination against individuals for other morally irrelevant reasons, but for ease of exposition, we will restrict our discussion to these features of persons.

3. For an example of this approach, see Reynolds (1986), pp. 372–375.

4. This account of a special recruitment measure is a variation of one described by L.W. Sumner. See Sumner (1987b), p. 208.

5. Ezorsky makes her point specifically with reference to "blacks and whites," but the point applies here too. See Ezorsky (1991), pp. 14–18.

6. For discussion of this, see Warren (1977), Purdy (1984) and (1994), and Sumner (1987b).

7. Judith Jarvis Thomson, for example, defends an argument like this. See Thomson (1973). Although there are various versions of this kind of argument, we need not consider them separately. For two examples, see Sher (1975), pp.160–161.

8. See O'Neill (1987).

9. For an interesting examination of this idea, see Friedman and May (1985).

10. See Boxill (1978), Part II. See also Thomas Nagel's discussion of the "free esteem" white men gain at the expense of the victims of sexual and racial discrimination (Nagel [1973], pp. 360–361).

11. English (1994), pp. 128–129.

12. Nagel briefly alludes to the idea of this type of justification. See Nagel (1973), pp. 362, note 12. For the clearest account and strongest defence of this strategy, see Sumner (1987b).

13. For more on this point, see Nagel (1973), p. 360; Thomson (1973), pp. 367–368; and Sumner (1987b), p. 214.

14. Pamela Courtenay Hall makes both of these points in Courtenay Hall (1993), pp. 29–30.

15. For more on this, see Nagel (1973), pp. 360–361 and Sumner (1987b), pp. 215–216. Sumner argues that the evil of traditional discrimination, and the qualitative difference in the effects of the two kinds of discrimination, helps explain why men may not have a moral right

enjoyed by women—the moral right not to be discriminated against on the basis of one's sex. See Sumner (1987b), Section 3.

16. Referring to a quota policy that employs reverse discrimination, Sumner writes:

    Since the alternative to a quota system appears to be the indefinite survival of traditional discrimination, there is, at least in the short run, no way to avoid imposing costs on some victims. (Sumner [1987b], p. 215.)

17. Williams (1962), pp. 124–125.

18. For a brief discussion of these reasons, see Sher (1987), pp. 192–193.

19. The view that the principle of equal opportunity, at least as it is popularly understood, is compatible with a worthy ideal of equality and is a principle of social justice has been vigorously criticized. For instance, critics claim that the principle offers everyone only an equal opportunity to compete for some good, not to win it. Thus it underplays the importance of one's natural talents and upbringing. By underplaying these factors, it encourages individuals to aim for unrealistic levels of success. It is also inegalitarian in spirit because its employment fosters a widening of the gap between those with abundant natural talents and those with few natural talents. Furthermore, since it encourages competitive attitudes, and since it encourages us to regard each other as mere locations of abilities, the principle undermines our sense of common humanity and discourages us from according each other the respect we are owed as persons. Moreover, because it offers us only an opportunity to find a place within the system as it is now, an acceptance of the principle presupposes a prior acceptance of the present flawed social order. Thus, according to this criticism, the principle mostly helps promote the status quo and effects only superficial change in the system.

    It is beyond our scope here to fully consider and respond to these objections. For discussions of these objections (and others), see Williams (1962), Plamenatz (1967), and Schaar (1967).

20. Sumner makes this point in response to the charge that since quota policies may sometimes encourage the hiring of a less qualified woman over a more qualified man, they promote inefficiency in the workplace. See Sumner (1987b), pp. 216–217.

21. Fishkin and Laslett (1992), pp. 8–10.

22. Moreover, "generation" is ambiguous in other ways we need not consider here. For an account of some other ambiguities, see Daniels (1988), p. 15.

23. Daniels (1988), p. 12.

24. Daniels (1988), p. 41.

25. Thanks to Tom Hurka for reminding me of this point.

26. See Sher (1992), pp. 54–57.

27. Sher (1992), p. 55.

28. Thanks to Larry Temkin for raising this objection, and thanks to Temkin and Arthur Ripstein for helpful discussion on this issue.

Exercises

Progress Check

1. Explain the distinction between the neutral and the traditional evaluative senses of the word "discrimination."

2. Explain the distinction between equal opportunity views and enhanced views.

3. How does a constant quota policy differ from an accelerated quota policy?

4. What is an enhanced quota policy?

5. What is restitution and how is it different from compensation?

6. Why is restitution that undoes or expunges past wrongs not generally available as a response to the harms of discrimination?

7. Outline the main reasons advanced by critics in opposition to regarding affirmative action programs as providing compensation to the victims of discrimination.

8. What is the main argument for justifying affirmative action programs employing reverse discriminatory measures from the perspective of distributive justice?

9. Why is discrimination inefficient?

10. Distinguish between the concept of a generation, an age group, and a birth cohort.

11. Why does Daniels think that treating people differently on the basis of their age is not necessarily discriminatory?

12. Why is treating people differently on the basis of their birth cohort membership discriminatory?

13. Outline the argument for adopting a policy of early mandatory retirement for redressing the harmful effects of discrimination.

Questions for Further Reflection

1. Some argue that whereas in the past there may have been some need for affirmative action policies, programs, and laws, nowadays we are much more vigilant in our opposition to discrimination. As a result, quota policies and laws like the *Employment Equity Act* are unnecessary. Critically evaluate this view.

2. Do you agree that past victims of discrimination are owed compensation for the harms they suffered? Why or why not? Explain and defend your view.

3. Critically evaluate the case for employing enhanced policies as a means of providing compensation to the victims of traditional discrimination.

4. Critically evaluate the case for employing enhanced policies as a means of advancing the cause of distributive justice.

5. Critically evaluate the case for a policy of mandatory early retirement on the grounds of promoting justice between contemporaneous birth cohorts.

Suggested Further Reading

The many works cited in the notes and referenced in the Bibliography provide a good entry into the literature on the ethics of affirmative action.

Weblinks

For an overview of the *Employment Equity Act* (1995), go to **laws.justice.gc.ca/en/E-5.401/ index.html**

The Treasury Board of Canada presents its report, Employment Equity in the Federal Public Service, 1999–2000, at **www.tbs-sct.gc.ca/report/ empequi/2000/ee-00-1_e.html**

The Public Service Commission of Canada's Employment Equity Positive Measures Program Web site is at **www.psc-cfp.gc.ca/eepmp- pmpee/index_e.htm**
This site contains a link to an informative report on the history of employment equity legislation and initiatives in Canada.

Group Work Activity:

Protection for Homosexuals?

The *Employment Equity Act* specifically protects women, Aboriginal peoples, persons with disabilities, and members of visible minorities. If the goal of the legislation is to address the harmful effects of discrimination in employment, does it go far enough? More to the point, should those discriminated against on the basis of their sexual orientation be protected? In arguing against the inclusion of gays and lesbians, among others, some have argued that sexual orientation, unlike being a woman or a visible minority, is relevant to work performance.

In your groups, consider this issue critically by answering the following questions:

1. In what professions and occupations, if any, do you think discrimination against a person on the grounds of her sexual orientation is relevant? Why? Defend your view.

2. (a) Is one's sexual orientation a relevant consideration in hiring for teaching positions? Should, for example, being a gay man or a lesbian count against someone applying for work as a teacher? If you think it does matter, explain and defend your view and then answer (b), (c), and (d).
(b) For how much, roughly, should sexual orientation count in hiring? Should gays and lesbians be disqualified from teaching? Why or why not?
(c) Would it be fair to select against a homosexual in the case where all other factors are roughly equal? Why or why not?
(d) Does the students' age matter? Why or why not?

If you think that sexual orientation is not relevant to being a teacher, defend your view and then move on to address (e) and (f).

(e) Does it matter if the gay man or lesbian is "openly" gay or lesbian? Why or why not (be sure to explain what you mean by "openly" in your answer)?
(f) Is being transsexual relevant?

16 Issues in Ethics and the Law: Law, Liberty, and Legal Moralism

Overview

Learning Outcomes

In this chapter we address a central question in ethics and the law: What is the rightful limit of the use of power by the state against the individual? In the course of considering some views on this topic, we examine the value of liberty and the contribution being free can make to living a good life. We also consider the question of the rightful use of law in enforcing morality.

Upon the successful completion of this chapter, you will be able to

1. outline Mill's Harm Principle and the main arguments for and against it concerning the question of the value of freedom;
2. explain and critically evaluate the debate over paternalism; and
3. explicate and assess Devlin's legal moralist position.

16.1 Introduction

As much as any other, our commitment to freedom collectively defines us. Although we regard ourselves as a caring society, we also regard ourselves as free, and we think this is as it should be. Our fundamental belief in the value of freedom is enshrined in the *Canadian Charter of Rights and Freedoms*, and we pay our respects each November 11 to those who fought and sacrificed to preserve our free way of life. Although part of the point of Remembrance Day is to reflect on what those who sacrificed their lives fought for, our deep-seated belief in the value of freedom is so strong that we rarely even question it. The notion that we could be better governed by giving up many of our liberties strikes most people as so absurd that it seems not to be an idea worthy of serious consideration.

Yet there is a serious point in questioning the value of freedom—not to discredit its importance, but to better appreciate it. It is easy to say that liberty is a good thing; it is more difficult to explain why, and it is even more difficult to identify the limits of the value of freedom. To some, the notion that freedom can be overvalued will seem preposterous, but we have noted several times in this book the dangers of exaggeration, and the lesson is no different in the case of freedom.

Arguably, to be an enlightened person in our society, we should be able to identify the liberties we need to thrive and explain both how such liberties contribute to our good and why they are necessary. Furthermore, an enlightened person should know when too much freedom is a bad thing, and why. When we consider the impact of freedom on our individual and collective welfare, it is no wonder that the subject of the value of freedom is one that attracts a study into ethics.

So, as with our approach to many of the other topics and issues we have considered, we begin our investigation into the value and the limits of the value of freedom with an open mind. Our aim is to gain greater insight into the argument for liberty and overcome the temptation to take our freedoms for granted. This in turn should help fill out our understanding of ethics, especially as it relates to various questions and topics in law, including the proper use of law to enforce morality. While this task may appear to be rather abstract and theoretical, our concern is practical, too. For example, gaining insight into the value of freedom will assist us in outlining what should be the proper limits of our *Charter* rights.

We first considered this project in the Introduction. As we noted there, whereas the *Charter* contains our fundamental rights and liberties, section 1 points to a method for determining the limits of our *Charter* rights. It states that "The *Canadian Charter of Rights and Freedoms* guarantees the rights and freedoms set out in it subject only to such reasonable limits prescribed by law as can be demonstrably justified in a free and democratic society."[1] So, according to the *Charter*, we have guaranteed rights and freedoms, but these are limited. The idea is that our collective interests in living in a free and democratic society can best be served by recognizing and placing limits on our basic legal rights. At first, this might seem odd. How can limiting freedom enhance freedom? How do we serve democracy by overriding our basic rights and liberties?

This puzzle dissolves, however, when we turn away from the temptation to exaggerate our claims to freedom and consider an actual case. Take, for instance, our right to freedom of action. We believe that we should be generally free to act as we please; but we also recognize that the government reserves the right to conscript men and women into the cause of defending Canada from external threats to our territorial integrity and our political sovereignty. This means we do not think that we are free to not defend our country in the cause of a just war, and here it is clear that limiting individual freedoms may be necessary for preserving our overall freedom and our democratic form of government. Indeed, upon reflection we can see that we do recognize limits to our basic rights and freedoms and that these are not absolute. For example, our basic right to freedom of expression does not cover the "right" to say whatever we please whenever we please. We do not think that we have a right to yell, "He's got a bomb!" in a crowded theatre just to see what will happen.

Given that, upon reflection, we can see our fundamental rights and freedoms are not absolute, how are we to identify their proper limits? More generally, to what extent is society justified in using the coercive power of law to compel us to act against our wishes? We will begin to address this question by turning to a well-known answer in a classic work on liberalism, John Stuart Mill's treatise *On Liberty* (1859).

16.2 Mill's Harm Principle

Mill's focus is our question, and in the first chapter of his work he outlines his response, the **Harm Principle.** Mill argues that individuals of mature age should be free to act as they wish, provided the exercising of their freedom does not harm others. Except for some exceptions, this is the rightful limit of the use of power by the state against the individual, according to Mill.

Mill asserts that, in the interests of society, individuals can rightfully be compelled to perform various acts including those that are necessary for society's defence and those that promote the basic institutions of justice. So, according to this view, our government could rightfully require us to bear our fair share of the defence of our country in the prosecution of a just war even if we don't want to. Similarly, according to this view, we have a responsibility to testify if called upon as a witness in court, and we have a responsibility to serve on a jury if we are needed. We can see the basic justification for these intrusions into our lives by considering the relationship between the individual and society that we discussed in Chapter 2. You may recall, there we noted that, as a result of agreeing to co-operate with others in our society, we enjoy benefits that are both substantial and that would otherwise not be available to us. In co-operating, we give up some of our freedoms, but in return for receiving the benefits of others' co-operation, they can expect that we will contribute to our joint co-operative efforts. In other words, these exceptions to the Harm Principle are justified as a simple matter of fairness: given that we benefit from our free society and the institutions of justice within it, it is only fair that we do our part to protect and promote the common good.[2]

Justification

Mill asserts that the Harm Principle is justified by appeal to general utility or the good of everyone weighted equally. As a Utilitarian, he supplies a welfarist defence of his view (see Chapter 4). He maintains that the state in which the laws satisfy the Harm Principle will be more likely to promote general utility or welfare than in a state that draws the limits of liberty rights in any other way, everything else being equal.

16.3 Sincland

According to Mill's account, freedom is valuable insofar as it promotes our overall well-being and by this measure, according to Mill, the Harm Principle provides us with the best balance between promoting the good of society on the one hand and respecting individual liberty on the other. This balance between respecting individual liberty and protecting the common good is precisely the sort of thing that the authors of the *Charter* sought to identify through the application of section 1. Section 1 says that our rights and freedoms can be overridden if doing so promotes the interests of a free and democratic society. Does Mill's Harm Principle provide us with the guide or test that we are seeking?

> The **Harm Principle**, according to John Stuart Mill, outlines the rightful limits of the use of power by the state against the individual. According to it, individuals of mature age should be free to act as they wish, provided the exercising of their freedom does not harm others.

To help test your intuitions and beliefs about this, consider the following thought experiment. Imagine that you live in Sincland, a country ruled by a benevolent dictator—me. Unlike most dictators who seek their own glory and who are driven by their desire for power, my goal as your ruler is to provide societal conditions that will enable you to live the best life possible. More broadly, my aim is to rule in order to best promote the overall good of all the citizens of Sincland. I am aware of Mill's Harm Principle, but I doubt his claim that life is better for individuals if they have the sort of robust set of freedoms that he recommends. Instead, I believe that individual welfare will be best promoted by severely limiting my subjects' liberty rights.

We know that people often make important decisions in their lives on the basis of insufficient or flawed information and on the basis of limited experience. Take, for example, the decision-making processes of many young adults as regards their future line of work. We all know people who make important educational and career decisions in the absence of careful research into potential jobs, or because of some perceived attraction of the work based on hearsay or media-driven perception. It is also common for people to regret such decisions later in life and for these decisions to subsequently cause them grief. So, although in Canada people are currently free to make these sorts of choices, it is doubtful whether having this freedom actually does lead to the best overall state of affairs.

Rather than leave you and others like you to make important career decisions, my officials will make these decisions for you. The officials' decisions will be based on the results of an exhaustive series of tests devised by my crack team of brilliant social scientists. Imagine that for the past several years these researchers have been working to develop and improve their exhaustive set of aptitude tests designed to determine the best field of work for an individual. The tests will reveal which line or lines of work in which individuals are both most likely to succeed and be happy. They are based on research drawing on the lives and experiences of literally thousands of people, and after years of development and fine-tuning, the researchers are confident of the predictive power of their tests.

Since it stands to reason that the testing process is more likely to predict what is best for you than you are, and given that our goal is to promote the good of everyone, people in Sincland are required to take these tests and live by their results. So, if you dearly wanted to go to law school, but the tests determine that you would be best off attending clown school, then you would be prevented from applying to law school and required to attend clown school instead. Alternatively you could go to jail. Given the research basis of the tests, why would anyone think that they would be better off making their own career decisions? Isn't our firm belief that life will likely go better for us if we make our own important choices just a dogmatic article of faith? Looking at it objectively, the notion that people who are free to make their own decisions will likely be better off than those streamed into the training, education, and work identified by the testing process seems like the wishful thinking of those raised on freedom propaganda.

Notice that the case for my method does not require that the tests be perfect predictors. Obviously, they are unlikely to be perfect and we can even imagine some people choosing better for themselves than the tests would. On the other hand, does it not seem likely that the scientists' tests will generally do a better job of selecting for

us than we would? Why would we think otherwise? We might assume that what we choose freely for ourselves must be better than what any tests can predict. However, it is false to say that whatever we choose for ourselves must also be good for us. We must discover what is good for us in life and we can—and often do—get it wrong. Certainly we are not infallible. In view of this, wouldn't the society where people are required to live by the results of these carefully developed tests minimize the sorts of terrible career-decision blunders that people in Canadian society so often make and later come to regret? Mill's argument for the Harm Principle rests on the debatable belief that we are best positioned to make our own important life choices. The method followed in Sincland challenges this.

We can imagine that once we have the career-decision testing process up and running, we could extend this process to other areas of personal life like, for example, decisions about personal relationships. The same reasoning applies. Just as with our work choices, we often make decisions about our friends and mates on the basis of flawed or insufficient information, and on the basis of limited experience. Yet these decisions greatly affect our overall well-being. Wouldn't we be better off having these sorts of decisions also determined by the exhaustive series of tests that we outlined in the case of the career decisions? Moreover, given the obvious potential of the tests to help us lead better lives, wouldn't people be clamouring to take them, especially when they come to appreciate their likely benefits? Perhaps what looks like a disconcerting aspect of the process—the threat of legal coercion hanging over those who do not voluntarily comply—is not so bad on reflection. Such legal sanctions should be needed only occasionally, because most people would willingly abide by the law, right?

Response: Freedom and the Conditions for Obtaining Self-respect

A critic might object that the main problem with requiring people to take these tests and have their future path determined by their results is that this method fails to appreciate the contribution that being a chooser makes to living a good life. Thus, we can distinguish between the instrumental value of our choices and the intrinsic value of being a chooser. In addition to the consequences of our choices, our welfare is also affected by our attitude toward ourselves, and this in turn is determined by our own self-esteem. By depriving people of the opportunity to make important life choices, we adversely affect their welfare by treating them as if they were incapable of being good choosers. The citizens of Sincland are treated like children, and the testing method is an insult to the dignity of those who must submit to it. In acting this way toward individuals, we rob them of an important source of self-esteem.

According to this analysis, freedom is valuable because it is necessary for obtaining self-respect, one of the most important goods in life. We can see this more clearly by considering what would happen to an individual's self-respect if she were completely deprived of freedom. If we are never free to make choices, we can never claim responsibility for what happens. However, just as we can take responsibility for our mistakes, we can also take credit for our successes and achievements. Moreover, freedom enables us to shape and choose our own identity-conferring commitments, and it is upon our successes and these commitments that our self-respect is based. Therefore, freedom is valuable because the opportunity to make free choices is necessary for developing self-respect. Since self-respect is one of the most important contributors to a prudentially good life, and since freedom is necessary for self-respect, freedom is prudentially valuable.[3] That is not to say all those who have freedom will have self-respect. Rather, the point is that freedom is needed as a pre-condition for obtaining self-respect.[4]

Thus, it seems the value of freedom cannot be cashed out merely in terms of the direct consequences of one's free choices. Mill seems to recognize this when he remarks that "Mankind are greater gainers by suffering each other to live as seems good to themselves, than by compelling each to live as seems good to the rest."[5] Mill appears to concede that, although we might have to suffer each other's choices because the consequences of the choices might not always be for the best, there is also an important source of value in determining one's own course in life. The flaw with the idea of Sincland is that it overlooks this important dimension of the value of freedom. When we factor this into the equation, the case for respecting people's choices, even granting that they sometimes will make mistakes, is decisive.

Counterresponse

A defender of the Sincland approach could agree that there is indeed value in respecting people's capacity for making autonomous choices but still maintain that this does not necessarily lead us to Mill's Harm Principle. The problem with allowing individuals as much scope to choose as Mill does is that he overestimates this value. The challenge, thus, becomes one of determining the best balance between respecting individual decision-making and ensuring that the best choices are made. It may be true that in completely depriving people of the power to make important life choices, we would sometimes go too far. However, it also seems likely that sometimes the disvalue of the choices that people actually make in life will cancel out the intrinsic value they derive from making their own choices. In other words, Sincland may offer better prospects for happiness for some than our own society does.

Minimally, the question whether we would be "greater gainers by suffering each other to live as seems good to [our]selves, than by compelling each to live as seems good to the rest" is empirical. There is no reason for presupposing that the best course must always be the one that decides in favour of allowing the greater scope to individual liberty.

Someone might insist that since we are talking about our rights to make important life choices, the curtailment of freedom would always be ultimately bad for individuals. But we must remember that we are trying to determine what the best degree of freedom would be. Even under Mill's Harm Principle, we are not completely free. It is absurd to think that individual self-esteem is crippled by society preventing us from doing whatever we want whenever we want. The method recommended in Sincland would merely curtail freedom more than would occur in a place ruled by the Harm Principle. We need some reason for thinking that this would be bad.

It seems the best strategy for a proponent of the method used in Sincland is to minimize intrusions into individual freedom while maintaining as much as possible the promised benefits of acting on the test results. How might we shape law and policy to both respect individual autonomy and minimize the occurrence of avoidable, important, life-decision blunders? Here, a defender of Sincland might respond by restricting the use of the testing process to important career decisions relatively early in adulthood and allowing as much freedom as possible to individuals otherwise consistent with Mill's Harm Principle. Alternatively, the test results could be limited so as to give individuals some range of career options. Such a process would therefore not be so draconian and would thereby not pose such a threat to individual self-esteem.

Modifying the policy in this way would also enable us to reply to another criticism. Critics of the Sincland approach to freedom argue that one of its principal failings is that it would be counterproductive, because it would severely restrict our abilities to become good decision-makers. If the aim is to help people become happy, productive contributors to society, then limiting their opportunities for developing their decision-making skills will be self-defeating. We learn from our mistakes and we can become good choosers only by making some mistakes. Given that having good decision-making abilities is important in living a good life for most people, the original conception of the testing method and policy would be severely flawed. On the revised conception, however, there would still be plenty of opportunities for people to make their own choices and to learn from their mistakes. The aim, thus, is not to eliminate all bad choices, but to restrict freedom to minimize major life-decision blunders.

Notice that this revised use of the testing method would still limit freedom much more than laws and policies based on the Harm Principle. The argument, however, is that this restriction on liberty would more likely promote both the good of individuals and the good of society as a whole. How might a defender of the Harm Principle respond?

16.4 Paternalism

Sincland's testing method requires people to adhere to the results of the tests for their own sake. Because it restricts individual freedom in this way, the policy is paternalistic. In contrast, Mill's Harm Principle explicitly forbids paternalistic interventions into an adult's life. By appreciating Mill's rationale for this, we can perhaps see why he presented his Harm Principle as a response to the question about the rightful limit of the use of power by the state against the individual. This in turn might enable us to marshal a stronger argument against the approach to freedom taken in Sincland.

In a widely read essay on Mill and **paternalism,** Gerald Dworkin explains.

> … by paternalism I shall understand roughly the interference with a person's liberty of action justified by reasons referring exclusively to the welfare, good, happiness, needs, interests or values of the person being coerced.[6]

In Mill, Dworkin detects opposition to paternalism both on grounds of general utility and for the sort of reason we just noted—that paternalistic interventions in an adult's life are an affront to his status as a being with dignity deserving of respect. We have already considered this latter argument, but what are we to make of the former one? Why does Mill think paternalistic laws are likely to lead to overall worse levels of well-being among the citizens of a state than laws that respect individual freedom that are not paternalistic? The argument for Sincland is that, sometimes at least, the gains in welfare to individuals by being treated paternalistically should

Paternalism is "the interference with a person's liberty of action justified by reasons referring exclusively to the welfare, good, happiness, needs, interests or values of the person being coerced."[7]

cancel out the disvalue of having their freedom restricted. What can Mill say in response?

An underlying assumption of the aptitude tests in Sincland is that the most suitable career or job for a particular individual can be predicted on the basis of how others with similar qualities have fared in various lines of work. This assumes, furthermore, that we are similar, or at least similar enough that we can make these sorts of generalizations across individuals. The same sort of idea lies behind the justification for all paternalistic laws. But is this idea reasonable? To test your intuitions and beliefs about this notion, we can consider an example of a paternalistic law. For example, it is illegal in Canada to play Russian roulette. (Russian roulette is a game in which a player fills one or more chambers of a gun with bullets, spins the chamber, and then points the gun at his own head and pulls the trigger.)

As Dworkin notes, it is difficult to identify purely paternalistic laws because there are often a number of justifications for a law. Nonetheless, it seems that at least part of the justification for the laws that prohibit Russian roulette is paternalistic. How could someone possibly benefit from playing this "game"? It seems that we do misguided people a service by preventing them from indulging in this apparently irrational activity. In making this sort of judgment, however, we are making a judgment about the rationality of a person's ends, and in doing this we need to proceed carefully. While judging the rationality of the means people employ to meet their ends is a fairly straightforward matter, judging the rationality of ends is not so simple. If your goal is to become Canada's foremost expert in tax law and your means consists of watching television 16 hours a day, seven days a week, then obviously you are acting irrationally. The means that you are using to achieve your goal are clearly inadequate. But on what basis do we similarly make judgments about the rationality of the ends people strive for in life?

The Russian Roulette Example

It seems the judgment that the end or activity of playing Russian roulette is irrational is due to its extremely dangerous nature. How could some-one rationally justify engaging in this activity, let alone claim that he suffers a loss by being prevented by law from partaking in it? We could argue that those who have dependants could not justify engaging in this activity, because to do so would be to act recklessly and run an unnecessary risk that places the dependants' welfare in jeopardy. Likewise, we could argue that those not mature enough or otherwise incapable of fully appreciating the risks of playing should be forbidden from doing so for their own sake. Although he opposes paternalistic interventions in the lives of mature adults, Mill accepts limitations on people's freedom in situations like these.

Imagine, then, that a group of mature, single, and likeminded dependant-less people form a club of Russian roulette players. They meet clandestinely to indulge in their passion once every three months or so. In response to the charge that they have a death wish, they argue instead that they play not in order to kill themselves, but rather to enhance their appreciation of life. Whereas the rest of us merely sleepwalk through life, they say, they savour each moment. Their goal is not necessarily to live as long as possible, but to live a life of the highest quality possible. For them, this means engaging in a risky pursuit that the majority of people in our society judge to be crazy.

In making their case, the players point out that they are not demanding the law be changed such that everyone be required to play. They recognize that this would not be good for everyone. Most people do not have the same attitude toward risk that they do. They are risk-takers, whereas the rest of us are risk averse by comparison. If they are not demanding that we play the game because they recognize that it would not be good for us, why, they wonder, do we think that we are justified in imposing our preferences and attitudes on them? They insist that they are not like us, that they are individuals who happen to share an unusual passion for Russian roulette. We do them wrong, they assert, by denying them the freedom to legally participate in an activity that adds value to their lives. However well-intentioned we are, we harm them by imposing our will upon them. And we all know where the road paved with good intention leads.

Not only are we doing them wrong by paternalistically prohibiting Russian roulette, but they further argue that our behaviour is hypocritical. Russian roulette is indeed a very risky activity, but many other risky activities are perfectly legal. Why the discrepancy? By what standard can we say that skydiving, race-car driving, and mountaineering are acceptable, but Russian roulette is not? The difference between these dangerous but legal activities and Russian roulette is simply a matter of the number of chambers in the gun. Who are we, they wonder, to decide what is an acceptable risk for others? Moreover, risk in life is unavoidable. To enjoy any quality of life, we must take risks. People die in their cars, their bathtubs, and while making love, but we don't ban driving, bathing, or sex. So why, they ask, do we think we are justified in paternalistically banning Russian roulette?

Whether we are convinced or not by this argument for the rationality of some people playing Russian roulette, the notion that it must always be irrational to play seems questionable. A decent case can be made for the view that, for some people, this sort of activity can be a good thing. If the purpose of the prohibition is to prevent people from harming themselves, then it seems that we might need to rethink the ban. Although he does not specifically mention this example, Mill notes that when people forbid others from engaging in some activity for their own good, it is often the case that they are really imposing their own values on others. Since we are individuals, and not all alike, this practice is questionable. Mill's case for his Harm Principle rests in part on the truth that we are different.

16.5 Consent and Competency

Despite this point about individuality, Mill's critics have argued that the issues surrounding paternalistic laws are not so simple. For example, H.L.A. Hart, although generally sympathetic to Mill, argues that before we accept Mill's argument against paternalistic law, we need to examine more carefully the conditions necessary for

individuals to make autonomous, mature, and informed decisions. Hart ventures that perhaps Mill was too generous in his attribution of these qualities to the typical adult, endowing him "with too much of the psychology of a middle-aged man." In support of his point, Hart argues we now recognize, in a way that Mill apparently did not, that there are many ways in which an adult's choices can fail to be free and informed. He explains that

> Choices may be made or consent given without adequate reflection or appreciation of the consequences; or in pursuit of merely transitory desires; or in various predicaments when the judgment is likely to be clouded; or under inner psychological compulsion; or under pressure by others of a kind too subtle to be susceptible of proof in a law court.[8]

In addition to the difficult question of how to determine that a person's choices are free and informed, we also face the challenge of ensuring that they are competent to make them in the first place. Mill's argument presupposes that the person who should be free to choose for herself be competent to make such choices. However, the task of determining this competency is not so straightforward.

In our day, the area in which the debate over consent and competency has mostly centred is Bioethics. Philosophers and health care professionals have investigated the question of the conditions necessary for determining whether someone is competent to give either their free and informed consent to or refusal of some treatment. James Drane argues that a good competency test should achieve a balance between protecting patients' welfare and respecting their autonomy. It should avoid two kinds of error:

1. preventing competent patients from deciding their own fate; and

2. failing to protect incompetent persons from the harmful effects of a bad decision.[9]

In the case of determining competency, the question thus arises whether anyone can be competent to refuse life-saving treatment where most people, including the person's physician, strongly recommend otherwise. If we simply assume that our choices reveal competency only if they are consistent with what most people would choose, or with what our physician would choose, then we overlook Mill's basic point about our individuality. Given our differences, it seems false that it is always in everyone's interests to accept the same health care treatment or course of treatment. This seems true especially when one considers that there are often a number of ways in which illnesses and diseases can be treated. So if we cannot simply rely on judging competency on the basis of the popularity of the decision made, then how are we to proceed? Although we cannot pursue this question here, supporters of Mill's Harm Principle will need to take steps to ensure that incompetent people are still protected.[10]

16.6 Appreciating the Value of Freedom

In our enquiry into the value of freedom, we have noted the connection between self-respect and liberty, and we have seen how Mill's point that we are individuals argues against the rationale for paternalistic interventions into the lives of mature adults. This point also calls into question the rationale underlying the research that leads to the aptitude testing in Sincland. That research proceeds on the assumption that we can predict which line of work likely is best for someone on the basis of inferring from what is good for others to what is good for an individual. But if we are all individuals, this sort of generalization seems questionable.

In support of his Harm Principle, Mill argues that, since we are individuals, we need to discover for ourselves what is best for us. It is dangerous to base our own choices in life on what is good for others or on what others believe is in our best interests. However well-intentioned they may be, if we do as others would choose for us, we run the risk of never discovering the sources of value that will make us happy. Furthermore, since we are likely to know our own preferences, character, and values better than others, we should decide for ourselves how

best to live our lives. This includes making decisions about our education, choice of work or career, and who will be our friends. In order to do this we need to be free. A legal system resting on Mill's Harm Principle will offer us this freedom.

Mill also maintains that extending this degree of freedom to individuals will promote general utility in other ways. Social progress will likely be better advanced by individuals pursuing their own good in their own way than if we place restrictions on people's pursuits based on what some think is best. How many advances in science have been made by those challenging orthodox views and methods to test their own theories? The same holds true in art and all other fields of human endeavour. If Michaelangelo had listened to his father, he would have gone into banking.

16.7 Legal Moralism, Devlin, and Sue Rodriguez

In considering Mill's response to our question of the rightful use of power by the state against the individual, we have briefly examined the question of the value of freedom. We have also challenged the paternalistic view that laws designed to protect individuals from their own supposed poor choices, assuming both competency and informed consent, seem to deny our individuality. According to this argument, paternalistic laws mistake an individual's true interests for what someone else thinks would be best for her. Although Mill's position seems to have some merit, there is another argument against legalizing activities like Russian roulette. Furthermore, since this argument presents us with an alternative answer to our question, we would do well to consider it.

Legal Moralism is the view that acts may be legally prohibited because they are immoral. According to the Legal Moralist, part of the proper function of law is to legislate against immorality. From this perspective, we can understand Mill's view as occupying one

> **Legal Moralism** is the view that acts may be legally prohibited because they are immoral.

spot on a continuum of possible legal moralist positions. If we identify immorality with the unjustified causing of harm, as perhaps some Welfarists might be inclined to do, then we can view Mill's Harm Principle as embodying a liberal outlook within Legal Moralism. Mill's view is liberal because it allows a rather wider scope for freedom than many other legal moralist approaches. To help round out our examination of our question, it will be useful to contrast Mill's approach to a more conservative and traditional one.

Lord Patrick Devlin was for many years a judge in Great Britain before his appointment as a Lord of Appeal. He famously took up the debate over Legal Moralism in his book *The Enforcement of Morality* (1965). Arguing against Mill's Harm Principle, Devlin held that society is justified in using the coercive power of law to preserve morality in addition to protecting individual life and property. Devlin uses a distinction between individual harm and public harm, or "offenses against society,"[11] and he argues for greater restrictions on individual liberty than does Mill. Devlin believes that the criminal law should be used to protect society against the public harms caused by sin or immorality. Furthermore, he believes that the Harm Principle is ineffective at protecting society against these offences to society because they cannot directly be identified in terms of harms to individuals. The problem with relying on a principle like Mill's is that there are cases where individuals act in ways that may not directly harm other individuals, but where their actions remain harmful to a society's collective interests. In support of this problem, Devlin cites the example of someone consenting to his own killing.

Sue Rodriguez and the Debate over the Illegality of Assisted Suicide

Sue Rodriguez suffered from amyotrophic lateral sclerosis (ALS), also known as Lou Gehrig's disease, a rapidly progressive neuromuscular disorder that is usually fatal. Wishing to end her life but physically unable to do so, Ms Rodriguez sought the help of her physician. However, physician-assisted suicide is illegal in Canada. According to section 241 of the *Criminal Code*

> Every one who (a) counsels a person to commit suicide, or (b) aids or abets a person to commit suicide, whether suicide ensues or not, is guilty of an indictable offense and liable to imprisonment for a term not exceeding fourteen years.

Rodriguez challenged the constitutionality of this law, arguing that it violated her *Charter* rights to privacy and freedom. In a 5–4 decision, the Supreme Court ruled against her, claiming that society has an interest in preserving the moral principle of respect for the sanctity of life, and judging that this interest outweighed the value of Rodriguez's autonomy rights.

Devlin on Moral Offences

Rodriguez's case illustrates Devlin's point. Assisted suicide may occur in private and may be conducted by someone who has no intention of ever participating in such an act again. Therefore, it may not directly harm anyone, including the person killed, now or in the future. The suicide can also explicitly demonstrate competency in requesting help, as Rodriguez arguably did. Given its self-directed focus, it seems that at least some acts of suicide and assisted suicide cannot justifiably be prohibited by laws based on Mill's Harm Principle. Yet Devlin argues that due to their immorality, the criminal law can rightly prohibit them. He adduces exactly the same sort of support that the Supreme Court adduced in their decision—the goal of promoting the sanctity of human life can outweigh an individual's right to freedom.

Devlin argues more generally that a class of actions like these threatens common decency and public standards of morality. As such, and despite the intrusion into individual liberty, we are justified in using the coercive power of law to prohibit such actions. Among these offences, besides suicide and assisted suicide, Devlin includes suicide pacts, euthanasia, duelling, abortion, incest, fornication, adultery, prostitution, sodomy, and cruelty toward animals. Devlin's argument is that Mill's Harm Principle may not prohibit these kinds of acts, but society can justifiably proscribe them nonetheless.

Devlin's Argument

Devlin's main argument in support of his legal moralist position unfolds in a few stages. He presents what he dubs an *a priori* argument for the view that there is such a thing as public morality. For Devlin, a society is defined by the political and moral ideas of its members. These ideas unify the society, and he reasons that just as the members of a family must live together under one set of rules, the citizens of a state must similarly live by the political and moral tenets that define their collective life together. Understood in this way, Devlin argues that just as a society's political framework is subject to attack from treason, its morality is subject to attack from public offences. Furthermore, he concludes the analogy by asserting that just as a society is justified in defending itself against treason, it is likewise justified in defending itself against immorality. He adds that

> An established morality is as necessary as good government to the welfare of society... The suppression of vice is as much the law's business as the suppression of subversive activities; it is no more possible to define a sphere of private morality than it is to define one of private subversive activity.[12]

16.8 Critical Response to Devlin's Legal Moralist View

Clearly Devlin believes that the state is justified in limiting the liberties of its citizens beyond the point for which Mill argues. A defender of Mill might respond by making a number of counter-arguments.

1. Devlin's endorsement of the moral status quo is both poorly defended and suspect.

A critic might wonder about Devlin's assumption that the accepted public morality is one that an enlightened person should accept. Certainly our common beliefs about morality are generally justified, but the many points at which there is doubt and controversy are typically points at which Devlin thinks the common view is right. It is precisely at these points, however, that we need to be reassured we already have it right. In addressing this issue, Devlin's definition of immorality is unhelpful. He claims that "Immorality then, for the purpose of the law, is what every right-minded person is presumed to consider immoral."[13] The problem with this definition is that it is circular. Presumably right-minded people will hold justified beliefs about ethics, but what makes a person right-minded? Moreover, why should we think that on controversial matters the status quo is correct?

On these questions, our critic might note, Devlin offers us little assistance. He declares that the right-minded man is the man who would react with intolerance, disgust, and indignation to an immoral act or practice. But toward what should we react with intolerance, indignation, and disgust? Although he does not state that all people are right-minded, he does assume that his society's morality is representative of what is right-minded. But what guarantee is there that what most people in his society would react to with disgust and indignation is not sometimes merely a product of ignorance and prejudice? People of Devlin's generation would have been ashamed of being divorced. Many people not so long before Devlin's time did not think twice about the morality of slavery. To repeat: Why should we think that on controversial questions the status quo is the right view?

Our critic might note that the example Devlin cites to illustrate his point about the right-minded man reacting properly with disgust to immorality is unhelpful. He takes the example of deliberate cruelty toward animals as a clear case of an offence to society rightly regarded with disgust by the right-minded man. This is also an example where Devlin thinks most people are right-minded. In response, however, the critic might argue that, whereas the deliberate infliction of cruelty upon non-human animals is immoral, it does not obviously count as an example of a public offence as Devlin supposes. A Welfarist, for example, would argue that since non-human sentient beings have a good of their own, they are logically among the class of those beings that can suffer harms. To suppose otherwise, as Devlin does, requires support and not just confident assertion. Indeed, our critic might add, we can view Devlin's appeal to what the "right-minded man" thinks here as being ironic. Rather than illustrate Devlin's point about the rightness of the "right-minded man," his appeal to this example arguably illustrates common ignorance and prejudice. For, our critic might contend, the fact that most people think that sentient non-human animals cannot suffer individual harms because they do not have a good of their own shows up the ignorance of the common view.

Our critic might conclude that in the absence of a persuasive defense for the status quo, Devlin's account is weak and should not be accepted over Mill's view. Furthermore, a more determined critic might challenge the view that the status quo in our time is the same as it was in Devlin's. Fornication is legal and common in Canada. Likewise, abortion and sodomy are legal and far more accepted now than they were then. This change in attitude undermines Devlin's assumption that these practices are immoral, and it undermines his belief that what his society regarded as wrong was wrong. Similarly, we should be cautious in unquestioningly accepting the status quo view of what is immoral and what is not. Rather than simply rely on the judgment of "decent society," we should apply Mill's Harm Principle for ourselves. According to this criticism, then, an unquestioning dependence on the status quo poses a threat to a society's genuine moral progress.

2. Devlin's account of a separate class of public harms is undefended and dubious.

A critic might also challenge Devlin's Legal Moralism on the basis that it rests upon a false and meaningless distinction without a difference. Devlin believes that over and above protecting individuals from threats posed to their lives and property, society is justified in using the law to legislate against public offence. This is supposed to warrant greater restrictions on individual liberty than is countenanced by Mill,

but the case for this rests on Devlin's claim that there are such public harms that do not reduce directly to harms to individuals. A critic might challenge this too and insist that there are three possibilities here, none of them friendly to Devlin's case:

1. Acts and practices are either harmful to individuals or they are not. If they are harmful to individuals other than the agent, they would be prohibited by the Harm Principle.

2. There are also those acts that are regarded as harmful to the agent, but that fall into the category of paternalistic interventions just discussed in Section 16.4.

3. Finally, there are those acts and practices merely regarded without justification to be dangerous or pernicious to society.

Our critic would claim that the example of acts of deliberate cruelty to animals fall into category (1). Likewise, insofar as the other morals offences are harmful, they too would fall into this category. Our critic would therefore place the burden onto Devlin to establish the public offence of the other kinds of acts he identifies, and to clearly distinguish this harm from direct harm to individuals. The challenge for Devlin is to show that once we subtract the direct harm to individuals of the acts that he thinks should be prohibited, that there is something left over that would justify the prohibition of the acts not recognized by Mill's Harm Principle.

Take, for instance, acts involving sex that are regarded by Devlin as injurious to society. One of Devlin's most controversial claims is that since even acts done in private can be publicly harmful, society is justified in legally banning them. In response, a defender of Mill would argue that Devlin's view that acts of fornication, adultery, and sodomy are publicly dangerous is unsupported. Insofar as they are harmful to others, they would be prohibited by the Harm Principle, but the idea that there is something over and above this that makes them injurious and justifies the prohibition is, our critic might claim, very doubtful. Although many people might be offended by the idea of someone engaging in an act of sodomy or fornication, the notion that their feelings of disgust and revulsion should cancel out the good to those engaging in the supposed disgusting practice needs to be more carefully defended.

The problem here is not with showing that some find some practices engaged in by others disgusting. That is obvious enough. Rather, the challenge is to determine *when* feelings of disgust justify overriding the wishes of those engaging in the supposedly disgusting conduct. Even if a majority of people regard a practice like sodomy as disgusting, it is a further question whether society is justified in legally banning sodomy. For we can make sense of the idea of feelings of disgust being appropriate and justified or not. If a majority of people on a public bus find the sight of a man wearing a turban to be disgusting, would their feelings of disgust justify their demand that the man remove the turban? Alternatively, if a group of racists find the sight of two people of different races holding hands disgusting and harmful to their children, would that justify a law banning such acts? Our critic would insist that in such cases, the fault lies with those who are intolerant, and what is required is not a law overturning our *Charter* rights to freedom of conscience and religious belief and freedom of association, but education to overcome ignorance and blind prejudice.

Defenders of Mill's Harm Principle must accept that their commitment to this account of the rightful limit of the use of power by the state against the individual commits them to tolerating acts and practices that they themselves would not engage in and that they may even find to be disgusting. However disquieting it may be to have to tolerate such acts, liberals believe that the alternative proposed by thinkers like Devlin is worse. On their view, such a society would unduly restrict personal freedom, and this repression would ultimately be worse for us than the costs of tolerance.

16.9 Conclusion

This brief discussion of the legal moralist positions advocated by Mill and Devlin presents a brief account of the issues involved in determin-

ing the rightful limit of the use of power by the state against the individual, but it is far from exhaustive. You are invited to further carry on the discussion and to read critically the claims set forth above. For example, in counterresponse to Mill, many feel Devlin is right to note that society is held together by collective values and that we are justified in protecting ourselves against threats to these values. Furthermore, many feel that the Harm Principle would not adequately do this. Can you develop Devlin's line of reasoning to further question Mill's support of the Harm Principle?

16.10 Review

In this chapter we considered some questions in ethics and the law. Specifically, we examined the value of freedom and the problem of determining what the rightful limits of the use of power by the state against the individual should be. After presenting J.S. Mill's Harm Principle, we considered the case for it by questioning Mill's assertion that a society governed by the principle would likely be best off. To this end, we examined the case for Sincland, a hypothetical place where people's major decisions are made for them by tests devised by social scientists. Sincland's proponents claim that people would be better off having fewer liberties because science is likelier to make better choices for us than we are, given our limited knowledge and experience.

In response, we considered the argument that there is value in choosing for oneself and that having freedom is a necessary condition for developing self-respect, one of the great goods in life. This point forced us to revise the extent of the interference in people's lives made in Sincland, but it did not conclusively show that people would likely be better off having the wide range of freedoms recommended by the Harm Principle.

To further consider Mill's case, we then examined the debate over paternalism. We noted that Mill's opposition to paternalistic law is grounded on his strong conviction in human individuality. With the help of the Russian roulette example, we noted how an activity that many would regard as irrational may not be irrational to others. This led us to think twice about imposing our values upon others through the coercive power of law.

After considering further questions surrounding the Harm Principle involving puzzles about informed consent, competency, and the nature of a harm, in the final part of the chapter we moved on to contrast Mill's case with the legal moralist position defended by Patrick Devlin. Devlin argues for a greater limitation on liberties than that recommended by Mill, on the grounds that society is justified in protecting itself from immorality that is not reducible to direct harms to individuals. Specifically, Devlin argues that in addition to individual harms there are also public harms caused by a range of activities. Since a society is defined by its common values, we have a right to protect those values even if the threat to them comes from acts carried out by consenting individuals in the privacy of their own homes. We examined two responding objections: (1) that Devlin's defence of the moral status quo is weak, and (2) that his distinction between public and private harms is unsupported.

Notes

1. The *Canadian Charter of Rights and Freedoms*, *Constitution Act*, 1982, Part 1, Section 1.

2. Mill also notes that we have general duties of beneficence, and we can reasonably require that individuals aid others in need when doing so is not overly demanding. This idea seems to accord with our intuitions. For example, we think that although we do not have a duty to rush into a burning building to assist those trapped inside, we do have an obligation to call for qualified emergency help. Recently, however, some have noted puzzles that can arise out of taking Mill's claim about our duty to aid others seriously. See, for example, Fishkin (1982).

3. The notion that self-respect is an important contributor to a prudentially good life seems obviously true. We might go even further and suggest that whatever other goods we enjoy—health, material comfort, education, meaningful work—if we lack self-respect, our lives will not be prudentially good. The negative attitude we may have toward ourselves as a result of a lack of self-respect or as a result of having only very low self-esteem will arguably poison our enjoyment and appreciation of all the other goods and opportunities we have in life.

4. Some will object that this way of putting it overstates the value of freedom for obtaining self-respect. For could not a slave take pride in his labour? In response, we might think of the present point as based on an extreme deprivation of freedom, such that an unfree person is not free to do anything.

5. Mill (1984), p. 81.

6. G. Dworkin (1971), p. 107.

7. G. Dworkin (1971), p. 107.

8. Hart (1963).

9. Drane (1985).

10. Critics also note that we need a clearer understanding of what a harm is. Although there are obvious cases of harm, there is also a grey area where determining whether something is harmful or not is not so clear.

11. Devlin (1965), p. 6.

12. Devlin (1965), pp. 13–14.

13. Devlin (1965), p. 15.

14. Feinberg (1985), p. 1.

15. Feinberg (1985), pp. 10–13.

Exercises

Progress Check

1. What does section 1 of the *Canadian Charter of Rights and Freedoms* state? What is its purpose?

2. What is J.S. Mill's Harm Principle?

3. What are the exceptions to the principle and the rationale for them?

4. What kind of justification does Mill cite in support of his principle?

5. What is the purpose of the Sincland example?

6. What limits are placed on freedom in Sincland? Why?

7. Outline the response to the example that appeals to the value of self-respect and the conditions necessary for obtaining self-respect.

8. What modification to the Sincland policy does this lead to?

9. What is paternalism?

10. Explain the Russian roulette example. What is the connection between the point of the example and the argument against the approach to freedom in Sincland?

11. What other reasons does Mill advance in support of his Harm Principle?

12. What is Legal Moralism?

13. What point of Devlin's is illustrated by the case of Sue Rodriguez?

14. What are the typical morals offences?

15. Outline Devlin's argument in support of his position and the criticisms of it.

Questions for Further Reflection

1. Explain and critically evaluate J.S. Mill's view of the rightful limit of the use of power by the state against the individual.

2. The Sincland example raises the idea that our good may be better promoted by limiting freedom in ways we currently do not. As we noted, Mill's argument rests in part on his belief about our individuality. How much force does Mill's point have in undermining the case for the limits on freedom recommended in Sincland? Defend your view.

3. Explain and critically assess the view that some very dangerous activities like Russian roulette can be rational for some people.

4. Mill argues that the Harm Principle should apply only to competent individuals. What problems do you see with determining a person's competency? How would you try to resolve these problems?

5. Explain and critically evaluate Patrick Devlin's argument for Legal Moralism.

6. Do you think the Supreme Court was right to uphold respect for the sanctity of human life at the expense of Sue Rodriguez's *Charter* rights to privacy and autonomy? Why or why not? Defend your view.

7. What is justified disgust? How is a case of justified disgust unlike the case of the disgusted racists? Explain.

8. What approach do you think we could take to develop a method for distinguishing between cases of justified and unjustified disgust and indignation?

Weblinks

The Internet Encyclopedia of Philosophy (hosted by the University of Tennessee at Martin) entry on Mill is at **www.utm.edu/research/iep/m/milljs.htm**

Group Work Activity:

Feinberg's Offense Principle and an Unusual Bus Ride

According to Joel Feinberg, Mill's Harm Principle is not comprehensive because it does not apply to those acts that may not be harmful but are offensive. He holds that society is justified in using the coercive power of law to limit an individual's freedom to offend others. He expresses this in his "Offense Principle" according to which

> It is always a good reason in support of a proposed criminal prohibition that it would probably be an effective way of preventing serious offense (as opposed to injury or harm) to persons other than the actor, and that it is probably a necessary means to that end.[14]

Feinberg's Offense Principle is designed to work together with Mill's Harm Principle. He argues for the

need to clarify this aspect of the law because legislatures have in the past tended to overreact to offence and punish mere offence more severely than harms. Feinberg argues that legal penalties for offence should be proportional, and less severe than penalties deterring harm. Furthermore, the Offense Principle focuses on wrongfully causing offence. Feinberg's emphasis is not on how an act is perceived, so it doesn't matter whether or not someone takes offence, nor is it on whether an offence is intended. Rather, the key question is whether a reasonable person would judge the act to be a wrongful offence.

For Feinberg, what a reasonable person would say is wrongfully causing offence involves making a normative judgment. What is offensive for the pur-

continued on next page

poses of the principle is not determined merely by what a poll or what a majority might say. Rather, to determine wrongful offence, we must use our judgment and defend our decisions. The difficulty is determining how to do this.

To help us address the practical problem of interpreting and applying the Offense Principle, Feinberg proposes that we try the following thought experiment.[15] Imagine that you are on a crowded public bus on your way to an important engagement for which you would not want to be late. In each scenario one or more people board the bus and begin to engage in conduct that many would regard as offensive. Although Feinberg discusses a colourful array of different kinds of offensive conduct involving a host of offensive states of mind, we can focus on one set of these: the cases involving nudity and sex. Here, then, are several scenarios.

1. A topless man or woman boards the bus and sits directly across from you.

2. A naked man or woman boards the bus and sits directly across from you.

3. The passenger next to you is wearing a T-shirt with a graphic depiction of a couple copulating.

4. The passenger next to you casually flips through a pornographic magazine.

5. Same as 4 except this time the passenger stimulates himself through his clothing while flipping through the magazine.

6. The couple across from you discuss in animated and explicit detail, complete with re-created sound effects, their love-making experience from the previous night.

7. The couple opposite you kiss and fondle each other through their clothes.

8. The male passenger sitting directly across from you quietly masturbates while gazing at the clouds floating by his window.

9. The male passenger sitting directly across from you begins to masturbate while leering at you and crudely commenting on your physical appearance.

10. A married, heterosexual couple discuss their upcoming 20th wedding anniversary. They profess their undying love for and devotion to each other. Their expressions of love lead to them engaging in an act of sexual intercourse.

11. Two strangers strike up a conversation on the ride. One proposes to the other that they have casual sex. They proceed to excitedly kiss and fondle each other while removing each other's clothing. Finally, they engage in an act of sexual intercourse.

12. Same as 11 except this time it is three strangers.

13. Same as 11 except this time the couple is homosexual and their interaction ends in either mutual fellatio or cunnilingus.

In your groups, answer the following questions:

1. What makes each activity different from the one that preceded it? Are the activities progressively more offensive, or not? Why?

2. To which activities, if any, would you apply the Offense Principle? Why?

3. Does it matter whether there are children on the bus? Why or why not?

4. If you think that any activity of those on the bus should be legally prohibited, how can you distinguish your appropriate feelings of being wrongfully offended from the offence experienced by the racist who objects to the sight of people from different races holding hands in public? In other words, what distinguishes wrongful offence in the cases introduced above from the morally unjustifiable offence experienced by the racist?

5. In the course of your discussion, did you disagree about how the law should deal with any of the scenarios? If so, did you manage to resolve your disagreement? Do you think that you could sketch out a model for resolving such disagreements in society at large or is this unworkable? Explain.

Appendix 1
Writing an Ethics Paper

The purpose of this brief appendix is to provide you with some practical advice and suggestions for writing papers in ethics. In most ethics and moral philosophy courses, students are required to write one or more essays for credit, either as separate assignments or for an exam. In order to do justice to your ideas, you will need to develop some proficiency in philosophy essay writing. Although following the advice below does not guarantee you will receive a high grade in your work, it will help you avoid the common mistakes that undermine the efforts of inexperienced students and writers. Keep in mind, however, that you should tailor this advice to your own situation. Follow the specific instructions or requirements set out by your professor, even if doing so conflicts with the suggestions set out below. Also, educational research has taught us that we prefer to think, learn, and work in different ways. Thus, you must judge for yourself which of the following points are especially relevant to you, and which ones you can safely disregard.

Getting Started

Most of the time you devote to working on your paper should consist in planning and thinking about the issues raised by your topic. The actual writing should come last. Before you put a pen to paper or fingers on a keyboard, think about some of the background issues and preparation that you will need to do.

1. Expectations

Most professors have read hundreds or even thousands of essays from students at your level, and as a result they have an excellent appreciation of the standards to which you should be working. They have realistic expectations for what you can accomplish, and you should, too. Many students fall into the trap of trying to do too much in their papers, and these excessive expectations can be crippling. By setting unrealistic goals for your work, you set yourself up to fail. Of course it is generally good to have high standards and to expect much from yourself. But you must be reasonable, too.

Consider that there are two main pedagogical purposes in having students write essays for credit in philosophy courses: to foster learning of subject matter and to provide an opportunity for developing thinking and writing skills under expert supervision and judgment. Set realistic expectations for yourself with respect to each of these goals.

The Subject Matter

There are two basic kinds of essays that you could be asked to write in philosophy, which develop two basic competencies—how to explain, and how to evaluate. The **expository essay** develops the first skill. In order to examine a debate in ethics, one must be able to fairly explain the positions and arguments of others who have advanced the discussion. In an expository essay your task is simply to fairly and clearly present a viewpoint or viewpoints. That's all.

Your professor has a realistic sense of what the depth and breadth of your understanding should be, and you should endeavour to learn what this standard is and to meet it. For example, to test your understanding of Aristotle's account of morality, you might be asked to explain his theory of virtue in 750 words. In this case, your goal would be to present Aristotle's position. Realistically, in 750 words you can expect to accurately explain the main features of Aristotle's view in some detail, but you cannot expect to present a comprehensive and exhaustive discussion of the scholarly interpretations of Aristotle's account.

Alternatively, you might be asked to write an **evaluative essay**. An evaluative essay (also referred to as a **position paper** or **critical essay**) provides you with an opportunity to demonstrate your ability to critically discuss a topic and advance argumentation in support of a thesis. A **thesis** is a succinct statement of your position as regards the topic, the explanation and defence of which will be the main focus of your essay. Again, for this sort of assignment, you should learn what your professor's expectations for your work are. Generally, however, you should set manageable goals. For example, do not try to present the final word on a complex issue or debate in, say, 1500 words. Strive instead to present some intelligent and informed discussion about some significant aspect of an issue.

> An **expository essay** is descriptive. The goal is to explain not evaluate or assess. An **evaluative essay,** also known as a **position paper** or **critical essay,** is a paper in which argumentation is advanced in support of a central thesis.
> A **thesis** is a succinct statement of an author's position as regards the topic of the essay, the explanation and defence of which forms the main focus of the work.

The Process

In addition to demonstrating your understanding of a topic, you will also be judged on how well you think and write. If you are completing an expository essay, focus on simply, clearly, carefully, and fairly presenting the view you are asked to explain. You will not be expected to entertain your reader, so don't try to. Avoid jokes, puns, and "amusing stories." The relevant substance of your essay, not your writing style, should hold your reader's attention. Your style should not intrude upon or distract your reader from your goal of explaining whatever it is you have been asked to present. To this end, employ simple, direct language. Avoid jargon, technical terms and expressions, and the thesaurus. Since your goal is to explain someone else's views, you should also avoid autobiographical comments, and any judgments or assessments whatsoever.

If you are writing an evaluative paper, focus on clearly and carefully explaining and defending your position. Avoid trying to present complex arguments. Similarly, steer clear of convoluted syntax and sentence structure.

2. Selecting a Topic

Just as you should have reasonable expectations for what you hope to accomplish in your paper, you should also select a topic that reflects these expectations. Choose a narrow as opposed to a broad topic that can be addressed within the time and space limitations within which you must work. By all means, reflect upon the big questions in ethics, but when it comes time to write your essay you should focus. If you are writing a 200 000-word book, then you can aim for both breadth and depth of treatment. In a 2000-word essay, however, you should aim for depth. In writing your paper, you will be engaging in an exercise in disciplined thought. You want to make as much progress on your topic as possible. If you write to a broad topic, you will make only superficial progress. If you write to a narrow topic, you are more likely to develop some depth in your discussion and argument. Since it is difficult to take your thought beyond the superficial, you will be better rewarded for developing depth in your analysis.

If you are required to select your own topic, or you are given a broad topic and encouraged to focus on some part of it, seek out the expert advice of your instructor to narrow down your task.

3. Research

In an introductory-level course in ethics, you will probably be encouraged to reflect on the readings in your text and limit outside research into your topic. Take this advice seriously. Although it is tempting to read the work of other thinkers on a subject, and although you will be required to do this as you advance in your studies, it is difficult to integrate secondary sources into the short essays that you will likely be asked to write. Assuming you are writing an evaluative essay, as you devote more space to explaining the views of others, you leave yourself less space to develop your own position. So, while it is generally easier to explain other people's views than to

develop your own arguments, doing this defeats the purpose of writing a position paper.

Some students believe that they must research their topic beyond what is requested by their professor in order to increase the quality of their work. The idea is that the experts are far more likely to provide insightful commentary than a student new to a topic could. This attitude, however, is based on a misunderstanding of the purpose of the essay. The point is to demonstrate your proficiency in explaining and defending your view about a topic in your course. The point is *not* to defend the best, true, strongest, or right view. Of course it is better to defend such views, but for now, your professor is likely more interested in the quality of the reasons and arguments you can advance to support your own position.

Related to this misunderstanding is a concern students often have with respect to originality. They worry that a novice cannot realistically hope to write an original and sensible essay on a topic debated by the experts. This outlook assumes that one is either doomed to writing original nonsense or reporting on the novel advances of others. Again this concern is based on a misunderstanding. To show originality in your introductory work on a topic, you need only carry your thought beyond where the discussion went in the text and in the classroom. Consider that in an undergraduate course in ethics or moral philosophy, you will likely cover a number of complex topics and issues in one term. In most cases, this means your treatment of the issues in class will be limited. This leaves you with an opportunity to develop your own thinking about the issues beyond your class discussion. Demonstrating this in your essays shows initiative and commendable effort.

Tips for Getting Started

1. Set realistic expectations for what you can accomplish in the word limit you have to work with. If you are unclear about your professor's expectations and standards, seek clarification.

2. Know what sort of essay you are writing. Is it expository or evaluative?

3. If you are writing an expository essay, aim at simply, clearly, carefully, and fairly presenting the view you are asked to explain.

4. If you are writing an evaluative essay, aim at clearly and carefully explaining and defending your position.

5. To foster depth in explanation and analysis, select a narrow as opposed to a broad topic.

6. Work to the goal of making as much progress on your topic as you reasonably can.

7. Limit your research to what is required.

8. Develop your thinking about your topic beyond the points raised in your text and your classroom.

Your First Draft

One of the keys to becoming a good writer is to practise, practise, practise. If there is an opportunity to have your work reviewed by your professor, or by a tutor or teaching assistant before you submit it for credit, you would be wise to do so. They will be able to mentor you and give you informed and expert advice. They will not pre-grade your work, but they should be able to identify areas that need improving—and some areas will need improving. An inescapable fact about good writing in philosophy is that it takes effort and revision. So do not think that you must have a *complete* and detailed version of your essay in your mind or in your notes before you write. Although it is smart to work from a plan or an outline, it is unrealistic to expect that you will not have to make changes. Trust your own ability to revise and rework your ideas. You do not have to get everything perfect the first time you express yourself. You also should reconcile yourself to the idea that for your paper to be good, you will probably have to leave some of your words and ideas on the floor.

In order to get the writing process going, it is probably best to focus on one aspect of your paper (other than the introduction or conclusion) and write that. A good place to begin is with explaining whatever it is you have been asked to explain, be it your view or someone else's. This is easier to compose, and since your own arguments (if these have been requested) will follow from what you are explaining, it makes sense to explain first. Write the introduction last, since it will likely be based on the final version of your essay.

In an evaluative essay, your own discussion will focus on explaining and defending your thesis statement. Think through your own view before you start to write, and then defend your position clearly and carefully. Ensure that everything you write is directly related to your topic. Remember that you are engaging in an exercise of disciplined and critical thinking. Once you have completed the body of your essay, you can compose your introduction and, if necessary, your conclusion. In a lengthy essay it may be necessary to include both an introduction and a conclusion that summarizes your progress through the topic. However, in a brief paper, it is reasonable to expect that your reader will remember what you wrote a few pages ago, so do not include a conclusion that merely repeats your points. Save the space for your argument.

Tips for Writing the First Draft

1. Write from a plan or outline, but be willing to revise this as the draft unfolds.

2. Don't procrastinate. You don't need to have a fully developed plan to begin writing.

3. Begin by explaining whatever it is you are asked to explain.

4. Expect to revise and rewrite. You do not have to get everything perfect the first time you express yourself.

5. Write your introduction last.

6. In a brief paper, do not repeat points from your introduction in a conclusion.

7. Focus on the topic. Everything you write should be directly related to your topic.

Revising and Rewriting

If you can, put away your essay for a few days, or even a few hours, and then read it over again. This will help you gain some perspective on revising your ideas and rewriting your prose. You might also consider having a friend or someone else in your class read your first draft, to gain their perspective and see how much sense your ideas make to them. This will help you gauge how clear your essay is. If it is clear, the reader should be able to correctly sketch out your view and the arguments you advance to support it. If it isn't clear, you will know what needs to be clarified. You might also engage in a mutual peer review process with someone else working on the assignment. If your professor organizes a session, participate. For a sample peer-review editing form, see Figure A-1 at the end of this appendix.

While editing and revising your draft, check to see that you have included a thesis statement and that you have defended this statement. Check, too, for clarity and relevancy. Your paper should be clear in two ways. Your prose should be clear—your sentences should be easy to follow and understand—and the organization of your ideas should be clear. If you find yourself repeating points, then you know that your essay can be more clearly and efficiently organized. Edit out all words, comments, and points that are not directly related to your topic. If you include something that is interesting but irrelevant, you are not telling your reader that you have interesting things to say. Instead, you are telling him that you cannot distinguish between what is relevant and what is irrelevant. Remember, you are not engaging in a creative writing exercise, so although you should use your imagination to reflect on the issues and devise your arguments, make sure you present your points clearly, simply, directly, and concisely.

Pay attention, too, to your use of examples. It's a good idea to use examples to illustrate subtle or complex points. However, examples should aid your reader's understanding, only; they are not a substitute for argument. Resist the temptation to meet your word or space limit by padding your essay with multiple examples packed with superfluous detail. If your goal is to make as much progress on the topic as possible, save your space for advancing and developing your argument. Think of your words as precious and of your reader's time as valuable. Your goal is to achieve the greatest effect in the fewest possible words. Usually one example will suffice to illustrate a point.

Tips for Editing

1. Gain a fresh perspective to carry out revisions by putting your first draft down for a few days, or even a few hours, before you begin to edit.
2. Do solicit advice from others and participate in a peer-review editing session.
3. Edit for consistency, clarity, and relevancy.
4. Use examples sparingly to illustrate subtle or complex points.

Advice about Content

Here is a simple model to follow in writing an evaluative essay, and some related advice.

Introduction

A brief, focused, and clear introduction provides your reader with some direction and demonstrates your planning and your command of your material. Since you are not writing a mystery novel, there is no need to withhold your view. Include your thesis statement and a brief outline of your plan. A few sentences will suffice.

In formulating your thesis, you need not aim to defend an extreme view. An evaluative essay involves evaluation, and although this sort of paper also is referred to as a critical essay, it need not be negative. You can positively evaluate a position by adding to the position, by developing the case for that particular view. You can also criticize a position or argue that there are some reasons for endorsing the view and some problems and limitations with it, too.

Regardless of the position you take, carefully measure what you will establish in your essay. Since you have limited space in which to work, it is entirely acceptable to acknowledge the limits of your own progress. Doing this shows your reader that you appreciate the scope of your argument. Consider the following two examples to illustrate this point. Both possible thesis statements respond to the following topic:

> In approximately 1000 words, explain and critically evaluate the view that abortion is never morally justifiable.

Thesis statement #1:

In this paper, I will prove beyond any shadow of a doubt that abortion is never morally justifiable.

Thesis statement #2:

In this paper, I will argue that, at least in some circumstances, there are good reasons for thinking

that abortion is morally justifiable. However, I will identify some limitations in my case and indicate where the debate needs to be developed further.

Notice that the first thesis is bold but far too ambitious. Abortion is a complex issue and although in 1000 words someone could advance *some* support for this thesis, it is not possible to sensitively and comprehensively present the sort of case one would need to to establish this claim (assuming that the claim could be established). In contrast, the second thesis sets out a realistic goal for a paper of this length.

Explanation

To improve your paper's clarity, it is wise to set off your explanation from your evaluation. The explanatory part of your paper consists of your exposition of whatever you have been asked to explain. Explanations can be judged by reference to the following four criteria. Endeavour to meet these standards.

1. Fairness and Accuracy

Your account of whatever you are asked to explain should be fair and accurate. In order for your evaluation to be relevant, it must address the view you are asked to evaluate. This means your explanation must be factual. It is also advisable to employ a principle of charity in interpreting someone else's view. Your goal is to make as much progress on the issues as you can, and you are more likely to do this if you address the strongest possible version of the position that you are asked to evaluate. This does not mean you must *misinterpret* someone's view to make it stronger. Rather, the principle of charity tells us to present the strongest possible account of a view consistent with what was actually said. If you have a doubt about what someone means in a passage, give her the benefit of the doubt and attribute the stronger interpretation.

Following the principle of charity in interpreting the ideas of others will help you avoid a common mistake in reasoning: the straw-man fallacy. The straw-man fallacy consists of attributing a weaker version of some position than the person actually held, and subsequently criticizing the weaker version. The straw-man fallacy is irrelevant because in criticizing a weaker version of someone's position, you do not address what he believed, and thus you do not make progress on the task at hand.

2. Clarity

Aim for clarity in your explanations. If your writing is so unclear that it is unintelligible, you will fail in your effort to communicate.

3. Concision

As we noted earlier, you should endeavour to write concisely. By explaining what you are asked to explain succinctly, you save your reader time and effort, and you save space for developing your evaluation in greater depth. This increases the probability that you will make more progress in your discussion.

4. Comprehensiveness

Use your judgment to determine what to include in your explanation and what to omit. Although you want your explanation to be as comprehensive as your allowable space permits, you must balance the competing demands of explanation and evaluation.

Evaluation

There are five main criteria by which your evaluation can be judged. Your case will likely be stronger if you work specifically toward addressing these criteria.

1. Cogency

The argument you advance in support of your thesis can be judged according to how convincing, or cogent, it is. You should aim to advance relevant and strong reasons to defend your view, as opposed to modest support, weak support, or no support at all. Moreover, your reasoning should be logically sound and sensible. Avoid outlandish, vague, and sweeping statements of support for your view. Instead, try to advance reasonable, true, and specific claims to make your case.

The depth of your analysis will also help determine the cogency of your argument. A superficial treatment of the issues will not be convincing. It is better to carefully defend your view, and, in relatively short papers 2000 words and under, this means you should carefully examine as few different points as you can to support your case. It is easy to briefly list several reasons for a position. But this shopping list approach to evaluation will not likely meet the concerns of a serious-minded critic. It is much more difficult to think through the argument in some detail. Imagine that your goal is to persuade someone of a serious but different mind than yours on the issue, or to persuade someone who has not yet made up his mind. To achieve this goal, you will have to examine and present the debate in some depth.

To add depth to your analysis you can adopt the following model.

Step 1: Explain your view on the issue and the main reason you have for thinking that your position is correct.

Step 2: Fairly and carefully present the strongest objection you can to your case. What is the main reason someone who disagrees with you on the issue has for thinking that your reason is weak?

Step 3: Present the strongest response to this objection. You have already reasoned through the debate and you are now explaining why you think your position is superior to the opposing view.

From this point, you can consider a counterresponse to your response and then respond to that, or alternatively you can consider a second serious objection to your view and respond to that.

Notice that by developing your argument in this way, you are focusing on defending your strongest reason in support of your position rather than superficially listing a number of reasons. This process takes considerable effort, imagination, flexibility in thinking, judgment, and background knowledge. Undertaking this process demonstrates your skill in analysis and your knowledge of the issues related to your topic.

2. Significance or Weight

In addition to advancing a cogent argument, your evaluation can also be judged according to its significance or weight. Do you address a central issue in the debate, or is your evaluation focused on a relatively minor issue, one that the opposing view can easily refute? The greater the significance of your argument, the more valuable it becomes. Remember, your aim should be to make as much progress on the topic as possible. If you make progress on a central issue in the debate, one with greater repercussions than a relatively minor point, then you will make more and better progress.

3. Originality

Your discussion may also be evaluated for its originality. As noted earlier, you can earn credit on this score by taking your thinking beyond where the discussion ended in the text or in your class. Although it is commendable to show that you have grasped the arguments presented on the topic in your text or class discussions, it is far more impressive to thoughtfully extend your analysis beyond that point. You don't need to be a professional philosopher to do this. You need only think clearly, carefully, and critically about the debate.

4. Clarity and Concision

For the reasons that these qualities are virtues of good explanations, as noted above, they are also virtues of strong evaluations.

Your Graded Work

It is normal to have an initial emotional reaction to reading your grade, but remember that your mark is not a reflection of your worth as a person. It is a judgment about the success of your essay in meeting the standards for the assignment. You can learn from the criticisms and comments on your essay; read them carefully and think about them. It is probably best to do this, however, after you have had some time to let the grade sink in. If after you have carefully reread both your paper and the comments, you either don't understand the comments or you think that you have been misunderstood, make an appointment to see the person who marked your paper and have that person further explain or clarify.

Figure A-1   Peer Editing Form: 20 Questions

Author's Name: _____   Editor's Name: _____

Introduction

What is the author's thesis?

Is it clear and directly related to the topic? If not, why not?

Outline any suggestions you have for improving this part of the essay.

Does the author provide an account of his or her plan in the essay?

If so, is it clear? Does the author do what she or he says she or he will do?

Explanation

Is the explanatory part of the essay clearly set out?

If the author is explaining someone else's view, does he or she do this fairly and sensitively? Explain.

Outline any suggestions you have for improving this part of the essay.

Evaluation

Is this part of the essay clearly distinguished from the explanation? If not, how can this be clarified?

What is the main reason that the author advances in support of his or her thesis?

Is this a good reason? Can you detect any problems or weaknesses? If so, briefly explain.

Briefly outline the author's main argument in a few sentences.

Does the author consider any serious objections to his or her view? If so, what is or what are these objections?

What response or responses are made to this objection or these objections?

Is this response or are these responses convincing? Why or why not?

Does the author follow up the response or the responses with any counter-objection or counter-objections? If not, do you have any suggestions for developing the discussion in this direction?

Overall, how many different reasons does the author advance in support of his or her view? Are these reasons related or are they disconnected?

Are too many reasons discussed? Too few? Explain.

Overall

What do you think is the main strength of this essay? Explain any constructive suggestions you have for building on this strength.

What do you think is the main weakness of the essay? Explain how you would address this weakness.

Appendix 2
Canadian Charter of Rights and Freedoms

Part I

Canadian Charter of Rights and Freedoms

Whereas Canada is founded upon principles that recognize the supremacy of God and the rule of law:

Guarantee of Rights and Freedoms

1. The *Canadian Charter of Rights and Freedoms* guarantees the rights and freedoms set out in it subject only to such reasonable limits prescribed by law as can be demonstrably justified in a free and democratic society.

Fundamental Freedoms

2. Everyone has the following fundamental freedoms:

   a) freedom of conscience and religion;

   b) freedom of thought, belief, opinion and expression, including freedom of the press and other media of communication;

   c) freedom of peaceful assembly; and

   d) freedom of association.

Democratic Rights

3. Every citizen of Canada has the right to vote in an election of members of the House of Commons or of a legislative assembly and to be qualified for membership therein.

4. (1) No House of Commons and no legislative assembly shall continue for longer than five years from the date fixed for the return of the writs of a general election of its members.

   (2) In time of real or apprehended war, invasion or insurrection, a House of Commons may be continued by Parliament and a legislative assembly may be continued by the legislature beyond five years if such continuation is not opposed by the votes of more than one-third of the members of the House of Commons or the legislative assembly, as the case may be.

5. There shall be a sitting of Parliament and of each legislature at least once every twelve months.

Mobility Rights

6. (1) Every citizen of Canada has the right to enter, remain in and leave Canada.

   (2) Every citizen of Canada and every person who has the status of a permanent resident of Canada has the right

   a) to move to and take up residence in any province; and

   b) to pursue the gaining of a livelihood in any province.

   (3) The rights specified in subsection (2) are subject to

   a) any laws or practices of general application in force in a province other than those that discriminate among persons primarily on the basis of province of present or previous residence; and

   b) any laws providing for reasonable residency requirements as a qualification for the receipt of publicly provided social services.

   (4) Subsections (2) and (3) do not preclude any law, program or activity that has as its object the amelioration in a province of conditions of individuals in that province who are socially or economically disadvantaged if the rate of employment in that province is below the rate of employment in Canada.

Legal Rights

7. Everyone has the right to life, liberty and security of the person and the right not to be deprived thereof except in accordance with the principles of fundamental justice.

8. Everyone has the right to be secure against unreasonable search or seizure.

9. Everyone has the right not to be arbitrarily detained or imprisoned.

10. Everyone has the right on arrest or detention

    a) to be informed promptly of the reasons therefor;

    b) to retain and instruct counsel without delay and to be informed of that right; and

    c) to have the validity of the detention determined by way of habeas corpus and to be released if the detention is not lawful.

11. Any person charged with an offence has the right

a) to be informed without unreasonable delay of the specific offence;

b) to be tried within a reasonable time;

c) not to be compelled to be a witness in proceedings against that person in respect of the offence;

d) to be presumed innocent until proven guilty according to law in a fair and public hearing by an independent and impartial tribunal;

e) not to be denied reasonable bail without just cause;

f) except in the case of an offence under military law tried before a military tribunal, to the benefit of trial by jury where the maximum punishment for the offence is imprisonment for five years or a more severe punishment;

g) not to be found guilty on account of any act or omission unless, at the time of the act or omission, it constituted an offence under Canadian or international law or was criminal according to the general principles of law recognized by the community of nations;

h) if finally acquitted of the offence, not to be tried for it again and, if finally found guilty and punished for the offence, not to be tried or punished for it again; and

i) if found guilty of the offence and if the punishment for the offence has been varied between the time of commission and the time of sentencing, to the benefit of the lesser punishment.

12. Everyone has the right not to be subjected to any cruel and unusual treatment or punishment.

13. A witness who testifies in any proceedings has the right not to have any incriminating evidence so given used to incriminate that witness in any other proceedings, except in a prosecution for perjury or for the giving of contradictory evidence.

14. A party or witness in any proceedings who does not understand or speak the language in which the proceedings are conducted or who is deaf has the right to the assistance of an interpreter.

Equality Rights

15. (1) Every individual is equal before and under the law and has the right to the equal protection and equal benefit of the law without discrimination and, in particular, without discrimination based on race, national or ethnic origin, colour, religion, sex, age or mental or physical disability.

(2) Subsection (1) does not preclude any law, program or activity that has as its object the amelioration of conditions of disadvantaged individuals or groups including those that are disadvantaged because of race, national or ethnic origin, colour, religion, sex, age or mental or physical disability.

Official Languages of Canada

16. (1) English and French are the official languages of Canada and have equality of status and equal rights and privileges as to their use in all institutions of the Parliament and government of Canada.

(2) English and French are the official languages of New Brunswick and have equality of status and equal rights and privileges as to their use in all institutions of the legislature and government of New Brunswick.

(3) Nothing in this Charter limits the authority of Parliament or a legislature to advance the equality of status or use of English and French.

16.1.(1) The English linguistic community and the French linguistic community in New Brunswick have equality of status and equal rights and privileges, including the right to distinct educational institutions and such distinct cultural institutions as are necessary for the preservation and promotion of those communities.

(2) The role of the legislature and government of New Brunswick to preserve and promote the status, rights and privileges referred to in subsection (1) is affirmed.

17. (1) Everyone has the right to use English or French in any debates and other proceedings of Parliament.

(2) Everyone has the right to use English or French in any debates and other proceedings of the legislature of New Brunswick.

18. (1) The statutes, records and journals of Parliament shall be printed and published in English and French and both language versions are equally authoritative.

(2) The statutes, records and journals of the legislature of New Brunswick shall be printed and published in English and French and both language versions are equally authoritative.

19. (1) Either English or French may be used by any person in, or in any pleading in or process issuing from, any court established by Parliament.

(2) Either English or French may be used by any person in, or in any pleading in or process issuing from, any court of New Brunswick.

20. (1) Any member of the public in Canada has the right to communicate with, and to receive available services from, any head or central office of an institution of the Parliament or government of Canada in English or French, and has the same right with respect to any other office of any such institution where

a) there is a significant demand for communications with and services from that office in such language; or

b) due to the nature of the office, it is reasonable that communications with and services from that office be available in both English and French.

(2) Any member of the public in New Brunswick has the right to communicate with, and to receive available services from, any office of an institution of the legislature or government of New Brunswick in English or French.

21. Nothing in sections 16 to 20 abrogates or derogates from any right, privilege or obligation with respect to the English and French languages, or either of them, that exists or is continued by virtue of any other provision of the Constitution of Canada.

22. Nothing in sections 16 to 20 abrogates or derogates from any legal or customary right or privilege acquired or enjoyed either before or after the coming into force of this Charter with respect to any language that is not English or French.

Minority Language Educational Rights

23. (1) Citizens of Canada
a) whose first language learned and still understood is that of the English or French linguistic minority population of the province in which they reside, or
b) who have received their primary school instruction in Canada in English or French and reside in a province where the language in which they received that instruction is the language of the English or French linguistic minority population of the province, have the right to have their children receive primary and secondary school instruction in that language in that province.

(2) Citizens of Canada of whom any child has received or is receiving primary or secondary school instruction in English or French in Canada, have the right to have all their children receive primary and secondary school instruction in the same language.

(3) The right of citizens of Canada under subsections (1) and (2) to have their children receive primary and secondary school instruction in the language of the English or French linguistic minority population of a province

a) applies wherever in the province the number of children of citizens who have such a right is sufficient to warrant the provision to them out of public funds of minority language instruction; and

b) includes, where the number of those children so warrants, the right to have them receive that instruction in minority language educational facilities provided out of public funds.

Enforcement

24. (1) Anyone whose rights or freedoms, as guaranteed by this Charter, have been infringed or denied may apply to a court of competent jurisdiction to obtain such remedy as the court considers appropriate and just in the circumstances.

(2) Where, in proceedings under subsection (1), a court concludes that evidence was obtained in a manner that infringed or denied any rights or freedoms guaranteed by this Charter, the evidence shall be excluded if it is established that, having regard to all the circumstances, the admission of it in the proceedings would bring the administration of justice into disrepute.

General

25. The guarantee in this Charter of certain rights and freedoms shall not be construed so as to abrogate or derogate from any aboriginal, treaty or other rights or freedoms that pertain to the aboriginal peoples of Canada including

a) any rights or freedoms that have been recognized by the Royal Proclamation of October 7, 1763; and

b) any rights or freedoms that now exist by way of land claims agreements or may be so acquired.

26. The guarantee in this Charter of certain rights and freedoms shall not be construed as denying the existence of any other rights or freedoms that exist in Canada.

27. This Charter shall be interpreted in a manner consistent with the preservation and enhancement of the multicultural heritage of Canadians.

28. Notwithstanding anything in this Charter, the rights and freedoms referred to in it are guaranteed equally to male and female persons.

29. Nothing in this Charter abrogates or derogates from any rights or privileges guaranteed by or under the Constitution of Canada in respect of denominational, separate or dissentient schools.

30. A reference in this Charter to a Province or to the legislative assembly or legislature of a province shall be deemed to include a reference to the Yukon Territory and the Northwest Territories, or to the appropriate legislative authority thereof, as the case may be.

31. Nothing in this Charter extends the legislative powers of any body or authority.

Application of Charter

32. (1) This Charter applies

    a) to the Parliament and government of Canada in respect of all matters within the authority of Parliament including all matters relating to the Yukon Territory and Northwest Territories; and

    b) to the legislature and government of each province in respect of all matters within the authority of the legislature of each province.

(2) Notwithstanding subsection (1), section 15 shall not have effect until three years after this section comes into force.

33. (1) Parliament or the legislature of a province may expressly declare in an Act of Parliament or of the legislature, as the case may be, that the Act or a provision thereof shall operate notwithstanding a provision included in section 2 or sections 7 to 15 of this Charter.

(2) An Act or a provision of an Act in respect of which a declaration made under this section is in effect shall have such operation as it would have but for the provision of this Charter referred to in the declaration.

(3) A declaration made under subsection (1) shall cease to have effect five years after it comes into force or on such earlier date as may be specified in the declaration.

(4) Parliament or the legislature of a province may re-enact a declaration made under subsection (1).

(5) Subsection (3) applies in respect of a re-enactment made under subsection (4).

Citation

34. This Part may be cited as the *Canadian Charter of Rights and Freedoms.*

Glossary

Accelerated quota policy: an affirmative action hiring policy that sets a target for hiring underrepresented individuals in the workforce that exceeds the percentage of currently available, minimally qualified job candidates from the targeted group. (See also *constant quota policy* and *enhanced quota policy*.)

Affirmative action: hiring programs and policies designed to promote the hiring of various groups of individuals who have suffered from traditional discriminatory hiring practices.

Anthropocentrism: in ethics, is the view that only humans can and should be given moral consideration.

Applied Ethics: the field of study within Normative Ethics that is devoted to examining ethical questions and issues that arise in distinct spheres of life. Bioethics, Business Ethics, Environmental Ethics, and Computer Ethics are all examples of areas within Applied Ethics.

Argument: (1) a dispute or (2) a set of claims in which one or more of these claims, called the *premise* or *premises*, is or are offered as support for another claim, called the *conclusion*. Except where explicitly noted otherwise, we use the word in this second sense.

Axiology, or **Value Theory:** the study of the nature of value.

Base pair: two nitrogenous bases, each part of separate nucleotides, connected by weak bonds and forming the basic units of DNA.

Biocentrism: the ethical view according to which the class of all beings that can be given moral consideration is limited to all living beings.

Birth cohort: the group of all individuals born between any two specified dates.

Blastocyst: a mostly hollow sphere with an outer lining of cells and a cluster of inner cells called the "inner cell mass"; forms at approximately the 100-cell stage in human embryonic development.

Blastomere separation: a method of cloning that consists of splitting a two-celled (or more) embryo to produce single totipotent stem cells that are then grown separately.

Categorical imperative: commands unconditionally and is derived from pure reason alone. As such, it expresses the autonomy of the will of rational beings. According to Immanuel Kant, it is the supreme principle of morality.

Cell: the basic unit of life in which the biochemical processes of life occur.

Chromosome: a self-replicating macromolecule of DNA sequence varying in size between roughly 50 million and 250 million base pairs in which genes are found.

Clone: an exact copy of biological material.

Compatibilist outlooks: assign a meaningful place to the study of ethics in both religious studies and philosophy.

(See also *Exclusive Assimilation* and *Extreme Temporalism*.)

Consciousness: the state of being sentient or aware of one's external surroundings.

Consequentialism: is marked by three defining traits. (1) Consequentialism is good-based. It endorses or renounces acts solely on the basis of the contribution that the acts make to furthering the overall good. (2) Consequentialism is a welfarist outlook. The good Consequentialism aims to promote is the well-being of particular individuals. (3) Consequentialism aims to promote individual welfare in a way consistent with its commitment to a principle of equal respect and consideration.

Constant quota policy: an affirmative action hiring policy that sets a target for hiring underrepresented individuals in the workforce that equals the percentage of currently available, minimally qualified job candidates from the targeted group. (See also *accelerated quota policy* and *enhanced quota policy*.)

Critical reasoning or analysis: refers to the process of identifying, clarifying, understanding, and evaluating the strength, truth, or rightness of a claim, view, or argument.

Crude Ethical Subjectivism: a non-cognitivist, meta-ethical view about the nature of moral judgments. According to it, all moral judgments are merely expressions of feelings because there are no moral facts or moral truths.

Cultural Relativism: the view that different societies and cultures follow different moral codes.

Deep Skeptical Challenge to Ethics: challenges the view that it is rational to care for anyone else for her or his sake.

Demandingness Objection: an integrity objection to Utilitarianism. According to this objection, the problem with Utilitarianism's demandingness can be traced to its conception of *the right*. Act Utilitarianism, for example, has a criterion of moral rightness that always requires agents to perform acts that will produce impersonally best states of affairs. Thus, Utilitarianism requires that individuals devote energy to their personal commitments, projects, and relationships only when and to the extent that doing so is most productive of *the good*, impersonally construed. Critics argue that the theory threatens that integrity or the continuity of the lives of all those persons who, to meet this requirement, must lessen or abandon their personal commitments.

Deontological ethical theories: right-based theories about the foundations of ethics. According to them, the morally *right* is logically prior to the *good* and is determined other than by appeal to the notion of what is morally good.

Descriptive Ethics: the study of what the morals of some group are. This is a scientific enterprise as is done, for example, by cultural anthropologists.

Determinism: the view that there is a causal explanation for everything that happens.

Dilemma of Determinism:

1. If Determinism is true, we can never do other than we do; hence we are never responsible for what we do.
2. If Indeterminism is true, then some events—namely, human actions—are random, hence not free; hence, we are never responsible for what we do.
3. Either Determinism is true or Indeterminism is true.
4. Therefore, we are never responsible for what we do. (Feinberg & Shafer-Landau [1999], p. 412)

Divine Command Theory: proposes that ethics is completely subsumed by religion because what is morally right, good, or obligatory is so simply and only because God commands or wills it to be so.

DNA: deoxyribonucleic acid; the double helix or double-stranded molecule that contains the chemically encoded information found in cells.

DNA sequence: the identity and ordering of the base pairs that comprise the genetic identity of an individual.

Ecology: the biological study of organisms' relations to each other and to their surroundings.

Ectogenesis: literally, the production of structures outside an organism; refers to the process of creating an artificial womb or uterus.

Embryo: a fertilized ovum; for humans from the two-cell stage to approximately six weeks gestation.

Emotivism: a non-cognitivist theory about ethics according to which moral judgments are really only the expressions of the feelings of those making the judgments. Typically, these expressions are ones of approval or disapproval.

Enhanced quota policy: an affirmative action hiring policy that sets a target for hiring underrepresented individuals in the workforce in numbers that exceed the threshold point for employing reverse discrimination. (See also *accelerated quota policy* and *constant quota policy*.)

Enhanced views: those views in the debate over affirmative action that endorse imposing some costs on individuals, typically white men, who have traditionally benefited from past discriminatory hiring practices. (See also *equal opportunity view*.)

Enlightened self-interest: an individual's actual good.

Equal opportunity view: the position in the debate over affirmative action that endorses the remedying of the underrepresentation of individuals traditionally discriminated against by past hiring practices through the scrupulous application of a principle of equal opportunity in hiring. (See also *enhanced views*.)

Ethical Absolutism: a normative and meta-ethical theory about the nature and justification of ethical claims and judgments. According to the Ethical Absolutist, there are universal moral demands for various reasons. Furthermore, under suitably similar circumstances, a moral judgment is true for all people at all times and in all places.

Ethical Egoism: a normative theory according to which humans should be motivated only by their own self-interest.

Ethical Relativism: a normative and meta-ethical theory about the nature and justification of moral judgments. According to the Ethical Relativist, moral judgments and any truths about morality are relative to someone's or some group's beliefs and values.

Ethical Subjectivism: a non-cognitivist theory about ethics according to which moral judgments are really only the reports or statements of the attitudes of those making the judgments.

Etiquette Relativism: a normative meta-etiquette theory about how we should regard the truths of etiquette. According to this view, the truths of etiquette are relative to particular and different local codes of etiquette.

Eugenics: the study of the production of fine or improved genetic offspring, typically human offspring.

Exclusive Assimilation: the view that the study of ethics is somehow dependent upon a particular religious doctrine. (See also *compatibilist outlooks* and *Extreme Temporalism*.)

Existentialism: primarily recognized as a post-World War II philosophical and literary outlook that emphasizes consideration of the concrete lives of individuals over reflections on so-called essential human qualities.

Extreme Deterministic Psychological Egoism: the view that humans lack free will and always behave in ways that promote their own good. According to this view, humans are never motivated by concern for another person.

Extreme Non-Deterministic Psychological Egoism: the view that humans act in ways that aim to promote their own good, and never act primarily or exclusively for the sake of another person.

Extreme Temporalism: the view that ethics is a worldly field of study properly divorced from religion. (See also *compatibilist outlooks* and *Exclusive Assimilation*.)

Fetus: an unborn or unhatched offspring; for humans, the stage from the development of major organs at approximately six weeks gestation until birth.

Gaia hypothesis: a hypothesis in science that the entire planet is itself a living being. James Lovelock and Lynn Margulis advanced this hypothesis.

Gamete: a mature sex cell; sperm or egg.

Gene: the basic unit of heredity controlling all the inherited characteristics of life consisting of a particular sequence of nucleotides.

Genetics: the study of inheritance patterns of particular traits in animals, plants, and bacteria.

Genome: the sum total of all DNA for any particular organism.

Germ cell: a sex cell. (See also *Gamete*.)

Germ line: the cells that pass genetic information from one generation to the next.

Germ-line genetic alteration: the technique of altering the genetic structure of germ cells to effect changes in subsequent generations.

Gonad: an organ that produces gametes.

Haploid: a single set of chromosomes, 23 in humans, as are found in sex cells. Two haploid sets, 46 chromosomes total in humans, are found in somatic cells that are diploid.

Harm Principle: according to John Stuart Mill, outlines the rightful limits of the use of power by the state against the individual. According to it, individuals of mature age should be free to act as they wish, provided the exercising of their freedom does not harm others.

Hedonistic Utilitarianism: the view that utility consists of the experience of pleasure, and that moral rightness should be understood in terms of the maximization of utility.

Holism (or the Land Ethic): the view in ethics that the moral community includes all the interdependent parts of entire ecosystems, including the Earth as a biotic community as a whole. Eschewing an individualistic perspective in ethics for a holistic perspective, and grounding ethics on ecology, Holists believe that acts are right insofar as they promote the integrity, stability, and beauty of the biotic community. Acts are wrong otherwise.

Human rights, natural rights, or **moral rights:** rights we have by virtue of our status as human beings.

Hypothetical imperatives: commands based on fulfilling worldly desires.

Impersonal Motivation Objection: an integrity objection to Utilitarianism. According to this objection, Utilitarianism threatens integrity because it requires that individuals adopt an impersonal motivation toward their personal commitments. Although Utilitarianism permits individuals to develop and maintain their personal commitments, it does so to promote the overall good: agents with such ties, it is claimed, are better able to promote impersonally good states of affairs than are agents without such concerns. The problem, however, is that Utilitarianism *requires* individuals themselves to adopt this attitude. This mediating, impersonal motivation has a destructive (or at least inhibiting) effect on the character of an individual's personal commitments. Thus, for example, rather than being committed to a friend as a friend, one is instead committed to a friend as a means or instrument for promoting impersonal value. But this mediating motivation undermines the essentially personal character of one's commitments, thereby destroying much of their (personal) value. This objection is an integrity objection because this change in motivation must reflect a change in values, which in turn threatens the integrity of a person's life.

Inalienable rights: see *human rights.*

Indeterminism: the view that some events are not caused.

Inner cell mass: the cluster of pluripotent stem cells inside the blastocyst, from which the fetus develops.

Instrumental value: refers to the value of something as an instrument or tool for achieving some purpose.

Interpersonal Ethics: See *Relationship Ethics.*

Intrinsic value: refers to the value of something as an end in itself.

Land Ethic: see *Holism.*

Legal Moralism: the view that acts may be legally prohibited because they are immoral.

Legal Positivism: a theory about the nature of law according to which law and ethics are conceptually distinct areas of study that refer to distinct social phenomena. This *Separability Thesis* is linked to the *Pedigree Thesis.*

According to this latter thesis, a law's validity is a matter of its pedigree, not its content. In other words, the Positivist argues that what makes a law a valid law of a system is determined by a social fact or social facts about the law coming into being in the right sort of way.

The lottery method or **fair lottery method:** involves resolving allocation or distribution problems of justice by according equal consideration to all who are vying for whatever is to be distributed. (See also *ranking method.*)

Maxim: in Immanuel Kant's ethics, a rule of conduct.

Mental State Accounts: accounts of well-being or prudential good according to which well-being can be understood entirely in terms of the mental states of sentient beings.

Meta-Ethics: broadly conceived, is the field of study within Philosophical Ethics that addresses the general background and framing issues that underlie Normative Ethics. Thus, Meta-Ethics examines the underpinnings and limits of questions in Prescriptive Ethics. These include questions about the analysis of moral language and epistemological and metaphysical questions about morality. More generally, Meta-Ethics addresses questions about the nature, justification, purpose, scope, and origins of morality.

Moral Absolutism: see *Ethical Absolutism.*

Moral rights: see *human rights.*

Multipotent stem cells: stems cells with the potential to develop into many kinds of tissue, but whose future possible development is more restricted than pluripotent stem cells. (See also *pluripotent stem cells* and *totipotent stem cells.*)

Natural Law Theories: maintain that there are universally applicable and objectively right moral principles that are discoverable by human reason. These objective moral principles, which are the natural laws, apply uniformly to all people at all times and in all places.

Natural rights: see *human rights.*

Non-Cognitivism: in ethics is the view that moral judgments do not express propositions. As such, they have no truth-value (they are neither true nor false) and therefore there is no such thing as ethical knowledge.

Normative Ethics or **Prescriptive Ethics:** the study of the particular moral theories, views, approaches, and frameworks that consist of the specific prescriptions and proscriptions of morality. More generally, the study of Normative Ethics is the systematic study of ethical conduct, character, and practice. It is also the study of practical ethical questions and issues that encompasses the fields of *Applied Ethics, Professional Ethics,* and *Relationship Ethics.*

Noumenal realm: a term used by Immanuel Kant to refer to the antithesis of the phenomenal realm of worldly experiences. In this realm, and from this perspective, the possibility of freedom, agency, and morality arise. (See also *phenomenal realm.*)

Nucleotide: a subunit of DNA consisting of one phosphate group, one sugar, and a nitrogenous base (A, G, C, or T).

Object: a dead being or inanimate thing.

Objective Consequentialism: the consequentialist view that "the criterion of rightness of an act or a course of action is whether it in fact would most promote the good of those acts available to the agent" (Railton [1984], p. 152). (See also *Subjective Consequentialism* and *Sophisticated Consequentialism*.)

Oocyte: an immature ovum.

Ovum: a mature egg or female sex cell.

Paternalism: "the interference with a person's liberty of action justified by reasons referring exclusively to the welfare, good, happiness, needs, interests or values of the person being coerced" (Dworkin [1971], p. 107).

Personal Ethics: see *Relationship Ethics*.

Phenomenal realm: a term used by Immanuel Kant to refer to the world of sensible experience. (See also *noumenal realm*.)

Pluripotent stem cells: stem cells with the potential to develop into most kinds of tissue. However, since they are not totipotent, they cannot develop into a complete individual. (See also *totipotent stem cells* and *multipotent stem cells*.)

Practical Reasoning Approach: this approach to the justification of morality indicates that the problem of justifying morality involves showing the rationality or practical benefit of being moral or leading a moral life.

Prescriptive Ethics: see *Normative Ethics*.

Professional Ethics: the field of study within Normative Ethics that examines ethical issues and concerns as they impact various areas of the lives, and especially the work, of professionals like physicians, lawyers, and engineers. Professionals are often subject to specific codes of conduct.

Prudential value: refers to the good or well-being of the person or being in question. Thus, an assessment of the prudential value of your life is a measurement of its value to you.

Psychological Egoism: a theory about human motivation according to which humans are motivated by a concern for their self-interest. In its extreme form, it is the view that humans always and only aim to advance their self-interest, where an individual's self-interest is understood narrowly to be independent of the self-interest of others.

Ranking method: a method for resolving allocation or distribution problems of justice that consists of ranking people who are vying for a good or resource according to one or more of their qualities. (See also *lottery method*.)

Relationship Ethics, Personal Ethics, or **Interpersonal Ethics:** the field of study within Normative Ethics that examines the ethical questions and issues faced by individuals in the course of their lives as social beings. Questions about the ethics of family and friend relations and issues involving the morality of sex and love are among those that are prominent in this area.

Reverse discrimination: the term sometimes used in the debate over affirmative action to refer to policies that unfairly impose costs on a targeted group of individuals (e.g., white men) who have traditionally benefited from existing hiring policies and programs.

Sociobiological explanation of ethics: explains ethics from the perspective of the study of the biological foundations of human social behaviour.

Somatic cell: any cell other than a gamete (egg or sperm). Somatic cells in humans contain a full complement of 46 chromosomes.

Somatic cell nuclear transfer (SCNT): the transfer of the nucleus of a somatic cell into an enucleated immature egg or oocyte.

Sophisticated Consequentialism: a Sophisticated Consequentialist is someone who has a standing commitment to leading an objectively consequentialist life. (See also *Objective Consequentialism* and *Subjective Consequentialism*.)

Stem cells: cells that renew tissue. There are three types: totipotent, pluripotent, and multipotent. Stem cells can transform into other kinds of cells (they are undifferentiated), and they can replicate many more times than non-stem cells.

Subject: the possessor or bearer of a life.

Subjective Consequentialism: the consequentialist view that "whenever one faces a choice of actions, one should attempt to determine which act of those available would most promote the good, and should then try to act accordingly" (Railton [1984], p. 152). (See also *Objective Consequentialism* and *Sophisticated Consequentialism*.)

Teleological ethical theories: good-based theories about the foundations of ethics. According to them, the morally right is determined by reference to the logically prior notion of what is morally good.

Totipotent stem cells: stem cells that have the total potential of developing into an individual. (See also *multipotent stem cells* and *pluripotent stem cells*.)

True friendship: true friendship involves mutually recognized and reciprocated well-wishing for the sake of one's friend.

Value Theory: see *Axiology*.

Valuer: someone who appreciates or realizes value.

Vector: that which delivers a gene to a cell to alter its genotype, like, for example, a genetically modified virus.

Virtue Ethics or **Virtue Theory:** the view that virtue is either a basic category in ethics or, less strongly, that virtue assumes a central role in ethics.

Weak Skeptical Challenge to Ethics: challenges the view that it is rational to act in ways that benefit others.

Welfarism: the foundational view in ethics according to which the purpose of morality is to promote the good of those beings that have a good of their own. According to the Welfarist, only welfare matters for ethics.

Will: according to Immanuel Kant, refers to our capacity for acting according to the conception of laws. Since we must use our reason to conceive of these practical laws, will is practical reason.

Xenotransplantation: the technique of transplanting organic material of one genetic type, usually a non-human, into a being of a different type, usually a human.

Zygote: a fertilized ovum or egg consisting of a unified sperm and egg cell; a single totipotent stem cell.

Bibliography

Aiken, William. (1984). "Ethical Issues in Agriculture," *Earthbound: New Introductory Essays in Environmental Ethics.* Tom Regan, ed. New York: Random House.

Anscombe, G. E. M. (1958). "Modern Moral Philosophy," *Philosophy,* 33, 1–19.

Aristotle. (1984). "Nicomachean Ethics," Books VIII and IX, *The Complete Works of Aristotle.* Jonathan Barnes, ed., vol. 2. Princeton, NJ: Princeton University Press.

———. "Politics," Books I.1–I.2, III.9, *The Complete Works of Aristotle.* Jonathan Barnes, ed., vol. 2. Princeton, NJ: Princeton University Press.

Arnal, William E. (2000). "Definition," in *Guide to the Study of Religion.* Willi Braun and Russell T. McCutcheon, eds. London: Cassell, pp. 21–34.

Attfield, Robin. (1981). "The Good of Trees," *Journal of Value Inquiry,* 15, 35–54.

———. (1983). *The Ethics of Environmental Concern.* Oxford: Basil Blackwell.

Badhwar, Neera Kapur. (1987). "Friends as Ends in Themselves," *Philosophy and Phenomenological Research,* vol. XLVIII, No. I, 1–23.

———. (1991). "Why It Is Wrong to Be Always Guided by the Best: Consequentialism and Friendship," *Ethics,* 101, No. 3, 483–504.

———. (1993). "Altruism Versus Self-Interest: Sometimes a False Dichotomy," *Social Philosophy & Policy,* vol. 10, no. 1, 90–117.

———. ed. (1993). *Friendship: A Philosophical Reader.* Ithaca, NY: Cornell University Press.

Baier, Annette. (1985). "What Do Women Want in a Moral Theory?" *Nous,* 19, no. 1, 53–63.

———. (1986). "Trust and Antitrust," *Ethics,* 96, no. 2, 231–260.

———. (1995). *Moral Prejudices.* Cambridge, MA: Harvard University Press.

Baird, Patricia A. (1994). "Altering Human Genes: Social, Ethical, and Legal Implications," *Perspective in Biology and Medicine,* 37, 566–575. Reprinted in *Contemporary Readings in Biomedical Ethics,* Walter Glannon, ed. Orlando, FL: Harcourt, 2002, pp. 266–273.

Baxter, W.F. (1974). *People or Penguins: The Case for Optimal Pollution.* New York: Columbia University Press.

Bentham, Jeremy. (1789). *The Collected Works of Jeremy Bentham. An Introduction to the Principles of Morals and Legislation.* J.H. Burns and H.L.A. Hart, eds. New York: Oxford University Press, 1996.

———. (1843). *Works.* Volume 2. Edinburgh: Tait.

Bernstein, Mark. (1998). *On Moral Considerability: An Essay on Who Morally Matters.* New York: Oxford University Press.

Bickenbach, J, ed. (1993). Chief Justice Brian Dickson, *R. v. Oakes,* Supreme Court of Canada, [1986] 1 S.C.R. 103, in *Canadian Cases in the Philosophy of Law,* 2nd ed., Peterborough, ON: Broadview Press, pp. 44–49.

Birsch, Douglas. (1999). *Ethical Insights: A Brief Introduction.* Mountain View, CA.: Mayfield Publishing Company.

Blum, Lawrence A. (1980). *Friendship, Altruism and Morality.* Boston: Routledge & Kegan Paul.

———. (1988). "Gilligan and Kohlberg: Implications for Moral Theory," *Ethics,* 98, no. 3, 472–491.

Boxill, Bernard. (1978). "The Morality of Preferential Hiring," *Philosophy & Public Affairs,* 7, no. 3, 246–268.

Boylan, Michael. (2000). *Basic Ethics.* Upper Saddle River, NJ: Prentice Hall.

Brandt, Richard. (1979). *A Theory of the Good and the Right.* Oxford: Oxford University Press.

Brink, David. (1986). "Utilitarian Morality and the Personal Point of View," *The Journal of Philosophy,* Volume 83, No. 8, 417–438.

Callicott, J. Baird. (1980). "Animal Liberation: A Triangular Affair," *Environmental Ethics,* pp. 311–328.

———. (1987). "The Conceptual Foundations of the Land Ethic," *Companion to a Sand County Almanac: Interpretive & Critical Essays.* J. Baird Callicott, ed. Madison, WI: University of Wisconsin Press, pp. 186–217.

———. (1989). "Animal Liberation and Environmental Ethics: Back Together Again," *In Defense of the Land Ethic: Essays in Environmental Philosophy.* Albany, NY: SUNY Press, Chapter 3.

Campbell, N., Reece, J., and Mitchell, L. (1999). *Biology,* 5th ed. Menlo Park, CA: Addison Wesley Longman, Inc.

Card, Claudia. (1996). *The Unnatural Lottery.* Philadelphia: Temple University Press.

Canadian Charter of Rights and Freedoms, Constitution Act, 1982.

Cocking, Dean and Kennett, Jeanette. (2000). "Friendship and Moral Danger," *The Journal of Philosophy,* 97, No. 5, 278–296.

Cooper, John. (1977). "Aristotle on the Forms of Friendship," *The Review of Metaphysics,* 30, No. 4, 619–648.

———. (1980). "Aristotle on Friendship," *Essays on Aristotle's Ethics.* A.O. Rorty, ed. Berkeley: University of California Press, pp. 301–340.

Cooper, W., Neilson, K., and Patten, S., eds. (1979). *New Essays on John Stuart Mill and Utilitarianism, Canadian Journal of Philosophy.* Supplementary Volume V. Calgary, AB: University of Calgary Press.

Copi, I and Cohen, C. (2002). *Introduction to Logic,* 11th ed., Upper Saddle River, NJ: Prentice Hall.

Copp, D. and Zimmerman, D., eds. (1984). *Morality, Reason, and Truth: New Essays in the Foundations of Ethics.* Totowa, NJ: Rowman & Allanheld Publishers.

Courtenay Hall, Pamela. (1993). "From Justified Discrimination to Responsive Hiring: The Role Model Argument and Female Equity Hiring in Philosophy," *Journal of Social Philosophy,* 24, 23–45.

Daniels, Norman. (1988). *Am I My Parents' Keeper? An Essay on Justice between the Young and the Old.* New York: Oxford University Press.

Danto, Arthur C. (1968). *What Philosophy Is: A Guide to the Elements.* New York: Harper & Row Publishers.

———. (1989). *Connections to the World: The Basic Concepts of Philosophy.* New York: Harper & Row.

Darwall, S., Gibbard, A., and Railton, P. (1992). "Toward *Fin de siecle* Ethics: Some Trends," *The Philosophical Review,* 101, 115–189.

Davis, H. and Munson, Ronald. (2000). "Germ-Line Therapy and the Medical Imperative," in *Readings in Health Care Ethics.* E. Boetzkes and W. Waluchow, eds. Mississauga, ON: Broadview Press, pp. 577–587.

Devlin, Patrick. (1965). *The Enforcement of Morality.* London: Oxford University Press.

Drane, James. (1985). "The Many Faces of Competency," *The Hastings Center Report,* 15, no. 2.

Dworkin, Gerald. (1971). "Paternalism," in *Morality and the Law.* Richard A. Wasserstrom, ed. Belmont, CA: Wadsworth Publishing, pp. 107–126.

Dworkin, Ronald. (1978). *Taking Rights Seriously.* Cambridge, MA: Harvard University Press.

———. (1986). *Law's Empire.* Cambridge, MA: Harvard University Press.

Elton, Charles. (1927). *Animal Ecology.* New York: Macmillan.

English, Jane. (October 1975). "Abortion and the Concept of a Person," *Canadian Journal of Philosophy,* vol. 5, no. 2, 233–243.

English, Parker. (1994). "Preferential Hiring and Just War Theory," *Journal of Social Philosophy,* 25, pp. 119–138.

Ezorsky, Gertrude. (1991). *Racism and Justice: The Case for Affirmative Action.* Ithaca, NY: Cornell University Press.

Feinberg, Joel. (1985). *The Moral Limits of the Criminal Law. Volume 2: Offense to Others.* New York: Oxford University Press.

Feinberg, Joel and Shafer-Landau, Russ, eds. (1999). *Reason & Responsibility: Readings in Some Basic Problems of Philosophy,* 10th ed. Belmont, CA: Wadsworth.

Fishkin, James S. (1982). *The Limits of Obligation.* New Haven, CT: Yale University Press.

Fishkin, James S. and Laslett, Peter. (1992). "Introduction: Processional Justice," in *Justice between Age Groups and Generations.* Peter Laslett and James S. Fishkin, eds. New Haven, CT: Yale University Press, pp.1–23.

Foot, Philippa. (1978). "The Problem of Abortion and the Doctrine of Double Effect," in *Virtues and Vices and Other Essays in Moral Philosophy.* London: Basil Blackwell, pp. 19–32.

Fox, Michael A. (1986a). *The Case for Animal Experimentation.* Berkeley: University of California Press.

———. (1986b). Letter in *Scientist,* December 15.

———. (1987). "Animal Experimentation: A Philosopher's Changing Views," *Between the Species,* 3: 55–60.

Frey, R. G. (1980). *Interests and Rights: The Case against Animals.* Oxford: Clarendon Press.

———. (1983). *Rights, Killing and Suffering: Moral Vegetarianism and Applied Ethics.* New York: Basil Blackwell.

Friedman, Marilyn. (1993). *What Are Friends For? Feminist Perspectives on Personal Relationships and Moral Theory.* Ithaca, NY: Cornell University Press.

Friedman, Marilyn and May, Larry. (1985). "Harming Women as a Group," *Social Theory and Practice,* 11, 207–234.

Gandhi, M.K. (1997). *Hind Swaraj and other writings.* Anthony J. Parel, ed. New Delhi: Cambridge University Press.

Gauthier, David. (1986). *Morals by Agreement.* Oxford: Clarendon Press.

Gilligan, Carol. (1982). *In a Different Voice: Psychological Theory and Women's Development.* Cambridge, MA: Harvard University Press.

Goodpaster, Kenneth. (1978). "On Being Morally Considerable," *The Journal of Philosophy,* 75, 6, 308–325.

Govier, Trudy. (2001). *A Practical Study of Argument,* 5th ed. Belmont, CA: Wadsworth.

Griffin, James. (1982). "Modern Utilitarianism," *Revue internationale de philosophie,* 141, 331–375.

———. (1986). *Well-Being: Its Meaning, Measurement, and Moral Importance.* Oxford: Clarendon Press.

Hare, R.M. (1981). *Moral Thinking: Its Levels, Method, and Point.* Oxford: Clarendon Press.

Harman, Gilbert. (1975). "Moral Relativism Defended," *The Philosophical Review,* 84, 3–22.

———. (1977). *The Nature of Morality: An Introduction to Ethics.* New York: Oxford University Press.

———. (1978a). "Relativistic Ethics: Morality as Politics," *Midwest Studies in Philosophy 3, Studies in Ethical Theory.* P. French, T. Uchling, Jr., and H. Wettstein, eds. Morris, MN: University of Minnesota, pp. 109–121.

———. (1978b). "What is Moral Relativism?" *Values and Morals.* A.I. Goldman and J. Kim, eds. Dordrecht, The Netherlands: D. Reidel, pp. 143–161.

———. (1982). "Metaphysical Realism and Moral Relativism: Reflections on Hilary Putnam's *Reason,*

Truth and History," *The Journal of Philosophy*, 79, 568–575.

———. (1984). "Is There a Single True Morality?" in *Morality, Reason, and Truth: New Essays in the Foundations of Ethics*. D. Copp and D. Zimmerman, eds. Totowa, NJ: Rowman & Allanheld Publishers, pp. 27–48.

Hart, H.L.A. (1961). *The Concept of Law*. Oxford: Clarendon Press.

———. (1963). *Law, Liberty, and Morality*. London: Oxford University Press.

Hinman, Lawrence M. (1998). *Ethics: A Pluralistic Approach to Moral Theory*, 2nd ed. Fort Worth, TX: Harcourt Brace.

Hobbes, Thomas. (1668). *Leviathan*. E. Curley, ed. Indianapolis, IN: Hackett, 1984.

Hohfeld, Wesley. (1913). "Some Fundamental Legal Conceptions as Applied in Legal Reasoning," *Yale Law Journal*, 23.

———. (1917). "Some Fundamental Legal Conceptions as Applied in Legal Reasoning," *Yale Law Journal*, 26.

Honderich, Ted, ed. (1985). *Morality and Objectivity: A Tribute to J.L. Mackie*. London: Routledge & Kegan Paul.

Hume, David. (1777). *An Enquiry Concerning the Principles of Morals*. La Salle, IL: Open Court, 1966.

———. (1739). *A Treatise of Human Nature: Books Two and Three*. P. S. Ardal, ed. Glasgow: Wm. Collins Sons & Co., 1972.

Hurley, Patrick. (2000). *A Concise Introduction to Logic*, 7th ed. Belmont, CA: Wadworth.

Jaggar, Alison M. (1991). "Feminist Ethics: Projects, Problems, Prospects," in *Feminist Ethics*, Claudia Card, ed. Lawrence: University Press of Kansas, pp. 78–104.

Joseph, Lawrence E. (1990). *Gaia: The Growth of an Idea*. New York: St. Martin's Press.

Kagan, Shelley. (1984). "Does Consequentialism Demand Too Much?" *Philosophy and Public Affairs*, 13, pp. 239–254.

Kahn, Charles. (1981). "Aristotle and Altruism," *Mind*, 90, 20–40.

Kant, Immanuel. (1963). "Duties towards Animals and Spirits," in *Lectures on Ethics*. trans. L. Linfield. New York: Harper & Row.

———. (1785). *Foundations of the metaphysics of morals, and What is enlightenment?* Indianapolis: Bobbs-Merrill Educational Publishing, 1980.

Kohlberg, Lawrence. (1981). *Essays in Moral Development, Volume 1, The Philosophy of Moral Development*. New York: Harper & Row.

———. (1984). *Essays in Moral Development, Volume 2, The Psychology of Moral Development*. San Francisco: Harper & Row.

Kruschwitz, R. and Roberts, R., eds. (1987). *The Virtues: Contemporary Essays on Moral Character*. Belmont, CA: Wadsworth.

Kymlicka, Will. (1988). "Rawls on Teleology and Deontology," *Philosophy & Public Affairs*, 17, Number 3, 173–190.

———. (1990). *Contemporary Political Philosophy: An Introduction*. New York: Clarendon Press.

Langenfus, William L. (1990). "Consequentialism in Search of a Conscience," *American Philosophical Quarterly*, 27, no. 2, 131–141.

Leopold, Aldo. (1949). *A Sand County Almanac*. New York: Oxford University Press.

Lovelock, James. (1979). *Gaia: A New Look at Life on Earth*. New York: Oxford University Press.

———. (1988). *The Ages of Gaia: A Biography of Our Living Earth*. New York: W.W. Norton.

Lovelock, James and Epton, Sidney. (1986). "The Quest for Gaia," *The Breathing Planet*. J. Gribben, ed. Oxford: Basil Blackwell, pp. 3–10.

Lovelock, James and Margulis, Lynn. (1974). "Atmospheric Homeostasis by and for the Biosphere: The Gaia Hypothesis," *Tellus*, 26 (1–2). 2–9.

MacIntyre, Alasdair. (1981). *After Virtue*. Notre Dame, IN: University of Notre Dame Press.

Mackie, J.L. (1977). *Ethics: Inventing Right and Wrong*. New York: Penguin.

Martin, Mike W. (2001). *Everyday Morality: An Introduction to Applied Ethics*, 3rd ed. Toronto: Wadsworth/Thomson Learning.

Marx, Karl. (1844). "Contribution to the Critique of Hegel's *Philosophy of Right: Introduction*," in *The Marx-Engels Reader*, 2nd ed. Robert C. Tucker, ed. New York: W.W. Norton, 1978, pp. 53–65.

McCloskey, H.J. (1963). "A Note on Utilitarian Punishment," *Mind*, 72, 599.

McDowell, J. (1985). "Values and Secondary Qualities," *Morality and Objectivity: A Tribute to J.L. Mackie*. Ted Honderich, ed. London: Routledge & Kegan Paul, pp. 110–129.

Mill, J.S. (1861). *Utilitarianism, On Liberty and Considerations on Representative Government*. H.B. Acton, ed. London: J.M. Dent and Sons, 1984.

Mowat, Farley. (1984). *Sea of Slaughter*. Toronto: McClelland and Stewart.

Nagel, Thomas. (1970). *The Possibility of Altruism*. Oxford: Oxford University Press.

———. (1973). "Equal Treatment and Compensatory Discrimination," *Philosophy & Public Affairs*, 2, no. 4, 348–363.

———. (1986). *The View from Nowhere*. New York: Oxford University Press.

Noddings, Nel. (1984). *Caring: A Feminine Approach to Ethics & Moral Education*. Berkeley: University of California Press.

Norton, B. (1988). *Why Preserve Natural Variety?* Princeton, NJ: Princeton University Press.

Nozick, Robert. (1974). *Anarchy, State, and Utopia*. New York: Basic Books.

O'Neill, Onora. (1987). "Rights to Compensation," *Social Philosophy & Policy*, 5, no. 1, 72–87.

———. (1989). *Constructions of Reason*. Cambridge: Cambridge University Press.

———. (1993). "Kantian Ethics," in *A Companion to Ethics*. P. Singer, ed. Cambridge: Cambridge University Press, pp. 175–185.

———. (1996). *Towards Justice and Virtue: A Constructive Account of Practical Reasoning*. Cambridge: Cambridge University Press.

Parfit, Derek. (1984). *Reasons and Persons*. Oxford: Oxford University Press.

Plamenatz, John. (1967). "Diversity of Rights and Kinds of Equality," in *Equality*. J. Roland Pennock and John W. Chapman, eds. New York: Atherton Press, pp. 79–98.

Plato. (1982). "Euthyphro" in *The Collected Dialogues of Plato*. E. Hamilton and H. Cairns, eds. Princeton, NJ: Princeton University Press, pp. 169–185.

———. "Republic," in *The Collected Dialogues of Plato*. E. Hamilton and H. Cairns, eds. Princeton, NJ: Princeton University Press, pp. 575–844.

Purdy, Laura M. (1984). "In Defense of Hiring Apparently Less Qualified Women," *Journal of Social Philosophy*, 15, no. 2, 26–33.

———. (1994). "Why Do We Need Affirmative Action?" *Journal of Social Philosophy*, 25, no. 1, 133–143.

Rachels, James. (1999). *The Elements of Moral Philosophy*, 3rd ed. Boston: McGraw-Hill.

Railton, Peter. (1984). "Alienation, Consequentialism, and the Demands of Morality," *Philosophy and Public Affairs*, 13, Number 2, 134–171.

———. (1988). "How Thinking about Character and Utilitarianism Might Lead to Rethinking the Character of Utilitarianism," *Midwest Studies in Philosophy*, XIII, 399–416.

Rawls, John. (1971). *A Theory of Justice*. Cambridge, MA: Harvard University Press.

———. (1980). "Kantian Constructivism in Moral Theory," *The Journal of Philosophy*, 77, no. 9, 515–572.

Regan, Tom. (1983). *The Case for Animal Rights*. Berkeley: University of California Press.

Regan, Tom, and Singer, Peter, eds. (1989). *Animal Rights and Human Obligation*, 2nd ed. Englewood Cliffs, NJ: Prentice-Hall.

Reynolds, William Bradford. (1986). "Equal Opportunity, Not Equal Results," *Business Ethics: Readings and Cases in Corporate Morality*, 2nd ed. W. Michael Hoffman and Jennifer Mills Moore, eds. New York: McGraw-Hill, Inc., pp. 372–375.

Rolston, III, Holmes. (1987). "Duties to Ecosystems," *Companion to a Sand County Almanac: Interpretive & Critical Essays*. J. Baird Callicott, ed. Madison, WI: University of Wisconsin Press, pp. 246–274.

The Royal Commission on New Reproductive Technologies. (1993). "Germ-Line Genetic Alteration" in *Proceed with Care*, Privy Council Office, 936–947.

Reprinted in *Readings in Health Care Ethics*, E. Boetzkes and W. Waluchow, eds. Mississauga, ON: Broadview Press, 2000, pp. 596–602.

Sagoff, Mark. (1984). "Animal Liberation and Environmental Ethics: Bad Marriage, Quick Divorce," *Osgood Hall Law Journal*, pp. 297–307.

Schaar, John. (1967). "Equality of Opportunity, and Beyond," in *Equality*. J. Roland Pennock and John W. Chapman, eds. New York: Atherton Press, pp. 228–249.

Scheffler, Samuel. (1982). *The Rejection of Consequentialism: A Philosophical Investigation of the Considerations Underlying Rival Moral Conceptions*. Oxford: Clarendon Press.

———, ed. (1988). *Consequentialism and Its Critics*. Oxford: Oxford University Press.

Schneewind, J.B. (1992). "Seventeenth and Eighteenth Century Ethics," *A History of Western Ethics*. L. Becker and C. Becker, eds. New York: Garland Publishing, pp. 80–95.

———. (1998). *The Invention of Autonomy: A History of Modern Moral Philosophy*. New York: Cambridge University Press.

Schneider, Stephen H. and Boston, Penelope J., eds. (1991). *Scientists on Gaia*. Cambridge, MA: The MIT Press.

Sen, Amartya. (1979). "Utilitarianism and Welfarism," *The Journal of Philosophy*, 76.

———. (1987). *On Ethics and Economics*. Oxford: Basil Blackwell.

Sen, Amartya and Williams, Bernard, eds. (1982). *Utilitarianism and Beyond*. Cambridge: Cambridge University Press.

Shackleton, R. (1972). "The Greatest Happiness of the Greatest Number: the History of Bentham's Phrase," in *Studies on Voltaire and the Eighteenth Century*, 90, 1461–1482.

Sher, George. (1975). "Justifying Reverse Discrimination in Employment," *Philosophy & Public Affairs*, 4, no. 2, 159–170.

———. (1987). "Predicting Performance," *Social Philosophy and Policy*, 5, no.1, 188–203.

———. (1992). "Ancient Wrongs and Modern Rights," in *Justice between Age Groups and Generations*. Peter Laslett and James S. Fishkin, eds. New Haven, CT: Yale University Press, pp. 48–61.

Sherman, Nancy. (1987). "Aristotle on Friendship and the Shared Life," *Philosophy and Phenomenological Research*, 47, No. 4, 589–613.

Sidgwick, Henry. (1907). *The Methods of Ethics*, 7th ed. London: MacMillan and Co., Ltd.

Singer, Peter, ed. (1986) *In Defense of Animals*. New York: Basil Blackwell.

———. (1990). *Animal Liberation*, Revised Edition. New York: Avon Books.

———. (1993). *Practical Ethics*, 2nd ed. Cambridge: Cambridge University Press.

———, ed. (1993). *A Companion to Ethics*. Oxford: Blackwell Publishers.

Slote, Michael. (1985). *Common-sense Morality and Consequentialism*. London: Routledge and Kegan Paul.

———. (1989). *Beyond Optimizing: A Study of Rational Choice*. Cambridge: Harvard University Press.

Smart, J.J.C. (1973). "An Outline of a System of Utilitarian Ethics," in *Utilitarianism: For and Against*. Cambridge: Cambridge University Press, pp. 3–74.

Sober, Elliot. (1986). "Philosophical Problems for Environmentalism," *The Preservation of Species*. B.G. Norton, ed. Princeton: Princeton University Press, pp. 173–194.

Solomon, Robert C. (1996). *A Handbook for Ethics*. Orlando, FL: Harcourt Brace.

Somerville, Margaret. (2000). *The Ethical Canary: Science, Society, and the Human Spirit*. Toronto: Penguin Books.

Sterba, James. (1994). "Reconciling Anthropocentric and Nonanthropocentric Environmental Ethics," *Environmental Values*, 3, 229–244.

———. (2001). *Three Challenges to Ethics: Environmentalism, Feminism, and Multiculturalism*. New York: Oxford University Press.

Stewart, David. (1998). *Exploring the Philosophy of Religion*, 4th ed. Upper Saddle River, NJ: Prentice-Hall.

Stocker, Michael. (1976). "The Schizophrenia of Modern Ethical Theories," *The Journal of Philosophy*, 73, 453–466.

Sumner, L.W. (1987a). *The Moral Foundation of Rights*. Oxford: Clarendon Press.

———. (1987b). "Positive Sexism," *Social Philosophy & Policy*, 5, no.1, 204–222.

———. (1995). "The Subjectivity of Welfare," *Ethics*, 105, 764–790.

———. (1996). *Welfare, Happiness & Ethics*. Oxford: Clarendon Press.

Taylor, Paul. (1982). "The Ethics of Respect for Nature," *Environmental Ethics*, vol. 3, 197–218.

———. (1986). *Respect for Nature*. Princeton: Princeton University Press.

Thomas, Lawrence. (1987). "Friendship," *Synthese*, 72, 217–236.

———. (1989). *Living Morally: A Psychology of Moral Character*. Philadelphia: Temple University Press.

Thomson, James, et al. (1998). "Embryonic stem cell lines derived from human blastocysts," *Science*, 282, 1145–1147.

Thomson, Judith Jarvis. (1973). "Preferential Hiring," *Philosophy & Public Affairs*, 2, no. 4, 364–384.

———. (1990). *The Realm of Rights*. Cambridge, MA: Harvard University Press.

Warren, Mary Ann. (1977). "Secondary Sexism and Quota Hiring," *Philosophy & Public Affairs*, 6, no. 3, 240–261.

———. (1983). "The Rights of the Nonhuman World," *Environmental Philosophy*. Robert Elliot and Arran Gare, eds. University Park, PA: Penn State University Press, pp. 109–134.

Watson, J. and Crick, F. (1953). "Molecular Structure of Nucleic Acids: A Structure for Deoxyribose Nucleic Acid," *Nature*, vol. 171, 737–738.

Williams, Bernard. (1962). "The Idea of Equality," in *Philosophy, Politics and Society* (second series). P. Laslett and W.G. Runciman, eds. Oxford: Basil Blackwell, pp. 110–131.

Williams, Bernard (1973). "A Critique of Utilitarianism," in *Utilitarianism: For and Against*. Cambridge: Cambridge University Press, pp. 75–150.

———. (1981). *Moral Luck*. Cambridge: Cambridge University Press.

———. (1985). *Ethics and the Limits of Philosophy*. Cambridge, MA: Harvard University Press.

Wilson, Edward O. (1987). "The Little Things that Run the World," *Conservation Biology*, 1, 344–346. Reprinted in *The Environmental Ethics and Policy Book: Philosophy, Ecology, Economics*. Donald VanDeveer and Christine Pierce, eds. Belmont, CA: Wadsworth, 1994, pp. 84–87.

Wolf, Susan. (1982). "Moral Saints," *The Journal of Philosophy*, 79, no. 8, 419–439.

Index